TEXAS
GARDENER'S HANDBOOK

First published in 2012 by Cool Springs Press, an imprint of the Quayside Publishing Group, 400 First Avenue North, Suite 400, Minneapolis, MN 55401

Cool Springs Press titles are also available at discounts in bulk quantity for industrial or sales-promotional use. For details write to Special Sales Manager at Cool Springs Press, 400 First Avenue North, Suite 400, Minneapolis, MN 55401

To find out more about our books, visit us online at www.coolspringspress.com.
First published as Texas Gardener's Resource, 2009

Library of Congress Cataloging-in-Publication Data

Groom, Dale.
  Texas gardener's handbook : all you need to know to plan, plant & maintain a Texas garden / Dale Groom and Dan Gill ; with Steve Dobbs ... [et al.].
      p. cm.
  Includes index.
  First published as Texas Gardener's Resource, 2009.
  ISBN 978-1-59186-543-8 (pbk.)
  1. Gardening--Texas. 2. Landscape plants--Texas. 3. Landscape gardening--Texas. I. Gill, Dan, 1954- II. Dobbs, Steve, 1959- III. Title.

  SB453.2.T4G763 2012
  635.09764--dc23
                              2012028128

President/CEO: Ken Fund
Group Publisher: Bryan Trandem
Publisher: Ray Wolf
Associate Publisher: Mark Johanson
Design Manager: Brad Springer
Design: S. E. Anderson
Layout: Erin Fahringer

Printed in China
10 9 8 7 6 5 4 3 2

Photography and illustration
Cool Springs Press would like to thank the following contributors to the *Texas Gardener's Handbook*.

William Adams	iStockphoto and its artists	Jerry Pavia
Liz Ball	Jackson & Perkins	Rick Ray
Michael Dirr	Dency Kane	Felder Rushing
Steve Dobbs	Bill Kersey Graphics	Ralph Snodsmith
Thomas Eltzroth	Todd Koske	Neil Soderstrom
Dan Gill	Charles Mann	Michael Turner
Lorenzo Gunn	Kevin Mathias	André Viette
Pamela Harper	Judy Mielke	
Heirloom Roses, Inc.	Scott Millard	

TEXAS
GARDENER'S HANDBOOK

DALE GROOM AND DAN GILL

WITH STEVE DOBBS, JAMES FIZZELL, JOE LAMP'L, AND JOE WHITE

COOL
SPRINGS
PRESS

Growing Successful Gardeners™

MINNEAPOLIS, MINNESOTA

CONTENTS

WELCOME TO GARDENING
in Texas

We Texans have excellent opportunities for establishing all kinds of gardens in our great state. Soils and climatic zones are quite diverse, and there are wonderful plants available to all of us. This book will provide an introduction to the many plants you can select for enjoyment in your Texas home landscape. Most of the plants are readily available. Some will be a bit difficult to locate, but all are worth seeking out. Remember that the hunt for those interesting and hard-to-find plants is part of the fun, too! Follow the suggestions in this book for assistance in enjoying your Texas gardening experience.

OUR DIVERSE STATE

Texas has four different hardiness zones, as shown on the United States Department of Agriculture (USDA) Cold Hardiness Zone map (page 17). The state reaches from Zone 6 in the Panhandle, where minus 10 degrees Fahrenheit is common, all the way down to Zone 9 in the valley, where freezes are the exception. Few states in the country have this diversity.

The colder zones are in the northwest areas of Texas, including Wheeler, Randall, and Bailey counties in the Panhandle. The warmer zones are in the south and include Cameron, Hidalgo, and Starr counties of our Rio Grande Valley. Keep in mind that the USDA Cold Hardiness Zone map doesn't tell the whole story of temperatures in our state. Temperatures in urban areas may be 10 degrees warmer than those in rural areas due to asphalt, concrete, masonry, and a denser population—all of which create what are called microclimates.

Microclimates can also be created in our own home landscapes by fencing, shrubbery, and by our homes and structures. You may discover that your yard has a location where particular plants will survive due to a microclimate that has been created, while your neighbor may not be able to grow the same plants.

Temperature range and rate of change greatly affect gardening in Texas. If, for example, one area were to drop to a sub-freezing temperature for a short period of time and climb right back up,

plants in that area would most likely receive little harm. But if the temperature dropped suddenly and remained there for several days, great damage could occur. When an unusual freezing spell struck North Texas, some of its live oak trees, which normally would be considered quite hardy in that area, were severely damaged.

The USDA Cold Hardiness Zone map provides general temperature guidelines for the state and each of its zones. Plant hardiness refers to each plant's ability to withstand the freezing temperatures that historically occur in the various zones. A plant that is barely able to withstand the temperatures in Zone 8 should not be planted in the colder Zone 7. Plants that will grow in Zone 6 will often grow in Zone 9. As you can see, Texas is a climatically diverse state, and it is important to pay attention to zone hardiness.

In Texas, one problem gardeners encounter is the challenge of raising plants that have been grown and acclimated in other parts of the country. While some plants will withstand all of our freezing temperatures, they may not be able to handle the blast furnace heat that we have. So, if you are ordering plants or buying them from another part of the country, make sure they will be able to handle Texas summertime heat. For best growing results, plants need to be placed where they will receive the proper amount of light. This book contains light requirements for the plants I have featured. This information can also be found at your local gardening retailer. Even the temperatures in our shade can be too hot for some northern plants, and they may not receive the sunlight needed to grow properly. Texas sun in July and August, for example, will fry some plants that can be grown in full sun in other parts of the country. I noticed an example of this when I was in Winnipeg, Canada, taping a television show in July, and I saw impatiens being grown in full sun. Impatiens grown in the full Texas sun of July would be cooked very quickly. When you read that particular plants can be grown in full sun, make sure the writer is referring to full sun locations in Texas and not New England, the Pacific Northwest, or other relatively cool locations.

FACING THE WIND

There is nothing like a Texas wind to affect your gardening activities. Make sure the plants that you select at your local garden center will be able to withstand the wind that is common in your area. Many Texans experience prevailing southwestern breezes, and in some locations they can be quite strong. I have seen significant landscape plants growing at an almost 45-degree angle due to these prevailing breezes. Make sure that trees or other tall shrubs are staked properly until they are large enough to withstand the strong breezes and are growing in a vertical position. Trees that are properly selected and placed can serve beautifully as breaks to block out strong winds.

THE IMPORTANCE OF MULCHING

Mulching can be a confusing topic for Texas gardeners. Whether it is compost, ground-bark mulch, or another type of material, mulch simply means a blanket of these materials on top of your soil. Whether we are planting vegetables, perennials, trees, or any other plant, mulch is a blanket we put on top of the ground that aids in moisture retention, weed control, and soil improvement.

The amount of mulch that you use is determined by the type. Generally, mulching three to four inches is quite sufficient. Lightweight materials, such as pine needles or clean hay will settle and may require a bit more coverage—but six inches placed between plants is usually adequate. In fact, all of the roses in the City of Tyler rose garden are mulched with pine needles.

Perhaps the most important benefit of mulching for Texas gardeners is conserving water. Plants that are properly mulched require less frequent watering, maintain even soil moisture content, and respond with better overall growth. If you take a walk through the woods, you will notice that our native vegetation is mulched by woodland floor debris or natural mulch. Mulching your finished plantings helps to approximate that natural environment.

Mulching is something that I encourage every gardener to do yearly, and I prefer the organic varieties. There are plenty of mulching materials from which to choose—pine, hardwood, peanut, pecan hulls, or shredded sugar cane. Select the one that works best for you and your plants.

GARDEN NUTRITION

Simply put, fertilization supplies nutrients to the soil for the plant to pick up. This process is sometimes misunderstood. While many gardeners think they are feeding the plant, they are actually adding nutrients to the soil for the plant to absorb. If the soil lacks sufficient amounts of naturally occurring plant nutrients, then your plants will not thrive.

Plants can be fertilized with various products including water-soluble, liquid, encapsulated, and premium-quality, slow-release fertilizers. Many different forms and types are available. Make sure that you read and understand the directions before you apply any type of fertilizer. When a container of fertilizer specifies an amount, we Texas gardeners may say, "Well, if that works well, then doubling that amount ought to be really great!" It doesn't work that way with fertilizers. Make sure you apply only the amount specified on the label.

My granny Miller said that Granddad was known to burn up crops in the vegetable garden by putting on too much cottonseed meal. Cottonseed meal is a 100-percent-natural organic fertilizer, but just because something is organic does not mean that you can't have problems by using too much. Soil nutrients are sometimes categorized as major or minor. Plants need more of the major nutrients than they do of the minor. Nitrogen (N), phosphorus (P), and potassium (K) are considered the three major nutrients. Some horticulturists classify sulfur, magnesium, and calcium as secondary nutrients. The remaining nutrients are called micronutrients because they are used by plants in extremely small amounts. This doesn't mean that major nutrients are more important, just that plants use more of them. Plants do not have the ability to determine where nutrients come from. As far as they are concerned, nutrients come from the soil reservoir. With the proper application of fertilizers, you can make sure that the soil has the nutrients necessary for good plant growth.

Nutrients occur naturally in our soil, originating from various materials, including stone and organic matter in the soil itself. Perhaps you have heard someone say, "The soil is just worn out." Soil doesn't really wear out, but we can deplete it of nutrients and damage soil structure. By re-supplying nutrients to soil that has been depleted and keeping soil structure in good shape, we can continue to grow in the same soils for generation after generation. If soils are deficient in naturally occurring nutrients, we can apply those nutrients in the form of fertilizers. I always recommend that you water thoroughly after applying any type of fertilizer.

When fertilizing your lawn, apply when the grass blades are dry. Follow label directions and then water thoroughly. You should be rewarded with a nice, thick, vigorous lawn if you also mow properly and water as necessary. Don't forget that your lawn may also need to be aerated if your soils are compacted or are the heavy clay types. Aeration allows oxygen, water, and nutrients to penetrate the soil and reach the root zones. In heavy clay soils or high traffic areas, aeration every two years is usually sufficient.

WHEN TO WATER

When droughts occur in Texas they remind us just how important water is to us. There are many demands on our water supply and water is not available in unlimited quantities. Described as "the essence of life," water is as necessary to plants as to humans in order to survive.

Water your plants deeply and thoroughly. Lawns, for example, need to be watered to a soil depth of six inches, and they prefer to be watered to eight inches. Don't set any of your plants, including your lawn, on a watering schedule. I have seen folks who turn on their lawn sprinklers, for example every morning at 6:38 A.M. for ten minutes. That is not desirable for individual plants, grass, shrubbery, or any other plant.

After watering, don't go back and re-water until your plants tell you they need it. Grass will tell you when it needs to be watered by changing from a nice pleasant green color to a kind of bluish gray. Or perhaps its sides will roll up, or it will not lie flat when you walk across it, not springing back. When you see these signs, water the lawn thoroughly. You can tell when shrubs need to be watered by simply sticking your finger in the soil. If the soil is dry, then irrigate or apply water thoroughly . . . did I mention to water thoroughly? Be sure that you soak the entire root zone of your plants when watering. If you water your plants frequently and very lightly, they will develop undesirable shallow root systems. When watering containers, water until there are no more air bubbles coming out of them. You will then know that all the pores have been saturated with moisture. The excess water will drain out. Be sure that all your containers drain properly.

Certain methods of irrigation can be good for water conservation; others can be quite wasteful. Sprinklers that throw a lot of water high in the air before the water strikes lawns or shrubs are not as efficient as other methods. Drip irrigation is the most efficient method of delivering water to landscape plants, including trees, shrubs, vines, groundcovers, annuals, and perennials. Drip irrigation can conserve as much as 50 percent of overall water usage. This water conservation translates into cost savings, plus it helps provide a beneficial environment for overall healthy plant growth. I have seen side-by-side comparisons of landscape beds that were planted and irrigated by drip irrigation and sprinkler irrigation. Drip irrigation is by far superior. Many hardware stores, sprinkler supermarkets, and nurseries carry drip irrigation systems, and they can help you select the best one for your home application.

Timing is important for watering at length. If watered at midday—especially with sprinklers that dispense water high into the air before it falls to the soil—lawns can lose a significant amount of moisture through evaporation. Early morning watering helps to prevent some of the evaporation.

THE SCOOP ON SOIL

Soil is the foundation for all of our successful gardening experiences. It is very important that we take care of our soil so it can perform at its best to meet personal gardening goals. Some Texas gardeners dream of running barefoot through the most luxurious lawn possible in the months of July and August. Others want the most gorgeous rose garden, azaleas, or beds of irises. I understand these desires. Soil testing is the tool that will help us obtain our gardening dreams.

It is worth performing soil tests every two years. If you are sampling several areas, the samples will need to be segregated. Each soil test stands alone. For example, your lawn soil needs to be separated from your landscape shrub bed, and from your perennial garden and annual plantings.

Make sure that the soil grade in the area to be landscaped is correct. If grading is necessary on new landscapes, complete the activity before installing grass, landscape beds, or any other plants. Grading can be done with small tractors, hand tools, or other methods.

If you don't feel comfortable performing the grading, contact a landscape contractor. In most communities, there are one or more members of the Texas Association of Landscape Contractors (TALC). When a contractor supplies an estimate, be sure you understand exactly what work is to be done and that you have the estimate and work plan in writing.

Drainage is very important and is one of the reasons we do grading in our landscape. Drainage can be improved with the addition of raised beds, which may necessitate additional soil and lots of organic matter. Soils that drain poorly tend to be oxygen-starved. This particular soil will not allow plants to grow healthy roots, and plants in this type of soil will suffer. Certainly there are plants that grow in damp-to-wet soils—including bald cypress, water-loving plants, bog plants, and weeping willows—but these are the exceptions. The general rule is that the majority of our landscape plants (including trees) need a well-drained soil in order to stay healthy.

SOIL PREPARATION

Before planting anything in your home landscape—annuals, shrubs, perennials, vines, or groundcovers—it is important to know exactly what kind of soil you have and the soil's pH. You may have your soil tested through our agricultural extension service. Most of us call the local representative of the Texas Agricultural Extension Service, "The County Agent." The number is found in the phone directory where all of the county office numbers are listed. Instructions, information sheets, and soil sample bags can be mailed to you, or you can pick them up. Offices are usually located in the county courthouse or county annex. The county agents' offices in Texas are always worth visiting for the opportunity to meet some good people who can be very helpful to you and your gardening goals. The Stephen F. Austin State University Soil Testing Laboratory is also available to you for complete soil testing. Contact the lab directly at (409) 468-4500. There are also some private testing labs throughout Texas, but be prepared to pay higher fees. After determining the soil's pH, you will need to prepare your soil for planting.

Preparing the soil includes breaking it up in some way. If planting a small area, a shovel or digging fork may be all you need. Those planting in larger areas traditionally use various types of tillers. The incorporation of organic matter into these areas will greatly improve the soil's drainage and moisture/nutrient holding capacity.

The benefits of organic matter cannot be overstated. Brown Canadian sphagnum peat moss, ground bark, compost you have made or purchased, and other types of organic matter will greatly improve the soil. Annuals and perennials usually require more extensive preparation than do shrubs and trees. When preparing for bedding plants, I recommend three inches or more of quality organic matter be blended with native Texas soil.

Trees require a simple loosening of the soil. In most cases, it is impossible to amend the soil in an area wide enough or deep enough for a tree's root system. Still, it is helpful to loosen the soil thoroughly before planting your tree, and be sure that you have selected the right tree for your soil type. The oak family is the number one shade tree grown in Texas, but some oaks do well in all areas, while others are very selective. For example, a water oak will grow in all areas of East Texas, but if you put it in the highly alkaline soils of Central or North Texas, results will be less than desirable.

PEST CONTROL

Pest control has several meanings. Weeds, insects, and diseases are all considered pests by most Texas gardeners. Weeds in our landscape beds can be controlled by the use of mulches. Mulching beds heavily with a three-to-four-inch layer makes it difficult for weed seeds to germinate and grow. In addition, there are various weed-prevention aids available for lawns as well as landscape beds.

Making sure our lawns are well-fertilized, mowed, and watered can also control weeds. A healthy, actively growing, thick lawn will normally have fewer weed problems. A well-selected and well-maintained landscape will have fewer insect and disease problems.

The crapemyrtle is a good example of the benefits of carefully choosing your plant's environment. When properly selected and planted in an ideal landscape location, crapemyrtle has few or no problems with powdery mildew. When planted in areas where there is poor air circulation and frequent watering, crapemyrtle is in a better environment for growth of this fungus.

Before you buy plants at your local nursery, always ask about potential disease and insect problems. If it sounds as if a plant may be too high-maintenance for your taste, make another selection. Remember, plants that tend to have problems in a certain landscape may have fewer problems when placed in other locations within a different environment.

PROPER PLANT SELECTION

Proper plant selection is extremely important for long-term success in Texas gardening. Many plants in magazines, catalogs, and on television will excite the gardener in you. They may look wonderful, but before you spend any money, be sure that these plants will grow and thrive in your area.

Through the years, I have found that the best place to shop for plant material is at local garden centers. These retailers tend to handle plants that do well in their particular area. For a list of trees, shrubs, vines, groundcovers, annuals, and perennials that are well-adapted to your home area, visit your local county agent's office. Additional information on some of the newer varieties and those well-tested is also available.

For long-term success with minimal maintenance, make sure that you select the proper plant. There are some wonderful selections of Texas-friendly plants from which to choose but—if they are shade grown—how much sun they receive can determine whether they thrive or die. The aucuba shrub, for example, is wonderful in shade areas in Texas but will not tolerate our sun. It will burn like my redheaded, fair-skinned wife, Judy.

Here are some questions to ask retailers before purchasing any type of plant:

- How tall and wide does this plant usually grow in my area?
- How much sun or shade is required?
- Does this plant have special soil requirements, and if so, what are they?
- Does this plant require well-drained soils, or will it grow in poorly drained or damp soils?
- Does it bloom? If so, when, for how long, and in what color(s)? In spring, summer, fall, or winter? For two weeks, six months, or longer?
- Does it have fall color? If so, what are the colors?
- Is it resistant to insect and disease pests that usually occur in my area?
- What are the watering/soil moisture requirements? Moist at all times? Tolerant of relatively dry soils?
- How often should it be fertilized, with what, and when?
- Are there any special pruning requirements? (Roses and certain other landscape plants, including edible-fruit-bearing plants, usually require special pruning and/or training to realize maximum benefits.)
- Is it deer-resistant (where applicable)?

SIZING UP YOUR OPTIONS

Most reputable garden centers will guarantee that the plants they sell will perform true to the variety, and that is important. Plants purchased from temporary retailers or other sources may not perform as promised. For the best overall value, buy plant material from the retailer in your area.

Buying from retailers who are members of the Texas Association of Nurserymen (TAN) will put you in touch with qualified help from Texas Certified Nursery Professionals (TCNP) and Texas Master Certified Nursery Professionals (TMCNP). These professionals are available to answer your questions and help you achieve your desired gardening goals.

Fall is for planting and is a wonderful time to landscape throughout our entire state. There is usually sufficient rain after the hot, dry Texas summer. The soil has adequate moisture, and the temperatures are cooler. Often you will find that nurseries put plant material on sale. The root systems of plants that are planted in the fall will continue to grow through the season, and you jumpstart their growth by almost a year.

With so many different sizes of landscape plants available, choices can sometimes get confusing. We use size measurements in the gardening industry that are relatively close to the actual gallon size. You will find plants in 2-, 3-, 5-, 7-, 10-, 15-, 20-gallon containers and larger. Certainly the sizes will be quite large for tree-type shrubs or trees. Sizes larger than twenty gallons are most likely trees.

Tall-growing shrubs such as crapemyrtles are sometimes sold according to height or caliper measurement (the diameter of the trunk). According to the American Association of Nurserymen (AAN), the caliper measurement of trees should be made approximately twelve inches above the soil line. This measurement provides the thickness, thus the diameter, of the trunk. If you see advertisements offering an oak tree of three inches, this is the thickness measurement of the trunk twelve inches above the soil line. You may also find plants sold in six to eight feet, eight to ten feet, and ten to twelve feet height ranges. Certainly the tall crapemyrtles, tall hollies, and some of the smaller-growing trees are classified in these ways.

PRUNING WITH A PURPOSE

From time to time our landscape plantings may require some pruning. But we want to prune for a purpose; we don't want to prune haphazardly. There are quite a few reasons for pruning. You may be pruning to shape a plant. You may want more light coming down through the trees. You may be pruning to do some specialized training. Perhaps you want to train a tree into an espalier or prune a rose for a particular type of growth to enhance selected blooms for shows. We often prune the tips out of the garden mums to induce branching and therefore thicken the overall planting so we have loads of buds that bloom in the fall.

The timing of pruning can be important. If you have a spring-blooming plant such as azalea, you certainly don't want to do any pruning until after the blooming season is completed in the spring. If you happen to have a group of overgrown azaleas that you wish to rework, do it after the major spring bloom is complete, just as you see the flush of spring growth beginning.

When pruning shrubs, select buds that are pointed outward and upward and then remove the branch just above the buds. That will give direction to the plant's branches. You can do similar types of pruning fairly often with certain types of roses. Pruning can be kept to a minimum if plants are selected and placed properly in your home landscape. Shrubs usually look best when allowed to grow into their natural form.

GREAT GARDENING

This book is an introduction to the plants that thrive in our great gardening state. We begin with a look at annuals—different varieties that offer fine possibilities. All can be tried in the home landscape, and don't forget to let little gardeners try their hand with annuals.

Texas gardeners grow a lot of bulbs. We need to be on the lookout for those lesser-used bulbs that have been around for generations and incorporate those varieties into our landscapes.

Nearly all Texas gardeners like to grow grasses in the home landscape. I've included grasses for every area of Texas. Try some of the ornamental grasses that are on the market, such as blue fescue or fountain grass.

Gardeners may not pay much attention to groundcovers, but if you need an alternative for lawn grass in a heavily shaded area, groundcovers are the answer. I've included some of the best available in Texas for your consideration.

Texans love to talk about our native plants. With a well-earned reputation for being the wildflower state, we also have shrubs, trees, and vines that are all native to Texas, and this book offers a good selection.

Perennials are the plants that re-grow each year and live for three years or more. Some of them grow for generations in our home landscapes. Some plants, such as the achillea or yarrow, are very tough and durable and can stand up to our Texas environment.

We have the world's headquarters for roses in Tyler, Texas, but we can grow roses in all areas of Texas. The American Rose Society (ARS) lists over fifty different classifications. I have profiled some of the most popular and successful ones for our state.

Another area that may interest you is raising your own vegetables, herbs, berries, and/or fruits. Many crops will thrive in our Texas climate, but be advised that raising your own food requires attentiveness and effort—all worthwhile!

There are many different types of shrubs available. I have listed several for your consideration, from abelia to winter jasmine.

Trees are near and dear to my heart. I like to climb trees, build tree houses for my children, and rest in their shade. You will find a good selection of trees in this book. These are generally what we call shade trees, including some that have been used in our landscapes for generations.

We will also take a look at vines and different ways to use them. If you enjoy flowering vines, you will find some interesting selections in these pages.

The Texas Gardener's Resource Guide has something for everyone. Great gardening . . . to YOU!

—Dale Groom, The Plant Groom™

TEXAS CLIMATIC CONDITIONS

CLIMATIC CONDITIONS

The climate of Texas is relatively mild. The United States Department of Agriculture divides the state into four hardiness zones based on the average minimum temperatures experienced during the winter. One-half of our state is in Zones 8 and 9, with average winter lows of 10 to 20 degrees Fahrenheit in Zone 8. Coastal areas around Houston, Corpus Christi, and Padre Island are in Zone 9 and experience average winter lows of 20 to 30 degrees. Our relatively mild climate allows a year-round gardening season for flower and vegetable gardens, particularly in the southern two-thirds of the state. Zone 7 may reach lows of 0 to 10 degrees, and Zone 6 in our Panhandle may reach -10 degrees. Texas is, overall, considered to have a relatively mild winter climate.

AVERAGE FREEZE DATES

Last freeze dates and first freeze dates are of great importance to many gardening activities, but it is important to understand that no one knows when the last or first freeze will actually occur during a particular year. Average dates can be helpful, but freezes can and do occur before the average first freeze date and after the average last freeze date. You must use experience and information from knowledgable local individuals (friends, professional horticulturists, local nurseries, and your County Agent with the Texas Agricultural Extension Service) when making planting decisions.

The first frosts usually occur in northwest Texas in early November, in areas around Dallas/ Fort Worth in mid- to late November, and along the Gulf Coast in early to mid-December. Experience shows that first freezes are more likely to occur later rather than earlier than these average dates.

Average last freeze dates are particularly important to gardeners who want to set out tender vegetables and bedding plants in the spring. North Texas freezes generally end in late March, freezes in areas south of Austin usually end in early to mid-March, and freezes along the Gulf Coast generally end in mid- to late February. Late freezes will occasionally occur after these dates. The conservative gardener should consider the frost-free date—when the chance of freezing temperatures is very unlikely—to be about four weeks after the average-last-freeze date.

AVERAGE RAINFALL AMOUNTS

Average annual rainfall is abundant in some areas. Amounts range from fifty-six inches in southeast Texas to nine inches in El Paso. Unfortunately, the rain does not appear regularly. Some areas of the state may receive five to ten inches of rain or more in a single rainfall and then go for weeks or months without significant precipitation. Well-drained beds are needed to handle periods of high rainfall, and proper irrigation is important during dry periods, especially during hot weather.

GARDENING SEASONS EXPLAINED

According to the calendar, spring, summer, fall, and winter begin and end at the same time everywhere in the United States. Common sense tells us, though, that the dates for spring-gardening activities must be very different between Maine and Texas.

Spring begins in early February in south Texas when deciduous trees like magnolias and redbuds begin to bloom and grow. When the calendar tells us that spring has officially begun, we in Texas can say, "It's passed in south Texas and arriving in north Texas," while at the same time in Maine it could be snowing. All Texas gardeners need to divide the year in a way that makes sense for us.

The terms spring, summer, fall, and winter carry strong associations with certain types of weather, and that can be a problem for Texas gardeners. Winter, for instance, brings to mind a picture of snow-covered dormant gardens with little or no activity. What we actually experience in

CROCUS

our state are episodes of cold weather interspersed with periods of mild temperatures. Planting and harvesting vegetables, planting hardy annuals, perennials, trees, and shrubs, and controlling weeds and insects may continue throughout the season in some areas of Texas.

To get around these preconceived notions, we can divide the gardening year into seasons that more accurately reflect the weather we have at that time. We can divide the gardening year into a first warm season (spring), a hot season (summer), a second warm/cool season (fall), and a cold/cool season (winter), depending on the zone you live in. There are no sharp boundaries between these seasons, and gardeners should always be aware that unusually high or low temperatures may occur at any time, especially during the season transitions.

The first warm season of the year runs from late March through mid-May. This warm season is characterized by mild to warm daytime highs generally in the 70s and 80s, cool nights in the 50s and 60s, and limited danger of nighttime freezes. It is a lovely time of year that is appreciated by gardeners and non-gardeners alike.

THE WARM SEASON

The first warm season is an excellent time to plant tender annuals and perennials in the landscape.

Trees, shrubs, and groundcovers, as well as lawns, can be fertilized to encourage the vigorous growth that takes place in this season. Tender vegetables such as tomatoes, peppers, squash, and snap beans can be planted now after all danger of frost/freeze has passed. New plantings of trees and shrubs in the landscape should be completed as soon as possible since the hot weather is right around the corner.

The first warm season also includes the peak blooming of the spring bulbs and cool-season bedding plants that were planted several months before, such as pansies, dianthus, petunias, snapdragons, and sweet peas. For new-bed planting, focus on warm-season plants such as marigolds, periwinkles, lantanas, and zinnias that will bloom for a long time, rather than cool-season plants that will play out as temperatures heat up in May.

THE HOT SEASON

May offers a transition into the hot season, which is characterized by brutally hot days in the upper 80s and 90s and warm nights in the mid- to upper 70s. The hot season is our longest season, and it can last through September. High humidity, rainy periods, drought conditions, insects, and diseases combine with heat to make this a stressful time of year for many plants. Numerous trees, shrubs, and perennials that are grown successfully up North cannot be grown here because they will not tolerate the hot season.

Tropical perennials such as hibiscus, gingers, blue daze, banana, and pentas really shine during the hot season, and many gardeners plant them every year even though they are prone to freeze injury or death.

If there is a down time in our gardens, the hot season is it. In July and August, and often September, it is so hot that many gardeners retreat to the air-conditioned indoors and spend less time in the garden than at any other season. But in spite of the heat, the hot season is a time of lush growth and abundant flowers from those plants that can deal with it.

There are a variety of things to do during the hot season. Controlling pests such as weeds, diseases, and insects is an important part of gardening at this time of year. Trees and shrubs grown in containers can be planted in the landscape but will require more care, and their survival is often not as sure as those planted during the cool season. Pruning is important to control the growth of a variety of plants, but avoid heavy pruning on spring-flowering trees and shrubs after June. Provide irrigation to the landscape during hot, dry periods.

THE WARM/COOL SEASON

Late September and early October offer a transition into the second warm season, which may last until late November. The weather at this time of year is similar to that of the first warm season, generally mild and pleasant. This is not the end of the gardening year as it is in the colder climates that have cold, harsh winters. For us, this time of year celebrates the flowers that are still lingering and looks toward a mild cool season.

As the heat diminishes, garden activities become more pleasurable . . . and there is lots to do. Many cool-season vegetables like broccoli, lettuce, cabbage, and turnips may be planted now. Flower gardeners can usually plant cool-season bedding plants like pansies, snapdragon, and dianthus. Deciduous trees, shrubs, and perennials begin to lose their leaves in November and finally enter dormancy, but we use so many broadleaf evergreen plants in our landscapes that they rarely look barren.

THE COOL/COLD SEASON

Late November to early December sees the arrival of the cool/cold season and the possibility of freezing temperatures. Although snow and severe freezes in the teens can occur, harsh weather rarely lasts long. Much of the time, the weather is mild with lows above freezing and highs in the 50s, 60s, and even 70s, particularly in the southern half of the state.

Tropical plants can be covered or brought in for protection on those occasional freezing nights. Along the Coast, the planting of cool-season vegetables and bedding plants can continue. This season is by far the best time to plant hardy trees, shrubs, groundcovers, and herbaceous perennials. In March and April, the cool season makes a transition into the first warm season, bringing us full circle.

TEXAS USDA COLD HARDINESS ZONE MAP

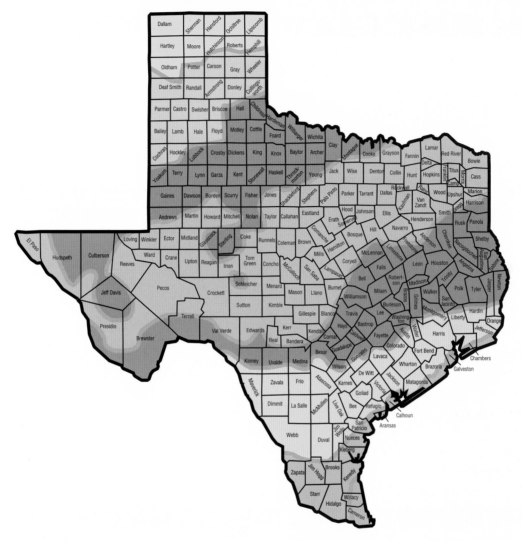

HARDINESS ZONES

Cold-hardiness zone designations were developed by the United States Department of Agriculture (USDA) to indicate the minimum average temperature for that region. A zone assigned to a plant indicates the lowest temperature at which the plant can normally be expected to survive. Texas has zones ranging from 6a (the coldest) to 9b. Though a plant may grow in zones outside its recommended zone range, the zone ratings are a good indication of which plants to consider for your landscape. Check the map to see which zone your Texas garden is in.

ZONE	Average Annual Minimum Temperature (°F)		
6b	0	to	-5
7a	5	to	0
7b	10	to	5
8a	15	to	10
8b	20	to	15
9a	25	to	20
9b	30	to	25
10b	35	to	30

KEY TO ICONS

Each entry in this guide provides information about a plant's characteristics, habits, and requirements for growth, as well as my personal experience and knowledge of the plant. Use this information to realize each plant's potential. You will find such pertinent information as mature height and spread, bloom period and seasonal colors, sun and soil preferences, water requirements, fertilizing needs, pruning and care tips, and hardiness zone and pest information. Each section is clearly marked for easy reference.

SUN PREFERENCES

Symbols represent the range of sunlight suitable for each plant. The symbol representing "Full Sun" means the plant needs 6 or more hours of direct sun daily. A ranking of "Part Sun" means the plant can thrive in 4 to 6 hours of sun a day. "Full Shade" means the plant needs protection from direct sunlight. Some plants can be grown successfully in more than one exposure, so you will sometimes see more than one light symbol with an entry.

Full Sun Part Sun Full Shade

ADDITIONAL BENEFITS

Many plants offer benefits that further enhance their appeal. These symbols indicate some of these benefits.

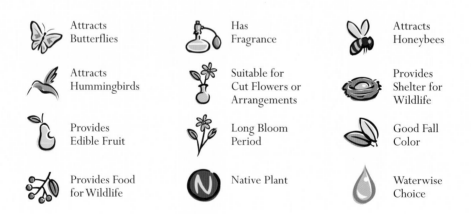

Attracts Butterflies

Has Fragrance

Attracts Honeybees

Attracts Hummingbirds

Suitable for Cut Flowers or Arrangements

Provides Shelter for Wildlife

Provides Edible Fruit

Long Bloom Period

Good Fall Color

Provides Food for Wildlife

Native Plant

Waterwise Choice

LANDSCAPING TIPS & IDEAS

For most of the entries, I offer landscape design ideas as well as suggestions for companion plants and other recommendations to help you achieve striking and personal results from your garden.

WORDS TO THE WATERWISE: CONSERVING WATER IN THE GARDEN

by Joe Lamp'l

Earth is sometimes referred to as the "water planet" because so much of it is covered by water. In fact, many of us learned in elementary school that about three-fourths of the earth's surface is covered by it. Unfortunately what we didn't usually hear was the sentence that should have followed: Even with all that water, 99 percent is unavailable to us as usable water—97 percent is salt water, and 2 percent is frozen (for now) in glaciers and polar ice caps. That leaves a miniscule 1 percent of all the water on earth for us to use for drinking, bathing, washing food, clothes, dishes, and cars, and watering our gardens, lawns, and landscapes. It sounds like a lot of demand on such a small reserve, and it is.

Perhaps if we had been told how precious this limited resource was then, we would have been doing more along the way to preserve and protect this finite supply. We didn't realize then that a global water crisis was looming, and it is here today . . . including in the mild-to-hot climate of the state of Texas.

But when confronted with the impending depletion of such a precious resource as water, we gardeners are not without our own resources—our own creative and significant solutions. The tips that follow are just some of the ways we can start making a difference right away. Now is the time to practice "waterwise gardening."

Please see the back of this book, pages 254 to 258, for further information on waterwise principles and recommended products such as rain barrels.

Supply only the water your plants need—know when to water and how much.

Get to know your plants—they'll tell you when to water.

You may not be aware that more plants die of too much water than not enough. We are literally killing them with kindness through overwatering, and it's simply not necessary. The problem is, most of us don't realize when our plants have received sufficient moisture, and so we overcompensate.

When we overwater, the soil becomes saturated, forcing out vital oxygen and literally drowning our plants. Although it is essential to provide ample water to new plants when they become established, once that is achieved, the water you supply should be reduced significantly.

After plants are established in the landscape, they should require supplemental watering only in the absence of rainfall. A good rule of thumb for many plants is, in the absence of rain, provide one inch of supplemental water each week, or whatever is necessary to make up the difference. Of course, this rule will vary from new seedlings to established, hardy natives.

As simple as it sounds, pay attention to what your plants and trees are telling you. Unfortunately, a plant that is underwatered or overwatered can show the same symptoms: limp droopy foliage, yellowing, and a lack of luster in the foliage. Similar symptoms can also occur in plants suffering from pests and diseases.

Since opposite causes may yield the same visual clues, you will have to do a bit of deductive reasoning. Given what you know, is it more likely that the plant has been getting too much water or not enough?

Just in case you're still not certain, and in the spirit of simplicity, here are a few easy ways to know for sure:

The finger test: Most of the time, you simply cannot tell what the moisture conditions are below the surface simply by looking. In fact, it's impossible if the soil under your plants is covered by mulch. Although not the most scientific approach, that pointer finger of yours can be a good indicator of the moisture conditions in the soil at the root level. Poke your finger into the soil around the base of the plant, down to the second

Less frequent, **deep watering** is the key to keeping plants healthy.

irrigation system, whether it's a soaker hose, drip irrigation, watering wand, or overhead sprinkler system, to soak the soil to the target depth. Check frequently, and you'll eventually determine the optimal time to get moisture down to the target level. Remember, the time determined in the above example assumes the soil started out dry. Once your soil maintains a consistent moisture level, it will take less time to keep it there. Note this as well and reduce the amount of time you water to maintain optimum levels.

Water deeply and less often.

Keep plants growing strong—encourage roots to explore deeper into the soil.

In many ways, plants are like some people I know. They don't work any harder than they have to! Consequently, if all the moisture needed is right near the surface, plants won't use extra energy and nutrients to grow roots deeper into the soil where moisture levels are consistently higher.

This is why the key is to water infrequently but deeply. Reducing the overall amount of water to plants (and especially lawns) keeps them growing stronger. Deep watering encourages deep roots, and roots that are encouraged to explore farther into the soil to find sustenance have better access to moisture when the area closer to the surface dries out. This upper layer always dries out first because soil at or near the surface warms faster and is subject to evaporation, and the drying effects of wind.

Now, deep watering doesn't mean turning on the sprinkler and leaving it on while you go and play a quick nine holes! The surface layer of most soils becomes quickly saturated after watering for only a few minutes, and then all the water applied from that point on runs off and is wasted.

Research shows that the most efficient way to get water down deep is to water an area for a short time until the upper surface is saturated—say, ten minutes for most soils (less if it's on a slope)—then stop and let that water soak in for thirty minutes to an hour, and then water again for a few minutes more. This allows the water to be deeply absorbed into the soil while reducing runoff, and ultimately lets you go much longer between watering.

knuckle. Pull it back out and take a look at your finger. If it's clean (relatively speaking), the soil is dry and in need of water. If your finger came back up with soil stuck to it, then there is sufficient moisture and no supplemental irrigation is needed at the time.

The dig test: Another easy and practical method is to conduct a dig test. Before watering, simply make a note of the moisture level of your soil, six to twelve inches below the surface (the target depth). Ideally, the soil will be dry at this point. Your goal is to determine how long it takes for your

Water at the right time of day.

The time of day that you water can have a significant effect on the water's efficiency.

The hotter it is, the more water is lost to evaporation. Add wind to the equation, and even more water is vaporized in the atmosphere before it ever reaches the ground. Depending on your irrigation system and the timing of when you water, as much as half the water can be lost to drift and evaporation, especially when using overhead sprinklers.

If you water at night, or very early in the morning, temperatures are cooler and winds are calmer. Late at night or very early in the morning is also the best time to use soaker hoses or drip irrigation. The coolness during darkness along with the calm skies allows soils to soak up the maximum amount of water, without the influence of drying winds or evaporating sunlight.

Mulch, mulch, mulch!

Mulch is an important tool for a gardener in more ways than one. As a way to conserve water, it can't be beat.

Mulch is one of the most versatile additions to any garden. It has many uses, which will be referred to throughout this book, but from the standpoint of water conservation, it is a star. A three- to five-inch layer of mulch will provide an insulating blanket that greatly reduces surface evaporation, slows runoff, moderates soil temperatures on hot days, and lowers the moisture requirements of the plants. It also dramatically cuts down on weed production, lowering the demand and competition for nutrients and water.

Mulch can be organic, such as leaves, straw, compost, or bark. It can even be gravel or plastic. In all cases, the mulch holds the moisture in place, in the ground, right where it is needed most.

Eliminate waste when watering your landscape.

Here are a few more ideas to employ, to make sure the ways you irrigate your plants and lawn are as efficient and waste-free as possible.

1. Fix leaky faucets and hoses. All those drips and drops add up to savings if you stop them. Take time to inspect all your outdoor faucets and connections, and call a plumber if the fixes are beyond your abilities. (Sometimes, all you need to do is replace old, worn-out equipment with new.)

2. Don't use water in place of a broom or blower. It's amazing how much water goes down the drain when we clean our walks and driveways with a hose. Besides saving precious water, broom power is good for you and leaves zero footprints on the environment.

3. Don't leave your hose running while unattended. Even for short periods of time, a running hose wastes hundreds of gallons of water. A hose without a nozzle shutoff can gush ten gallons of water a minute! Look for the nozzles that have spring-loaded automatic shutoffs—let the nozzle go and it shuts off automatically. Now that's easy!

4. If you have one, program your irrigation system to supply the right amount of water. Measure its output to know just how much is enough. If possible, try to fine-tune your system or adjust your spray pattern so all areas are receiving about the same amount each week. You'll be surprised to find how much water coverage may vary from even a single sprinkler head.

Use plants that need less water.

Waterwise gardening involves prudent planting. Many of the plants profiled in this book qualify as drought-resistant, especially once established. When you peruse the profiles in the pages that follow, watch for the "Waterwise Choice" icon with applicable entries. In all cases, the "Water Needs" of each plant are noted, to further inform you and help you decide if this is a plant you want in your home landscape.

See also the list on pages 255-256 at the back of this book.

ANNUALS
for Texas

Annuals are plants that sprout from seeds, grow, mature, flower, set seed, and die in a single growing season. The group is divided into warm-season annuals and cool-season annuals, with classification depending on cold hardiness and heat tolerance.

WARM-SEASON ANNUALS

Warm-season annuals are killed or damaged by freezing temperatures and therefore grow best during the warm to hot months of April to early November. Seeds or transplants may be planted into the garden from late March through August. They usually thrive during the long, hot months, although the performance of some will diminish during the hottest weather in late summer.

Since we have a growing season that is seven months long, it is unusual for true annuals to last from April to November. There is a group of plants called tender perennials that do have the stamina to last the entire season. Since they are often killed during winter freezes, and so last for just one season, these plants are grown as warm-season annuals and are generally grouped with them even though they are perennials. Unlike true annuals, tender perennials are not programmed by their genes to die after flowering and setting seed. Beds planted with tender perennial bedding plants usually will not have to be replanted in July or August as is typical for some true annuals. This makes them a good choice for lower-maintenance landscapes. As a bonus, some tender perennials can survive mild winters and may live to bloom another year. Tender perennials on the Warm-Season Annuals chart (see pages 24-25) are marked with single plus marks (+).

COOL-SEASON ANNUALS

Flower beds can remain colorful through the winter when planted with cool-season annuals, a wonderful group that will grow and bloom from November to May or whenever it gets warm in the spring. Seeds for many may be planted in flats or direct-seeded from August through November.

Transplants should be planted from September through February, depending on which hardiness zone you live in.

Cool-season bedding plants will generally tolerate freezing temperatures into the low 20s and even teens without protection (nasturtiums are the exception, as they are damaged by temperatures below 30 degrees Fahrenheit). Some will bloom all winter during mild weather, peaking in March and April. With the onset of hot weather in May, most cool-season annuals are quick to decline. Pansies are the most cold-hardy annuals we use in Texas.

There are several hardy perennials that are commonly used as cool-season annuals. Although foxglove, delphinium, and hollyhock are reliable perennials in cooler zones, they have a hard time surviving our summers. Transplants are set into the garden from October through February for blooms in April through early June. Planting dates are determined by the zone you live in.

GROWING ANNUALS SUCCESSFULLY

Successful annual growth depends on selecting varieties that do well, good bed preparation, planting each type in the growing conditions that it prefers, and paying attention to proper care after planting.

Don't scrimp on bed preparation, as this is essential for plants to perform their best. Good bed and soil preparation is the foundation for successful long-term annual growth and bloom.

First remove any weeds or other unwanted plants from the bed. Growing weeds may be controlled with a non-selective herbicide, which does not leave a residue in the soil. Be sure to follow label directions carefully.

Turn the soil to a depth of at least 8 inches with a shovel, fork, or tiller.

Spread a 4-inch layer of composted, rotted leaves, aged manure, finely ground pine bark, or peat moss over the bed. Blend the organic matter into the top 4 inches of the soil thoroughly, rake smooth, and then plant. Add small amounts of slow-release fertilizer to each planting hole according to label directions.

NASTURTIUM CLOSE-UP

PLANNING THE ANNUAL FLOWER GARDEN

Before you go to the nursery and buy annuals, look carefully at the growing conditions in the area to be planted. Most annuals do best with six to eight hours of sun a day (partial to full sun). Make sure you select plants that will thrive in the light conditions they will receive. Annuals generally need good drainage, so plant in a raised bed if the area tends to stay damp. Measure the size of the bed and calculate how many plants you will need to create the desired effect. Although spacing varies with the plant's known average spread, about 8 inches can be used for estimating.

It is also a good idea to make some decisions on the color or colors that will be used in the flower bed, as well as desirable heights (usually taller plants in the back of beds, shorter in the front) and general layout to meet your desire. You can always make changes or adjustments if necessary, but it is a good idea to have developed your ideas as completely as possible before buying plants.

PLANTING ANNUALS

When planting annual transplants, make sure you space them properly. Too close, and the plants will crowd one another and be less healthy. If planted too far apart, the plants will not grow together to completely fill the bed. Plant transplants so the top of the rootball is level with the soil in the bed. If the roots are in a dense mass, open the mass slightly to encourage the roots to grow into the surrounding prepared soil.

Many annuals are easy to direct-seed into the garden—but in this day of instant gratification, many gardeners don't have the patience for this (or only want a few plants of specific types/varieties) and rely on transplants instead. If you have the patience, plant seeds at the proper depth in a well-prepared bed and keep moist until they come up. When direct-seeding, it is important to thin seedlings so they are spaced properly. Check the seed package for recommendations.

GENERAL CARE

Proper care of annuals will keep the garden attractive for a long time. Annual beds may be relatively high maintenance, and this should be remembered when deciding how many beds you want and how large the beds will be. Water as needed and weed if necessary, although both of these jobs can be reduced with the use of a mulch. A 3- to 4-inch layer of pine bark mulch will work well.

Thorough watering during dry weather, especially when it's hot, is important to keep annuals growing vigorously and blooming. Soaker hoses, where suitable, are a great way to water without getting the flowers or foliage wet. This can reduce disease problems and damage to open flowers.

Whenever it is practical, remove the old flowers to keep the plants looking attractive and to encourage continued flowering. This practice is called deadheading.

Insect and disease problems may occur, especially with warm-season annuals. Keep a watchful eye out for symptoms and act promptly before significant damage occurs. Some annuals will not recover well if badly damaged. Remember, it is important to properly identify the cause of a problem before taking action.

WARM SEASON ANNUALS

Ageratum
Alyssum
Amaranthus*++
Angelonia*
Bachelor's Button/Gomphrena*+
Balsam++
Begonia, Wax
+Blue Daze+++
Celosia*
Cleome++
+Coleus+++
Copper Plant*
Cosmos++
Dahlberg Daisy++
Diascia
Dusty Miller+
Esperanza
Gaillardia*
Geranium
+Impatiens+++
Joseph's Coat
Lantana
Licorice Plant
Marigold*++
Melampodium
Million Bells
Narrow-leaf Zinnia
+Ornamental Pepper*
+Pentas+++
+Periwinkle*
Persian Shield
Portulaca*++
+Purslane*
Rudbeckia*
Salvia (some varieties)+
+Scaevola+++
Sunflower*++
Torenia
Verbena+
Zinnia*++
* Heat tolerant
+ Tender Perennials
++ Easily direct-seeded
+++ Best to buy transplants

At the beginning of the planting season, you can plant seed in flats or directly in beds, or you can use transplants. (Use transplants if you are planting towards the end of an annual's planting season.)

COOL SEASON ANNUALS

Alyssum+
Annual Baby's Breath
Annual Candytuft
Annual Phlox+
Calendula+
Dahlberg Daisy+
Delphinium++
Dianthus
Dusty Miller
English Daisy
Forget-me-not
Larkspur+
Nasturtium+
Nicotiana
Ornamental Cabbage and Kale
Pansy**++
Petunia++
Poppies+
Snapdragon
Statice
Stock
Sweet Pea+
Viola

** The most cold-hardy annual we use
+ Easily direct-seeded
++ Best to buy transplants

At the beginning of the planting season, you can plant seed in flats or directly in beds, or you can use transplants. (Use transplants if you are planting towards the end of an annual's planting season.)

Although many bedding plants prefer partial to full sun (about 6 to 8 hours of direct sun), the following will do well in shade, or even prefer shade to partial shade (about 2 to 4 hours of direct sun).

Warm-season: Balsam*, Cleome*, Impatiens, Pentas*, Salvia* (some varieties), Torenia*.

Cool-season: Forget-me-not, Nasturtium*, Nemophila, Nicotiana*.

* Also will do well in full sun.

COSMOS

ALYSSUM
Lobularia maritima

Color(s)—White, pink, rose, lavender, and purple

Bloom period—Fall, winter, and spring; warm-season

Mature Size (H x W)—4 to 6 in. x 10 in.

Water needs—Water once or twice a week during dry weather, especially the first few weeks after planting when the plants are getting established or if it's hot.

Planting/Care—Plant in full sun or part shade in fall or early spring. If direct-seeding, do not cover the seeds, water daily, and thin to 6 to 8 inches apart. In midseason, plants may begin to look shaggy. Shear to revitalize or tear out and replace with other annuals.

Pests/Diseases—No major problems

Landscaping Tips & Ideas—Indispensible in the spring flower garden, it is outstanding when used as an edging, planted in pockets, or as filler in garden beds. 'Snowcloth' and 'Carpet of Snow' are compact, low-growing white varieties. 'Rosie O'Day' is dark pink. The Wonderland series is known for its especially bright colors.

ANGELONIA
Angelonia angustifolia

Color(s)—Purple, white, and pink

Bloom period—Summer; warm-season

Mature Size (H x W)—18 to 24 in. x 10 to 15 in.

Water needs—Provide irrigation during drought periods to keep the blooms coming.

Planting/Care—Plant after frost is past, in full to part sun. Fine in average soil, but thrives in rich, fertile ground. The blooms are self-cleaning—no pruning or deadheading necessary. Fertilize at planting time; additional fertilizer is generally not needed.

Pests/diseases—Of minimal concern. Watch for aphids and spider mites.

Landscaping Tips & Ideas—Thrives in the heat! The colors complement almost any flower in the landscape. Use them in masses in beds, in containers, and in the garden. Look for 'Carita', 'Angel Mist', or 'Serena'. They come in various shapes, heights, and colors. The 'Serena' ones stay under 12 inches and are excellent for beds.

COCKSCOMB
Celosia argenta var. cristata

Color(s)—Hot colors in shades of red, magenta, purple, pink, and yellow

Bloom period—Spring, summer, and fall; warm-season

Mature Size (H x W)—6 to 36 in. x 6 to 12 in.

Water needs—Maintain a moist, not wet, soil throughout the entire growing season.

Planting/Care—If given a spot in full sun with well-drained soil, it grows easily. Remove any damaged or spent blooms or leaves as needed.

Pests/diseases—Usually has no serious pests or problems.

Landscaping Tips & Ideas—Works well when used in color gardens to outline other varieties and colors. There are basically two types. One is the plume type—they look like feathery flowers. The older of the two is the cockscomb type—these are crested with very tight flowers that resemble the comb of a rooster. Both work well in mass plantings or planters.

COLEUS
Solenostemon scutellarioides

Color(s)—Vivid shades of green, chartreuse, red, pink-white, maroon, bronze, and yellow

Bloom period—Not grown for flowers, grown for colorful foliage; warm-season

Mature Size (H x W)—6 to 36 in. x 12 to 48 in.

Water needs—Maintain a moist soil throughout the entire growing season (apply a layer of mulch).

Planting/Care—Plant in early spring after frost is past. Best in full sun to shade (depending on variety) and moist soil. Pinch back terminals, along with blooms, to induce branching and more colorful foliage. Add a slow-release fertilizer at planting time, or water-soluble fertilizers as needed.

Pests/diseases—Sucking insects may visit. Your local garden center can offer several control possibilities.

Landscaping Tips & Ideas—Works well in front of evergreen shrubbery in shaded areas or in beds among shade trees. Try hanging baskets, tubs, and planters. Most varieties currently available grow in sun, but need constant moisture to survive.

COPPER PLANT
Acalypha wilkesiana

Color(s)—Foliage in copper, red, bronze, pink, and green

Bloom period—Not grown for flowers, grown for foliage; warm-season

Mature Size (H x W)—2 to 4 ft. x 8 to 12 in.

Water needs—Water sufficiently to prevent soil dryness. Do not overwater.

Planting/Care—Very tough! Loves warmth and sun, so do not set them out until the air temperature is consistently above 65 degrees F—70 degrees F is even better—both day and night. Mulch well, and use fertilizer for optimum growth. Pinch back growing tips or terminals to induce fast growth and branching.

Pests/diseases—None serious

Landscaping Tips & Ideas—A wonderful background plant, it will take all the heat the sun can dish out. Use virtually anywhere in your home landscape where there is full sun. Do not plant in heavily shaded areas. In containers, use a lightweight potting mix. Often survives winters in Zone 9.

COSMOS
Cosmos spp. and cultivars

Color(s)—White, pink, rosy red, burgundy, yellow, gold, orange, and brick red

Bloom period—Spring through fall; warm-season

Mature Size (H x W)—1 to 4 ft. x 1 to 2 ft.

Water needs—Water often when plants are getting established, and thereafter only about once a week during hot, dry weather.

Planting/Care—Easy to grow, and the blazing heat of midsummer does not slow this plant down. Plant in spring or early fall, and mulch to control weeds and conserve soil moisture. Deadhead frequently to encourage longer flowering. Little need for fertilizer.

Pests/diseases—None serious

Landscaping Tips & Ideas—C. bipinnatus performs best in spring and early summer, and again in fall. Cultivars of C. bipinnatus look great with spring- and early-summer flowering plants; 'Gazebo' and 'Sonata' are favorites. Combine C. sulphureus with other heat-tolerant summer bloomers such as torenia, stokesia, verbena, and Mexican petunia.

DIANTHUS
Dianthus chinensis

Color(s)—White, pink, red, and blends

Bloom period—Spring, summer, and fall; cool-season

Mature Size (H x W)—4 to 18 in. x 6 to 12 in.

Water needs—Maintain a moist, but not wet, soil.

Planting/Care—Mulch to maintain soil moisture, keep weeds at bay, and moderate soil temperatures. Fertilize at planting time in the spring, or as needed with water-soluble fertilizers. Remove spent blooms and stems to encourage additional flowering. These do best in cool weather.

Pests/diseases—Aphids may visit tender growth, but they usually aren't a serious problem. If needed, visit nurseries that offer a wide range of control possibilities.

Landscaping Tips & Ideas—Some are classified as biennials or short-lived perennials, but often behave and are used as annuals in Texas landscapes. Excellent border plants, the taller standard varieties make for great backgrounds and cut flowers. May be grown solo in large containers or with additional flowering plants such as lobelia and verbena. Adaptable to rock gardens and detail designs, forming low mats and drifts of color.

DIASCIA
Diascia spp. and hybrids

Color(s)—Pink, rose, and salmon

Bloom period—Summer; warm-season

Mature Size (H x W)—10 to 14 in. x 10 to 14 in.

Water needs—Supplemental moisture is required during a drought.

Planting/Care—Plant in spring after the last frost, and avoid extremes of full sun or full shade. Good, rich garden soils are ideal. Mulch to retain soil moisture, to moderate hot summer temperatures, and to minimize weed growth. Apply water-soluble fertilizers on a regular basis when watering.

Pests/diseases—Aphids and spider mites are a possibility, but not a major concern.

Landscaping Tips & Ideas—These dainty, cascading plants, covered with masses of tubular flowers, are perfect for flower beds, windowboxes, containers, and hanging baskets. Recommended varieties include 'Ruby Field', 'Pink Queen', 'Elliott's Variety', 'Summer's Dance', and 'Strawberry Sundae'.

ESPERANZA
Tecoma spp. and cultivars

Color(s)—Yellow and orange

Bloom period—Summer; warm-season

Mature Size (H x W)—2 to 4 ft. x 2 to 4 ft.

Water needs—Water two to three times a week when rainfall is not present. Though relatively drought-tolerant, do water in severe dry periods or the plants will stop blooming.

Planting/Care—Plant after the last frost. They like full sun in fertile, organic sites, but accept half-day shade in sandy and limestone conditions. Use slow-release fertilizer; don't overfertilize or you may get all foliage and few flowers.

Pests/diseases—Potential pests include mealybugs, spider mites, and aphids; your local garden center can advise you on controls.

Landscaping tips & ideas—Amazing fortitude—gets bigger and better as the season progresses. Use as a seasonal container or bedding plant. Named cultivars include 'Lonesp' (yellow), 'Orange Jubilee' (orange), and 'Burnt Out' (burnt orange flowers). Tends to be perennial in Zone 9.

GERANIUM
Pelargonium x hortorum

Color(s)—Pink, red, bronze, maroon, white, and salmon

Bloom period—Spring, summer, and fall; warm-season

Mature Size (H x W)—12 to 24 in. x 8 to 18 in.

Water needs—Water thoroughly, taking care not to over-water—geraniums will not tolerate a wet soil.

Planting/Care—Maintain a three-inch layer of bark mulch throughout the entire growing season. Need to be well-nourished in order to do their best. Apply a slow-release fertilizer that will last throughout the growing season. Remove spent blooms.

Pests/diseases—No serious pests

Landscaping tips & ideas—Unlike in other parts of our country, geraniums are not considered full-sun summer annuals due to Texas's intense heat and sun. Enjoy them in the cooler spring and fall periods, and provide some shade in summer. May be grown as bedding plants in masses or in large terra-cotta pots, planters, windowboxes, and hanging baskets.

GLOBE AMARANTH
Gomphrena globosa

Color(s)—Purple, magenta, red, reddish-orange, orange, pink, white, and yellow

Bloom period—Summer to fall; warm-season

Mature Size (H x W)—9 in. to 2 ft. x 6 to 8 in.

Water needs—Water enough to prevent soil dryness. Do not overwater. These are tough and drought tolerant.

Planting/Care—Plant after danger of frost is past. For best results, plant in improved soil. Deadhead if desired. Apply liquid, water-soluble fertilizer as needed throughout the growing season.

Pests/diseases—This plant has no serious pests or diseases.

Landscaping tips & ideas—Try these very heat-tolerant beauties for summerlong color. Use the shorter dwarf varieties such as the purple-flowering 'Buddy' or the Gnome series (in shades of pink, white, and purple) in border plantings. For background color, use the standard types such as *G. haageana* in pale red to orange, or 'Lavender Lady' in pale purple.

JOSEPH'S COAT
Alternanthera spp.

Color(s)—Foliage in shades of green, copper, yellow, pink, rose, white, and gray

Bloom period—Not applicable; warm-season

Mature Size (H x W)—6 to 15 in. x 8 to 24 in.

Water needs—A good soaking twice a week suffices in drought periods, depending on your soil type and mulch.

Planting/Care—Plant in spring after the last frost, in full sun. Soil type is not critical as long as it drains well. The plant responds well to doses of water-soluble fertilizer. Shear to keep the growth busy and compact.

Pests/diseases—The larva of the ghost caterpillar feeds on the foliage at night, causing unsightly damage. Treat with organic and synthetic insecticides.

Landscaping tips & ideas—A truly tough and handsome foliage plant, it provides an ever-changing display. Use it with colorful annuals, in the garden or in containers. An especially good one is 'Ruby Amaranth', with bushy, three-foot growth and brilliant, large, purple-wine foliage.

IMPATIENS
Impatiens walleriana

Color(s)—White, red, scarlet, mauve, orchid, purple, pinks, orange, rose, and bicolors

Bloom period—Spring to frost; warm-season

Mature Size (H x W)—6 to 18 in. x 10 to 14 in.

Water needs—Maintain a moist soil throughout the growing season (try drip irrigation). Overwatering will cause the fleshy stems and plant crown to rot.

Planting/Care—Plant in shade in improved soil, in a spot that is easy to water. Conserve soil moisture with mulch. Impatiens respond quite favorably to seasonal applications of fertilizers. Midsummer pruning may be necessary.

Pests/diseases—Mealybugs, slugs, and snails may visit, but serious insect problems are rare.

Landscaping tips & ideas—Enjoy the super colors during the spring and early summer in shady areas only. The shorter varieties make excellent border plants and are striking in windowboxes and hanging baskets. Use in large masses beneath trees and to fill spaces in shaded shrub plantings. The New Guinea ones—such as 'Blake', 'Spectra Salmon', and 'Tango'—are dependable and attractive in sunnier spots.

KALE/CABBAGE, ORNAMENTAL
Brassica oleracea

Color(s)—White, carmine, purple, cream, and soft gray

Bloom period—Grown for foliage, not for flowers; cool-season

Mature Size (H x W)—10 to 18 in. x 10 to 12 in.

Water needs—Apply sufficient water to ensure moist growing conditions, but do not overwater.

Planting/Care—Plant in very early fall. Avoid shade and heavy clay soils. Maintain a season-long mulch layer. If a slow-release bedding-plant fertilizer was applied at planting time, no additional feeding is necessary. Remove unsightly leaves.

Pests/diseases—Cabbage loopers or aphids may visit but normally are not serious problems. Should controls be necessary, visit your local garden centers for pest-control advice.

Landscaping tips & ideas—Plant in very early fall when temperature is cool and transplants are available. In the southern part of our state in Zones 8 and 9, these may provide winter color all through the season till spring heat arrives. In Zones 6 and 7, it is still worth planting because of its spectacular early-fall colors.

LANTANA

Lantana camara

Color(s)—Yellow, white, pink, red, lavender, and orange

Bloom period—Summer; warm-season

Mature Size (H x W)—2 to 5 ft. x 3 to 6 ft.

Water needs—Drought tolerant after established, but bloom more consistently with supplemental irrigation.

Planting/Care—Plant after frost in any well-drained soil, in full sun. Mulch. Shear larger ones if they grow out of bounds. Routine feeding assures continuous bloom. Trim off berries if they appear, then fertilize to stimulate reflowering.

Pests/diseases—White flies, spider mites, and occasional lacebugs. Powdery mildew occurs if grown in too much shade.

Landscaping Tips & Ideas—A great rotational plant to follow cool-season plants like pansies, which start to decline in the heat. Use as a bedding plant or display in pots. Esperanza, sun coleus, and torenia are good companions with similar growing heights.

LICORICE PLANT

Helichrysum petiolare

Color(s)—Foliage in gray-green, white, yellow and green, and chartreuse

Bloom period—Not applicable; warm-season

Mature Size (H x W)—6 to 28 in. x 12 to 24 in.

Water needs—Keep soil consistently moist but not waterlogged. (Overwatering causes rotting, while overly dry situations cause the foliage to scorch.)

Planting/Care—Plant after the last frost, in a spot with some afternoon shade if possible. Fertile, well-drained soil is best. Control size by pruning. Supplemental feedings initiate vigorous growth.

Pests/diseases—Other than occasional whiteflies, pests are rare. Sometimes these plants are host to the larval stage of beautiful butterflies—so tolerate the chewed foliage, which will recover.

Landscaping Tips & Ideas—A designer's dream! Use with flowering annuals in ground beds or containers of all shapes and sizes. Combine gray licorice with purple verbena in hanging basket or lemon licorice with 'Fancy' sun coleus and pink million bells. The nice blend of colors and textures appears almost like a living bouquet.

MARIGOLD

Tagetes spp. and hybrids

Color(s)—Orange, yellow, mahogany, gold, lemon, near-white, and blends

Bloom period—Early summer through fall; warm-season

Mature Size (H x W)—6 to 36 in. x 10 to 18 in.

Water needs—Water sufficiently to prevent soil dryness. Do not overwater.

Planting/Care—Maintain even soil moisture with bark mulch. Marigolds benefit from a fertile soil. Use fertilizer as needed. Remove old blooms to encourage more flowering.

Pests/diseases—When it gets hot and dry late in the season, spider mites may visit your plants. (To avoid them, plant during late fall till first frost.) Snails and slugs may occur on young plants; if they become a problem, visit local garden centers for the best control possibilities.

Landscaping Tips & Ideas—Marigolds offer an effective mass of color in the garden at low cost. Short, bushy varieties work well in hanging baskets. All marigolds shine in containers, but because of their vigorous nature, use a container at least 12 inches in diameter.

MELAMPODIUM
Melampodium paludosum

Color(s)—Yellow

Bloom period—Summer; warm-season

Mature Size (H x W)—14 to 36 in. x 12 to 24 in.

Water needs—Established plants are fairly drought tolerant, but water if it wilts during hot, dry weather.

Planting/Care—Plant anytime in late spring through the summer and water well until established. It thrives in any average garden soil and likes full sun. Do not be generous with fertilizer, or the plants become enormous. It's also a good idea to mulch, not only to prevent weeds and conserve soil moisture, but to curb its prolific self-seeding. It is sometimes necessary to stake taller-growing cultivars.

Pests/diseases—Caterpillars sometimes eat holes in the leaves. Control with Bt as needed, following label directions.

Landscaping Tips & Ideas—The taller ones are best planted toward the back of the beds. It also looks great with ornamental grasses and 'Homestead Purple' verbena. Compact cultivars—such as 'Showstar', 'Million Gold', and 'Derby'— tend to be less floppy in the garden.

MILLION BELLS™
Calibrachoa hybrids

Color(s)—Pink, rose, yellow, and white, solids and various shades

Bloom period—Summer; warm-season

Mature Size (H x W)—4 to 6 in. x 24 to 36 in.

Water needs—Moisture seems to be the key to growing these delightful plants. Without supplemental irrigation, the plants stop blooming.

Planting/Care—Plant in spring after the last frost. Full sun sites are fine. They will accept partial shade, but with too much shade, the plants become spindly and bloom sporadically. Any soil type is fine as long as drainage is satisfactory. Seldom need pruning or trimming. Prolonged mid- to late summer heat can reduce flowering.

Pests/diseases—Watch for whiteflies.

Landscaping Tips & Ideas—Does well in containers and baskets but is even better as a bedding plant or groundcover. 'Trailing Pink' is a favorite.

NARROW-LEAF ZINNIA
Zinnia angustifolia

Color(s)—Orange, yellow, and white

Bloom period—Early summer to first frost; warm-season

Mature Size (H x W)—12 to 15 in. x 12 to 15 in.

Water needs—Little additional water is needed after plants are established and growing. It is well adapted to hot and dry conditions.

Planting/Care—Plant in spring or summer, in sun, in average soil. Water in well, and mulch. Shear plants back lightly in late summer or fall if they become rangy; if you do this, follow up with a light application of fertilizer.

Pests/diseases—None

Landscaping Tips & Ideas—This plant is prized for its sprawling habit, prolific flowering, and natural toughness. It also looks charming cascading over the edge of a raised planter or windowbox. The brilliant color is not always easy to use, but it combines well with rudbeckia, yellow purslane, gold portulaca, butterfly weed, or white periwinkle—other plants that enjoy hot, dry, sunny locations.

NASTURTIUM
Tropaeolum majus

Color(s)—Orange, yellow, red, and white

Bloom period—Summer; warm-season

Mature Size (H x W)—8 to 15 in. x 12 to 15 in.

Water needs—Water regularly throughout the growing season, and provide extra during dry spells.

Planting/Care—Easy from seed, nasturtiums thrive in a sunny spot in average soil (rich soil favors foliage at the expense of flowers). Protection from blazing sun may be needed. Fertilizing is not necessary.

Pests/diseases—Leafminers are a minor problem at times; simply pick off and discard affected leaves and they will soon be replaced.

Landscaping Tips & Ideas—Use these perky, bright flowers in pots, in hanging baskets, as an edging in the garden, and tucked in at the feet of taller flowers. Climbing and trailing ones can be trained to cascade down a rock wall or up over a trellis. Alaska Mix has variegated leaves. 'Peach Melba' has a vanilla-white flower with maroon markings.

PANSY
Viola x wittrockiana

Color(s)—White, blue, mahogany, rose, yellow, apricot, purple, violet, lavender, orange, and bicolors

Bloom period—Fall, winter, early spring; cool-season

Mature Size (H x W)—8 to 12 in. x 12 in.

Water needs—Maintain a moist soil during the growing season.

Planting/Care—Plant in early fall when nighttime temperatures have cooled. Do not plant in shaded areas or where the soil drains poorly. Feed occasionally for better flowering. Deadheading also encourages more flowering and tidies up the pansy.

Pests/diseases—Aphids, slugs, or snails may visit. Try your local garden center for several control possibilities.

Landscaping Tips & Ideas—Good with spring bulbs such as daffodils and tulips, and other spring-blooming annuals. They make colorful masses among rocks and informal paths in rock gardens. They also work well in containers in areas that need some splash of color in the fall, winter, and early spring. Plant groups of single colors; do not plant a "hodge-podge" with these beauties.

PENTAS
Pentas lanceolata

Color(s)—Red, pink, white, and lavender

Bloom period—Summer; warm-season

Mature Size (H x W)—10 to 36 in. x 10 to 24 in.

Water needs—Water once or twice a week during hot, dry weather.

Planting/Care—Plant in full sun to part shade in well-prepared beds. It does not require perfect drainage, but doesn't do well in spots that are constantly wet, either. Feed every six to eight weeks, or use your favorite slow-release fertilizer at planting. Taller cultivars may be cut back in late summer to control their size and shape.

Pests/diseases—Occasionally, caterpillars chew holes in the foliage, and damage can be significant if not caught early. Hand-pick, or spray with Bt (do not spray in butterfly gardens!).

Landscaping Tips & Ideas—Dwarf pentas perform well in containers alone or in combination with other summer annuals. They are outstanding combined with perennials, shrubs, and annuals in beds or in butterfly gardens with lantana, verbena, and butterfly weed.

PERIWINKLE
Catharanthus roseus

Color(s)—White, pink, purple, hot pink, deep rose, and bright lavender

Bloom period—Spring, summer, fall; warm-season

Mature Size (H x W)—6 to 12 in. x 12 to 24 in.

Water needs—Water as needed.

Planting/Care—They need full sun and fertile soil. Do not plant in heavy clay soil, wet locations, poorly drained locations, or heavily shaded areas. Need to be nourished throughout the growing season with a quality fertilizer.

Pests/diseases—Overwatering can encourage fungal diseases.

Landscaping Tips & Ideas—Periwinkles are truly "Texas flameproof" and continue to bloom and do well in spite of all the heat. Often used en masse to create groundcover and filler effects, these plants work equally well when container-grown. Proven varieties include 'Apricot Delight', 'Pacifica Red', 'Parasol', 'Peppermint Cooler', 'Velvet Rose', 'Tropicana', and 'Terrace Vermilion'.

PERSIAN SHIELD
Strobilanthes dyerianus

Color(s)—Silvery-purple foliage; occasional small purple flowers

Bloom period—Late summer; warm-season

Mature Size (H x W)—15 to 38 in. x 12 to 32 in.

Water needs—Water regularly throughout the growing season.

Planting/Care—Plant as the soil temperatures warm up and danger of frost is past. The foliage intensity is best achieved in organic soils in partial shade. Space 18 to 24 inches apart in groups; diagonal planting offers better design and allows the plants to fill in the space. Mulch, but don't let it get angled up on the plant stem because rotting can occur. Responds well to fertilizing, especially in poor soils. Pinch back to maintain compact habit.

Pests/diseases—Rare

Landscaping Tips & Ideas—Use as a specimen or background plant. Also appealing massed in ground beds. Flower colors of pink, purple, and white are perfect companions. Often survives winters in Zone 9.

PETUNIA
Petunia x hybrida

Color(s)—Pink, salmon, red, rose, burgundy, violet, lilac, cream to pale yellow, and variations

Bloom period—Spring, summer, and fall; cool-season

Mature Size (H x W)—6 to 18 in. x 12 to 24 in.

Water needs—Maintain a moist, but not wet, soil.

Planting/Care—Plant in very early spring or very early fall. They will resist light frosts. Give them moist, fertile soil that drains well. Nutrition can be added through fertilizer applied once at planting time. Deadheading can be beneficial.

Pests/diseases—Not common. For help with chewing pests, visit your local nursery.

Landscaping Tips & Ideas—Work well as beds of color early in the spring and even during early fall. Use in mixed annual and perennial beds. The most striking effect is accomplished by using many of one variety or color together. The single varieties such as 'Wave', 'Easy Wave', and 'Tidal Wave' tend to be more heat resistant.

PORTULACA
Portulaca grandiflora

Color(s)—Bright colors and pastels of white, red, cerise, rose pink, orange, and yellow

Bloom period—Spring to fall; warm-season

Mature Size (H x W)—4 to 12 in. x 8 to 12 in.

Water needs—Water enough to prevent soil dryness. It will not tolerate prolonged wet-soil conditions; the fleshy stems can be damaged with overwatering.

Planting/Care—Plant in spring after all danger of frost is past. It can stand the heat—even in nearly pure-sand locations. Apply fertilizer throughout the season. Cut back terminals to induce branching, and thus more blooms.

Pests/diseases—None

Landscaping Tips & Ideas—Marvelous in outlying beds in sunny locations. It works well as a container plant. It may also be grown successfully in hanging baskets of all sizes. Ideal for hot rock gardens and along sunny borders, trails, and paths. Use these varied and versatile plants in your favorite colors or in single colors in mass plantings in beds, pots, or in baskets for season-long color.

SALVIA
Salvia splendens

Color(s)—White, pink, rose, red, violet, burgundy, salmon, purple, and cream

Bloom period—Spring to fall; warm-season

Mature Size (H x W)—6 to 12 in. x 8 to 10 in.

Water needs—Maintain even soil moisture (drip irrigation is ideal). A mulch layer over the growing area will help.

Planting/Care—Plant in early spring after all danger of frost is past in well-drained, rich, moist soil. Get best results by planting where they will receive morning sun with some afternoon shade. Properly nourished salvia will survive stressful situations. Pinch spent bloom spikes to maintain a more compact and desirable plant.

Pests/diseases—Spider mites may appear during hot, dry summers. Visit local retail garden centers for proper pest controls.

Landscaping Tips & Ideas—Experiment with mass plantings in your home landscape. Plant salvia in entryways and yard beds. Use in containers on decks, gazebos, or by swings.

SNAPDRAGON
Antirrhinum majus

Color(s)—Red, white, yellow, orange, maroon, fuchsia, carmine, and pink

Bloom period—Fall and early spring; cool-season

Mature Size (H x W)—6 in. to 4 ft. x 6 to 8 in.

Water needs—Water sufficiently to maintain a moist soil, but don't overwater.

Planting/Care—Plant in the fall as a cool-season annual or to enjoy in late winter/early spring until our summertime heat takes them out. They need a very rich, moist, well-drained soil. Best in full sun. Provide good nutrition by fertilizing according to label directions. Remove spent blooms.

Pests/diseases—Rust may be a problem. Tender, new growth may be visited by aphids, but this is not usually a serious problem. Visit local garden centers for pest controls.

Landscaping Tips & Ideas—Group shorter varieties for plantings in mass effect or as border plants. The taller ones work very well as background with shorter snapdragon varieties or pansies in front. Create all sorts of effects by simply using various types, colors, and sizes.

SUNFLOWER
Helianthus annuus

Color(s)—Dark-centered; gold, lemon, bronze, mahogany, white, and bicolors

Bloom period—Summer and fall; warm-season

Mature Size (H x W)—18 in. to 10 ft. x 2 ft.

Water needs—To prevent wilting and dryness, supply sufficient moisture. Sunflowers are drought tolerant.

Planting/Care—Plant seeds directly in the soil after temperatures have warmed; follow directions on seed packet. At least six hours direct sun is ideal. Fertilize at planting time with a slow-release fertilizer, or use granular, liquid, or water-soluble fertilizers as needed. Larger varieties require some staking and tying. Smaller ones may benefit from the removal of spent blooms and leaves to encourage additional blossoms.

Pests/diseases—Some chewing insect pests, including grasshoppers, may visit. Consult your local garden center for appropriate controls.

Landscaping Tips & Ideas—Use with other summer-color annuals, shrubs, or perennials. Plant en masse to create a fun "forest" for the little ones.

TORENIA
Torenia fournieri

Color(s)—Blue, violet, purple, pink, and rose

Bloom period—Summer; warm-season

Mature Size (H x W)—12 in. x 14 in.

Water needs—Water weekly during hot, dry weather, and keep beds mulched to conserve soil moisture and to prevent weeds.

Planting/Care—Thrives in any average garden soil without preparation. Performs equally well in full, hot sun or in shady areas. Fertilize once in mid-summer to keep plants vigorous. It self-seeds with abandon, but rarely becomes a nuisance.

Pests/diseases—No major problems

Landscaping Tips & Ideas—The cool blue flowers blend well with any color scheme. In shady areas, combine with caladiums, impatiens, wax begonias, ligularia, and hosta. In sunnier areas, combine with lantana, melampodium, gaillardia, and coneflower. Clown, Dutchess, and Panda strains all have compact plants in a variety of colors and are excellent. Vigorous spreading types, such as the Wave and Catalina series, are outstanding.

VERBENA
Verbena x hybrida

Color(s)—White, pink, red, purple, magenta, wine, blue, apricot, salmon, and bicolors

Bloom period—Spring to fall; warm-season

Mature Size (H x W)—4 to 12 in. x 12 to 18 in.

Water needs—Maintain a moist soil, but don't overwater.

Planting/Care—Plant in a sunny location in well-drained ground. Use a bedding-plant fertilizer at planting time or through the season. Remove spent blooms.

Pests/diseases—Where air movement is poor or they are kept too damp, powdery mildew can occur. Few insect pests.

Landscaping Tips & Ideas—Use in any type of bed planting. Makes a vivid groundcover, complementing background seasonal annuals and perennials. Well-suited to embracing rocks and growing along gravel walks and paths. Due to its trailing nature, it also makes a wonderful hanging-basket plant and is particularly useful if you have limited space or want to create a vertical effect. Try in containers or windowboxes in sunny areas.

WAX BEGONIA
Begonia semperflorens-cultorum hybrids

Color(s)—White, red, pink, and blends

Bloom period—Spring, summer, and fall; warm-season

Mature Size (H x W)—6 to 16 in. x 8 to 12 in.

Water needs—Maintain a moist soil, but do not overwater. Mulch to conserve soil moisture.

Planting/Care—Plant in early spring in rich, deep, moist, and fertile soil. Apply bedding-plant fertilizer at planting time. Apply liquid, water-soluble, and granular fertilizers as needed. Remove spent blooms or damaged leaves.

Pests/diseases—Slugs or snails may visit, but they are usually not a serious problem. Your local garden center will have several control options.

Landscaping Tips & Ideas—These are the annual bedding plant of choice for Texans who wish to have season-long color in the shade or sun from the same plant. Use around walkways and in landscape beds or as edging plants with taller plants as background. Attractive with caladiums (in the shade) and verbena, marigolds, and periwinkle (in the sun).

ZINNIA
Zinnia elegans

Color(s)—Red, orange, rose, cherry, pink, salmon, lavender, gold, yellow, cream, white, green, and bicolors

Bloom period—Summer and fall; warm-season

Mature Size (H x W)—6 to 40 in. x 6 to 12 in.

Water needs—Maintain even soil moisture. Don't allow to become extremely dry or wet.

Planting/Care—Plant in the spring, in beds that drain well and have good air movement. Use a season-long bedding-plant fertilizer, and liquid, water-soluble, or granulated fertilizers throughout the season. Remove spent blooms. Tall ones may require staking due to the weight of their blooms in wind and rain.

Pests/diseases—May have powdery mildew if air circulation and drainage are poor. Leafminers also visit occasionally; if this becomes a problem, visit your local garden center for controls.

Landscaping Tips & Ideas—Spectacular when massed as a bedding plant, they also work well with other annuals such as salvias and marigolds. Use in entryways or as background plants. These are much at home in cottage gardens as well as in the vegetable garden for cutting. Dwarf varieties work well in containers.

JANUARY

- Make a New Year's resolution to start a Texas gardening journal. An important part of planning for the future is remembering what was done in the past.

- Look through the many seed catalogs that arrive now. There is still plenty of time to decide what to plant when the cool-season annuals finish, but it won't hurt to start coming up with some new ideas. Note the All-America Selections winners for the new year, as well as past winners.

- In some Texas zones, there is still time to purchase and plant seeds of fast-growing, cool-season annuals such as alyssum, annual phlox, calendula, forget-me-not, and nasturtium.

- Keep beds mulched to suppress weed growth, retain soil warmth, and conserve soil moisture.

- Cool temperatures and normal rainfall generally make watering unnecessary this month. Do watch rainfall amounts, and if the weather is dry, water thoroughly. Annuals in container plantings will need to be watered regularly.

FEBRUARY

- Purchase seeds of warm-season annuals locally this month. Many seeds can be planted in flats or outside in beds in late March.

- Draw simple sketches of your flower beds and begin to plan what will go into them for the warm season. Decide on a color scheme and the texture and forms your plantings will have.

- Spring is here in Zones 8b and 9. Flowering trees and spring bulbs are blooming, but February can still produce bitterly cold weather and most often will. If severe weather is predicted, it doesn't hurt to place some old blankets, sheets, tarps, or grow cover over a bed if you are concerned about cold damage.

- If beds seem to be staying too wet, pull back mulch to allow water to evaporate.

- Remove wood sorrel from cool-season flower beds using a trowel or weeding tool so you get the roots and bulbs attached.

MARCH

- Some gardeners who did not plant in the fall may notice the amazing display of pansies, dianthus, and alyssum in other gardens and just have to go out and buy some. If you want to plant cool-season plants, choose well-established ones in 4-inch pots.

- It is time to seriously begin planning your warm-season flower beds.

- In Zones 8 and 9, some warm-season bedding plants may be direct-seeded into the garden now, including cleome, cosmos, Dahlberg daisy, marigold, and rudbeckia. Once the shoots come up, cover them if nighttime lows are predicted to go below the low 30s.

- Stay on top of the weeds! Keep beds well mulched. Mulches should be at least 3 inches thick. Pine straw, cypress mulch, pine bark, leaves, and dry grass clippings are just some of the suitable choices.

- Snails and slugs can be a major problem, chewing holes in leaves and flowers, particularly pansies. Use selected baits per label directions.

APRIL

- Most of the warm-season bedding plants can be planted this month statewide.

- The flowers of many cool-season annuals that are blooming so beautifully now are edible. They make colorful garnishes or attractive additions to fresh salads. Some are: pansy, viola, dianthus, nasturtium, calendula, and ornamental cabbage and kale (flowers and foliage). Be sure to wait prescribed periods before using after pest-control aids are applied.

- Caterpillars are on the prowl. Look for their droppings, which can be the size of a BB or pencil eraser and dark green to black. Look for holes in the leaves also. Visit retail garden centers for help in identifying insect pests and selecting appropriate aids.

- As the weather warms and plants grow larger, cool-season annuals growing in containers will need more frequent watering.

- Annuals growing in containers need regular fertilization, as constant watering leaches available nutrients quickly. Fertilize once a week with soluble fertilizer at half the recommended rate.

MAY

- In May we often seed a transition from warm weather to intense heat. Many cool-season annuals are in decline. Clean out the beds and replant with warm-season annuals.

- Do not plant transplants too deeply, and make sure they are spaced properly. If anything, annuals have a tendency to grow larger in our climate than their tags predict. Water them well with root stimulator to get the young plants off to a good start.

- Newly planted beds will need thorough watering if the weather is dry. (Do not water lightly every day.)

- Get ready: here they come. Crawling, hopping, flying, and walking, there are lots of insect pests out there ready to damage your annuals. Regularly inspect your plants for early signs. Some damage is inevitable—just don't let it get out of hand.

- Make notes in your Texas gardening journal; this will be valuable when planning future plantings.

JUNE

- Think of ways to deal with the intense heat of the next three or four months. Try to work on days that are overcast, or work in shady areas of the landscape, moving as the shade moves from one location to another. We enjoy very early morning times—give them a try.

- Pay careful attention to the weather and rainfall amounts. Always water deeply and thoroughly when irrigating.

- Group outdoor container plants in a shady location, as this will help slow water loss.

- If plants are pale and low in vigor, try an application of soluble fertilizer (use a hose and applicator for faster, easier application).

- Hot, dry weather favors the outbreak of spider mites. Damage starts as tiny pale or white speckles on the upper surface of foliage. Fine webbing may be seen on plants that have heavy infestations. Visit your local nurseries for information and aids to control them.

JULY

- Some annuals planted back in March or early April may be winding down toward the end of this month or in early August, especially those that can't handle the heat. Evaluate them and make plans for their replacement as they finish.

- If you need to add some color to your landscape, most nurseries carry a decent selection of warm-season bedding plants through the summer. You can also direct-seed some of the quick, easy ones such as amaranthus, cosmos, gaillardia, marigold, portulaca, sunflower, and zinnia.

- High temperatures place great stress on annual flower beds, and this time of year can be very hot and dry. Watch the weather, and water appropriately. Annuals in containers may need to be watered twice a day.

- In the cool of air-conditioned rooms, make notes and entries in your Texas gardening journal about what was done in your summer annual plantings and what you would like to do next season.

AUGUST

- August is a month of evaluation. True annuals planted earlier will often need to be replaced unless they are heat tolerant. Hanging baskets of annuals may also be past their prime and need to be replanted. Next year, use more heat-tolerant varieties.

- Plant replacements for annuals that are no longer attractive. Check local nurseries for colorful, heat-tolerant bedding plants. Don't overlook colorful foliage plants such as ornamental sweet potatoes, copper plant, Joseph's coat, coleus, dusty miller, purple leaf basil, lantana, 'Lady in Red' salvia, and blue daze.

- Stake, support, trim back, or even remove larger-growing annuals that are overly enthusiastic, to make sure everybody has enough room.

- Even though many tender perennials are in bloom, trim them back one-third to one-half their height. It is worth the temporary loss of flowers to have shapely, attractive plants for the late summer to fall period.

- Fertilize those annuals that you have pruned back to encourage regrowth.

SEPTEMBER

- Cool-season annual seeds can be sown this month. If you have not begun to think about plans for the cool-season annual garden yet, perhaps you should.

- We aren't out of the hot season yet. Continue to monitor rainfall, and water thoroughly when necessary.

- After months of growth, annuals in containers will have filled them with their roots. Frequent watering is critical to plantings in this condition since the roots will deplete water in the soil rapidly. Consider repotting into a larger pot if watering once or twice a day is not sufficient.

- Whiteflies are often a major pest on lantana, hibiscus, and a variety of other ornamentals. Control is difficult once they get out of hand. Visit local nurseries for information on control aids.

- Even if only for 10 or 15 minutes in the early morning or evening, spend a little time two or three times a week on weed control.

OCTOBER

- Once again, it becomes a pleasure to get into the garden, and there's lots to do. It is time to think about your cool-season annual garden.

- You can direct-seed poppies, larkspur, sweet pea, calendula, and alyssum now. Chrysanthemums are often planted in flower beds this month, but marigolds are becoming a popular substitute—they provide some of the same yellow, gold, mahogany, and orange colors but bloom longer.

- October may be a relatively dry month. Water plants as needed, paying special attention to any newly planted areas.

- After transplants have been in new pots for about three weeks, begin to fertilize them. Fertilize new plantings in beds at the time they are installed.

- Caterpillars can be a major problem on annuals now, and moths have had all summer to build up populations. Treat promptly with an approved insect-control according to label directions.

NOVEMBER

- Finalize your plans for beds of cool-season bedding plants and plant them. Have a good idea of the colors, heights, and amounts needed, as well as light conditions, before you go to the nursery.

- Along with May, November is the most active month for planting beds of annuals. Pansies are our most cold-hardy and usually produce a colorful show all cool/cold season.

- The hard decision now is what to do with the tender perennials that may still be looking attractive. Tempting as it may be to leave them in the bed, they will eventually have to make way for cool-season plants.

- You generally don't need to change the mix in containers when changing plantings. If it seems to be dense and compacted, blend in some sifted compost or peat moss along with some vermiculite or perlite or toss the old mix into your compost pile or a garden bed and start with fresh potting soil.

DECEMBER

- Things should be coming together in your cool/cold-season flower beds in early December. Try to get most planting done well before the holidays. You know you won't have time later.

- Make notes in your Texas gardening journal on which plants were planted where.

- Should temperatures below freezing be predicted, bring flats or pots of transplants into a protected location for the night. Direct-seeded annuals will probably be fine, but if they are newly germinated and temperatures will drop to the mid- to low 20s, cover them.

- Annual beds should be mulched—maintain a mulch 3 to 4 inches deep.

- Fertilize only if plants show deficiency symptoms such as pale leaves, stunted growth, and yellow lower leaves.

- It is a relief to see insect and disease problems diminish. Weeds, however, are not so kind. Wood sorrel is a persistent perennial weed—keep after it.

PERENNIALS
for Texas

Perennials are a flower gardener's delight. Though showy and colorful like annuals, their longer lives make them a less transient part of the garden. The ability of some varieties to live for years allows them to become old friends that can provide you with beauty for many seasons. As with annuals, though, perennial beds and borders can be a high-maintenance part of the landscape.

Perennials are plants that live for three years or longer. Unlike annuals and biennials, perennials do not die after flowering and setting seed. Technically, trees, shrubs, lawngrasses, and bulbs are all perennials, but gardeners use the term "perennial" as an abbreviation for "hardy, herbaceous perennial"—a group of nonwoody, hardy plats grown for their attractive flowers or foliage. Some herbaceous perennials are evergreen and never go completely dormant, while others go dormant, lose their leaves, and essentially disappear at certain times of the year, usually winter.

Success with perennials in Texas depends largely on proper selection, beginning with a rejection of perennials that only grow well north of Zone 6. To survive here, perennials must be able to endure the summer heat, humidity, and rain or lack of rain, along with the diseases that may visit. Stop planting perennials recommended in books written for the rest of the country and focus on those that will thrive in our climate. You will discover that not only is perennial gardening possible here, but we can plant beds that rival those in any part of the world.

COREOPSIS

garden blooming throughout much of the year. Some other important questions you need to answer about the perennials you want to use: What species or cultivars are best for Texas? How tall will the plants grow? What colors are the flowers? What light conditions does the plant prefer—full or part sun, part shade or shade? Do they need excellent drainage? Are they evergreen? If they go dormant—when? How fast will they spread?

With some thoughtful planning, perennials can serve many purposes and attractively embellish the landscape in a variety of ways. They are impressive in perennial borders or mixed borders (which could include annuals, bulbs, shrubs, and even small trees). Tucked in pockets among shrubs, they can brighten up an area when the shrubs are not in bloom. Many perennials make outstanding specimens in containers.

PLANNING THE PERENNIAL GARDEN

Gardening with perennials is something that gardeners often develop an interest in as they become more experienced. When you finally reach that "been there, done that" stage with annuals, perennials offer exciting challenges and great fun. Utilizing perennials effectively does, however, require learning and careful planning to achieve best results.

Different perennials have various seasons of bloom—some over a long period, some for just a few weeks. Utilizing a variety of perennials that bloom at different times can keep your perennial

PLANTING AND TRANSPLANTING

The first step in planting perennials is bed preparation. It is important to do a good job at each of the following stages:

1. Remove weeds and other unwanted plants from the bed. Growing weeds may be eliminated with a non-selective weed-control aid that does not leave residue in the soil.

2. Turn the soil to a depth of at least 8 to 12 inches.

LAVENDER

through early December, and late summer- or fall-flowering perennials are planted from February through early April, or in fall. Many gardeners plant perennials throughout the winter when weather is mild, especially in south Texas.

PLANTING TRANSPLANTS

1. Space plants according to label information, references, or local advice. Most perennials will grow considerably larger than the size of the transplant. Do not crowd them.

2. Plant transplants with the top of the rootball even with or slightly above the soil. Many perennials will rot if planted too deeply. If the roots are in a tightly packed mass, separate before planting. A small amount of granular slow-release fertilizer may be placed in each planting hole. Firm the soil around the plant once you have finished planting.

3. Water newly planted transplants thoroughly. A root stimulator may be applied according to label directions.

4. Mulch the bed 3 to 4 inches deep to control weeds.

Some perennials are relatively easy to grow from seed. Seeds are generally planted directly into garden beds or in containers outside to raise transplants. This is best done after the danger of frost or freeze is past and early enough for the plants to become established before winter—April through August.

CARING FOR YOUR PERENNIALS

Perennial beds require watering, fertilizing, grooming, staking, cutting back, dividing, transplanting, weeding, and mulching. Do not plant more beds of perennials than your time will allow you to properly care for.

Providing support for tall-growing perennials is important and often neglected by gardeners. Sprawling perennials may be unattractive and can damage the plants around them. Plan to stake, cage, tie up, or otherwise support perennials that need it early, before they fall over.

3. Spread a 4-inch layer of compost, rotted leaves, aged manure, finely ground pine bark, or sphagnum peat over the bed. If needed, add sand, lime, or sulfur at this stage. Have your soil tested through your county office of the Texas Cooperative Extension Service to learn more about what will improve your soil's fertility.

4. Thoroughly blend the amendments into the top 4 to 6 inches, rake smooth, and you're ready to plant.

Perennials are most often planted using purchased transplants or divisions. Transplants may be purchased in 4-inch to gallon-sized or larger pots. Generally, spring- and early-summer-flowering perennials are planted in October

WATERING

Watering is critical for newly planted perennials, especially during hot, dry summer weather. Water deeply and thoroughly by applying water slowly over a period of time. Sprinklers may be used, but water can damage flowers and encourage leaf diseases. Soaker hoses provide a good alternative. The use of 3 to 4 inches of mulch in perennial gardens will conserve moisture and reduce irrigation need.

FERTILIZATION

A small amount of granular slow-release fertilizer can be added to the planting hole at planting. Always apply any fertilizer according to label directions. During the growing season, fertilize established perennials beginning in March or early April and then according to package directions using a general-purpose, premium-quality, long-lasting, slow-release fertilizer appropriate for your area. Follow package directions. Scatter the fertilizer granules evenly throughout the bed and water-in to wash the fertilizer off the foliage and into the soil. In Texas, premium-quality granular rose fertilizers and multipurpose 3:2:1 ratio fertilizers (including 21-7-14, 15-5-10, and 18-6-12) work well in perennial plantings.

PINK IRIS

PEST CONTROL

Pest control is usually a part of perennial gardening, but the use of tough, well-adapted perennials will minimize problems. Remember, when using pest-control aids, always read the label thoroughly before purchase and use.

Caterpillars damage plants by chewing holes in leaves. The whitefly can be a difficult insect to control, especially in mid- to late summer when populations can get way out of hand. The adults are small, snow-white flies; the larvae appear as small disks under the leaves. Aphids cluster on new growth and flower buds, sucking the sap from the plant. They are relatively easy to control but may return, requiring additional applications of pest-control aids. Various sucking insects, such as leaf hoppers, thrips, and plant bugs, cause small white flecks to appear on the foliage of many perennials. The damage is generally little more than cosmetic but can weaken the plant if extensive.

Spider mites can be devastating on some plants, especially during hot, dry weather. Snails and slugs love hostas and other plants that have succulent leaves and grow in shady areas. Control with baits used according to label directions, handpicking, or traps.

Well-adapted perennials planted in the right location generally have minor disease problems. Leaf spots caused by various fungi and powdery mildew will sometimes occur and can be treated with fungus-control aids. Root and crown rot may occur if drainage is inadequate, during periods of excessive rain, or if perennials not well adapted to Texas are planted.

BEEBALM
Monarda didyma

Hardiness—Hardy throughout Texas

Color(s)—Pink, rose, purple, and white

Bloom Period—Summer, on and off

Mature Size (H x W)—1 to 3 ft. x 2 to 4 ft.

Water Needs—Provide supplemental irrigation during periods of drought. Mulch to retain soil moisture.

Planting/Care—Plant in fertile soil in early summer and allow plants plenty of elbow room. Deadhead spent flowers to ensure additional color. Remove dormant foliage in the fall or early spring. Replace decomposed mulch as needed.

Pests/Diseases—Powdery mildew is a common problem, alleviated by good air circulation, removing and disposing of infected foliage, and spraying with a fungicide as directed. Alternatively, seek out the newer, mildew-resistant cultivars.

Landscaping Tips & Ideas—Taller ones are good background plants in perennial borders. Crowding them with other perennials tends to help keep them in their allotted space.

BLACK-EYED SUSAN
Rudbeckia spp.

Hardiness—Hardy throughout Texas

Color(s)—Yellow

Bloom Period—Summer

Mature Size (H x W)—1 to 3 ft. x 6 to 8 in.

Water Needs—Water sufficiently to prevent complete soil dryness, but do not overwater.

Planting/Care—Fall planting is best, and early spring planting is fine. Choose a well-drained spot that gets at least eight hours of sunlight per day. Add some organic matter to the soil. Fertilize once a growing season. Cut back old or spent flower stems.

Pests/Diseases—None

Landscaping Tips & Ideas—Some are short-lived perennials (R. fulgida), some are annuals (R. hirta)—all will work well in the home landscape in full-sun locations. Try in difficult-to-water areas that beg for great summertime color. Old-fashioned fragrant petunias and globe amaranth make good companions, or try a "native garden" look with some ornamental grasses.

BLAZING STAR
Liatris spp. and cultivars

Hardiness—Hardy throughout Texas

Color(s)—Shades of purple, white

Bloom Period—Summer and fall

Mature Size (H x W)—1 to 5 ft. x 1½ ft.

Water Needs—Water often enough to keep soil moderately moist, but beware: overwatering on heavy soils can rot the plant.

Planting/Care—Plant in spring or early fall, although fall is better. For best results, plant in full sun and fertile, well-drained soil. Fertilizer is not required, but will help improve vigor and foliage color and encourage larger flower spikes. Plants top-heavy with blossoms should be staked.

Pests/Diseases—Uncommon

Landscaping Tips & Ideas—Use with yellow, daisy-type annuals such as Black-eyed Susan and small species of sunflowers. The taller cultivars are excellent as the rearmost flower in perennial borders. 'Kobold' has very deep purple flowers.

BUTTERFLY WEED
Asclepias tuberosa

Hardiness—Hardy throughout Texas

Color(s)—Orange to orange-red

Bloom Period—Mid- to late summer

Mature Size (H x W)—1½ to 3 ft. x 1 ft.

Water Needs—Drought tolerant once established. Provide water in extremely dry, hot weather.

Planting/Care—Plant in spring in full sun, in sandy or infertile soil. If soil is acidic, change it to alkaline by adding appropriate amounts of lime. Little additional fertilizer or water is needed. Pull out competing weeds. Be sure to mark the location of dormant plants so that resting ones will not be disturbed or destroyed.

Pests/Diseases—None

Landscaping Tips & Ideas—Plant with African marigold, annual salvia, sunflower, cosmos, calendula, and zinnia. Use a mixture of these in a wildflower or butterfly garden. 'Gay Butterflies' is a standout for its red, orange, and yellow flowers.

CARYOPTERIS
Caryopteris x clandonensis

Hardiness—Hardy in USDA Zones 6 and 7

Color(s)—Blue-lavender

Bloom Period—Late summer into early fall

Mature Size (H x W)—3 to 4 ft. x 3 to 4 ft.

Water Needs—Water to keep soil from drying out, especially during droughts.

Planting/Care—Best in full sun in well-drained, fertile soil. Fertilizing is not necessary. Trim back in late winter or early spring.

Pests/Diseases—Spider mites and lace bugs are possible—both cause speckled foliage from their sucking feeding habits.

Landscaping Tips & Ideas—A great background in a perennial garden, especially in association with evergreens. Plant as a border near fence rows. Can stand alone, also looks good in groups of three. Do not locate in a heavy-traffic area, however, because it attracts lots of bees. For an eye-catching display, pair it with pink flowers.

CATMINT
Nepeta x faassenii

Hardiness—Hardy in USDA Zones 6 and 7

Color(s)—Violet-blue and pink

Bloom Period—Summer and fall

Mature Size (H x W)—1 to 3 ft. x 2 to 3 ft.

Water Needs—Water to get established, and during prolonged dry spells.

Planting/Care—Plant in spring or summer. It likes afternoon shade in hot, humid locations. Fertilizing is not needed. Prune to initiate new growth during a lull in flowering periods.

Pests/Diseases—Since it is related to catnip, keep cats away until it is well-established (by the second year, a plant should be able to bounce back from such chewing).

Landscaping Tips & Ideas—Use in a border to frame other, taller perennials. Use as filler plants grouped in clusters of three or more. The violet blooms complement pastel hues. 'Blue Wonder' has compact, upright growth. 'Sweet Dreams' has soft, two-tone pink flowers.

COREOPSIS
Coreopsis spp. and cultivars

Hardiness—Hardy throughout Texas

Color(s)—Yellow, white, pink, and rose

Bloom Period—Late spring to fall frost

Mature Size (H x W)—12 to 32 in. x 15 to 24 in.

Water Needs—A durable plant, but irrigate in severe drought.

Planting/Care—Plant in spring or summer in full sun. Requires good drainage. More robust in moist, fertile soil. Fertilize if the foliage appears nutrient-deficient. Deadhead to force continued bloom. Trim in late winter or early spring as new growth emerges.

Pests/Diseases—Caterpillars and spittlebugs may appear. In severe infestations, cut plant to the ground and fertilize as foliage regrows. Mildew can occur, especially during prolonged rainy periods.

Landscaping Tips & Ideas—Use it as border, background, or filler plant. It is a favorite in wildflower gardens. Two outstanding, tried-and-true cultivars are pale yellow 'Moonbeam' and brighter yellow 'Zagreb'.

DAYLILY
Hemerocallis spp. and hybrids

Hardiness—Hardy throughout Texas

Color(s)—Yellow, orange, pink, red, apricot, lilac, cream, white, and bicolors

Bloom Period—Summer

Mature Size (H x W)—1 to 4 ft. x 1 to 2 ft.

Water Needs—Water as necessary to prevent wilting, especially during the blooming periods.

Planting/Care—Daylilies are so tough and durable, they can be dug, divided, or planted any time of the year in Texas. Plant in deep, rich, improved soil. Fertilize in springtime. Remove spent stalks.

Pests/Diseases—Daylily rust can be a serious problem. Aphids and thrips may appear in spring, and grasshoppers in late summer. Visit your local nursery for appropriate controls.

Landscaping Tips & Ideas—Versatile! Use as bedding plants for mass plantings, or display in tubs. Or mix with other colorful perennials, bulbs, or late-spring and summer annuals. Good planted with dwarf cannas or iris.

DUSTY MILLER
Centaurea cineraria

Hardiness—USDA Zones 7 to 9, varies with varieties selected

Color(s)—Foliage, white to silver

Bloom Period—Not grown for flowers

Mature Size (H x W)—8 to 18 in. x 12 to 18 in.

Water Needs—Water as necessary to prevent soil dryness.

Planting/Care—Plant in spring after frost, in sun. Good drainage is key. Fertilize in the spring when new growth begins. Remove any blooms and prune through the growing season to maintain a more compact, uniform habit.

Pests/Diseases—Considered virtually insect- and disease-free

Landscaping Tips & Ideas—The neutral yet vibrant silver foliage brings out the mixed colors of other flowering annuals and perennials. Shorter varieties may be used in masses to create a groundcover effect. Taller ones are excellent background plants. When planting in a border, use a dwarf variety such as 'Frosty' or 'Silver Queen'.

ECHINACEA
Echinacea spp.

Hardiness—All coneflowers are hardy in Texas

Color(s)—Purple, pink, white, rose, yellow, and orange

Bloom Period—Spring, summer, and into fall

Mature Size (H x W)—1½ to 3 ft. x 1 to 2 ft.

Water Needs—Water as necessary to prevent soil dryness, and mulch well.

Planting/Care—Will grow in clay, loam, or sandy soils, so long as the site is well drained. Dappled shade is best. Dig in some organic matter. Fertilize in the spring as growth gets started. Remove spent blooms and stems.

Pests/Diseases—None serious

Landscaping Tips & Ideas—Grow the native species, E. angustifolia, or the popular E. purpurea, or cultivars of these, which come with showier flowers and colors beyond the traditional pale purple. Grow them en mass (planted a foot apart), as clumped accents in a flower bed, or in large tubs or containers.

FALSE INDIGO
Baptisia spp.

Hardiness—Hardy throughout Texas

Color(s)—Purple, yellow, or white

Bloom Period—Late spring and summer

Mature Size (H x W)—3 to 5 ft. x 3 to 5 ft.

Water Needs—Water after planting to establish them, but then reduce as the plants mature.

Planting/Care—Plant in the fall or spring, in full sun and average soil with good drainage. This is a legume plant forming nitrogen-fixing bacteria along its fibrous roots, so supplemental feedings are often not needed.

Pests/Diseases—Of little concern

Landscaping Tips & Ideas—Use as a specimen plant or background border plant. It complements ornamental grasses, coreopsis, daylilies, and artemisia. 'Purple Smoke' has blue-gray foliage with elongated purple flower spikes; 'Screamin' Yellow' has vibrant yellow flowers. Both need plenty of space.

FOUR O'CLOCK
Mirabilis jalapa

Hardiness—Hardy in all zones in Texas except USDA Zone 6

Color(s)—White, pink, salmon, lavender, yellow, magenta, and blends

Bloom Period—Summer

Mature Size (H x W)—3 to 4 ft. x 3 ft.

Water Needs—Water as necessary to maintain a moist soil; mulch to conserve soil moisture.

Planting/Care—Will grow in sand or heavy clay, but prefer moist, loamy soils. Provide room to grow and multiply (thin out unwanted plants as they come up in the spring). Fertilize when growth emerges.

Pests/Diseases—Virtually none

Landscaping Tips & Ideas—Use as tall background plants. They also look great in containers with white annual vinca trailing over the edges. Use as filler plants, border plants, or in mass plantings. They can be used in an out-of-the-way garden area, as they are virtually maintenance free and will form large plantings.

GARDEN MUM
Dendranthema x grandiflorum

Hardiness—Hardy throughout Texas

Color(s)—All colors except blue

Bloom Period—Fall

Mature Size (H x W)—12 to 18 in. x 12 to 18 in. or more

Water Needs—Water as necessary to maintain a moist soil. Do not let them become totally dry.

Planting/Care—Plant either in the fall in full bud, or in the spring after frost. Fertilize as new growth appears, and apply every eight weeks through the growing season. Start pinching back to 4 in. in springtime, and continue till mid-July. Stake taller ones with heavy blooms.

Pests/Diseases—Select locally adapted varieties, and there should be no problems with insects or diseases.

Landscaping Tips & Ideas—Plant along walkways and around garden structures such as decks, gazebos, benches, ornamental pools, or water fountains. They also work well in large containers.

GAURA
Gaura lindheimeri

Hardiness—Hardy throughout Texas

Color(s)—White and pink

Bloom Period—Summer

Mature Size (H x W)—3 to 5 ft. x 3 to 4 ft.

Water Needs—Water during extremely dry periods.

Planting/Care—It prefers full sun, and good drainage is critical. A site with good air movement minimizes pest problems and allows for more movement of the flowering spikes. Mulch to control weeds and retain soil moisture.

Pests/Diseases—Spider mites can occur if air circulation is poor, and leaf spots are more likely in heavily shaded spots.

Landscaping Tips & Ideas—A tall, mounding plant ideal for the background of a perennial border. Delightful in association with evergreen shrubs. May be grown in a large container. 'Franz Valley' is a compact choice. 'Carrie's Gold' has variegated foliage and pink-and-white flowers. 'Crimson Butterflies' has burgundy foliage and a compact habit. 'Siskiyou Pink' is also lovely.

GOLDENROD
Solidago canadensis

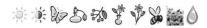

Hardiness—Hardy throughout Texas

Color(s)—Yellow

Bloom Period—Late summer and fall

Mature Size (H x W)—I to 6 ft. x 2 to 4 ft.

Water Needs—Water established plants only during prolonged dry spells.

Planting/Care—Plant in partial or full sun in well-drained soil. Apply slow-release organic fertilizer instead on a yearly basis. Prune to remove dormant foliage before new growth begins. Stake larger, upright-growing selections.

Pests/Diseases—Potential pests include spider mites, thrips, and leafminers, and occasional disease include leaf rust and powdery mildew. Properly spaced plants with good air circulation and afternoon shade are less likely to succumb to these problems.

Landscaping Tips & Ideas—Plant taller ones toward the back of borders. Use dwarf ones as border plants or in masses. Good with ornamental grasses, fall asters, and mums.

HARDY HIBISCUS
Hibiscus moscheutos

Hardiness—Hardy throughout Texas

Color(s)—White, pink, purple, and red

Bloom Period—Spring to autumn

Mature Size (H x W)—2 to 6 ft. or more x 3 to 6 ft.

Water Needs—Water as needed to maintain a moist soil.

Planting/Care—Plant early spring to early summer, in afternoon shade or dappled light. Good air movement is advised. Plant in an easy-to-water area, so you can keep the soil moist. Will grow in boggy conditions. Fertilize at the beginning of the season, approximately 10 weeks later, and once in the fall. Mulch. Prune very low to the ground by the end of winter.

Pests/Diseases—Not a problem

Landscaping Tips & Ideas—Adds color to beds, nooks, and corner plantings, mass plantings, or planters. Works well in front of broadleaf evergreen foundation plantings; not suitable for primary foundation plantings. 'Texas Star' (H. coccineus) is also recommended.

HOSTA
Hosta spp.

Hardiness—Hardy throughout Texas

Color(s)—Blooms in white, blue, lavender; foliage in green, chartreuse, gray, blue, and combinations

Bloom Period—Summer, varies by cultivar

Mature Size (H x W)—12 to 18 in. x 18 to 36 in.

Water Needs—Water as necessary to maintain a moist soil throughout the growing season.

Planting/Care—Plant in shade in early spring, in beds well-prepared with organic matter. Fertilize in early spring and again throughout the growing season as needed.

Pests/Diseases—If slugs and/or snails are already a problem in your landscape, get the situation under control before planting any hostas. See your local garden center for control measures.

Landscaping Tips & Ideas—Grow singly as accents in the shady garden, or in masses to create a groundcover effect. Grow in tubs to provide portable color for shady areas. Lovely in natural, woodland settings.

IRIS
Iris spp. and cultivars

Hardiness—Hardy throughout Texas

Color(s)—All colors, plus bicolors

Bloom Period—Spring to early summer

Mature Size (H x W)—3 to 4 ft. x 12 to 16 in.

Water Needs—Keep soil moist but not wet.

Planting/Care—Not all irises do well in our warm Texas climate—make selections with help from your local garden center. Best in fertile soil. Fertilize when new growth emerges. Remove spent bloom stalks but leave the foliage for as long as possible, as it is sending food reserves down into the rootstock to fuel next year's show.

Pests/Diseases—If iris borers or grasshoppers appear, ask at your local garden center for the best controls.

Landscaping Tips & Ideas—Use smaller types in mass plantings in borders or as groundcovers. Taller ones make excellent cut-flower plantings and contribute to perennial borders, in or out of bloom.

LAVENDER
Lavandula angustifolia

Hardiness—Hardy throughout Texas (needs winter protection in USDA Zone 6)

Color(s)—Purple, violet-blue, pink

Bloom Period—Summer

Mature Size (H x W)—10 to 36 in. x 12 to 36 in.

Water Needs—Once established, water sparingly and allow the soil to dry out between waterings.

Planting/Care—Best in well-drained soil. Healthy plants need not be fertilized. Shear off old blooms to promote new ones. Cut back winter-damaged foliage in early spring.

Pests/Diseases—Not a problem. Root rot is the biggest concern in poorly drained soils. Caterpillars and leaf spot may visit if the site is too shady, humid, or damp.

Landscaping Tips & Ideas—Terrific in perennial beds. Nice in rows as a small hedge. May be grown in containers and windowboxes, or added to a vegetable or herb garden. 'Hidcote' and 'Munstead' are the most popular and readily available.

LIGULARIA
Farfugium japonicum

Hardiness—Hardy throughout Texas

Color(s)—Yellow

Bloom Period—Summer to fall

Mature Size (H x W)—10 to 12 in. x 12 to 14 in.

Water Needs—Water new plants once or twice a week during hot spells; established ones need less.

Planting/Care—Plant in fall or early spring in a spot that receives two to four hours of sun a day. Allow at least a foot between plants—even though this may seem like too much space at first. Fertilize in spring. Remove spent flower stalks and leaves. Divide clumps every two or three years.

Pests/Diseases—None

Landscaping Tips & Ideas—Due to its low, mounding growth, it is suitable for the front or middle of shady beds or in containers. The bold texture contrasts wonderfully with ferns, acorus, hydrangeas, gingers, liriope, impatiens, and begonias.

MEXICAN BUSH SAGE
Salvia leucantha

Hardiness—Hardy in USDA Zones 9 and 10, or grow as an annual. Protect from north winds.

Color(s)—Purple-and-white

Bloom Period—Fall

Mature Size (H x W)—4 to 6 ft. x 3 to 5 ft.

Water Needs—Drought tolerant, but provide extra water later in the summer and early fall.

Planting/Care—Plant after last frost through June, in rich garden soil with good drainage. Fertilize sparingly—too much and the plants become too tall and risk blowing over. No pruning is necessary.

Pests/Diseases—Other than the occasional spider mite, pests are rare.

Landscaping Tips & Ideas—Use as a background plant in a perennial garden or flower bed or as a specimen plant among shrubs. Use as a hedge or screen along fencerows or to hide eyesores. You can grow a single specimen in a pot, though it will be smaller.

MEXICAN PETUNIA
Ruellia brittoniana

Hardiness—USDA Zones 7 to 9

Color(s)—Lavender, purple, white, and pink

Bloom Period—Spring and summer

Mature Size (H x W)—10 to 36 in. x 12 to 18 in.

Water Needs—Water to prevent soil dryness, and mulch to conserve soil moisture.

Planting/Care—A very tough plant. Plant anytime. Will grow in light, sandy soil as well as heavy clay, tolerating both damp and dry conditions. Fertilizing is not necessary. Pruning is rarely needed except to remove spent bloom stalks. An enthusiastic self-seeder; can become a nuisance.

Pests/Diseases—None

Landscaping Tips & Ideas—If you have an area in your landscape where other perennials have not survived, try this plant and enjoy season-long color. Taller varieties may be used in and among other perennials. Its color is accentuated when planted with some dusty miller.

MEXICAN TARRAGON
Tagetes lucida

Hardiness—Hardy throughout Texas; needs winter protection in colder areas

Color(s)—Golden yellow

Bloom Period—Fall

Mature Size (H x W)—2 to 3 ft. x 1 to 2 ft.

Water Needs—Drought tolerant, but water once or twice a week during hot, dry periods.

Planting/Care—Plant after frost, in sun, in a spot with excellent drainage. Fertilize in spring and once again in summer. Prune off faded blooms. When the top growth is browned by winter freezes, cut back almost to the ground and mulch to protect from the cold. Divide large clumps in spring.

Pests/Diseases—None significant

Landscaping Tips & Ideas—Looks outstanding with other late bloomers, including asters, ornamental grasses, ruellia, salvias, and society garlic. Best placed toward the back or middle of beds. An excellent addition to herb gardens—the aromatic foliage may be used in cooking.

PHLOX
Phlox paniculata

Hardiness—Hardy throughout Texas

Color(s)—Pink, rose, lavender, purple, white, and bicolors

Bloom Period—Summer to early fall

Mature Size (H x W)—2 to 5 ft. x 1 to 2 ft.

Water Needs—Water to prevent soil dryness (at ground level to avoid wetting the foliage).

Planting/Care—Plant in spring, in sun to part sun in an area with good air circulation and good drainage. Mulch well. Remove spent blooms to encourage continued flowering.

Pests/Diseases—Pests are rare. If powdery mildew becomes a problem, get advice from your local garden center.

Landscaping Tips & Ideas—Add to your perennial plantings or grow as a bedding plant. For best results, plant in large drifts or masses. Enjoy their beauty and fragrance in large tubs stationed near an entryway. There are many related species and cultivars; check your local garden center in the spring.

PINCUSHION FLOWER
Scabiosa columbaria

Hardiness—Hardy throughout Texas

Color(s)—Pink, purple, yellow, and white

Bloom Period—Spring through fall frost

Mature Size (H x W)—12 to 18 in. x 12 to 18 in.

Water Needs—Water to get established, then the plants will be relatively drought tolerant. Provide supplemental irrigation in severe drought, or the plants will shut down.

Planting/Care—Survives in many settings and soils, but for best results, grow in fertile, organic, well-drained sites. Fertilize at planting time. Deadhead the flowers for a tidier appearance. Plants occasionally spread and can be divided in the spring or fall.

Pests/Diseases—Rare, but watch for spider mites, lace bug, and mildew.

Landscaping Tips & Ideas—An attractive, long-blooming low grower, ideal for a perennial garden when tucked in among appropriate-height companions. Also works in container displays. Two good varieties, 'Butterfly Blue' and 'Pink Mist', also look great together.

PINKS
Dianthus spp.

Hardiness—Hardy throughout Texas

Color(s)—Rose, salmon, pink, lavender, magenta, white, and bicolors

Bloom Period—Fall, winter, and spring

Mature Size (H x W)—4 to 15 in. x spreading

Water Needs—Maintain moist soil, but do not overwater. Mulch.

Planting/Care—Plant in early fall or spring after frost is past. Site with plenty of morning sun and afternoon shade. They bloom best under cooler conditions. Remove spent blooms.

Pests/Diseases—Leaf spot can occur in cloudy, humid conditions. This is corrected when the sun comes out, humidity decreases, and with good air movement. Get control advice from your local garden center.

Landscaping Tips & Ideas—Excellent in areas where you wish to create a mass effect for early-season bloom. The taller ones make nice background plantings. Due to the various colors, entire drifts with shades of color may be created. Pinks are super in country-cottage garden themes.

RED-HOT POKER
Kniphofia hybrids

Hardiness—Hardy throughout Texas

Color(s)—Yellow, orange, red, and creamy white

Bloom Period—Summer

Mature Size (H x W)—2 to 4 ft. x 2 ft.

Water Needs—Water new plantings during hot, dry weather. Established plants are drought-tolerant, rarely need watering, and will resent being kept too wet.

Planting/Care—Plant in spring or fall in sun, in well-drained soil. Mulch. Fertilize every spring. Trim off spent flower stalks. Cut foliage to the ground in winter. Divide mature clumps in fall or early spring.

Pests/Diseases—No major problems

Landscaping Tips & Ideas—Striking in a border. Without crowding the clump, surround it with other interesting perennials. Works well as a single specimen or accent, but looks good in groups of three. Avoid planting in large areas or drifts. Good companions include salvias, canna, beebalm, stokesia, ruellia, goldenrod, melampodium, lantana, and torenia.

RUSSIAN SAGE
Perovskia atriplicifolia

Hardiness—Hardy throughout Texas

Color(s)—Lavender-blue

Bloom Period—Summer to fall

Mature Size (H x W)—3 to 4 ft. x 3 to 4 ft.

Water Needs—Water to establish, if rainfall is not adequate. After that, it is quite drought tolerant.

Planting/Care—Plant in full sun in a spot with good drainage. No need to fertilize. Trim occasionally to promote more growth. Shear all dead growth in early spring.

Pests/Diseases—None serious, though spider mites may appear.

Landscaping Tips & Ideas—The shrublike growth requires plenty of background space and looks best in large perennial beds—it looks out of place in smaller ones. The cool colors are nice for contrasting displays. Try with pink- or yellow-blooming perennials, hardy hibiscus, daylily, phlox, Black-eyed Susan, and canna. 'Blue Haze' has pretty pale-blue flowers. 'Blue Spire' has darker, more violet blooms.

SALVIA
Salvia spp. and hybrids

Hardiness—Hardy throughout Texas

Color(s)—Red, purple, blue, pink, magenta, yellow, and white

Bloom Period—Summer through fall

Mature Size (H x W)—1 to 6 ft. x 1 to 5 ft.

Water Needs—New plantings need water once or twice a week, while established ones need water once a week during hot, dry weather.

Planting/Care—Best in average, well-drained soil. Fertilize once in spring and once in summer. Trim off faded flower spikes. Prune in late summer for a shorter, bushier, fall-blooming plant.

Pests/Diseases—None

Landscaping Tips & Ideas—Excellent for mixed beds and borders, as well as containers. There is a size and color for every location. The hybrid 'Indigo Spires' is a real winner, with long spikes of bluish-purple flowers on a somewhat sprawling plant over a very long season.

SEDUM
Sedum spp.

Hardiness—Hardy throughout Texas

Color(s)—Yellow, red, pink, pink-purple, and bronze-pink

Bloom Period—Spring, summer, and especially fall

Mature Size (H x W)—4 to 18 in. x 12 in.

Water Needs—Water as needed to prevent total soil dryness, but do not keep wet.

Planting/Care—Plant in early spring or early fall, in sun. Avoid shade and poorly drained areas. Fertilize once in the spring. Cut back any old flower stems if they appear unsightly.

Pests/Diseases—Usually pest-free

Landscaping Tips & Ideas—Depending on the species, sedums are appropriate in perennial borders, rock gardens, banks, and even containers and hanging baskets. They work well along gravel or natural, sunny walks or trails. Because of similar cultural needs, santolina is an excellent companion plant. 'Ruby Glow' and related border sedums are fabulous in the fall.

SHASTA DAISY
Leucanthemum x superbum

Hardiness—Hardy throughout Texas

Color(s)—White with yellow centers

Bloom Period—Spring, summer, and fall

Mature Size (H x W)—12 to 30 in. x 24 in.

Water Needs—Water as needed—especially during the blooming and growing season—to maintain a moist soil. Do not allow the soil to become dry, and never overwater.

Planting/Care—Plant in early fall or very early spring, in improved soil. Fertilize in spring as new growth appears. Prune out spent blossoms. Shasta daisies benefit from annual or biannual digging up, dividing, and replanting—do this in the fall.

Pests/Diseases—If spider mites or other "critter" pests visit your plantings, get help at your local garden center.

Landscaping Tips & Ideas—Use along walkways, around garden structures, and even in large containers. Use with daylilies, salvia, summer phlox, and rose plantings.

SOUTHERNWOOD
Artemisia abrotanum

Hardiness—Hardy throughout Texas

Color(s)—Yellow

Bloom Period—Summer

Mature Size (H x W)—12 to 24 in. x 36 in.

Water Needs—Water only when soil becomes dry. Do not allow prolonged periods of drought, but do not overwater.

Planting/Care—Plant in early spring or early fall in well-drained soil. If you have heavy clay, improve it first by digging in organic matter. In sandy soil, add composted bark. Feed in spring with a slow-release fertilizer. Prune to maintain more compact growth, and remove spent blooms.

Pests/Diseases—None serious

Landscaping Tips & Ideas—Pair with other easy-to-grow plants such as lantana or Mexican bush sage. It blends beautifully with seasonal, colorful annuals and perennials. Good accent plant for rock gardens and in the Japanese garden. The feathery, fragrant foliage is popular for many uses when cut and dried.

SPIDERWORT
Tradescantia virginiana

Hardiness—Hardy throughout Texas

Color(s)—Sky-blue, white, pink, and purple

Bloom Period—Summer

Mature Size (H x W)—2 ft. x 1 ft.

Water Needs—Water once or twice a week during hot, dry spells, especially while it is in bloom.

Planting/Care—Plant in fall or spring. Fertilize once in spring. If the plants get floppy, support with a ring of green twine. Plants enter a semidormant state in midsummer's blazing heat. Once flowering is over, cut the plants back hard.

Pests/Diseases—Caterpillars occasionally chew holes in the leaves and can be controlled with Bt, if needed.

Landscaping Tips & Ideas—To avoid gaps in your garden when fading occurs, plant among other plants that are more active in the summer. Combine with liriope, mallow, coneflower, torenia, purple heart, and salvia.

STOKES' ASTER
Stokesia laevis

Hardiness—Hardy throughout Texas

Color(s)—Powder blue

Bloom Period—Summer

Mature Size (H x W)—18 to 24 in. x 12 in.

Water Needs—Water weekly during hot, dry weather, especially during midsummer when the plants are in bloom.

Planting/Care—Plant in full or part sun in a spot with good drainage. Fertilize in spring and again in midsummer. Remove individual flowers as they fade. When blooming is finished, cut the flower stalks level with the plant's foliage. Divide in early spring or fall to create more plants.

Pests/Diseases—No major problems

Landscaping Tips & Ideas—Look best when planted in groups. The color is a welcome addition to any bed or border, and an excellent choice for butterfly gardens. Look great with daylilies, perennial verbena, lantana, crocosmia, and melampodium.

VERONICA
Veronica spicata

Hardiness—Hardy throughout Texas

Color(s)—Deep blue, lavender-blue, pink, and white

Bloom Period—Summer

Mature Size (H x W)—12 to 24 in. x 12 to 24 in.

Water Needs—Water once or twice a week during hot, dry weather. Mulch.

Planting/Care—Plant in fall to early spring. Full sun and excellent drainage are requirements. Fertilize in spring and once again in summer. Prune off faded flower spikes to extend blooming. When a plant has finished flowering, you may cut it back by half.

Pests/Diseases—No problems, except a vulnerability to root rot, which is prevented by good drainage.

Landscaping Tips & Ideas—Adds color to midsummer. Combine with 'Indian Summer' rudbeckia, gaura, purple fountain grass, Disco Belle mallows, Russian sage, and lantana. Because the bloom season is not extensive, about six weeks, surround with longer-bloomers.

YARROW
Achillea cultivars

Hardiness—Hardy throughout Texas

Color(s)—White, yellow, and pink flowers; grayish foliage

Bloom Period—Late spring to early fall

Mature Size (H x W)—6 in. to 3 ft. x 8 in. to 3 ft.

Water Needs—Water to prevent soil dryness, but never overwater.

Planting/Care—Plant in spring after frost. Plant in any location that receives at least six hours of daily sunlight and drains well. Fertilizing is normally not needed. Prune as necessary to maintain desired shape, usually by removing old flowers.

Pests/Diseases—None serious

Landscaping Tips & Ideas—The taller-growing ones make excellent back- ground plnats. Smaller varieties can be used in mass plantings or in borders. Also grows well in containers. Works well with other easy plants such as Mexican bush sage and salvias.

PERENNIALS

Name	Light	Type and Size	Flowers	Comments
Achillea millefolium **Yarrow**	Full sun to part shade	Evergreen in mild winters; 12 inches	Flat clusters of various colors on stalks to 24 inches; early summer	Ferny, aromatic foliage; very easy to grow; flowers dry well; native and non natives
Artemisia ludoviciana *A. 'Powis Castle'* **Artemisia**	Full to part sun	Semi-dormant in winter; 2 to 3 feet	Not significant	Outstanding silvery foliage; cut back winter/spring
Asarum spp. **Wild Ginger**	Part shade to shade	Evergreen; 6 to 8 inches	Small brown, not significant	Shiny kidney-shaped dark green leaves
Asclepias curcassavica *A. tuberosa* **Butterfly Weed**	Full to part sun	Dormnt in winter; 1 to 3 feet	Showy orange flowers in summer	Excellent nectar food for butterflies, larval food for Monarchs; native
Asparagus densiflorus 'Sprengeri' **Asparagus Fern**	Full sun to shade	Evergreen, dormant if low 20s occur; 1 to 2 feet (zone 9 only)	Tiny, white to pale pink, summer; scarlet pea-size fruit	Tough, indestructible in the garden or in containers; mulch crown in winter
Aspidistra elatior **Cast-Iron Plant**	Shade to full shade	Evergreen; 2½ feet	Not significant	Prune out unattractive leaves as necessary; tough; easy to grow
Aster spp. and hybrids **Aster**	Full to part sun	Dormant in winter; 1 to 5 feet, depending on type	Showy, daisy-like in clusters, many colors; late summer, fall	Excellent for late-season color; cut back hard after bloomings; native and non natives
Canna x *generalis* **Canna**	Full sun to part shade	Dormant in winter; 18 inches to 7 feet tall, depending on varieties planted	Spikes or stems with several blooms in yellow, orange, pink, red, coral, and cream	Dwarf to tall varieties are available and very easy to grow
Centaurea cineraria spp. *cineraria* **Dusty Miller**	Full to part sun	Dormant evergreen, depending upon the winter	Colorful, prune as needed, gray foliage	Virtually pest free
Chlorophytum comosum 'Variegatum' **Spider Plant**	Part shade to full shade	Evergreen, dormant if low 20s occur; 1 foot (zone 9 only)	Not significant; remove flower stalks to keep the plants looking neat	Normally thought of as a houseplant; the roots will survive the low teens
Coreopsis lanceolata **Coreopsis**; **Tickseed**	Full to part sun	Dormant in winter; 24 inches	Yellow, gold, mahogany daisy-like flower; early to midsummer	Very showy flowers and easy to grow from seed; native

PERENNIALS

Name	Light	Type and Size	Flowers	Comments
Cuphea micropetala **Cigar Plant**	Full to part sun	Dormant after first freezes; 2 to 5 feet	Yellow and red-orange fall to winter, and spring if mild winter; early to midsummer	Cut back hard after freezes brown the foliage; can spread aggressively
Dendranthema x *morifolium* cultivars **Garden Mums**	Full to part sun	Dormant in winter; 1 to 2 feet	Showy daisy-like flowers in many colors; fall	Cut back hard in winter, divide in early spring
Echinacea purpurea **Purple Coneflower**	Full to part sun	Dormant in winter; 2 feet	Purple or white daisy-like flowers with a prominent cone; summer	Cut back after flowering; easily grown native
Eupatorium coeolestinum **Wild** or **Hardy Ageratum**	Full sun to part shade	Dormant in winter; 2 to 3 feet	Soft lavender-blue fluffy flowers, primarily in fall; some blooms in early summer	Spreads rapidly; native; Joe-Pye Weed (*E. maculatum* and *E. purpureum*) are also good
Hemerocallis hybrids **Daylily**	Full to part sun	Semi-dormant in winter; 1½ to 3 feet in bloom	Larger flowers on stalks in many colors; early to late summer	Reliable, easy perennial; divide in Sept. or Oct.
Hibiscus moscheutos **Hardy Hibiscus**	Full to part sun	Dormant in winter; 2 to 4 feet	Very large plate-sized blooms in white, pink, or red; early to late summer	Reliable; spectacular in bloom; easy to grow from seed; cut back in fall
Hosta spp. and hybrids **Hosta; Plantain Lily**	Shade	Dormant in winter; 6 to 24 inches	Lavender or white, bell-shaped flowers on stalks to 3 feet, some fragrant; summer	Excellent for shady areas; snails and slugs may be a major problem
Leucanthemum x *superbum* **Shasta Daisy**	Full sun to part shade	Dormant in winter; 24 inches in bloom	White daisy flowers with yellow centers; spring	Problems with rotting out in summer increase closer to the coast; provide good drainage
Ligularia tussilaginea **Ligularia**	Shade	Evergreen; 18 inches	Clusters of 1-inch yellow daisy-like flowers; late summer to fall	Excellent texture plant for shady beds; leaves look like lily pads
Mirabilis jalapa **Four-o'Clocks**	Full sun to part shade	Dormant in winter; 3 to 4 feet tall and 3 feet wide	Dark green foliage with white, pink, salmon, lavender, yellow, fragrant blooms	Old favorite in Texas, a "can't miss" perennial; may be invasive

PERENNIALS

Name	Light	Type and Size	Flowers	Comments
Monarda fistulosa *M. didyma* **Beebalm**	Full to part sun	Dormant in winter; 2 to 3 feet	Flower heads in various colors; summer	Cut back hard after flowering for repeat bloom; aromatic foliage
Phlox divaricata **Blue Phlox** or **Louisiana Phlox**	Full sun to part shade	Dormant in winter; 12 inches	Lavender-blue to purple flower clusters; spring	Flowers occur about four weeks; trim back when finished
Phlox paniculata **Garden Phlox** (Summer or Border)	Full to part sun	Dormant in winter; 2 to 3 feet	Various colors; early to late summer; most varieties will not thrive here in zones 8 and 9	Those with magenta flowers, such as 'Robert Poore', are most reliable
Physostegia virginiana **Obedient Plant**	Full to part sun	Dormant in winter; 2 to 3 feet	Spikes of rosy purple or white; midsummer	Staking is recommended; spreads rapidly
Rudbeckia hirta 'Angustifolia' **Black-Eyed Susan**	Full to part sun	Dormant in winter; 2 feet	Golden daisies with dark brown centers; midsummer	Reliable, long-lived, and easy; cut back after flowering; native
Ruellia brittoniana **Ruellia**; **Summer** or **Mexican Petunia**	Full sun to part shade	Dormant after first freezes; 1 to 5 feet, depending on cultivar	Lavender, purple, or pink; blooms spring to early winter	Very easy and reliable; self-seeds readily; new cultivars include dwarfs and variegated foliage; native and non natives
Salvia spp. and hybrids **Salvia**; **Sage**	Full sun to part shade	Evergreen in some areas if winter is mild; 1 to 6 feet, depending on type	Spikes in various colors, especially purples, reds, and blues; spring, summer, and especially fall	A large group that includes many excellent plants for Texas gardens; trim in late summer and cut back in late winter; native and non natives
Sedum spp. **Sedum**; **Stonecrop**	Full to part sun	Usually evergreen succulent; 4 to 12 inches	Various colors of star-shaped flowers generally in clusters	Many types; some do better than others; needs well-drained soil
Solidago spp. and hybrids **Goldenrod**	Full to part sun	Dormant in winter; 2 to 6 feet, depending on type	Spikes of golden yellow; late summer to fall	Does not cause hayfever; excellent tough natives for late-season color
Veronica spicata **Veronica**; **Speedwell**	Full to part sun	Dormant in winter; 1 to 2 feet	Spikes of purple, blue, or rose in early to midsummer	Cut back faded flower spikes to encourage more bloom

LIGHT REQUIREMENTS:
FULL SUN: 8 hours or more of direct sun; PART SHADE: About 4 hours of direct sun; FULL SHADE: Little or no direct sun;
PART SUN: About 6 hours of direct sun; SHADE: About 2 hours of direct sun

JANUARY

- Visit local nurseries. Become familiar with which perennials they have on hand now, ask when additional ones will be available.

- Want to move a perennial? Now is a good time.

- Apply mulch over the crowns and roots of the less hardy perennials during the coldest part of winter.

- Do not water on any preset schedule, but if the weather turns mild and/or dry, water beds containing perennials as needed.

- Few herbaceous perennials are in active growth now, and this is not the time to fertilize.

- Any time a stretch of mild weather occurs, cool-season weeds will be in active growth. Promptly pull up any that appear.

- Cut back and remove old, dead upper portions of dormant perennials. Some don't go dormant until the first freezes hit, and in the southern parts of the state freezes may not occur until late December or January (or sometimes not at all in the Rio Grande Valley area).

FEBRUARY

- Work on getting beds ready and in shape for planting. Eliminate any weeds and remove turf from new beds. Turn the soil, and add organic matter.

- Plant spring- and summer-blooming perennials as soon as possible. Canna, daylily, daisy, and blue phlox are in this group.

- Note where dormant perennials are located and do not damage them while digging.

- Water in newly planted perennials and continue watering as needed.

- In south Texas, perennials that are in active growth may be fertilized in late February.

- Use a pest-control aid as needed—if the winter has been mild, you may see aphids on new growth.

MARCH

- Finish transplanting and dividing perennials. If they are transplanted now, most will barely miss a beat if moved with most of their roots.

- Protect tender perennials from the possibility of a sudden freeze. Tender new growth is most susceptible. Mulch, fabric sheets, or cloth may be placed over them.

- Apply water slowly over time with a sprinkler or soaker hose. It is far better for the health of your perennials to water

them thoroughly as needed, than to water them lightly and frequently.

- Fertilize established perennials this month. This is most efficiently and economically done using a granular fertilizer applied evenly throughout a bed.

- Get an early start on control snails and slugs, which may be active in some zones during mild weather. Various baits and traps, and handpicking, help reduce their populations.

APRIL

- If you are planting this late, choose larger plants in larger containers.

- Allow perennials enough space. If you are accustomed to planting annuals, you may be tempted to plant them too close. Most grow considerably larger than the small transplants you set out.

- Deadhead (remove the faded flowers) regularly from your bloomers—such as blue phlox—to keep plants attractive and to encourage more flowers.

- Water deeply if sufficient rain does not fall. This will encourage your perennials to develop deep root systems that will make them stronger and more drought resistant later in the summer.

- Finish fertilizing this month.

- As your perennials grow, make sure your layer of mulch is at least 3 inches thick.

- Look for a white, powdery substance coating perennial leaves. Powdery mildew is a common disease; treat with a fungus-control aid.

MAY

- Install supports for vigorous growers. Some are less noticeable and more effective when used earlier rather than later. Short tomato cages are useful and effective, and of course there are many other designs available.

- It's late to plant—maybe too late. If it doesn't like the heat, a plant may be stunted and sulk the rest of the season, but you never know. You can try planting healthy container-grown selections.

- Snake a soaker hose through a perennial bed to cover the entire area. This is an effective way to water without getting any on the flowers and foliage.

- If for some reason you have not fertilized yet—better late than never. Apply a premium-quality, slow-release granular fertilizer at the rate recommended on the label.

- Watch your plants and try to eliminate pests before they do too much damage. On the other hand, don't reach for the spray bottle every time you see a hole in a leaf.

JUNE

- Take pictures of your perennial garden. Dated pictures are an invaluable way to record how things looked at particular times. Support these by also making notes in your Texas gardening journal.

- If you plant perennial transplants growing in containers now, disturb the roots as little as possible, and water well for the first several weeks.

- Water deeply and thoroughly when rain has not occurred. In a surprisingly short time, 95-degree days and 75-degree nights can dry out the soil.

- Make another application of fertilizer to beds last fertilized in March or April. Evaluate the plants first; if they are growing vigorously (or too vigorously) and have a rich green color and plenty of flowers, fertilizing is optional.

- Make sure you properly identify any pest problems. Check with your local cooperative extension office or your local retailers. These sources can give you assistance and suggestions on various methods and aid for preventing and controlling problem insects.

JULY

- Do most of your gardening work during the cooler morning or evening hours. The heat this time of year is brutal.

- Record failures as well as successes in your Texas gardening journal. Perennials that aren't going to make it should be showing signs of stress by now.

- Use soaker hoses, drip irrigation, or sprinklers and leave them on long enough for the water to moisten the soil about 4 to 6 inches down. Morning is the preferred time so plants are well-supplied with water going into the hottest time of the day.

- Don't fertilize if you aren't sure your plants need it. High temperatures stress plants and can actually slow down the growth of many perennials.

- Apply nonselective weed-control aids to the foliage of the weeds only. If any spray gets on the foliage of a desirable plant, wash it off immediately. Better yet, use a barrier of some kind to protect desirable plants.

AUGUST

- Plan ahead for fall planting. Visit local nurseries to see what is currently available and ask what will be; this should help you in planning fall plantings. If you let your wants be known, many nurseries will call you when the plants arrive.

- Now would be a good time to look over your perennial beds and evaluate how things are growing. Note these observations in your Texas gardening journal and make decisions about what to remove, divide, or transplant this fall.

- Prune back overgrown perennials, especially those that bloom over a long period and well into fall.

- Water spring-planted perennials deeply once or twice a week during dry periods. If you notice them wilting, you are waiting too long.

- Whiteflies can be a major problem in late summer. Consider cutting back heavily infested plants. If you spray, you will need repeated applications of whatever you choose, and you'll need to spray under the foliage thoroughly.

SEPTEMBER

- Evaluate the performance of your perennials this summer and record information in your Texas gardening journal.

- While it is still too hot to transplant or divide most perennials, you may divide daylilies and irises (including Louisiana irises).

- Cut back flower stalks and old faded flowers to keep your perennials looking attractive.

- Replenish mulch layers that may have decayed and thinned out over the summer.

- Continue to water as needed using sprinklers, soaker hoses, or drip irrigation, as September can still be dry.

- Perennials showing nutrient deficiencies may be fertilized this late in the year, but use a soluble fertilizer to deliver available nutrients immediately.

OCTOBER

- Plant new perennials this month. Space plants according to information on the label, references, or local advice.

- Water in transplants with a soluble fertilizer mixed half-strength.

- Plant a few chrysanthemums if you need to "punch up" the color in some of your flower beds, or develop entire beds of garden mums.

- As perennials finish and are cut back, remove stakes, cages, and other supports when they are no longer needed. Clean them up and store them out of the way.

- Keep beds mulched 3 to 4 inches deep, to thwart cool-season weed seeds that will be germinating soon.

- Armyworms are large, dark caterpillars that can chew up a perennial planting in no time. They feed during the day and are easily seen if you look carefully. Control as needed with appropriate aids.

NOVEMBER

- If freezes threaten in north Texas, plan on covering some of the blooming perennials—such as butterfly weed, cigar plant, ruellia, and the salvias—that could be damaged. The plants will survive without protection, but it would be a shame to lose out on some of the flowers.

- Garden mums are still available at local nurseries. Buy ones that have few open flowers and mostly buds—the plants will be attractive longer.

- When digging up and transplanting a perennial, get as much of the root system as possible. If the soil falls away, immediately wet the roots and wrap them with plastic to keep them from drying out. Replant immediately after removing the plastic.

- Tall-growing, fall-blooming perennials, like narrow-leaf sunflower, goldenrod, and cigar plant, may need to be staked. Remember how windy some of those cold fronts can be.

- Water newly planted, transplanted, and divided perennials as needed to maintain a moist soil if the weather is dry.

DECEMBER

- This is a good time to inventory your gardening tools. How many were broken or lost last summer? What needs to be replaced? Are there tools you need but don't have? With gift-giving season right around the corner, now would be a good time to let people know what you want.

- Cut back fall-bloomers that have finished blooming or been killed back by freezes. Mulch 3 to 4 inches deep over the roots and the base of the plants.

- No fertilizer is required by perennials this month. Even if the weather has been mild and late-flowering ones like salvias are still in bloom, don't feed them. Winter is on its way and little of the fertilizer would be used effectively. Late fertilizing may also decrease the hardiness of your perennials by stimulating growth.

- A few evergreen perennials (strawberry begonia, for example) may have problems with snails and slugs eating holes in their leaves. Set out traps.

BULBS
for Texas

Gardeners tend to use the term "bulb" for any fleshy, underground organ produced by a plant, and we'll conform to that tradition in this chapter. But the term actually refers to several botanically distinct structures including true bulbs, corms, rhizomes, tubers, and tuberous roots.

A true bulb consists of a compressed stem and a growing point or flower bud enclosed with thick, fleshy modified leaves. In some bulbs, the fleshy leaves form concentric rings (such as onions), and in others (such as lilies), they look like thickened, overlapping scales. Examples of plants that produce true bulbs include allium, amaryllis, crinum, clivia, garlic chive, hyacinth, lily, narcissus, oxalis, rain lily (Zephyranthes), society garlic, spider lily (Lycoris), tuberose, and tulip.

A corm is a compressed, fleshy stem with a growing point on top. Roots grow only from the base. Corms can develop small buds around their base called cormels, which are useful in propagation. Examples of corms are crocus, freesia, and gladiolus.

Rhizomes are fleshy, horizontal, underground stems. Shoots occur from the top and roots grow from the bottom. Plants that produce rhizomes include canna, calla lily, agapanthus, gingers (hedychium, alpinia, zingiber, curcuma, costus, kaempferia), iris (bearded, Louisiana, Siberian, Japanese), and walking iris (Neomarica).

Tubers tend to be more irregular in shape and have more growing points. Both shoots and roots arise from these growing points. Examples of tubers are caladium and Jack-in-the-pulpit.

Tuberous roots are thickened, fleshy roots. Often, as with dahlias, a portion of the crown or stem containing buds must be attached to the tuberous root in order for it to grow. Others, such as sweet potatoes, are able to grow shoots directly from the tuberous root. Some plants grown from tuberous roots are dahlia, gloriosa lily, ornamental sweet potato, and ranunculus.

Bulbs are divided into two groups according to their season of growth and bloom: spring or summer. Spring bulbs are planted in the fall and early December (tulips in late December and early January) and bloom from January through April. Summer bulbs, generally planted between March and May, are in active growth from March through November and bloom at some time during that period.

PLANNING THE SPRING BULB GARDEN

Unfortunately, most spring-flowering bulbs originate in climates cooler than ours and do not rebloom well in our state, especially in south Texas.

Determine where spring bulbs would make a nice addition to the landscape. Since several provide only one season of bloom, it may make better sense economically to use them to embellish rather that to provide lavish displays. Plant groups or drifts of bulbs among existing shrubs, flower beds, and groundcovers, especially in areas where they can be appreciated up close.

Bulbs become available in local nurseries as early as September. Go ahead and purchase them, but there is no hurry to plant them. Purchasing early provides you the opportunity to choose from a good selection and get the bulbs you desire.

SELECTING SPRING BULBS

Buy the largest bulbs of the best quality your budget will allow. With bulbs, you definitely get what you pay for. When choosing loose bulbs at a local nursery or garden center, pick the plumpest bulbs. They should be firm with no obvious cuts, soft spots, or insects or disease damage. When purchasing daffodils, look for double-nosed bulbs, which look like two bulbs joined together at the base.

PLANTING SPRING BULBS

Most spring-flowering bulbs require excellent drainage, so avoid low, wet areas or use raised beds as necessary. Prepare the area for planting:

Remove any unwanted weeds. Turn the soil 8 to 10 inches deep. Spread 4 to 6 inches of organic matter (compost, rotted manure, ground bark, peat moss) over the area and blend thoroughly.

Rake smooth, dig appropriate holes, apply slow-release fertilizer, and plant.

It is important to plant bulbs at the proper depth. Dig individual holes, or excavate to the recommended depth the entire area to be planted and plant all the bulbs at once.

Bulbs that are expected to rebloom reliably should be planted in areas that receive at least six hours of direct sunlight. This allows them to build up food reserves for next year's bloom. Bulbs that will be grown for just one season may be planted in shadier locations since they are discarded after blooming, although some amount of direct sunlight is still preferred.

CARING FOR YOUR SPRING BULBS

Keep areas planted with spring bulbs mulched and weed free. Little supplemental watering is needed during our usually rainy months.

Bulbs grown as annuals may be removed from the bed anytime after they finish flowering. Repeat-blooming bulbs may simply be left in the ground from year to year. This works best in settled situations such as the front of shrubs, at the base of deciduous trees, or in areas of low-growing groundcovers. If the bulbs are growing in a location where you intend to plant something else to bloom during the summer, they may be lifted, stored, and replanted in the fall. Another option is to mark the location of the bulbs and plant around them.

In order for repeat-blooming bulbs to bloom the following year, you must allow the foliage to persist after flowering. Do not cut back the leaves until they have turned mostly yellow.

PLANNING YOUR SUMMER BULB GARDEN

Most summer-flowering bulbs are native to tropical or subtropical climates and will reliably bloom here for many years in Zones 8 and 9. Indeed, for some of these plants, the trick is not getting them to grow but keeping them under control. In Zones 6 and 7, mulch heavily and hope for regrowth, or lift, store, and replant each year.

These plants offer a wide variety of uses in the landscape, providing valuable additions to flower beds, perennial borders, groundcovers, and containers. Think carefully about the characteristics of each type of bulb and the growing conditions it needs. Then determine where the bulbs will grow and look best before you plant.

PLANTING YOUR SUMMER BULBS

Generally, dig 2 to 4 inches of organic matter (such as compost, finely ground pine bark, rotted manure, or sphagnum peat moss) into the area before you plant your bulbs. Raise beds to improve drainage if necessary. A light sprinkling of premium-quality, long-lasting, slow-release granular fertilizer every six to eight weeks during active growth (beginning in March and ending in August) is sufficient for most summer bulbs. A granular rose fertilizer applied according to label directions usually works well for summer bulbs.

CARING FOR YOUR SUMMER BULBS

No matter what situation you have—from shady to sunny and from dry to wet conditions—at least a few kinds of bulbs with thrive there. Most summer bulbs prefer good drainage. Calla, canna, crinum, spider lily (Hymenocallis), Louisiana iris, blue flag, yellow flag, and some gingers are a few exceptions. Full to partial sun (six or more hours of direct sunlight) is needed by most of these plants for healthy growth and flowering, although many, such as achimenes, caladium, gingers, and bletilla, do fine in shadier spots. Crinum is one of the most dependable summer-flowering bulb plant groups we grow in Texas.

Many summer bulbs have a dormancy period when the foliage dies off and the bulb rests. This period generally occurs during winter. At that time, yellow or brown foliage may be trimmed back to the ground. Place markers where the dormant bulbs are located so you won't accidentally dig into them later. Avoid removing any of the bulb's foliage when it is healthy and green.

RANUNCULUS

Most summer bulbs are best propagated by dividing the clumps in early March. Some bulbs, such as bearded iris, do best when divided every year or two, while others, like agapanthus, prefer to be left alone.

See pages 70 71 for a list of summer-flowering bulbs that are best suited to Texas.

AUTUMN CROCUS
Colchicum autumnale

Hardiness—Hardy throughout Texas

Color(s)—White, lavender, and pink

Bloom Period—Fall; fall-flowering

Mature Size (H x W)—4 to 6 in. x 4 to 6 in.

Water Needs—If planted in organically rich, well-drained soil, you can rely on fall rains.

Planting/Care—Plant corms in mid- to late summer. Feed in late fall after the flowers have faded. Leave the foliage be until it dies down naturally, since this is what feeds the corms for next year's show.

Pests/Diseases—No serious problems

Landscaping Tips & Ideas—Large groups in perennial borders are great, but because the foliage is unsightly in the spring, plant things that cover them but don't overpower the blooms in the fall. Groundcovers like ajuga, mondo grass, compact sedums, and low-growing veronica make good companions. They also work well in rock gardens, and can complement sidewalks, pathways, and garden art.

BEARDED IRIS
Iris x germanica

Hardiness—Hardy throughout Texas

Color(s)—Purple, yellow, blue, white, pink, and wine

Bloom Period—Spring to early summer; summer-flowering

Mature Size (H x W)—2 to 3 ft. x 2 ft.

Water Needs—Water weekly during dry weather.

Planting/Care—Plant in fall, where they will get at least six hours of daily sun. Avoid wet areas. Plant so the rhizome is just below the soil surface, and mulch. Fertilize after flowering. Trim off spent flower stalks and yellowed foliage. Divide in the fall. Less reliable in the southern, hottest parts of the state.

Pests/Diseases—No major problems

Landscaping Tips & Ideas—These look great with roses and perennials, such as phlox, Shasta daisy, and salvias. Plant in the middle or front of beds to show off the flowers and attractive foliage.

BUTTERFLY GINGER
Hedychium coronarium

Hardiness—Hardy throughout Texas

Color(s)—White

Bloom Period—Summer to fall; summer-flowering

Mature Size (H x W)—4 to 6 ft. x 3 ft.

Water Needs—Water weekly during hot, dry weather.

Planting/Care—Plant in spring and summer. No more than four to six hours of sun a day is best. Moist, fertile soils encourage vigorous growth. Set the rhizomes just below the soil surface, and mulch. Stake as needed. Fertilize once in spring and once in summer. Each shoot produces only one bloom spike; cut it off once it is spent, or cut down the entire shoot at that time. Mulch for the winter. Divide in spring.

Pests/Diseases—None serious

Landscaping Tips & Ideas—Outstanding planted close to an outdoor sitting area where the lovely fragrance can be enjoyed. Combines well with ferns, spider lilies, agapanthus, and firespike.

CALADIUM

Caladium x hortulanum

Hardiness—USDA Zones 9 to 10; in other areas, dig up and store for the winter

Color(s)—Foliage in blends of green, white, pink, red, and metallics

Bloom Period—Not applicable; summer-flowering

Mature Size (H x W)—12 to 16 in. x 12 to 18 in.

Water Needs—Maintain moist growing conditions.

Planting/Care—For best results, plant in shade where drainage is good and there is easy access for watering. Fertilize regularly throughout the growing season. Prune out any flower stems that appear.

Pests/Diseases—If slugs and snails visit, get advice from your local garden center on controls.

Landscaping Tips & Ideas—Use in background plantings or in beds of ferns, English ivy, ajuga, liriope, azalea, aucuba, or other shade-loving plants. They mix well with shade-loving annuals such as impatiens and wax-leaf begonias. Good for edgings. Try them in various sizes and types of containers.

CANNA

Canna x generalis

Hardiness—USDA Zones 7 or 8 to 11

Color(s)—Yellow, orange, pink, red, coral, and cream; some have colorful foliage as well

Bloom Period—Spring and summer; summer-flowering

Mature Size (H x W)—18 in. to 8 ft. x 18 to 24 in.

Water Needs—Maintain moist growing conditions.

Planting/Care—Plant in the spring after conditions have warmed up. Best in deep, moist, rich soil. Fertilize in springtime and repeat later as desired. Prune out spent bloom stalks. Remove plants' tops after the fall killing freezes.

Pests/Diseases—Slugs, snails, and leaf rollers may visit—if they become problems, get advice at your local garden center.

Landscaping Tips & Ideas—Colorful and easy, in the ground or in tubs. Wide range of sizes—the smaller ones are suitable for beds with other bulbs, annuals, or perennials. The most striking effect comes from mass plantings in multiple rows.

CRINUM

Crinum spp.

Hardiness—USDA Zones 7 to 10

Color(s)—White, dark or pale pink, cream, and wine

Bloom Period—Spring and summer; summer-flowering

Mature Size (H x W)—1 to 4 ft. x 2 to 3 ft.

Water Needs—Water as necessary to prevent soil dryness.

Planting/Care—Plant in spring after the soil has warmed up (planting too early may cause bulb rotting). Full sun and well-drained loamy soil is ideal. Plantings usually take two or more years to establish and start flowering well. Nudge them along with regular feedings. Remove spent flower stalks.

Pests/Diseases—Snails or mealybugs appear on occasion. Consult your local garden center for controls.

Landscaping Tips & Ideas—Plant in old-fashioned or country garden themes. They grow well in tubs and with other summer bulbs. They are good mixers with summer perennials and annuals, and are desirable around landscape pools.

CROCOSMIA
Crocosmia x crocosmiiflora

Hardiness—Hardy throughout Texas

Color(s)—Orange, yellow, red, scarlet

Bloom Period—Mid- to late summer; summer-flowering

Mature Size (H x W)—2 to 3 ft. x 1 to 2 ft.

Water Needs—Provide supplemental irrigation during drought.

Planting/Care—Plant the corms in spring in moist, well-drained soil. Fertilize at planting time and again during the growing season as needed. Mulch for the winter in cold-climate areas.

Pests/Diseases—Spider mites like this plant, especially in sites stressed with drought, poor soil, and poor circulation.

Landscaping Tips & Ideas—The upright, spiky foliage and arching flower spikes are compatible with daylily, coneflower, and salvias. They are tall enough to plant in the back or middle of a perennial garden. Plant some in your cut flower garden, since they are long-lasting in arrangements. 'Lucifer', a more cold-hardy cultivar, has hot red color.

DUTCH IRIS
Iris x hollandica

Hardiness—Hardy throughout Texas

Color(s)—Blue, purple, white, yellow, and bronze

Bloom Period—Spring; spring-flowering

Mature Size (H x W)—18 to 24 in. x 6 in.

Water Needs—While the foliage is green, water once a week if the weather is dry.

Planting/Care—Plant in the fall in a well-drained spot that gets four to six hours of daily sun. Fertilize in early spring. Cut off the flowers as they fade, but allow the foliage to die down naturally so it can help the bulb store food reserves for next year.

Pests/Diseases—No major problems

Landscaping Tips & Ideas—Since the foliage isn't particularly attractive, plant clumps among other plants—particularly warm-season annuals such as salvia, cosmos, or torenia. Blooms about the same time as Louisiana irises and spirea, adding to the celebration of spring.

ELEPHANT EAR
Colocascia and Alocascia spp.

Hardiness—Only to USDA Zone 7; elsewhere, treat as an annual or overwinter indoors

Color(s)—Foliage, sometimes variegated, in green, black, burgundy, and purple

Bloom Period—Not applicable; summer-flowering

Mature Size (H x W)—2 to 6 ft. x 2 to 6 ft.

Water Needs—Plentiful moisture is key. However, the site should be drier in the winter (slow, dormant) months.

Planting/Care—Plant the tuber in late spring or early summer in rich, organic soil (in subsequent years, they will tend to emerge later in the spring or early summer, so be patient). The massive plants are heavy feeders and respond to any fertilizer.

Pests/Diseases—None serious

Landscaping Tips & Ideas—The large, dramatic leaves provide great backdrops for other plants. Combine with other large-foliage plants like canna, coleus, and even ornamental grasses. They also make nice container plants or water-garden bog plants.

GLADIOLUS
Gladiolus spp. and hybrids

Hardiness—USDA Zones 8 to 10; in colder zones, dig up and store corms for the winter

Color(s)—All colors except true blue; bicolors, too

Bloom Period—Spring and summer; summer-flowering

Mature Size (H x W)—18 in. to 6 ft. x around 12 in.

Water Needs—Maintain a moist soil. Do not allow soil to dry out, especially during blooming.

Planting/Care—Start planting in late spring, and stagger additional plantings every two weeks through midsummer to ensure a continuous show. Full sun and sandy loam is best. Stake taller, top-heavy ones.

Pests/Diseases—Thrips may appear in warmer weather; consult a local garden center for control advice.

Landscaping Tips & Ideas—Often planted in rows in cutting or vegetable gardens and harvested for spectacular bouquets. Dwarf ones can be added to mixed flower borders or perennial gardens or used as background plants.

HARDY GLAD
Gladiolus byzantinus

Hardiness—Hardy throughout Texas

Color(s)—Magenta, fuchsia, pink, and white

Bloom Period—Spring; spring-flowering

Mature Size (H x W)—1 to 3 ft. x 2 to 4 ft.

Water Needs—If spring rainfall is lacking, irrigation should be provided.

Planting/Care—Plant corms in the fall in well-drained, organically rich soil. Mix slow-release organic fertilizers into the bed in the fall. Remove spent flower stalks and let the foliage die down naturally before cutting it back in midsummer. Staking isn't mandatory.

Pests/Diseases—Pests are of minimal concern. Heavy shade and poorly drained soils can cause rot, lanky growth, foliar disease, and poor flowering.

Landscaping Tips & Ideas—Good in a perennial bed or border. Plant corms close together to form a larger flower display. Late-emerging companions include 'Moonbeam' coreopsis, trailing lantana, and purple heart.

HYACINTH
Hyacinthus orientalis

Hardiness—USDA Zones 5 to 9

Color(s)—White, pale yellow, pink, red, blue, and purple

Bloom Period—Late winter and spring; spring-flowering

Mature Size (H x W)—8 to 12 in. x 6 to 8 in.

Water Needs—Water as necessary to prevent soil dryness. Mulch.

Planting/Care—Plant in late fall, in good soil. Will need shade from our hot, western, afternoon sun. Fertilize at planting time and again every spring. Cut away spent bloom stalks.

Pests/Diseases—None serious

Landscaping Tips & Ideas—Stunning in mass plantings, as an addition to a spring border, or as a potted plant. Their stiff, formal appearance lends them to formal plantings. Showy in large drifts combined with other spring bulbs, flowering trees, and shrubs. Site where you can savor the pretty hues and heady, perfumed fragrance.

LILY
Lilium spp. and hybrids

Hardiness—Hardy throughout Texas

Color(s)—Many colors and bicolors

Bloom Period—Varies; summer-flowering

Mature Size (H x W)—1 to 7 ft. x 1 to 3 ft.

Water Needs—Regular water is key, especially leading up to and during blooming.

Planting/Care—Plant in spring or early summer (or fall in Zones 8 and 9) in well-drained, sandy loam. Allow foliage to die down on its own. Stake taller varieties. Apply slow-release fertilizer in fall or early spring.

Pests/Diseases—Poorly drained sites can lead to basal root rot. If aphids appear, consult a local garden center.

Landscaping Tips & Ideas—Plan an ongoing show by planting a range of different types. Site towering varieties in large groups or in the back of a layered perennial bed. Great for cut-flower gardens. Some lower-growing plants that hide the "bare knees" are: ferns, million bells, salvia, liriope, and verbena.

LOUISIANA IRIS
Iris spp. and hybrids

Hardiness—Hardy throughout Texas

Color(s)—Burgundy, red, pink, blue, purple, lavender, white, and yellow

Bloom Period—Spring; spring-flowering

Mature Size (H x W)—16 to 36 in. x 14 to 24 in.

Water Needs—Keep soil constantly moist during the growing season.

Planting/Care—Plant in the fall in at least six hours of sun a day. Mulch to conserve moisture and prevent sunscald. Plants are semidormant in late summer, especially in drier locations, and the unattractive foliage can be trimmed off.

Pests/Diseases—Leafminers cause white streaks in the foliage, but rarely cause serious damage. Control with a systemic insecticide. Dispose of leaves infected with rust.

Landscaping Tips & Ideas—Plant in shallow water or on the banks around ponds—conditions similar to their natural habitat. They also look good planted in clumps among perennials and shrubs in traditional beds.

NARCISSUS
Narcissus spp. and hybrids

Hardiness—Hardy throughout Texas

Color(s)—Yellow, gold, orange, white, red, pink, and bicolors

Bloom Period—Spring; spring-flowering

Mature Size (H x W)—3 to 18 in. x 6 to 8 in.

Water Needs—Water to prevent soil dryness.

Planting/Care—Plant daffodils, jonquils, and narcissus species in the fall in well-drained soil. Fertilize at planting time and again every spring. Cut away spent bloom stalks, but allow the foliage to die down naturally. In mild-winter areas, they may not repeat bloom and you will have to plant new bulbs each year.

Pests/Diseases—Rot can occur in poorly drained locations. If slugs or snails become a problem, get advice from your local garden center.

Landscaping Tips & Ideas—Use as bedding or border plants, around entryways, as well as in woodland plantings, rock gardens, and containers. Use "naturalizing mixtures" in mass plantings.

OXALIS
Oxalis spp.

Hardiness—Hardy throughout Texas; require winter protection in cold-winter areas

Color(s)—White, pink, rose, and yellow

Bloom Period—Early summer and fall; summer-flowering

Mature Size (H x W)—1 ft. x 1 ft.

Water Needs—Supplemental irrigation in times of drought is a must.

Planting/Care—Plant these tiny bulbs in spring, in part-day sun or dappled shade. A well-drained, organically rich, slightly acidic soil is ideal. Mulch to retain moisture and hold off weeds. Apply a slow-release fertilizer every spring.

Pests/Diseases—Bulbs can rot in water-logged sites. Watch for occasional spider mites.

Landscaping Tips & Ideas—The nice compact growth is perfect for borders in perennial shade gardens or along a garden path. Add them to beds with other bulbs, which will easily emerge from among them. Good companions are ajuga, moneywort, dwarf Solomon's seal, and barrenwort.

PHILIPPINE LILY
Lilium formosanum

Hardiness—Hardy throughout Texas

Color(s)—White

Bloom Period—Late summer; summer-flowering

Mature Size (H x W)—5 ft. x 2 ft.

Water Needs—Water only if conditions are dry.

Planting/Care—Plant in spring or early summer in a well-drained spot in the sun (at least six hours daily). Fertilize with half-doses in spring and again in summer. Stake if they become tall and top-heavy. Cut back the foliage when it yellows in the fall.

Pests/Diseases—None serious

Landscaping Tips & Ideas—Tall and dramatic, so position them where the white trumpets can preside over the display below. Companions in bloom at the same time include rudbeckia, lantana, ruellia, verbena, and lots of warm-season annuals.

SNOWFLAKE
Leucojum aestivum

Hardiness—Hardy throughout Texas

Color(s)—White

Bloom Period—Early spring; spring-flowering

Mature Size (H x W)—1 ft. x 6 in.

Water Needs—Winter and spring rains usually provide adequate moisture; water weekly during dry, hot weather.

Planting/Care—Plant in fall in average soil in four to six hours of sun a day. Trim off faded flowers, but delay cutting back the foliage until it turns yellow. Divide every three to five years.

Pests/Diseases—None

Landscaping Tips & Ideas—For the best effect, plant in clusters of six or more. Pair with low-growing, cool-season annuals such as pansy, viola, lobelia, alyssum, and petunia. When those start to flag, replace with heat-tolerant bedding plants that help hide snowflake's fading foliage. They also do well in more settled situations, as among groundcovers or at the bases of trees, or in front of shrubs.

SPIDER LILY
Lycoris spp.

Hardiness—USDA Zones 8 or 9 to 10

Color(s)—Red, pink, white, and yellow

Bloom Period—Late summer and fall; summer-flowering

Mature Size (H x W)—1 to 2 ft. x 6 in.

Water Needs—Water in winter as necessary to maintain moist soil, and mulch well.

Planting/Care—Plant the bulbs in well-drained soil; sandy loam is best. Apply a slow-release fertilizer every fall. Prune off spent flower stalks.

Pests/Diseases—Combat slugs or snails with remedies suggested by your local garden center.

Landscaping Tips & Ideas—Work great naturalized in drifts if left undisturbed, so remember to avoid constant mowing around these areas. Also work well grouped in beds, where they will multiply readily.

TULIP
Tulipa spp. and hybrids

Hardiness—USDA Zones 3 to 8; not perennial in warmer parts of the state

Color(s)—All colors except true blue

Bloom Period—Spring; spring-flowering

Mature Size (H x W)—12 to 40 in. x 8 to 10 in.

Water Needs—Maintain a moist soil, neither too wet nor too dry.

Planting/Care—Plant in late fall/early winter. Prechill the bulbs in your refrigerator for approximately six weeks. Sunny locations with well-drained soil are best. Feed at planting time. Cut away spent blooming stalks.

Pests/Diseases—If aphids, mice, rats, squirrels, and other pests become a problem, seek control possibilities at your local garden center.

Landscaping Tips & Ideas—The best shows are masses of single colors. In small-space areas, grow in containers. They combine well with spring annuals, other spring bulbs, and spring-flowering trees and shrubs. They bring spring charm to rock gardens and garden paths.

77

SPRING BULBS

Name	Plant	Depth	Spacing	Blooms
Allium (Flowering Onion)	Sept. to Dec.	2 in. to 4 in.	4 in. to 12 in.	April to May
Anemone	Oct. to early Dec.	1 in.	6 in. to 8 in.	March to May
Arisaema	Oct. to early Dec.	2 in. to 4 in.	8 in. to 12 in.	March to May
Bletilla (Ground Orchid)	Sept. to April	1 in.	6 in. to 8 in.	March to April
Crocus	Oct. to early Dec.	2 in.	2 in. to 3 in.	Feb. to March
Hippeastrum (Amaryllis)	Sept. to Dec. in pots. April in garden.	Neck exposed	8 in. to 12 in.	Nov. to Jan. in pots. April in garden.
Hyacinth	late Dec. to early Jan.	3 in. to 4 in.	4 in. to 6 in.	March
Iris, Dutch (bulbous)	Oct. to early Dec.	2 in. to 4 in.	4 in. to 6 in.	March to April
Iris, Louisiana, Siberian, Japanese, Bearded (rhizomatous)	Sept. to Feb.	Just below soil surface	12 in. to 18 in.	March to May
Leucojum (Snowflake)	Oct. to early Dec.	4 in.	4 in. to 6 in.	April
Lily, Easter	Oct. to early Dec.	4 in.	8 in. to 12 in.	April to May
Muscari (Grape Hyacinth)	Oct. to early Dec.	2 in.	2 in. to 4 in.	March to April
Narcissus (including Daffodils)	Oct. to early Dec.	4 in.	4 in. to 6 in.	Jan. to April
Ornithogalum (Star of Bethlehem)	Oct. to early Dec.	4 in.	4 in.	April
Ranunculus	Oct. to early Dec.	1 in.	8 in.	April to May
Spanish Bluebell (Hyacinthioides hispanicus)	Oct. to early Dec.	4 in. to 6 in.	4 in.	April
Spring Starflower (Ipheion uniflorum)	Oct. to early Dec.	2 in. to 3 in.	3 in. to 6 in.	March to May
Sisyrinchium (Blue-eyed Grass)	Oct. to early Dec.	2 in.	4 in. to 6 in.	April
Tulip	Late Dec. to early Jan.	4 in. to 6 in.	4 in. to 8 in.	March to April
Zantedeschia (Calla Lily)	Sept. to Nov. (bulbs). March to May (plants).	2 in. to 3 in.	12 in. to 18 in.	April to May

Notes: Because they bloom in the spring, amaryllis, Louisiana iris, calla lily, and bletilla are grouped with the spring bulbs. However, their foliage persists through the summer, and they should be handled as summer bulbs.

Check with local nurseries and/or Extension Service/County Agent offices when uncertain of exact planting dates for your garden. Texas has four USDA Plant Hardiness Zones with two subzones in each of these. The planting dates listed usually work for a large part of Texas.

SUMMER-FALL BULBS

Name	Plant	Depth	Spacing	Blooms
Achimenes	May to June	1 in.	4 in. to 6 in.	June to Oct.
Agapanthus	March to Aug.	1 in.	8 in. to 12 in.	May to June
Alpinia (Shell Ginger)	March to Aug.	1 in.	1 ft. to 5 ft.	May to June
Belamcanda (Blackberry Lily)	March to April	1 in.	8 in. to 12 in.	June to Aug.
Caladium	April to July	1 in. to 2 in.	6 in. to 12 in.	Foliage May to Oct.
Canna	March to Aug.	1 in. to 2 in.	12 in. to 18 in.	May to Nov.
Clivia	March to Aug.	1 in.	18 in. to 24 in.	March to May
Costus (Spril Ginger)	March to Aug.	1 in.	1 ft. to 2 ft.	June to Oct.
Crinum	March to Aug.	Neck exposed	1 ft. to 3 ft.	April to Oct.
Curcuma (Hidden Lily Ginger)	March to Aug.	1 in. to 2 in.	1 ft. to 2 ft.	May to Aug.
Dahlia	March to May	4 in.	8 in. to 18 in.	May to Oct.
Daylily (*Hemerocallis*)	Oct. to Dec.	4 in.	12 in. to 18 in.	May to June
Dietes (African Iris)	March to Sept.	1 in.	1 ft. to 3 ft.	April to June
Elephant Ear (Colocasia, Alocasia)	April to Aug.	Neck exposed	2 ft. to 3 ft.	Foliage spring to frost
Eucomia (Pineapple Lily)	Sept. to Nov.	Neck exposed	18 in.	May
Gladiolus	Feb. to March	4 in. to 6 in.	6 in.	April to June
Globba (Dancing Lady Ginger)	April to Sept.	1 in.	1 ft.	July to Oct.
Gloriosa Lily	March to April	4 in.	8 in. to 12 in.	May to Aug.
Habranthus	Sept. to Dec.	1 in.	8 in.	May to July
Hedychium (Butterfly Ginger)	March to Sept.	1 in.	1 ft. to 2 ft.	May to Nov.
Hymenocallis (Spider Lily)	March to Sept.	Neck exposed	1 ft. to 3 ft.	June to Aug.
Kaempferia (Peacock Ginger)	April to Aug.	1 in.	8 in. to 12 in.	June to Sept.
Iris (Bearded, Siberian)	Oct. to Feb.	1 in.	12 in.	April to May
Lily (Philippine, Tiger)	March	4 in. to 6 in.	1 ft.	July to Sept.
Lycoris (Spider Lily, Naked Ladies)	March to Aug.	3 in. to 4 in.	4 in.	Sept. to Oct.
Neomarica (Walking Iris)	March to Aug.	1 in.	8 in. to 12 in.	May
Oxalis (*Oxalis regnellii* and *O. triangularis*)	March to Sept.	1 in. to 2 in.	6 in. to 8 in.	March to Nov.
Sprekelia (Aztec Lily)	March to April	Neck exposed	8 in. to 12 in.	May
Tigridia (Tiger Flower)	March to May	4 in.	8 in.	May to June
Tuberose (Polianthes)	Feb. to April	1 in. to 2 in.	8 in.	June to July
Tulbaghia (Society Garlic)	March to Sept.	1 in.	10 in.	April to Nov.
Zephyranthes (Rain Lily)	Oct. to Feb.	1 in. to 2 in.	2 in. to 3 in.	Spring to fall
Zingiber (Pine Cone Ginger)	March to Sept.	1 in.	1 ft. to 2 ft.	July to Sept.

Note: Plant dormant bulbs, divisions, or container-grown plants early in the planting time given. Later in the planting time given, it's best to choose container-grown bulbs in active growth.

Texas has four USDA Plant Hardiness Zones; Zones 6 through 9 with subzones in each of these. Suggested planting dates listed above usually work for a large portion of Texas. Check with local nurseries and/or your County/Extension Agent's office for exact planting dates for your area.

JANUARY

- Start keeping simple records of your bulb-gardening efforts. This information is invaluable for future projects.

- If it was not done in December, it's time to get those tulips and hyacinths out of the refrigerator and plant them—about 4 inches deep in well-prepared beds. This task needs to be finished by mid-month.

- During the rooting and sprouting phase, water potted bulbs and allow them to drain thoroughly. When the sprouts are about an inch tall, place in a sunny location.

- Spring bulbs planted in the fall are up and growing. Don't be concerned about freezing temperatures damaging the leaves.

- Little additional water or fertilizer is needed by most bulbs growing in the landscape now. Keep beds weeded, mulched, and watered when needed.

- If the foliage of summer bulbs is frost-damaged and unattractive, cut it to the ground. Make sure tender bulbs have a 6-inch layer of mulch over them for protection, especially in north Texas.

FEBRUARY

- If you are still haunting retailers who offer colorful summer bulbs or drooling over catalogs that have pictures of these bulbs, make your decisions soon and purchase locally or send in your order.

- Resist spring-flowering bulbs that are put on clearance sale. They are unlikely to do well if planted this late. Exceptions are amaryllis and paperwhite narcissus.

- Plant gladiolus bulbs starting in February in south Texas and in March in north Texas.

- In Zones 8b and 9, in mid- to late February, plant caladium bulbs in flats of sifted compost or potting soil to get a head start. Individual bulbs may also be potted in 4-inch pots.

- A light application of slow-release granular fertilizer is appropriate for Louisiana iris, calla lily, and fall-planted spring-flowering bulbs that are in active growth.

MARCH

- The coldest weather has passed and spring bulbs really begin to "wow" us this month. Don't forget to take notes on the performance of bulbs in your landscape.

- Make decisions about where to plant summer-flowering bulbs. The location should provide the growing conditions needed for best performance.

- Decide if established plantings have grown beyond their designated spot—plan to lift and divide them this month, or April at the latest.

- Most bulbs benefit from being divided every two or three years, including bearded iris.

- Remove faded flowers and developing seedpods from spring-flowering bulbs that are to be kept for blooms next year. Do not remove any of the green foliage, and fertilize them if you did not do so last month.

- Do not let weed problems get ahead of you. Remove weeds promptly and keep beds mulched 3 to 4 inches deep.

APRIL

- Spring-flowering bulbs continue to grace flower beds with their charming beauty. Don't let the season pass without making some notes in your Texas gardening journal. Take pictures or videotape for a visual record.

- Louisiana irises reach their peak this month in south Texas and next month in north Texas. Now is a good time to assess color combinations and how crowded plantings are becoming.

- It's time to plant bulbs you started in pots or flats, in well-prepared beds.

- Do not remove the foliage of repeat-blooming spring-flowering bulbs until it is mostly yellow.

- April can be somewhat dry. Mulch beds to conserve moisture and reduce drying. Water established beds as needed. When you irrigate, do so thoroughly.

- Warmer weather increases pest problems. Caterpillars may be a problem, especially the destructive canna leaf roller. Treat with appropriate aids as needed.

MAY

- The foliage of spring-flowering bulbs may be cut back if yellow, and most gardeners are quite ready to do so after watching it gradually flop over and turn yellow.

- Continue to add summer bulbs to the landscape. The nurseries will have container-grown agapanthus this month. If you haven't tried dwarf cannas, they are available in super colors and great foliage—mass plantings make an outstanding impact in the landscape.

- As flowers fade, trim them off to keep plants looking neat.

- As weather gets hotter, bulbs will usually require more frequent watering if there is not enough rain. It is better to water thoroughly and occasionally than to water lightly and frequently. Use sprinklers or soaker hoses.

- Bulbs growing in the ground can be fertilized as needed to encourage vigorous growth.

- Regularly fertilize bulbs growing in containers with your favorite soluble or slow-release fertilizer. The constant watering they require washes out available nutrients.

JUNE

- Bulbs in the landscape have pretty much filled in their spaces by now, and you can assess the need for any additional planting. Avoid overcrowding beds. Evaluate and make notes.

- Canna and iris may be planted this month.

- Seedpods will sometimes form after a summer bulb has bloomed. Allowing them to develop is a waste of the plant's energy. Remove them as well as old flower spikes when you notice them.

- If needed, stake or otherwise support taller-growing bulbs such as the larger gingers, gladiolus, lilies, and dahlias. Bamboo stakes and nylon stockings work well for this task.

- Fertilize actively growing bulbs in garden beds.

- Aphids and leaf hoppers may be a threat this month. Thrips may be a problem on gladiolus. Keep your eyes open. Apply pest-control aids as needed, according to label directions.

JULY

- Note in your Texas gardening journal when bulbs bloomed, how long they stayed in bloom, major insect or disease problems, and comments on their overall appearance.

- You can still purchase and plant summer bulbs growing in containers. Check local nurseries for new types of ginger.

- Tropical bulbs like ginger, crinum, gloriosa lily, achimenes, oxalis, caladium, and society garlic live it up in the midsummer heat. They certainly enjoy it more than we do. Perhaps you can look out a window from your air-conditioned house and appreciate the show. This is but one reason they should be planted earlier in the season so we can enjoy them now.

- Water thoroughly and deeply as needed. Remember, do not water on any preset schedule—watch the weather.

- In particular, watch the fertilizer needs of container bulbs. If the need to apply soluble fertilizer every two weeks is too much of a bother, use a slow-release fertilizer.

AUGUST

- Get out those spring bulb catalogs. Now is the time to start looking through them for what you want to plant next season.

- Wrap up planting container-grown bulbs this month. Most are left in the ground over the winter in Zones 8b and 9 if the soil drains well, and they need time to become well-established before cold weather arrives. For all other Texas zones, leave summer bulbs in the ground after their tops die, mulch heavily, and keep your fingers crossed.

- Thin out shoots of already-bloomed cannas and gingers if clumps are becoming overly thick.

- Dig up, divide, and transplant Louisiana iris and calla lily this month.

- Continue to water bulb plantings deeply and thoroughly as needed.

- Make your last application of granular fertilizer to actively growing bulbs in the ground this month.

SEPTEMBER

- It's time to finalize those spring bulb ideas and visit local retailers to purchase or send off your orders. Bulbs should be in your hands for October or November planting.

- Standard or hybrid tulips and hyacinths may be placed in the bottom of your vegetable crisper for chilling prior to planting.

- It is time to divide and transplant iris and calla lily, as they are dormant now.

- Good, drenching rains may spare you the chore of watering. Otherwise, water as needed, especially if the weather is hot.

- Achimenes in containers and in the garden may begin to lose steam this month. Those in containers should be given less water.

- Pests that have been a problem all summer are still around, often in greater numbers after a summer of breeding. Don't let your guard down now. Continue to watch for and control pests as they appear.

OCTOBER

- Local nurseries and garden centers are usually good sources for spring bulbs. It's good to look at bulbs in person so you can see and feel them prior to making your selections.

- All bulbs except tulips and hyacinths may be planted into the garden this month in northwest Texas. Planting depth and spacing are important. Generally, we plant bulbs shallower than is recommended for the North.

- Caladiums may be dug up in early to mid-October. Don't wait until all the foliage is dead. Brush off any dirt clods clinging to the bulbs and store them in a frost-free location.

- Watch for the foliage on spider lilies to appear after they finish blooming. Don't cut the foliage once it appears.

- Remember, do not water your bulbs on any present schedule. Do water as needed, deeply and thoroughly.

- Summer bulbs may still be growing but should not be fertilized now, with colder weather approaching.

NOVEMBER

- Finish planting most of your spring bulbs this month.

- Paperwhite narcissus (and other Tazetta narcissus, such as 'Soleil d'Or') may be planted in pots this month and are easily grown for winter bloom as well. Plantings approximately every two weeks will provide fragrant blooms all winter long. Children love to plant and grow them.

- Some summer bulbs have gone dormant, some are winding down, and some are still growing, especially in south Texas.

- In north Texas, the first freezes often occur in November. Cut back the foliage that has browned and mark the locations of dormant summer bulbs to avoid digging into them later on. Mulch tropical bulbs with 10 to 12 inches of leaves or pine straw to protect them from winter cold.

- Be vigilant for insects, especially in south Texas. If insect pests are damaging your plantings, select approved aids and apply according to label directions.

DECEMBER

- Go over your Texas gardening journal notes on your spring bulb plantings. Make sure everything has gone according to plan. (You did have a plan, didn't you?) If you simply have to, you may still make some final additions to your plantings early this month.

- Begin planting tulips and hyacinths in the garden late this month, or in early January.

- Keep beds mulched and weed-free.

- Provide proper light and water to bulbs growing in containers indoors. Do not allow the soil to dry out in pots of tulips, hyacinths, and other spring-flowering bulbs that are outside forming roots.

- Check on any stored summer bulbs occasionally to make sure they are fine.

- During a quiet winter day when the weather is too rough to go out and work in the garden, try to find out more about unfamiliar summer bulbs you might want to try growing next summer.

TULIPS AND DAFFODILS

LAWNGRASSES
for Texas

Almost every landscape includes a lawn. These areas of mowed grass provide important spaces for outdoor activities and a restful contrast to beds of flowers and shrubs. For some, the lawn is a source of pride and is lavished with as much attention as a prized rose garden. For others, the lawn is just something that has to be mowed—as long as it's mostly green, they're happy. Most of us fall somewhere in between.

Lawn care does not have to be complicated, but there are certain necessary elements. Knowing how to select the right grass, providing the right care at the right time, and dealing appropriately with problems that may arise are all important to success.

Our relatively mild climate and long, hot summers dictate the types of lawngrasses that will grow here. The warm-season grasses we use grow vigorously at 80 to 95 degrees Fahrenheit in spring, summer, and fall. They typically go dormant and turn brown with the first frost, greening up again as the weather warms in March and April. Properly maintained, they are long-lived and rarely need to be replaced. The primary warm-season turfgrasses include common Bermuda, hybrid Bermuda, centipede, St. Augustine, and zoysia.

In the warm Texas zones, cool-season grasses may be planted, but not to create permanent lawns as they are in the northern United States. They are used to oversee warm-season lawns in the fall, maintaining a green lawn during the winter when those grasses are brown and dormant. The cool-season grasses are temporary residents in the lawn and die during the early-summer heat. The cool-season grasses generally used for overseeding are annual ryegrass and perennial ryegrass.

SELECTING THE RIGHT GRASS
New homeowners rarely change the type of grass in an existing lawn but occasionally will if sufficient reasons arise. New construction generally allows you to decide which type of grass you want to plant. The choice of grass and how it is planted is a matter of taste, available labor, growing conditions, predicted use, and economics.

Historically, St. Augustine has been the most popular lawn grass, and it is still the most commonly seen in yards around the state. Centipede has become increasingly popular for new lawn installation (especially in east Texas with its acidic soils), owing primarily to its lower maintenance needs. It requires less mowing and fertilization and has fewer insect and disease problems than St. Augustine. However, centipede is not a grass for alkaline or prairie soils. See the following page for lawn grasses appropriate for planting in Texas.

PLANTING A LAWN
Have a soil test done through your local Cooperative Extension Service office of the Stephen F. Austin State University soil-testing lab to determine needed fertilizer, lime, sulfur, etc. Remove any weeds growing in the area and debris (especially around newly constructed homes). Till the soil 4 to 6 inches deep. Apply soil amendments recommended by the soil test and work into the soil. Establish the grade and rake smooth. Use the planting method of your choice.

The following are the most commonly used lawn planting methods:

SEEDING:
1. Broadcast half the seed walking east to west, the other half walking north to south, to ensure even coverage.
2. Let the soil cover the seeds when initial irrigation occurs.
3. Water lightly every day until seeds come up, then as needed to maintain a moist soil until the plants are established.

Plant Bermuda April through August, and centipede April through July.

PLUGGING:
1. Plant 2- to 4-inch diameter plugs 6 to 12 inches apart (greater spacing may be used, but coverage will take longer).
2. Once planted, step on them to firm them

into place.

3. Water lightly every day for one week, every other day for another week, then less frequently but more thoroughly, especially if weather is dry.

Plugging is best done April through August.

SODDING:

1. Lay the sod in a brick pattern (alternate ends and middles) with the seams pressed tightly together.

2. Roll the area to firm the sod into the soil if needed.

3. Water lightly every day for a week, every other day for another week, then less frequently but more thoroughly, especially if water is dry.

Sodding is best done April through September.

CARING FOR YOUR LAWN

Regular mowing is important during the growing season. This may mean mowing every five to seven days during hot and rainy summer weather. Mow often enough so that no more than one-third of the grass blade is removed each time. Mowing height is very important, and your mower blades must be sharp. Set your mower to the following recommended heights:

Common Bermuda: 1 to 1½ inches (rotary or reel mower)

Hybrid Bermuda: ½ to 1 inch (reel mower recommended)

Centipede: 1 to 2 inches (rotary or reel mower)

St. Augustine: 2 to 3 inches (rotary or reel mower)

Zoysia: ½ to 1½ inches (rotary or reel mower)

Irrigation is generally needed only during hot, dry weather, but when necessary, it is very important. Water deeply and thoroughly, applying ½ to 1 inch of water. Lawns are generally fertilized in April, June, and August for maximum growth and quality. Fertilize centipede lightly in April and July. Insect and disease problems are most common during the summer growing season (although brown patch fungus attacks in the spring and fall). Watch carefully for damage, get an accurate diagnosis, and treat appropriately. Practice good weed control when necessary.

LAWNGRASSES

COMMON BERMUDA

Characteristics: Fine texture, dark green color; used on athletic fields; coarser texture than hybrids; new, improved named varieties becoming available. Plant seed, sod, or plugs.

Strengths: Rapid establishment rate; excellent wear tolerance; good ability to recover from damage; excellent drought tolerance; good salt tolerance; can be seeded.

Weaknesses: Poor shade tolerance; medium to high maintenance.

HYBRID BERMUDA

Characteristics: Very fine texture; dark green; excellent quality; used extensively on golf courses and athletic fields; high fertility requirements. Plant sod or plugs.

Strengths: Rapid establishment rate; excellent wear tolerance; good ability to recover from damage; excellent drought tolerance; good salt tolerance.

Weaknesses: Very poor shade tolerance; very high maintenance; should use reel mower.

CENTIPEDE

Characteristics: Medium texture; slow growth; low fertility requirements; requires acid soils; popular for home lawns. Plant sod, plugs, or seed.

Strengths: Good disease and insect resistance; low maintenance; fair tolerance to partial shade. Advantages over St. Augustine are: finer leaf texture, better cold tolerance, better resistance to chinch bugs and brown patch, can be seeded.

Weaknesses: Poor wear tolerance; quality can decline if overfertilized; lighter green leaf color; poor drought tolerance; poor salt tolerance; seed is slow to establish; for acidic soils only.

ST. AUGUSTINE

Characteristics: Coarse texture; rich green color; popular for home lawns. Generally, plant sod or plugs; seed very rarely available, but not best quality.

Strengths: Best grass for part-shade; excellent salt tolerance; medium maintenance; establishes fairly quickly.

Weaknesses: Poor cold tolerance; very susceptible to chinch bugs, brown patch; coarse texture.

ZOYSIA

Characteristics: Several species and cultivars; medium-fine to fine texture; dark green color; very dense growth; used on golf courses and home lawns. Plant sod or plugs.

Strengths: Excellent wear tolerance; good tolerance to part shade ('Emerald' and 'El Toro' varieties); excellent cold tolerance.

Weaknesses: Slow establishment rate; accumulates thatch, readily requiring removal; medium to high maintenance.

LAWN WITH IVY AND ASSORTED BEDS

BERMUDA GRASS, COMMON
Cynodon dactylon

Type/Hardiness—Warm-season grass; hardy throughout Texas

Color—Blue-green

Texture—Fine

Recommended Mowing Height—1 to 1½ in., and 2 in. or taller in midsummer

Water Needs—Water to a minimum soil depth of 6 to 8 in.

Planting/Care—Plant in spring when night temperatures have warmed up. Begin fertilizing in spring after new growth emerges. Reapply about every ten weeks during the growing season, and once again in the fall. Mow with a sharp-bladed mower.

Pests/Diseases—May be attacked by brown patch, dollar spot, leaf spots, and other diseases; grubs, Bermuda mite, sod webworms, army worms, and other insects. Visit your local garden center for controls.

Landscaping Tips & Ideas—Best in sunny landscape areas where you want a tough grass that is wear-tolerant. There is no companion planting—it spreads by under-ground runners and may be invasive in neighboring garden beds.

BLUE FESCUE
Festuca glauca

Type/Hardiness—Clumping; hardy throughout Texas

Color—Blue-gray

Texture—Coarse

Mature Size (H x W)—10 to 12 in. x 12 to 16 in.

Water Needs—Water only as necessary to prevent total soil dryness.

Planting/Care—The best planting times are very early spring or very early fall. Site in full sun in well-drained ground. Fertilize no more than once in early spring and once in early fall, watering in well after each application.

Pests/Diseases—None serious

Landscaping Tips & Ideas—Although used as a border or edging plant, it is great for mass plantings as a lawnlike substitute in waterwise landscaping schemes. May also be grown in large containers. It is a tough and durable plant, very drought tolerant, and averse to shade and too much water.

BLUE GRAMA
Bouteloua gracilis

Type/Hardiness—Warm-season; hardy throughout Texas

Color—Light green

Texture—Fine

Recommended Mowing Height—2 to 3 in.

Water Needs—Very drought tolerant once established.

Planting/Care—Best in heavier, drier soils. Has a bunching rather than spreading habit, so occasional reseeding is necessary to keep a nice turf appearance. Minimal need for mowing. Cold-hardy native.

Pests/Diseases—None serious

Landscaping Tips & Ideas—A great choice for prairie restoration and landscaping sites that require minimal mowing. Occasionally mixed with buffalograss seed for a prairie, warm-season mix, and is somewhat easier to establish than buffalo.

BUFFALOGRASS
Buchloe dactyloides

Type/Hardiness—Warm-season; hardy throughout Texas

Color—Green

Texture—Soft, wavy

Recommended Mowing Height—2 to 3 in.

Water Needs—Minimal. Do not overwater.

Planting/Care—Thrives in semi-arid areas on neutral or alkaline soils. Relatively slow-growing, so may not need mowing at all or very often.

Pests/Diseases—None serious

Landscaping Tips & Ideas—If it achieves a tufted appearance at 6 to 8 inches, it should not be fertilized and seldom watered. A native grass, it is well-suited to naturalistic or informal gardens and landscapes.

CARPETGRASS
Axonopus affinis

Type/Hardiness—Warm-season; hardy throughout Texas

Color—Medium green

Texture—Coarse

Recommended Mowing Height—1 to 2 in.

Water Needs—Prefers moist ground

Planting/Care—Plant in spring. A low-maintenance choice for areas with poor, wet, acidic, or infertile soil. Doesn't require frequent fertilization and makes a dense, thick lawn. During the growing season, the quickly emerging seedheads make frequent mowing necessary.

Pests/Diseases—Various insects may appear, including armyworm, cutworm, white grub, mole cricket, and sod webworm. Potential diseases include brown patch, dollar spot, leaf spot, pythium blight. Nematodes can also occur. Get advice locally for diagnosing and treating any of these.

Landscaping Tips & Ideas—Noted for its heat tolerance and ability to grow well in problem sites with poor soil.

CENTIPEDEGRASS
Eremochloa ophiuroides

Type/Hardiness—Warm-season; hardy throughout Texas, but best for eastern third/acidic soils

Color—Bright yellow-green

Texture—Medium

Recommended Mowing Height—2 to 3 in., or taller in midsummer

Water Needs—Water to a soil depth of 6 to 8 inches. Sufficient water is required in the blazing heat of July and August.

Planting/Care—Thrives in acidic soils and fails in alkaline ones (due to severe chlorosis problems). Plant in spring and keep moist until established. Use fertilizer especially for this grass, because it includes iron (necessary to avoid yellowing). Mow once a week.

Pests/Diseases—If insects or diseases such as brown patch occur, visit your local garden center for control options.

Landscaping Tips & Ideas—Use as a stand-alone grass; should not be used in conjunction with Bermuda or St. Augustine lawns. Lower-maintenance than the other two.

KENTUCKY BLUEGRASS
Poa pratensis

Type/Hardiness—Cool-season; hardy in northern areas

Color—Dark green

Texture—Medium

Recommended Mowing Height—2 to 3 in.

Water Needs—Needs more water than warm-season grasses, though it can survive a drought better than expected, even when allowed to go dormant.

Planting/Care—Cannot tolerate high heat and humidity. Prefers a slightly acid pH and plenty of sun (though it tolerates partial shade). Plant in fall or early spring. Not invasive.

Pests/Diseases—Insects—armyworm, billbug, cutworm, sod webworm, white grub. Diseases—brown patch, gray leaf spot, rust, powdery mildew, fusarium blight. Also vulnerable to nematodes. Consult a local garden center for controls if necessary.

Landscaping Tips & Ideas—Best grown at higher elevations or in the northernmost counties. A blend of two or more cultivars is recommended, since different varieties exhibit different levels of tolerance for pests and adverse environmental conditions.

ROUGH BLUEGRASS
Poa trivialis

Type/Hardiness—Cool-season; hardy in northern areas

Color—Bright green

Texture—Coarse

Recommended Mowing Height—2 to 2½ in.

Water Needs—Best in cool, moist sites.

Planting/Care—Overseed into zoysia or Bermuda lawns in the fall; the small seed size is a plus, making applying or reapplying easier. It adapts to wet and shady conditions. It goes dormant in summer heat.

Pests/Diseases—None serious

Landscaping Tips & Ideas—Used as an annual cool-season grass on warm-season lawns. Particularly good for overseeding zoysia and Bermuda since it is tolerant of partial shade and does not make a thick, dense sod. It is very winter-hardy. Sometimes combined with Kentucky bluegrass seed in mixes; avoid this combination in the cooler, high elevation growing zones, as the rough bluegrass can potentially live through the summer, overtaking the Kentucky bluegrass.

RYEGRASS
Lolium spp.

Type/Hardiness—Warm-season; hardy throughout Texas

Color—Medium to dark green

Texture—Medium

Recommended Mowing Height—2 to 2½ in.

Water Needs—Water as necessary to prevent drying and wilting.

Planting/Care—Fertilizing throughout the growing season is not necessary if the grass is healthy. Mow with a sharp blade throughout the fall, winter, and spring.

Pests/Diseases—Brown patch, leaf spot, and rust may appear; your local garden center can help you with controls.

Landscaping Tips & Ideas—Ryegrass can be used to overseed St. Augustine, Bermuda, zoysia, and centipede to maintain a green year-round appearance. Annual ryegrass greens an existing lawn as the permanent grass goes dormant, then dies out as spring heats up and the other begins to green up. Its bright springtime green complements blooming trees, shrubs, and flowers. Does well under deciduous trees.

ST. AUGUSTINE
Stenataphrum secundatum

Type/Hardiness—Warm-season; hardy throughout Texas

Color—Dark green

Texture—Coarse

Recommended Mowing Height—2 in., or more in midsummer

Water Needs—Water often during establishment, then reduce frequency. Water to avoid prolonged and severe wilt.

Planting/Care—Plant in spring after frost. Needs at least four hours of sun a day, or eight hours of mixed sun and shade. Fertilize in springtime as new growth begins.

Pests/Diseases—Susceptible to brown patch, leaf spot, and gray leaf spot. Sometimes visited by grubs, chinch bugs, and other unwanted pests. If problems persist, seek control advice locally.

Landscaping Tips & Ideas—Use as a stand-alone in any type of design desired. There are no companions; it will crowd out Bermuda and other grasses. Will not tolerate high traffic. Because it doesn't have underground runners or rhizomes, it's relatively easy to prevent intrusions into flower beds.

TALL FESCUE
Fescue arundinacea

Type/Hardiness—Cool-season; hardy throughout Texas

Color—Dark green

Texture—Medium to coarse

Recommended Mowing Height—2 to 3 in., or taller in midsummer

Water Needs—When establishing, maintain moist soil. Thereafter, water to prevent wilting. The demand for summer water is best supplied by automatic sprinklers.

Planting/Care—Plant in sun or under deciduous trees. Fertilize in early fall, late fall, and early spring (never in summer), and water in well after each application. May thin out in dry Texas summers. To ensure a thicker lawn, apply extra seeds each fall.

Pests/Diseases—May have unwelcome visits from fusarium blight, leaf spot, or even brown patch. Army worms, cutworms, and white grubs may visit as well. Visit your local garden center for controls.

Landscaping Tips & Ideas—Should be used as stand-alone pure plantings. Ideal for smaller shaded lawns with automatic sprinkler systems.

ZOYSIA
Zoysia japonica

Type/Hardiness—Warm-season; hardy throughout Texas

Color—Dark green

Texture—Very fine

Recommended Mowing Height—½ to 1 in., or taller in midsummer

Water Needs—Routine watering to prevent wilting.

Planting/Care—Plant in early spring after frost. Tolerates shade, but not heavy shade. Grows slowly, but should still be mowed often to maintain an even turf. A reel mower is best. Fertilize in spring and again in fall. Yearly dethatching may be necessary in thick-growing lawns.

Pests/Diseases—May be visited by the common white grub. Brown patch, rust, and leaf spot may occur. If problems persist, get advice from your local garden center.

Landscaping Tips & Ideas—Best for small, detailed areas such as Japanese gardens or small courtyards and lawns. It is a more expensive investment than most other grasses, but one of the best-looking available and lower in water use than St. Augustine.

MOWING INFORMATION AND ADVICE

Hi-ho, hi-ho, it's off to work I go . . . and then I come home and mow the lawn! Mowing is the single most stressful practice for the grass—and the owner—in lawn care. Yet it is done more frequently that any other practice, generally taken for granted, and more often than not, done incorrectly.

MOW OFTEN

Most homeowners mow every seven to ten days. But if the truth be told, we really should be mowing every four to five days, especially if you follow the "one-third" rule, which says to mow when the lawn gets one-third taller than the recommended growing height. For my own lawn, using this rule would mean mowing every four days during the growing season, even with minimal fertilization.

But I do find that more frequent mowings keep the lawn in the best shape. The smaller clippings easily fall into the grass, quickly breaking down with sunlight and moisture. Realistically, it is tough for even professional lawn companies to mow that often, but if you get as close as possible to following the one-third rule, success will be just around the corner.

MOW, THEN MEASURE

It is a good idea to measure the actual leaf blade length following mowing to determine exactly how the height compares to the mower deck setting you are using. Most mowers have mechanisms that allow adjustments to raise or lower the body of the mower. Instead of just depending on guesswork to find the right setting, take a ruler and measure the height of the grass blades in several locations immediately after mowing. The ground level will vary across your lawn, so an average measurement will give you a better idea of the height at which each setting really cuts.

MOW HIGH

One common mistaken belief is that the closer you cut the lawn, the slower it will grow, so you won't have to mow it as often. If you keep cutting the grass so short you are almost scalping it, you may not have to mow as often, because it will likely die. The effect of mowing too close is that weeds will take over, and you will have to mow even more frequently. The more sunlight that reaches the soil surface, the more weed seed that germinates. Taller grass also filters pollutants better and serves as a living mulch for the lawn, minimizing soil temperatures and reflective heat.

Generally, grass roots mirror the grass blades, so the taller the blades, the deeper the roots. You want the roots to be deep because that will make the grass more drought-, cold-, and pest-resistant.

SHARP BLADES ARE BETTER

Dull mower blades chew, rip, or tear grass blades. So if you haven't sharpened or replaced your blades and think you are mowing at a particular height, you are fooling yourself. Sharp mower blades give a clean, smooth cut. They also make the mowing process more efficient, causing less stress on both the mower and the grass. Also start with new blades each year. This is a minimal investment that pays big dividends in the health of your lawn.

DON'T BE SET IN YOUR WAYS

Soil compaction occurs over time, usually from the weight of mowing or gardening equipment, pet runs, or frequent foot traffic. Areas near sidewalks and pathways are likely to become compacted first. Soil type also plays a role. Clay soils are more likely to compact than sandy, silty, or loamy soils. Soil compaction causes problems such as poor root growth, poor oxygen penetration to the roots, and poor water filtration, all of which mean poor plant performance.

One of the biggest contributors to soil compaction in your lawn is mowing in the same direction week after week, year after year. It is easy to change directions every time you mow. If you mow in a perpendicular direction, then the next time a diagonal one, you can go at least four different ways, spreading the path of the lawnmower tires over a larger surface area. You'll also be surprised at how different the view looks when you vary the direction of your mowing.

TO BAG OR NOT TO BAG?

A 1,000-square-foot lawn can generate 200 pounds or more of clippings annually depending on how often you fertilize. The clippings contain nutrients somewhere around 4 percent nitrogen (N), 2 percent phosphorus (P), and 0.5 percent potassium (K). So it doesn't make much sense to pay to fertilize the lawn, then cut the grass and throw away part of the fertilizer. Frequent mowings, minimal feedings, and proper watering practices allow you to leave the clippings where they fall and benefit the lawn at the same time. If you shred the clippings with a mulching mower, you can reduce your fertilizer needs by as much as 25 percent.

On the other hand, leaving thick clumps of grass on the lawn after mowing can be detrimental. If rain, vacation, or other cause permits your grass to get too tall between mowings, you most likely will need to rake and remove the clippings—unless you are using a mulching mower or a bag attachment.

Mulching mowers and mulching blades pulverize and shred cut grass into smaller pieces, which helps eliminate the need for bagging or removing lawn clippings.

Many municipalities limit or even prohibit grass clippings form their landfills in order to encourage recycling or composting of this valuable organic garden product. Use caution when applying clippings from a lawn recently treated with a post-emergent herbicide as a mulch for vegetables and flowers. It is better to compost these clippings thoroughly before use, turning the pile often to encourage heat and microorganisms to break down the chemicals.

GETTING READY FOR WINTER

Most lawns respond well to gradually raising the mowing height by ¼ to ½ inch in preparation for winter. The taller leaf blades encourage deeper root growth, and increase cold tolerance and winter protection. Also, remove tree leaves from the lawn either by raking or mowing. Many mulching mowers pulverize the leaves into small-enough pieces that will quickly decompose, adding valuable organic matter back into the soil.

If you are not up to the challenge of raking but don't have a mulching mower, try mowing in a diminishing circle in the same direction, blowing the leaves into a narrower pile for easier pickup by hand. You can also shred the leaves fairly well by mowing over them several times in early winter.

THATCH—THE REAL STORY

Thatch consists of layers of undecayed grass located between the soil and the leaf blades of the turf plants. Thatch is primarily composed of roots, rhizomes, and stolons, not grass clippings. Thatch formation is a routine part of the growth cycle, in which plant parts age, die, and decompose into humus.

The problem occurs when something upsets this natural cycle, causing thatch to build up quicker than it can break down. Rapid, excessive lawn growth is the major cause of thatch, and over-fertilization and over-watering are the biggest culprits. They produce excessive amounts of grass clippings, preventing normal breakdown of thatch.

Excessive thatch inhibits water penetrations into the soil, harbors insects and diseases, and leads to shallow root systems susceptible to heat, cold, and drought. The potential for thatch to become a problem depends on the turfgrass species and management practices. A half-inch layer of thatch might be a problem for some grasses, but not others. To determine the thickness, take plugs from your lawn so you can easily see and measure the thatch layer.

If you have too much thatch, there are several ways to deal with it. Scalping the lawn in the spring to loosen thatch is not recommended.

- Vertical mowers and dethatching equipment, which can be rented, mechanically reduce the thatch layer. They have blades, knives, or tines that lift the dead vegetation to the surface where it can be gathered and then composted.
- Use a hand rake to pull thatch to the surface. This can be very time-consuming, strenuous work.

Warm-season grasses should be dethatched shortly after the grass begins active growth. If you do it too early, it may cause early green-up, with the chance of late-season cold injury. Cool-season grasses should have thatch removed in the fall or early spring when the lawn is growing vigorously. It is a good idea to reseed cool-season lawns after dethatching to promote thicker lawn coverage.

In severe cases, spread removal over a two- to three-year period. This will minimize stress to the lawn and invite fewer weed problems. Adequate soil moisture also makes the process much easier and less stressful to the lawn.

IDENTIFYING TURFGRASS PESTS
DAMAGE SYMPTOMS OF COMMON TURFGRASS PEST PROBLEMS AND POSSIBLE CAUSES

Symptom(s):   Possible causal agent(s):

A. Disruption of soil:
  1. Hills, piles, or structures of loose dirt on turf . . . . *ants*
      a. Mounds up to 18 inches tall with no visible entrance(s), or mound with ants emerging in mass when disturbed . . . . *red imported fire ant*

Controlling Fire Ants

      b. Small mounds with rims around single central entrance holes and presence of small ($\frac{3}{16}$ in.) grayish-black ants . . . . *pyramid ants*
      c. Many hills of coarse soil with central exit holes and presence of large ($\frac{3}{8}$ in.) red-brown ant with spines on the thorax . . . . *Texas leafcutting ant*
      d. Flat cleared areas up to 3 ft. in diameter made of coarse soil particles with a single central exit hole and with the presence of large ($\frac{3}{8}$ in.) reddish-brown ants with square heads . . . . *red harvester ant*
  2. Trails of raised, loose dirt roughly ½ inch wide in an "S" shaped pattern through turf . . . . *mole crickets*
  3. Small piles of dirt "pellets" ($\frac{3}{16}$ in.) scattered through thatch . . . . *earthworms*
  4. Earthen "chimneys" with central holes (about ½ inch diameter) . . . . *crawfish*

| White Grub | Sod Webworm |

Reprinted from: The Texas Agriculture Extension Service publication B#-5083

5. Small piles of loose dirt associated with exit holes . . . .*green June beetle larvae*

6. Round holes (up to ½ inch diameter) in soil . . . . *digger wasp nests or cicada exit holes*

B. Direct damage to grass causing yellowing or plant death:

  1. Grass blades chewed or missing . . . . *caterpillars*

    a. Presence of gray-brown caterpillars up to 1 in. long with an inverted cream-colored "Y"
      on the fronts of the head capsules . . . . *army worms*

    b. Presence of gray-brown caterpillars up to 1 in. long that curl into a tight "C" position when disturbed . . . .*cutworms*

    c. Presence of translucent greenish caterpillars up to ¾ in. long with black raised spots
      on each body segment . . . .*tropical sod webworm*

  2. Yellow or dead grass:

    a. Roots missing and presence of cream-colored "C" shaped grubs with three legs on body segments
      behind brown head capsule . . . .*white grubs*

    b. No tissue removed, with presence of pinkish-orange, white and black nymph and adult stages
      of bugs up to ³⁄₁₆ in. long . . . . *chinch bugs*

    c. No tissue removed, but "galls" or globular objects (scales) in the root zone . . . . *Rhodesgrass scale or ground pearls*

    d. No tissue removed, but with shortened internodes producing a typical rosetting
      and tufted growth, or "witch broom" effect; grass may be very yellow
      or whitish in appearance with no insects visible to the naked eye . . . *Bermudagrass (stunt) mites or buffalograss (stunt) mites*

COMMON LAWN DISEASES

Diseases are caused by pathogens, referred to as causal agents or organisms, which feed on or disturb plant tissue. They are typically fungal or bacterial in nature and spread by rain, wind, and in some cases, contact with lawn mower tires. For a disease to become infectious, there must be a host (turfgrass), pathogen, and the right environmental conditions such as temperature or moisture. And those conditions must occur for the right amount of time for the pathogen to grow and become infectious. This means that some diseases are more prominent during certain times of the year.

Just as with insects, homeowners must be observant of their lawns to spot symptoms early. Diseases sometimes spread very quickly, and early identification is the key to implementing the appropriate management strategy. Some diseases can be managed by changing cultural habits, such as fertilizer applications, watering, and mowing. If chemical treatments are required, early detection can help in treating only the infected area rather than the entire lawn. This saves time and money and helps protect the environment from an overuse of chemicals.

If you do make a habit of routinely scouting your lawn, it is likely that by the time you see the symptoms of the disease, the pathogen may no longer be active. In other words, the damage is already done, and any kind of control may be a waste of time.

If so, it may be time for a little lawn renovation. On the other hand, some diseases worsen with time, proper environmental conditions, and poor lawn management, even to the point of killing the grass, roots and all.

FUNGICIDES

There are several fungicides on the market that can help in lawn disease control. Remember that in many cases, simple cultural or management practices can do the job without spraying. In situations where they can't, you must match the chemical product to your particular disease and lawn grass. Some are preventative, some systemic, and others kill on contact. I can't emphasize enough that reading the label is essential in applying the treatment correctly and safely.

ALTERNATIVE DISEASE-CONTROL PRODUCTS

There are many alternative disease-control products available. Look for products such as copper, fungicidal soaps, Neem, baking soda, and sulfur, to mention a few. Again, be sure to read the label. Some products, even organic ones, can burn plant foliage when used in the heat of the day or if air temperatures are too high. Be careful with home concoctions, since application amounts and plant sensitivity are hard to determine.

COMMON LAWN DISEASES

BROWN PATCH

Symptoms and Signs: Individual leaf blades are affected, starting with small, dull tan lesions, enlarging and turning brown with reddish-brown margins near the soil. The leaf blades do wilt and are easily pulled from the base of the plant. The grass can wilt because water and nutrient uptake are interrupted. The overall appearance of the lawn shows brown spots or patches from a few inches in size up to several feet.

Management: Select a low fertility program avoiding excess nitrogen. Water early in the morning, deeply and infrequently. Mow when the grass foliage is completely dry using a sharp blade. Fungicides are recommended and can be applied in the impacted and adjoining areas rather than on the entire lawn. Remove and compost clippings during warm, moist weather to avoid spread. Avoid thatch buildup.

DOLLAR SPOT

Symptoms and Signs: Individual leaf blades first turn yellowish-green, progressing to a water-soaked appearance, and finally turning a straw color with reddish-brown margins. Overall the lawn looks to have distinct, off-color, almost bleached circular patches several feet across.

Management: Water early in the morning, deeply and infrequently. Mow when leaf blades are completely dry. Apply nitrogen fertilizer at the proper rate. Adopt a routine fertility program. Use appropriately labeled fungicides. Avoid thatch buildup.

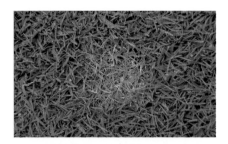

DOWNY MILDEW *(Similar in appearance to powdery mildew)*

Symptoms and Signs: Initially white, raised, linear streaks appear parallel to the midvein of the leaf blade. Leaves eventually become yellow and die at the tips. Distortion of the foliage may also occur.

Management: Avoid watering in the evening. Instead water early or late in the morning. Water deeply and infrequently. Control thatch problems. Fertilizer programs should be reviewed, avoiding high nitrogen applications. Fungicides are available and should be labeled for downy mildew. The pathogen subsides with drier conditions.

FUSARIUM BLIGHT

Symptoms and Signs: Stunted grass with scattered patches of light green foliage that turn reddish brown, then tan, and finally a straw color. Tufts of healthy green grass will remain in the impacted areas. Fusarium can also affect the roots and crowns of the plants, characterized by brown to reddish decay and pinkish growth of the pathogen during high incidences of rainfall and irrigation.

Management: Reduce thatch layer at appropriate time, reduce or eliminate high nitrogen fertilizer applications, water deeply and less often, employ fungicide products labeled for your particular turfgrass.

GRAY LEAF SPOT

Symptoms and Signs: Individual leaf blades get obvious grayish-brownish-red dots, or spots that enlarge to circular or elongated lesions heavily concentrated along the center of the leaf. During optimum wet conditions the spots develop depressed, blue-gray centers with irregular brown margins and a border of yellow-green tissue. With time and severe infection, entire leaf blades can wither and turn brown.

Management: Reduce nitrogen, water deeply and less often early in the morning, select resistant grass cultivars, use appropriately labeled fungicides, delay overseeding with ryegrass until later in the season. Avoid soil compaction. Manage any thatch buildup.

HELMINTHOSPORIUM LEAF SPOT

Symptoms and Signs: Circular lesions appear as small purplish spots that increase in size, turn brown, then fade to yellow with a brown or darker margin. Some folks even describe the spots as "eye-like." The entire leaf blade can also turn yellow. The older, infected blades can wither and dry, causing a melting effect in the lawn.

Management: One of the easiest diseases to manage by proper maintenance, using recommended mowing height, sharp blades, moderate fertility, supplement deep and infrequent irrigation, and thatch control. Apply a fertilizer with a moderate rate of nitrogen at the time of infection. Maintain even moisture if possible. Raise mowing height and especially avoid scalping. Remove and compost grass clippings from infested areas. Use appropriately labeled fungicides.

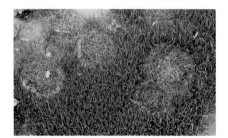

POWDERY MILDEW

Symptoms and Signs: Grayish-white, powdery, mildew-like growths on the leaf blade, which can spread, making areas of the lawn have a grayish-white appearance. Blades can eventually turn yellow.

Management: Bag clippings in severe cases and dispose of properly. Avoid watering in the evenings. Use a sharp mower blade. Thin tree branches for more light and air circulation. Use appropriately labeled fungicides according to directions.

PYTHIUM BLIGHT

Symptoms and Signs: Individual leaf blades have a water-soaked, grayish-green appearance, shriveling and eventually turning brown. The leaf blades tend to mat together with a slimy look and feel to the foliage. As the disease progresses, irregularly shaped areas of turf, usually a few inches across, develop. As it spreads, it encroaches on larger areas. There will also be healthy patches of green in the affected areas, leaving a "frog-eye" appearance. The lawn patches can appear to be irregular, crescent-shaped, or even streaks of blighted grass. In early morning, with heavy dew or irrigation, cotton-like growth may be seen on the foliage.

Management: Provide good drainage and air circulation. Irrigate early in the morning and avoid frequent irrigation. When the disease is present, avoid foot and mower traffic in the affected area. Labeled fungicides are also available.

RUST

Symptoms and Signs: Yellow flecks on leaves that enlarge and become a fuzzy orange-red. The pustules tend to be oriented in rows up and down the leaf blade. If the disease progresses, the leaves turn completely yellow, starting at the tips and moving down toward the sheath. In such cases, the entire area of affected grass appears yellow.

Management: Fertilize with a slow-release nitrogen product. Remove and compost clippings properly. Mow frequently. Choose resistant cultivars when available. Use appropriately labeled fungicides.

JANUARY

- Gardeners in the southern part of the state can still overseed dormant lawns with ryegrass or a blend this month, but it is risky if severe cold weather occurs before the grass has had a chance to establish. More seed may be spread over lawns overseeded earlier to thicken up sparse areas.

- Mow overseeded lawns as needed. If the weather is moist and mild, this could be every week. If the weather is cold, grass will grow more slowly.

- Cool, moist weather generally makes irrigation unnecessary this month. Water as needed.

- In south Texas, cool-season grasses should have been fertilized last month and can be fertilized again in early February. In north Texas, fertilizer may be applied in late November (once the warm-season grass goes dormant) and again around the middle of this month.

- Winter weeds may be growing in the lawn now. Mow them back if you like.

FEBRUARY

- Review the notes you made last year on the performance of your lawn and make decisions on what needs to be done this spring. If you don't have any notes from last year, don't you wish you did? Plan to keep at least a few simple records in your Texas gardening journal this year for future reference.

- Mow overseeded lawns as needed. If the weather is moist and mild, this could be every week. Ryegrass falls over, mats, and looks unattractive if allowed to grow too tall.

- If the weather turns dry and you have ryegrass growing, irrigation may be necessary.

- In south Texas, overseeded lawns may be fertilized early this month. Water in fertilizer immediately after application.

- Mild weather will encourage enthusiastic growth from cool-season weeds in the lawn. Use a weed-control aid to eliminate broadleaf weeds.

- Pythium blight may attack ryegrass, causing areas to "melt." Treat with fungus-control aids.

MARCH

- Regular mowing is just around the corner, and you may need to begin mowing occasionally. Get your lawn mower in good repair for the coming season. It is especially important to have sharp blades.

- As spring progresses, new vigorous grass roots will begin to grow. This month is a particularly critical time in this process, and care need to be taken not to interfere with the reestablishment of a strong root system. Do not disturb or stress the grass this month. This would not be a good time to aerate, fill over, or dethatch the lawn.

- As turf wakes up from dormancy, warm days and dry weather may make watering necessary. If needed, water thoroughly.

- Brown patch thrives in cool, moist weather this month. St. Augustine is particularly vulnerable, although centipede is occasionally damaged by this disease. One course of action is to treat with a fungicide labeled for this problem.

APRIL

- This month begins the prime planting season for warm-season grasses, which runs till August or September. With the exception of common Bermuda, solid sodding is the preferred method of establishing a lawn.

- Ideally, wait until next month to do filling, aerification, or dethatching, when the grass is growing more vigorously.

- April can be one of the drier months, though mild weather generally keeps the grass from getting too stressed. Watch the weather, and if things get too dry, water thoroughly and deeply as needed.

- Lawns that have been damaged or are in low vigor certainly should be considered for fertilization. Do not guess; follow the label directions on lawn fertilizer carefully. Water the lawn immediately after.

- Apply broadleaf weedkillers now and next month. Be sure to read the label for tolerant grasses and application rates.

- Mowing becomes a regular job this month, though not as often as will be needed during midsummer.

MAY

- Planting lawns now has the advantage of allowing the grass to grow and establish over the long summer months. Grass planted in early summer will also better endure the cold of its first winter.

- If your lawn has some low places in it, now is a good time to correct this situation. Choose a soil that matches your native soil for the fill. For example, do not use light sandy soils to fill areas where the native soil is heavy clay.

- Temperatures in the 90s generally make their debut this month. Calibrate your sprinkler system to apply ½ to 1 inch of water when irrigation becomes necessary.

- This month is the last chance to apply many broadleaf weedkillers before the weather becomes hot.

- Do not wait too long before mowing, especially as the rate of growth speeds up during summer.

JUNE

- Lawns that feel spongy when you walk on them may have developed a thick layer of thatch. Plan on dethatching with a vertical mower (best handled by a professional lawn-care company), or core aerification (you can rent a machine that does this).

- Water newly laid sod for 15 to 20 minutes every day for a week. The roots are mostly lost when sod is harvested, and the sod easily dries and will die if not kept moist.

- Water established turf only as needed during hot, dry weather.

- Lawns (other than centipede) that were fertilized in April may need to be fertilized again this month. Also, fertilize lawns sodded in April or early May.

- Be cautious about using weedkillers the rest of the summer. Many could damage the lawn if temperatures are high.

JULY

- Mow, edge, and deal with pest problems before you go on vacation.

- As landscapes mature, shade trees may create more shade than your lawn grass can tolerate. They will begin to thin and disappear when that happens. Increase the amount of sunlight reaching the turf by selective pruning of lower branches and inner branches to allow more light to reach the lawn below.

- Do not water needlessly. Overwatering your lawn wastes water and promotes disease problems. Wait at least 7 to 10 days after the last good rain before you consider irrigation.

- If you last fertilized in April, you might fertilize again this month, especially if the grass is not growing fast enough and you would like to mow more often. Fertilizer will also create a deeper green color.

- This is prime chinch bug season for St. Augustine, especially if the weather turns dry. Do not delay controlling this pest!

AUGUST

- This is a good month to evaluate your lawn. If it's in poor shape, try to identify the problems and plan how to do a better job preventing them. Record your notes in your Texas gardening journal.

- Finish up seeding common Bermuda grass this month. Every week of delay is now one week less of growing season for the turf to establish. This is also true for plugs.

- Areas of your lawn that still need to be renovated should also be handled now. Remove any weeds, loosen the soil, and plug or sod new turf into the area.

- These long, hot days coming at the end of a long, hot summer are especially stressful. Watering continues to be important. Do not be fooled by quick thundershowers. Unless at least ½ inch of rain falls, you'll need to water.

- Those who want maximum quality and growth should make their third and last fertilizer application this month.

SEPTEMBER

- Continue to lay sod this month, but it's too late for planting plugs and really too late to plant seeds of centipede or even fast-growing Bermuda.

- September is a prime month for hurricanes. If one threatens your area, pick up and store all loose objects in the lawn, including sprinklers, tools, lawn ornaments, and anything else that could be picked up by strong winds. Should one hit your area, rake and hose off debris from your lawngrass as soon as possible after the storm.

- Water as needed, especially newly laid lawns or lawns that are recovering room dethatching or aerification.

- This month or the first week of October is the time to winterize your Texas lawn. Apply with a broadcast or rotary spreader. Water thoroughly afterwards.

- Watch for caterpillars such as army worms or sod webworms. They chew grass blades and can make the lawn look terrible. Control with insect-control aids.

OCTOBER

- Plant ryegrass seed this month and in November. Water lightly every day for the 7 to 10 days it takes them to germinate.

- Some gardeners are afraid that existing warm-season turf will be damaged if overseeded. Don't worry. It won't be. In fact, overseeding tends to reduce competition from cool-season weeds.

- Do not allow turfgrass to go into dormancy when it is drought-stressed. Water deeply and thoroughly if a good rain does not occur for 10 to 14 days.

- If you didn't winterize your lawn during September, the first week of this month is the time to do so, especially in north Texas. Anytime in October works for south Texas lawns.

- Watch for and treat brown patch if it appears in your St. Augustine.

- Apply pre-emergent herbicides in early to mid-October to prevent problems with cool-season annual lawn weeks (do not apply to overseeded lawns).

NOVEMBER

- In the northern part of the state, warm-season grasses are going dormant with the first freeze. Down south, mowing is greatly reduced as the weather cools.

- Continue to overseed ryegrass if you have not already done so. You will need to continue mowing through the winter, but many people think it is worth it.

- In north Texas, fertilize ryegrass planted in October in late November after the warm-season grass in your lawn has gone dormant.

- Apply a pre-emergent herbicide early this month if you did not do so in October.

- In south Texas, watch for brown patch on St. Augustine and treat promptly with an appropriate aid.

- Mow ryegrass regularly. Set the mower to a height of 1 to 2 inches.

DECEMBER

- Unless you overseeded with ryegrass, lawns are wonderfully care-free this month. Review your notes and make sure you have recorded everything you need to do in your Texas gardening journal before you forget.

- Before you store your lawn mower, be sure to service it properly.

- If there are some areas of the lawn where the ryegrass seems a little thin, feel free to scatter some seed to thicken up those spots a bit.

- Cool to cold weather and a dormant condition make watering warm-season grasses unnecessary this month. Continue to irrigate lawns overseeded with ryegrass as needed if the weather is mild and dry.

- Fertilize ryegrass around the middle of the month after warm-season grasses go dormant. This will make it darker green and encourage vigorous growth.

- Mow ryegrass to a height of 2 inches if it was used to overseed centipede or St. Augustine.

GROUNDCOVERS & ORNAMENTAL GRASSES

for Texas

These plants can be valuable problem-solvers for Texas gardeners. Both groundcovers and ornamental grasses offer a wide range of looks in terms of color, texture, and flowers or seedheads. They tolerate a wide range of growing conditions, including poor soil and shade, so they can be employed where lawn grass won't grow well. In general, they are lower maintenance than lawn grasses and flower beds as well. Just be sure to match your choice to the growing conditions of the site you have in mind.

GROUNDCOVERS

What is a groundcover?

The term groundcover generally refers to low-growing plants, other than turfgrasses, used to cover areas of the landscape—creepers, vines, prostrate shrubs, low-growing shrubs, and dwarf shrubs—all may qualify.

Perennial, evergreen plants having a running, sprawling, or spreading habit are generally used. Many have variegated foliage or produce colorful flowers while others are more subdued. Groundcovers establish an effect in the landscape that provides variation in height, texture, and color that enriches their surroundings. Yet they require less maintenance than flower beds.

Best uses

In addition to the beauty they provide, groundcovers have practical uses as well. Some groundcovers are effective in erosion control while others, because they don't have to be mowed, reduce maintenance in problem areas such as steep slopes or under low-branched trees and shrubs. Where the roots of large trees protrude, groundcovers hide the roots and prevent mowing problems. They provide barriers to foot traffic (most people won't walk through them) and can guide traffic movement through a site. Groundcovers are probably used most commonly in confined areas where lawn mowing is difficult or in shade where grass will not grow.

Groundcovers or groundcover-type plants allow home gardeners to have something green growing under their wonderful, cooling shade trees. Keep in mind that these plants do not tolerate the foot traffic that is tolerated by turfgrass. However, with a little ingenuity, wonderful pathways can be made through groundcovers. Also, not all groundcovers will grow in heavily shaded areas; some require full sun. Groundcovers are perfect for very steep areas or other "no mow" areas. Look for plants that can weep down the slopes, holding the soil together along with providing an attractive look.

Groundcovers reduce maintenance in hard-to-maintain areas in the landscape, such as areas between the drive and the house—eliminating the need to mow and edge turf.

Design-wise, groundcovers can be a unifying element, tying plant groupings together as well as providing interest and accents of texture, color, form, contrast, and pattern in the garden design. For example, groundcover areas serve as a welcome relief and contrast from often harsh, boring, surfaced areas. Pockets of groundcovers in gravel walk areas can add interest with color, form, and texture.

Choosing

When choosing groundcovers, it is helpful to first visit several nurseries to inspect groundcover varieties. When choosing one for your landscape, ask questions like: Will this grow in sun? Will it grow in full shade? Is it winter-hardy in my area? Does it prefer dry or moist soil? Does it prefer sandy or clay soil? Ideally, you should find a match for existing conditions in your yard, rather than set yourself up for modifying a site to suit the plant.

It is equally important to carefully consider the characteristics you would like the groundcover to have (height, texture, color, etc.). Take your time, look at everything, and make the decision that is right for you and your landscape.

Planting & Care

You should also look at the size of the area to be planted. Only the most reliable, fast-spreading, and reasonably priced groundcovers should be considered for large areas. Mondo grass (*Ophiopogon japonicus*) and monkey grass (*Liriope muscari*) are good choices

ORNAMENTAL GRASS IN A CONTAINER

Container-grown grasses are best planted in spring so you can enjoy them all season long. Those in the cooler, northern counties may need to provide extra protection if they want their potted specimens to survive the winter. There are two ways to do this: cover or envelop the entire thing with hay, or insulate the roots by temporarily sinking the pot in the ground.

The right pot has only two simple requirements. It needs a drainage hole so excess water can get out, and it must be big or deep enough to accommodate the extensive root system.

Matching pot size to the plant is mainly an aesthetic decision. You don't want the display to look top-heavy or for a plant to be dwarfed by its container. When growing colorful grasses, it's fun to use a pot that has a matching or complementary color. And while ornate or "busy" pots may be a tougher patch for certain flowering perennials and annuals, they work very well with the natural simplicity of many ornamental grasses.

In addition to beauty—and perhaps portability, if you choose to move your potted grass around over the course of the season—a good reason to grow one this way is control. A vigorous or large plant can been kept in bounds, managed more easily.

for shade to part sun. Asiatic jasmine (*Trachelospermum asiaticum*) is excellent for sun to part shade.

Whatever type of groundcover you choose, proper preparation of the planting area will help ensure good establishment and faster growth. Maintaining groundcovers involves some weeding, trimming back, watering, and fertilizing, but most groundcovers are not too demanding.

Prepare the soil by tilling the area. The planting area must be totally weed- and grass-free prior to planting. If it is poorly drained or lacks nutrition, add organic matter and perhaps some slow-release fertilizer. There are materials called erosion mats that can be placed on top of prepared beds to hold the soil in place until your groundcover becomes established. Groundcovers and fertilizers may all be found at your local nursery, along with the assistance of trained professionals.

Non-shrub groundcovers will usually achieve total coverage of an area two seasons after planting from 4-inch containers on 12-inch centers. The more aggressive plants may accomplish total coverage in one season if planted early in the spring and provided with proper care.

Fertilization helps to encourage the spreading of groundcovers. Start applying approximately six weeks after planting, or as new growth begins. Always read and follow label directions, and water thoroughly after each application. You may apply fertilizer to established plantings as new growth begins, and reapply as needed. Water your groundcover plantings deeply and thoroughly as needed.

Controlling weeds is also important to the successful establishment of groundcover plantings and is especially true for recently planted areas. Mulching with bark will help, but hand-to-hand combat/weeding may be needed to remove persistent weedy pests. Local nurseries will have pre-emergent herbicides, should you wish to prevent weed growth in this manner; always read and follow label directions.

ORNAMENTAL GRASSES

What is an ornamental grass?

Ornamental grasses are an often-overlooked group of herbaceous perennials that thrive in Texas gardens, and they will grow beautifully with minimal effort. The term ornamental grass is applied to grasses and grasslike plants that are used chiefly for their beauty. They are a large and complex group of plants with a wide range of growth habits and culture. This versatile group of plants is becoming increasingly popular all across the United States but still deserves to be more widely utilized in Texas landscapes.

Some of our worst garden weeds are grasses. Crabgrass and Johnson grass are persistent, difficult-to-control pests that many of us are all too familiar with. As a result, many gardeners are reluctant to deliberately plant grasses into flower beds or borders in their landscape.

Ornamental grasses, however, are truly attractive and not rampantly aggressive. Like their weedy cousins, they are tough and susceptible to virtually no insect or disease problems. Ornamental grasses are an excellent choice for gardeners trying to create a landscape that is more self-reliant, requiring less spraying, fertilization, and maintenance.

Best uses

Ornamental grasses may be added throughout your home landscape. In simple mass plantings or in combination with other ornamentals, annuals, perennials, and shrubs, ornamental grass is a valuable, functional plant. It adds interest and beauty to a landscape.

The strong vertical or fountaining form of many ornamental grasses combined with their feathery flower heads makes a unique contribution. This is true whether they are planted solo, in groups, masses, or displayed here and there in large containers.

Grass foliage moves in breezes and catches the light like few other plants. It adds fine texture and colors such as metallic blues, burgundy, white, creamy yellow, and every shade of green imaginable. Grasses also offer an impressive array of flower plumes and seedheads for added interest at various times.

Choosing

There are many different types. Maidengrass, *Miscanthus sinensis*, is an ornamental bunch grass often seen growing in striking clumps at the Texas State Fair. The white-plumed pampas grass, *Cortaderia selloana*, may very well be the oldest, ornamental, clumping grass used in Texas (there is also a pink-plumed variety). Fountain grass, *Pennisetum alopecuroides*, is a group of grasses best known as purple fountain grass. These, and other worthy selections, are profiled in the pages ahead. You would also do wise to check over the selections at your local garden centers and decide what look you like best.

Planting & Care

Most ornamental grasses grow best in full to part sun, but they are tolerant of a side range of growing conditions. If you are planting them into an existing bed, little improvement will be needed. Turn the soil and then incorporate a 2-inch layer of organic matter in the area to be planted. Water them thoroughly as needed until they are established, then just sit back and relax.

Some ornamental grasses are evergreen, but most go dormant for the winter. At some point before the end of February, you should cut the plants back to within a few inches of the ground. Other than that, occasional watering and fertilizing is all they need. They are as easy to care for as most perennial plants, and certainly less effort than lawn grasses and many groundcovers.

ACORUS
Acorus gramineus

Hardiness—Hardy throughout Texas

Color(s)—Evergreen foliage

Bloom Period—Not applicable

Mature Size (H x W)—6 to 12 in. x 6 to 8 in.

Water Needs—Water once or twice a week during hot, dry summer weather.

Planting/Care—Spring and early-summer planting is best. Needs a sufficiently moist site, but not particular as to soil type. Provide some shade during the day. Fertilize in spring. Cut back every few years in spring to encourage fresh growth and improve appearance.

Pests/Diseases—White scale and spider mites can occur. Control either with oil sprays.

Landscaping Tips & Ideas—Excellent in containers, as edging along pathways, in front of perennial beds, as individual clumps, or in drifts. Make a dynamic display by combining with red impatiens, cardinal flower, or red wax begonias. Also an attractive addition to a water garden. 'Variegatus' has creamy white stripes.

AJUGA
Ajuga reptans

Hardiness—Hardy throughout Texas

Color(s)—White, blue, purple, and rose

Bloom Period—Spring

Mature Size (H x W)—3 to 8 in. x 1 ½ to 2 ft.

Water Needs—Maintain a moist, but not wet, soil. Do not allow it to go totally dry.

Planting/Care—Plant in well-drained soil. Add organic matter first if sandy or clay. Fertilize approximately three times over the course of the growing season.

Pests/Diseases—Wilt disease can occur in summer heat—apply fungicide at first signs. Spider mites may visit during hot, dry weather. Consult your local garden center about controls.

Landscaping Tips & Ideas—Ideal for natural spreading along walks or in informal settings. It is excellent cascading over low walls or edgings. Its blue-purple flowers complement spring bulb blooms. Ajuga lends itself to detail designs in small pocket plantings and in rock gardens.

ASIAN JASMINE
Trachelospermum asiaticum

Hardiness—Hardy throughout Texas

Color(s)—Grown for foliage (turns bronze in cold weather)

Bloom Period—Not applicable

Mature Size (H x W)—12 to 16 in. x 10 ft.

Water Needs—Maintain moist soil.

Planting/Care—Plant in early spring through early fall. Tolerates sandy as well as heavy clay soils, but is best in well-prepared beds, and needs good drainage. Fertilize in the spring and again every time you feed your lawn (use the same fertilizer) and water well after each application. In spring, remove winter-damaged growth.

Pests/Diseases—None

Landscaping Tips & Ideas—Excellent in beds with standard landscape plants, or use to accent taller plants such as tall crapemyrtles. (Not good with dwarf plants, which it will overpower.) Use beneath trees, in curb strips, and areas where mowing is difficult or dangerous.

ASPIDISTRA
Aspidistra elatior

Hardiness—Hardy in Zones 7 to 9

Color(s)—Evergreen foliage

Bloom Period—Not applicable

Mature Size (H x W)—2 to 3 ft. x 2 to 3 ft.

Water Needs—In the first year, water weekly during hot, dry weather. Established plantings rarely need irrigation.

Planting/Care—Plant anytime, even in the heat of the summer if kept well-watered. Mix organic matter into the soil. Mulch to conserve soil moisture and suppress weeds. Fertilize in spring. Prune out yellow or brown leaves; if entire planting gets like this, cut it to the ground in spring—it may take two seasons, but it will recover.

Pests/Diseases—White scale may be controlled with an oil spray.

Landscaping Tips & Ideas—Grows well under trees, competes well with their roots. Forms slowly spreading clumps. 'Variegata' has creamy white streaks. 'Milky Way' has smaller, low-growing leaves spotted white.

CREEPING JUNIPER
Juniperus spp.

Hardiness—Hardy throughout Texas

Color(s)—Evergreen foliage

Bloom Period—Not applicable

Mature Size (H x W)—6 in. to 2 ft. x 4 to 8 ft.

Water Needs—Water to maintain moist growing conditions, but do not overwater.

Planting/Care—Plant in fall or early spring, in sun (perhaps with some shade from the hot western afternoon sun). Will grow in practically any Texas soil. Fertilize in spring as growth begins, reapply twice during the growing season, and once more in the fall.

Pests/Diseases—Spider mites may visit in late summer in hot, dry locations. Consult your local garden center for control advice.

Landscaping Tips & Ideas—Excellent for slopes and inclines, is ideal for rock gardens. May be grown in planters and containers to cascade over the sides; looks wonderful when allowed to weep over stone walls.

CREEPING PHLOX
Phlox subulata

Hardiness—Hardy throughout Texas

Color(s)—Pink, purple, and white

Bloom Period—Early spring

Mature Size (H x W)—3 to 6 in. x 24 in.

Water Needs—Provide supplemental water during drought.

Planting/Care—Plant in spring, in at least four to five hours of daily sun, in well-drained fertile soil. Space plants 12 to 18 inches apart to get the best fill. Use a slow-release fertilizer at planting time. Shear plants after blooming to keep mounding growth habit.

Pests/Diseases—In drought-stressed, full-sun locations, spider mites can become a problem.

Landscaping Tips & Ideas—Plant on slopes or near walls where the plants can cascade, or use in foreground of perennials. For more dramatic impact, plant groups of five or more. Good with spring bulbs—the bulb growth and flowers will emerge through the phlox foliage for an added surprise each spring.

FOUNTAIN GRASS
Pennisetum alopecuroides

Hardiness—In USDA Zones 7 to 9

Color(s)—Green foliage; yellow-green, cream, or rose flower spikes

Bloom Period—Summer and fall

Mature Size (H x W)—10 in. to 3 ft. x 1 to 2 ft.

Water Needs—Quite drought tolerant, but don't let it go bone-dry in mid-July or August. Water as necessary to prevent complete soil dryness.

Planting/Care—Plant in spring after frost, in improved soil. Maintain bark mulch around the base. Apply a lawn fertilizer two weeks after planting, weeks later, and perhaps again in early fall.

Pests/Diseases—None serious—though an occasional grasshopper may stop by for a bite.

Landscaping Tips & Ideas—A neat, upright, clumping plant with attractive flower spikes, gorgeous in any area where you rarely have a chance to water. 'Little Bunny' and 'Hameln' are good dwarf varieties that can also be raised in containers.

GIANT REED GRASS
Arundo donax

Hardiness—Hardy throughout Texas

Color(s)—Tan flowers, bluish foliage

Bloom Period—Late summer

Mature Size (H x W)—10 to 15 ft. x 8 ft.

Water Needs—During their first year, water weekly during hot, dry weather; established plants are drought tolerant. Mulch to conserve soil moisture and control weeds.

Planting/Care—Plant in spring after frost. Becomes a very large plant, so leave ample space around it. Fertilize each spring as new growth appears. At winter's end, cut down brown foliage to keep the plants looking tidy; fresh new canes will appear and grow rapidly. Tall ones tend to lean—either stake them or shorten them with loppers.

Pests/Diseases—None

Landscaping Tips & Ideas—Make an effective screen; plant 5 to 8 feet apart. Also makes a large, dramatic accent. An excellent choice for creating a lush, tropical look.

GRAY SANTOLINA
Santolina chamaecyparis

Hardiness—Hardy throughout Texas

Color(s)—Yellow

Bloom Period—Summer

Mature Size (H x W)—1 to 1½ ft. x 3 to 5 ft.

Water Needs—Water only to prevent soil dryness; do not overwater.

Planting/Care—Plant in early spring or early fall. Requires good soil drainage and sun in order to thrive. Fertilizing is usually not required. You may wish to perform minimal shearing of branches that tend to grow out of the compact form. If so, shear once or twice a year.

Pests/Diseases—None

Landscaping Tips & Ideas—Try it cascading down a rock or concrete wall, or even over a bed edge raised with railroad ties or landscape timbers. Especially attractive in rock gardens, mounding over rocks, or pea-gravel walks. Its unique gray foliage makes a strong contrast with green foliage, or with colorful annuals and perennials, accenting vivid colors.

HARDY FERNS
Many genera, species, and varieties

Hardiness—Hardy throughout Texas

Color(s)—Evergreen or deciduous green foliage

Bloom Period—Not applicable

Mature Size (H x W)—1 to 3 ft. x spreading

Water Needs—Maintain a moist soil during the growing season.

Planting/Care—Plant in early spring, in soil with lots of organic matter. Mulch to keep weeds at bay and conserve soil moisture. Fertilize three times during the growing season. Prune out dead parts every spring as new growth begins.

Pests/Diseases—Normally, none, but if any pests happen to bother a planting, get control advice at your local garden center.

Landscaping Tips & Ideas—Fine for formal or informal beds. Use as background plantings with colorful shade-lovers such as caladiums, spring bulbs, impatiens, or azaleas. Also good in large tubs or planters; holly fern, *Cyrtomium falcatum*, evergreen in most of Texas, is excellent for this.

HARDY ICE PLANT
Delosperma cooperi

Hardiness—Hardy in most areas of Texas (more difficult near the coast)

Color(s)—Purple

Bloom Period—Summer through fall

Mature Size (H x W)—2 to 12 in. x 8 to 24 in.

Water Needs—Water occasionally while plants are getting established; thereafter, they are very drought tolerant.

Planting/Care—Plant in early spring or summer. Does well in well-drained soil such as sandy loam. Few supplemental feedings are needed. Cool, damp conditions of early spring may delay emergence.

Pests/Diseases—Spider mites sometimes occur. Rotting is typical in poorly drained soils. Generally trouble-free.

Landscaping Tips & Ideas—Use as a border plant near sidewalks or in a rock garden. Spreads, but is noninvasive. Bulbs and other perennials readily grow through it. Pair with yellow- and purple-flowering perennials for a brilliant show. 'Starburst' has nice design features because of its lilac flowers highlighted with a distinct yellow and white center.

JAPANESE ARDISIA
Ardisia japonica

Hardiness—Hardy in USDA Zones 8 and 9

Color(s)—Pink flowers, red berries in winter

Bloom Period—Summer to fall

Mature Size (H x W)—10 in. x 18 in.

Water Needs—Water weekly during hot, dry weather.

Planting/Care—Plant in fall or spring. Well-drained soils improved with ground pine bark or compost are best. Mulch to conserve soil moisture, control weeds, and allow the rhizomes to spread. Fertilize in spring; apply more in summer if the area is not fully covered. In spring, cut back winter-damaged growth.

Pests/Diseases—Control fungal leaf spots with fungicide. Control scale insects with horticultural oil spray.

Landscaping Tips & Ideas—Beautiful planted under trees or in front of large shrubs. Not terribly aggressive, combines well with ferns, hostas, toad lily, and other shade-loving perennials. The bright-red berries add a cheerful note to the winter garden.

JAPANESE BLOOD GRASS
Imperata cylindrica

Hardiness—Hardy in USDA Zones 6 and 7

Color(s)—Red foliage

Bloom Period—Not applicable

Mature Size (H x W)—15 to 20 in. x 15 to 24 in.

Water Needs—Supplemental irrigation is a must in dry conditions or the plant will scorch.

Planting/Care—Plant in spring or early summer in well-drained soil. Afternoon or lightly dappled shade is best. Fertilize only if soil is infertile. Trim back the growth every spring to make way for new. In highly organic, moist soils, can slowly creep into unwanted areas.

Pests/Diseases—None serious

Landscaping Tips & Ideas—Site where it will be backlit with morning sunlight—beautiful. Good as a mass planting near borders or edges of water gardens. Combine it with bolder, broader-foliaged plants or variegated or yellow-leaved shrubs or perennials. 'Red Baron' has showy red foliage that intensifies in the fall.

LAMIUM
Lamium maculatum

Hardiness—Hardy throughout Texas (less reliable in coastal areas)

Color(s)—White, pink, and yellow

Bloom Period—Late spring to early summer

Mature Size (H x W)—8 to 12 in. x 12 to 24 in.

Water Needs—SWater during dry conditions.

Planting/Care—Plant in fertile, moist, well-drained soil in spring or fall. Best in dappled or afternoon shade. Mulch well. Fertilize only if the plants are not vigorous; they will respond well. Trim back taller selections to keep the planting looking tidy.

Pests/Diseases—Spider mites and heat scorch are occasional problems in sunnier locations. Fungal leaf spots and powdery mildew are not common but do occur.

Landscaping Tips & Ideas—Terrific as a border or foreground plant in perennial shade gardens. Or use it as companion with shade-tolerant flowers, especially white, purple, or yellow. Hostas are good companions but can overgrow lamium. Suitable as filler in containers and hanging baskets.

LIRIOPE
Liriope muscari

Hardiness—Hardy throughout Texas

Color(s)—Purple, lilac, and white

Bloom Period—Summer

Mature Size (H x W)—8 to 30 in. x spreading

Water Needs—Maintain a moist soil—not wet, not continuously dry.

Planting/Care—Plant in spring after the last frost, or in early fall. Fertilize regularly during the growing season. Prune out dead outer leaves in early spring before new growth emerges.

Pests/Diseases—None serious, though grasshoppers may visit—look for controls at your favorite nursery.

Landscaping Tips & Ideas—Use to line walkways, pathways, or driveways, though it does not respond well to heavy foot traffic. Use carefully placed stepping stones as walkways. Also makes a good groundcover, growing in shady locations under trees where others will not grow. Some are low-growing ('Lilac Beauty', 'Silver Midget'), some get quite tall ('Evergreen Giant', 'Majestic')—so choose the right variety to fit your plans.

MAIDEN GRASS
Miscanthus sinensis

Hardiness—Hardy throughout Texas

Color(s)—Tan plumes

Bloom Period—Summer to fall

Mature Size (H x W)—2 to 10 ft. x 8 ft.

Water Needs—Water as needed to prevent soil dryness.

Planting/Care—Plant in early spring after frost, in well-prepared soil. Fertilize regularly throughout the growing season. Every year in very early spring, chop back to about 6 inches to remove all the dead growth.

Pests/Diseases—None serious.

Landscaping Tips & Ideas—A wonderful, easy-care plant. Site in pockets among existing landscape plants, particularly Texas natives. Not ideal for entryways or walk-ways, which it may overpower. Plant in large containers, in rock gardens, in a courtyard, and in patio designs. Beautiful in the fall garden, when the foliage may turn golden bronze and the plumes change to a silvery color. 'Yaku Jima' is a good dwarf selection for smaller spaces.

MONDO GRASS
Ophiopogon japonicus

Hardiness—Hardy throughout Texas

Color(s)—Evergreen foliage

Bloom Period—Not applicable

Mature Size (H x W)—3 to 10 in. x spreading

Water Needs—Water as needed to prevent wilting.

Planting/Care—Plant in early spring or fall, in beds prepared with organic matter. Fertilize in early spring with a slow-release plant food. Shear or mow each spring after frost is past, to maintain a compact and uniform look.

Pests/Diseases—None serious

Landscaping Tips & Ideas—Works best in shade and can fill in a broad area. Planting in a checkerboard pattern will usually lead to a "grass" look in one or two seasons. Not a turfgrass, so it will not tolerate a lot of foot traffic. May be used to line borders or walkways. Can even be grown in a hanging basket. Do not expose to daylong full sun or reflected heat.

MONEYWORT
Lysimachia nummularia

Hardiness—Hardy in USDA Zones 6 and 7

Color(s)—Yellow

Bloom Period—Spring

Mature Size (H x W)—2 to 4 in. x 12 to 24 in.

Water Needs—Soil must be consistently moist. Provide supplemental water in droughts.

Planting/Care—Plant in well-drained, moist ground. Prefers afternoon shade. Mulch. If you fertilize, be careful not to burn the foliage with granular fertilizers; always water it in. The foliage will scorch in severe winters but rebound. Trim back if planting exceeds its boundaries.

Pests/Diseases—None

Landscaping Tips & Ideas—Because it is low-maintenance, it is perfect for sidewalk and landscape borders. Its low-growing habit allows flowering bulbs to emerge through it each spring. It will fill in around hosta, coral bells, cardinal flower, and other shade-loving perennials. It will cascade over walls and out of containers or hanging baskets.

PACHYSANDRA
Pachysandra terminalis

Hardiness—Hardy throughout Texas (less reliable in coastal areas)

Color(s)—White

Bloom Period—Early spring

Mature Size (H x W)—6 to 8 in. x 12 to 18 in.

Water Needs—Water weekly when rainfall is lacking. During severe droughts, soak the plants or they wilt and thin out.

Planting/Care—Plant in spring or early summer. Needs moist, fertile soil with a slightly acidic pH. Space plants about 15 in. apart.; it will spread without being invasive.

Pests/Diseases—Drought-stressed plants: spider mites and scale. In too much shade or damp: fungal leaf diseases and root rot.

Landscaping Tips & Ideas—A great filler in shade gardens. Plant in and around deciduous plants, and the evergreen foliage will command attention, especially in dormant winter landscapes. It mixes well with shade-loving perennials. Try in a shaded courtyard, around trees, or in a shady rock garden.

PAMPAS
Cortaderia selloana

Hardiness—Hardy throughout Texas

Color(s)—White and pink

Bloom Period—Late summer to fall

Mature Size (H x W)—6 to 10 ft. x 13 ft.

Water Needs—Water sufficiently to prevent soil dryness.

Planting/Care—Plant in early spring. Fertilizing makes it grow aggressively; if you do this, apply a lawn food on a regular basis throughout the growing season. In very late winter or early spring, particularly if there has been winter damage, you may cut it back to about a foot high. Use a hand-pruner, lopper, or even a chainsaw.

Pests/Diseases—None serious

Landscaping Tips & Ideas—Makes a great screen, blocking out views, noise, and wind. Makes an interesting specimen plant. Not good for high-traffic areas due to its razor-sharp blades; not good for the end of your driveway, as it may block your view. 'Pumila' and 'Monvin' are smaller-size selections.

PERIWINKLE
Vinca minor

☀ ☀ ☀ 💧

Hardiness—Hardy throughout Texas (not as reliable in coastal areas)

Color(s)—White, purple, and blue

Bloom Period—Spring

Mature Size (H x W)—4 to 18 in. x 4 to 18 in.

Water Needs—Maintain a moist soil, especially during the growing season. Though drought tolerant, it is quick to wilt when dry. In heavy clay soils, do not overwater.

Planting/Care—Plant in early spring or early fall. Will grow in sand or clay, as long as there is good drainage. Tolerates morning sun, but must have afternoon shade; all-day dappled shade is ideal. Give a slow-release plant fertilizer in early spring.

Pests/Diseases—Caterpillars can appear and strip a planting of its leaves. Consult a local garden center for control options.

Landscaping Tips & Ideas—Ideal for large areas, such as beneath shade trees. Attractive when planted with spring bulbs and dwarf azaleas. Nice in hanging baskets and other containers.

PROSTRATE ROSEMARY
Rosmarinus officinalis 'Prostratus'

☀ 🦋 🧴 🌱 🐝 💧

Hardiness—Hardy throughout Texas

Color(s)—Blue

Bloom Period—Spring and summer

Mature Size (H x W)—2 to 4 ft. x spreading

Water Needs—Water as needed only to prevent complete soil dryness.

Planting/Care—Plant in spring after frost or in early fall; a slightly alkaline soil is preferred. Excellent drainage is critical. No need to fertilize. You may prune to obtain a desired shape.

Pests/Diseases—None serious

Landscaping Tips & Ideas—An excellent groundcover in hot, full-sun, hard-to-water locations. Gorgeous when grown poolside and on decks, balconies, and patios, as well as hanging baskets. Serves well as an accent plant. A must for herb and kitchen gardens, and ideal for rock gardens.

SEDGE
Carex spp.

☀ 🍃

Hardiness—Hardy throughout Texas

Color(s)—Tan to brown spikes

Bloom Period—Spring

Mature Size (H x W)—1 to 2 ft. x 1 to 2 ft.

Water Needs—Water regularly to keep soil moist.

Planting/Care—Plant in rich, humusy soil, and mulch. Space plants 15 to 18 inches apart. Feed when new growth reaches 3 or 4 in., then wash off any trapped in or on the foliage. In early spring, remove any winter-burned foliage. Cut back heat-damaged foliage in the fall.

Pests/Diseases—Occasional leaf fungus or rust spot; if either becomes severe, treat with a foliar-disease product.

Landscaping Tips & Ideas—Its colorful and versatile foliage enhances any garden; it is one the few grassy plants that prospers in shade. Use the small mounding plants along shaded paths or as a border with sidewalks. Mass in groups of 3 to 5.

SILVER GRASS
Miscanthus sinensis 'Variegata'

Hardiness—Hardy throughout Texas

Color(s)—Pinkish-tan

Bloom Period—Summer to fall

Mature Size (H x W)—4 to 6 ft. x 4 to 6 ft.

Water Needs—Water weekly the first year in hot, dry weather; thereafter little if any water is necessary.

Planting/Care—Plant in spring or early summer. Grows best in well-drained to damp conditions.

Pests/Diseases—None serious

Landscaping Tips & Ideas—Excellent in the background of flowerbeds or perennial borders or a specimen plant to accent an area of your landscape.

STRAWBERRY GERANIUM
Saxifraga stolonifera

Hardiness—Hardy throughout Texas

Color(s)—White

Bloom Period—Spring

Mature Size (H x W)—4 in. x 4 in.

Water Needs—Needs moist soil. Water weekly during warm, dry weather.

Planting/Care—Plant in late fall to early spring. Needs plenty of shade. Do not bury the crown when planting, or it may rot. Cut back faded flower stalks.

Pests/Diseases—Rare. Treat mealybugs, if they appear, with the appropriate insecticide.

Landscaping Tips & Ideas—Best for small areas and detail work. Beautiful around shady pools, along walkways, or for edging beds. Use in front of caladiums, hostas, ferns, and acorus. Given its small size, be careful not to overwhelm it with surrounding plants. Also nice in containers and windowboxes, where the runners of young plants dangle attractively over the sides. Cultivars such as the variegated 'Tricolor' are best used in containers.

STONECROP
Sedum spp.

Hardiness—Hardy throughout Texas

Color(s)—Red, pink, and yellow

Bloom Period—Spring, summer, or fall

Mature Size (H x W)—2 to 24 in. x 12 to 24 in.

Water Needs—Most are drought tolerant.

Planting/Care—Generally takes care of itself. Plant in spring or summer; well-drained soil is key. Don't fertilize unless the plants show deficiency symptoms. Overfertilizing causes them to become leggy and fall over; overwatering causes rot.

Pests/Diseases—Seldom. Black aphids favor some sedums early in spring, but are easily controlled.

Landscaping Tips & Ideas—Textures and flower colors and bloom times vary. Overall, one of the best choices for hot-sun landscape beds. A great companion plant for bulbs planted in the fall or as an accent in rock gardens. Cascade the spreading, prostrate forms over rock walls. Combine with hardy ice plant, which produces blooms longer in summer.

SWITCH GRASS
Panicum virgatum

Hardiness—Hardy throughout Texas

Color(s)—Purplish-red to beige plumes

Bloom Period—Mid- to late summer

Mature Size (H x W)—4 to 8 ft. x 2 to 4 ft.

Water Needs—Once established, the plants are drought-tolerant.

Planting/Care—Accepts poor soils as long as they drain well. Full-sun locations are best. Space plants 2 to 3 ft. apart. Feed when new growth reaches 10 to 12 in. and again in midsummer, but don't overdo. Cut spent stalks back to the foliage.

Pests/Diseases—Minimal

Landscaping Tips & Ideas—Use as a background plant in a perennial garden, cluster it in groups of three, or plant in double rows for a screen later in the summer. It is a natural for wildflower or meadow gardens or as a specimen. Due to its deep, fibrous root system, it is perfect for erosion control in problematic sites.

WILD OATS
Chasmanthium latifolium

Hardiness—Hardy throughout Texas

Color(s)—Green to bronze spikes

Bloom Period—Late summer to fall

Mature Size (H x W)—2 to 4 ft. x 2 to 3 ft.

Water Needs—Water regularly.

Planting/Care—Plant in late fall or early spring. Moist, sandy-type soil is ideal. Fertilize only in poorer soils as new growth begins. Cut back early every spring to remove last season's growth. Will self-sow; prevent this with a thick mulch so seeds are hindered from penetrating the soil, and trim the seedheads before they turn brown.

Pests/Diseases—Highly unlikely

Landscaping Tips & Ideas—A good choice for the shade garden. Use these upright plants as a background or feature plants, grown in clusters of 3 or more, or plant them to give a hedge-like appearance. Also good as an edging plant near water or bog gardens.

WINTERCREEPER
Euonymus fortunei

Hardiness—Hardy throughout Texas

Color(s)—Grown for its evergreen foliage

Bloom Period—Not applicable

Mature Size (H x W)—6 in. to 2 ft. x 2 to 8 ft.

Water Needs—Do not keep wet, but do not allow the soil to become dry.

Planting/Care—Plant in early fall, or early spring, in improved soil that has good drainage. Fertilize at the start of the growing season, again in early summer, and once again in the fall. Form a denser planting by cutting back tip or terminal growth.

Pests/Diseases—Scale insects may visit; apply dormant oil during the winter season according to label directions.

Landscaping Tips & Ideas—Good for large areas that need a winter-hardy groundcover. The relatively large-leaved 'Coloratus' may be used successfully to secure soil on difficult-to-maintain slopes and inclines.

ZEBRA GRASS
Miscanthus sinensis 'Zebrinus'

Hardiness—Hardy throughout Texas

Color(s)—White

Bloom Period—Summer

Mature Size (H x W)—6 ft. x 4 ft.

Water Needs—Water weekly the first summer. After that, little irrigation is needed.

Planting/Care—Plant after the last spring frost. Growth is sturdier and less likely to lean over in full sun, but the plant will do well in some shade. Any good garden soil will do. You may fertilize in spring. Cut back the clump in early spring to make way for new growth. (New growth is bright green; the variegation will show up as the foliage matures.)

Pests/Diseases—No major problems

Landscaping Tips & Ideas—Use this big plant toward the back of beds. Its striking variegation makes it an outstanding accent plant, in the ground or in a large container. Try combining it with rudbeckia, lantana, or forsythia sage.

GROUNDCOVERS

Name	Height	Light	Comments
Asian Jasmine *Trachelospermum asiaticum*	12 to 16 inches	Full sun to part shade	Excellent fast-growing vine for covering large areas; shear back to 4 to 6 inches annually; edge sides of bed as needed; evergreen or semi-evergreen.
Aspidistra, Cast Iron Plant *Aspidistra elatior*	2 feet	Shade to full shade	Tall ground cover for deep shade; sword-shaped dark-green leaves; evergreen.
Autumn Fern *Dryopteris erythrosora*	12 to 18 inches	Shade to full shade	Attractive new growth has a coppery-red tint; tough, reliable evergreen fern.
Creeping Juniper *Juniperus horizontalis*	18 inches	Full sun	Needs excellent drainage and air circulation; good for hot, dry, sunny areas; watch for spider mites.
English Ivy *Hedera helix*	8-inch-deep mat	Shade to part sun	Useful for covering large areas and slopes; may be damaged by root rot; use vigorous, fast-growing cultivars as ground cover; evergreen.
Holly Fern *Cyrtomium falcatum*	12 to 20 inches	Shade to part sun	Bold, coarse texture almost shrublike; tolerates drier soil than most ferns; evergreen or semi-evergreen.
Japanese Ardisia *Ardisia japonica*	10 inches	Shade to part shade	Bright red berries in winter, but few in number; choose plain green cultivars for ground cover planting; evergreen.
Lily Turf *Liriope spicata*	8 to 10 inches	Shade to part shade	Grasslike foliage; reliable for large areas, better than L. muscari as a ground cover since it spreads faster; evergreen.
Mondoor Monkey Grass *Ophiopogon japonicus*	8 to 10 inches	Shade to part sun	Grassy appearance; thin dark-green leaves; one of best for planting large areas; evergreen.
Sedum *Sedum* spp.	4 to 18 inches tall, depending on variety	Full sun to part shade	Evergreen–deciduous. Fleshy relatively light green leaves; yellow, red, pink, pink-purple, and bronzy-pink blooms; hardy statewide; needs well-drained locations.
Strawberry Geranium *Saxifraga stolonifera*	4 inches	Shade to part shade	Delightful plant for small detail planting; round dark-green leaves with silver veins; stalks of small white flowers in spring; evergreen.

ORNAMENTAL GRASSES

Name	Size	Light	Comments
Acorus *Acorus gramineus*	6 to 12 inches	Part shade to shade	Small grasslike plant excellent in moist to wet area; effective as a groundcover or detail planting; evergreen.
Blue Fescue *Festuca ovina*	10 to 12 inches	Full sun	Bunching grass with blue-gray color; good in hot dry spots; requires well-drained locations; evergreen.
Fountain Grass *Pennisetum alopecuroides*	10 inches to 3 feet, depending on variety.	Full to part sun	Fine-textured grass, not too large; dwarf cultivars such as 'Hameln' are only 18 inches; attractive plumes in midsummer; hardy in zones 8 and 9 to statewide, depending on variety.
Giant Reed Grass *Arundo donax*	10 to 15 feet	Full to part sun	Large, coarse-textured upright grass suitable for accent or screen; cut back if damaged by winter freezes; produces 2-foot tan plumes in late summer.
Lindheimer's Muhly *Muhlenbergia lindheimeri*	3 to 4 feet	Full to part sun	Very attractive dome of fine-textured leaves are bluish-gray-green in color; flower plumes appear in fall.
Pampas Grass *Cortaderia selloana*	8 to 10 feet	Full to part sun	Large, mounding fine-textured grass suitable for accent or screen; cut back if damaged by winter freezes; produces attractive creamy white to silvery plumes in late summer; hardy in zones 7, 8, and 9.
Variegated Japanese Silver Grass *Miscanthus sinensis* 'Variegata'	5 to 6 feet	Full sun to part shade	Mounding fine-textured grass with creamy white variegated foliage; outstanding specimen or accent; pinkish-tan plumes in midsummer; there are many outstanding cultivars of this grass species; hardy statewide.
Zebra Grass *Miscanthus sinensis* 'Zebrinus'	5 to 6 feet	Full sun to part shade	Upright to mounding medium-texured grass; blades are striped horizontally with pale yellow bands; attractive plumes in late summer; cut back in February; hardy statewide.

JANUARY

- Virtually all hardy perennial groundcovers can be planted or transplanted this month.

- If needed, now is a good time to transplant or divide your ornamental grasses. Cut back the brown foliage, lift the clump, divide it into two or four pieces, and replant them into your landscape or share with friends.

- Some groundcovers may also be divided or transplanted now. This is a good way to create new areas of groundcover without having to buy any plants. Liriope, lily turf, strawberry geranium, ajuga, Japanese ardisia, aspidistra, and ferns can all be divided now, especially in Zones 8b and 9.

- Do not allow your groundcovers to stay covered by fallen leaves. Rake out, vacuum, or mow leaves and use them for mulch or put them in your compost pile.

- Consider planting monkey grass or creeping lily turf in areas under trees where you will need to rake out leaves.

• FEBRUARY

- Are there areas where it is difficult to mow or where grass will not grow due to shade? These are ideal locations for groundcovers. Remove all unwanted vegetation first, then till the soil to loosen it, and add organic matter.

- Combine a few perennials that you find relatively care-free with some ornamental grasses to create a bed that is interesting, attractive, and low-maintenance.

- Water newly planted groundcovers and ornamental grasses thoroughly when they go in the ground, and throughout the month as needed.

- It is a bit too soon to fertilize existing plantings. But any new groundcovers or ornamental grasses can be given a dose of slow-release fertilizer at planting time.

- Keep an eye out for scale insects and spray with a lightweight oil as needed.

- Rejuvenate established groundcover areas by shearing them back every two or three years at this time . . . before new growth begins next month.

MARCH

- After you cut back your ornamental grass, lay the clippings on the lawn and run your mower (with a bag attached) over them. The chopped blades make a great mulch, or they can be added to your compost pile.

- Finish up groundcover plantings so they will have some time to become established before the fierce heat of summer arrives.

- When deciding how far apart to space new groundcover plantings, look at your budget and buy what you can afford. Space them evenly and wait for them to fill in (or buy more later and install them evenly among the originals).

- Maintain a moist soil for your newly planted ornamental grasses and groundcovers.

- Fertilize established groundcovers and ornamental grasses this month.

- Cut back brown ornamental grass foliage as soon as possible. Don't wait till you see new growth.

APRIL

- Many ornamental grasses work well as container plants. Try a display on a patio, porch, or deck.

- Groundcovers need to be planted as soon as possible. Grasses are so tough they can be planted throughout the summer, but if you want to transplant or divide some that are already growing in your landscape, do it now.

- Tree roots will compete with groundcover plants for water. Make sure there is enough for both.

- Fertilize groundcovers this month if you did not do so in March. This helps those still growing to fill an area. Water immediately to wash the fertilizer off the foliage and down into the soil.

- Ornamental grasses will benefit from fertilizer scattered throughout a mixed bed. (But overly generous fertilizing will cause them to produce tall, weak stems that are prone to lying over, so be careful.)

- Help control weeds with a mulch and/or weed-control aids.

MAY

- Planting groundcovers this late means you'll have to put extra effort—especially watering—into getting them established in the heat. Ornamental grasses are tougher and can be planted throughout the summer.

- Established ornamental grasses often share beds with other plantings. If you water the area enough to keep the other plants happy, chances are the grasses will be happy too.

- It's late to be fertilizing groundcovers, particularly those that are still filling in, but you may. Remember to water-in. Ornamental grasses usually don't need much fertilizer.

- Snails and slugs may attack low-growing groundcovers such as ajuga, strawberry geranium, and hosta. Set out homemade traps or treat the area with snail-and-slug-control aids.

JUNE

- If you don't want to wait till this fall to plant a bare shady area, decide what kind of groundcover you would like and plant it now. Just make sure you keep it well-watered and mulched. Tough, easy groundcovers such as monkey grass, creeping lily turf, and Asian jasmine should do okay if planted this late.

- If it has not rained for more than ten days, water established groundcover plantings.

- Ornamental grasses rarely need to be watered once established; newly planted ones will appreciate irrigation if the weather is dry.

- Container-grown ornamental grasses may need daily water in hot weather.

- In hot, muggy weather, leaf-spot disease is worse. Trim off any badly damaged foliage and spray with an appropriate aid.

- Weeds invading groundcovers can be a problem. A mulch helps keep them at bay, but you may have to hand-pull and/or treat the area with a specialized weed-control aid.

JULY

- Take some time, while you escape the heat indoors, to make some notes on your groundcovers and ornamental grasses.

- Keep groundcover beds well-mulched, especially those that have not yet filled in. There is an old saying about the growth of groundcovers: "The first year they sleep, the second year, they creep, and the third year, they leap." So be patient.

- Many ornamental grasses begin to bloom in July. Notice

how attractive the plumes are waving about the foliage in different hues.

- Water is especially critical this time of year. It is much better to water deeply and occasionally than lightly every day.

- Groundcover areas fertilized this spring can be fertilized again this month.

- Watch for crown rot on ajuga—the disease can spread rapidly. At the first sign of trouble, drench the bed with a disease-control aid, and repeat every two to four weeks until the weather cools down in October.

AUGUST

- If you take a vacation this month, leave your plantings in good shape: water thoroughly, make sure everything is weeded and mulched, edge groundcover plantings that need it, and remove spent flowers.

- Local nurseries may be offering containerized ornamental grasses this month. You can plant now to fill gaps in borders, but be prepared to water as needed to maintain a moist soil.

- Watering continues to be critical, and it is much more efficient to use soaker hoses and sprinklers than to water by hand. Morning is the best time so that the plants will go into the hottest part of the day well supplied.

- If you did not fertilize filling-in groundcovers last month, you should do so this month. Follow label directions, and remember to water-in well.

- Spider mites thrive this month, especially in groundcovering junipers. Treat with appropriate aids.

SEPTEMBER

- Now that the summer season is coming to a close, take some time to walk around and evaluate plantings in your landscape. Make notes in your Texas gardening journal for future reference.

- Flower plumes or seedheads of ornamental grasses can be cut and used in arrangements. Spray with a little clear shellac to keep them from shattering.

- Strong, gusty winds can blow down stalks of tall ornamental grasses. Often they straighten themselves up, but sometimes they need a little help. Either loop around the plants with green twine to hold them up again, or cut them back if they insist on laying over.

- September can be hot and dry, so continue to water when necessary. When watering, do a thorough job.

- Pests have had all summer to build up population levels. Inspect plants frequently. To minimize the impact on beneficial insects, spray only infested plants, if at all.

OCTOBER

- With careful planning and selection of plants, there can always be something wonderful going on in your landscape.

Ornamental grasses are all decked out with attractive, often colorful feathery plumes.

- October begins fall-planting season, especially for groundcovers. Prepare an area well to help ensure good establishment and faster growth.

- Mulches in your beds have probably decayed and thinned over the summer, but this is not a bad thing. Organic mulches add organic matter to the soil as they decay. They do, however, lose their effectiveness in controlling weeds as they become too thin. So, if needed, add new mulch over the old to create a depth of about 3 inches.

- If cool-season weeds could threaten your groundcover beds, control them with pre-emergents, also called weed preventers. Apply before weed seeds germinate!

- October may be dry and mild to hot some years, so watch the weather and water if needed.

NOVEMBER

- Continue to plant hardy perennial groundcovers this month. They will not grow over the winter, but they will send out new roots and get existing roots established. As a result, they will outgrow spring-planted ones and not have to be tended so much next summer.

- You can also dig, divide, and transplant groundcovers this month.

- Water newly planted or transplanted plants as needed if the weather turns mild and dry.

- Fertilizer is not needed now.

- Check groundcovers for the presence of scale insects. They look like white or tan bumps on leaves and stems that detach easily when pushed with your thumbnail. Apply a control aid if desired.

DECEMBER

- Early December is an especially good time to plant hardy groundcovers in most of the state. The weather is generally still mild, and the soil is warm from summer. If planted now, plants will make strong root growth and be ready to grow vigorously next spring and summer.

- Nearly all groundcovers can be dug, divided, and transplanted during this month. If you live in Zones 6a to 7b, you may want to wait until February to do any transplanting.

- Water-in newly planted additions, to maintain a moist soil.

- To keep things looking neat, selectively prune brown, damaged, or diseased leaves.

- When cold weather browns the foliage of ornamental grasses, you can cut them back immediately or wait. Some gardeners admire the way they look when they are dormant—others just think they look like dead grass.

WILDFLOWERS &
NATIVES
for Texas

There's absolutely no place like Texas—and no natives like Texas native plants! Some of the best and easiest-to-grow ones have become standards in the nursery industry as well as our home landscapes.

Native annuals and perennials are commonly called "wildflowers," and Texas is blessed with them in variety and abundance. While there are certainly more than the ones profiled in the following pages, this is an excellent selection of specimens that will thrive in our unique Texas climate.

Depending on which Texas natives you select, they have the ability to provide plentiful color in our environment. They are a diverse group, adapted to most landscape situations. They can handle our weather and soils and are resistant to many pests and diseases that trouble some cultivated plants.

AMERICAN BEAUTYBERRY

CHOICES THAT STOP TRAFFIC

Cenzino, or Texas sage, *Leucophyllum frutescens*, has become widely available across the state. Native shrubs, including American beautyberry, *Callicarpa americana*, perhaps are less widely known but super in the landscape. I have been growing one planting of American beautyberry for nineteen years and it looks great. This is especially so during late summer and early fall when it is loaded with tight clusters of purple berries. Outstanding!

Autumn sage, *Salvia greggii*, is another native plant that does beautifully in well-drained Texas soils. It is not only easy to grow but also offers us bloom color in sunny spots. The large native myrtle, *Myrica cerifera*, has also become a welcome addition to our landscapes. I grow a planting of this native as a screen, and it works well. If you are looking for a native, tall-growing (up to 20 feet) shrub to utilize as a specimen, screen, or other application, wax myrtle will work well for you. It performs well in clay or sandy soils in urban or rural landscapes.

Everyone is, or should be, familiar with our native Texas bluebonnet, *Lupinus texensis*. Take a look at Black-eyed Susan, *Rudbeckia hirta* 'Angustifolia'. Both plants provide wonderful color throughout

the long growing season. Clasping-leaf coneflower, *Rudbeckia amplexicaulis*, coreopsis, *Coreopsis lanceolata*, Indian blanket, *Gaillardia pulchella*, and Texas bluebells, *Eustoma grandiflora*, are other wonderful native wildflowers available to us.

ADDING NATIVES TO YOUR GARDEN

One of my favorite wildflowers is Black-eyed Susan, mentioned above. This pretty flower is sometimes called Brown-eyed Susan. I enjoy mine in a west-facing bed along with salvias, daylilies, and ornamental grasses. It is one wildflower I recommend if its colors of golden yellow and dark brown fit in with your other landscape colors. You will not be disappointed.

While a stand-alone planting of Indian paintbrush, *Castilleja indivisa*, will make a great color planting, it is super when utilized in

EVENING PRIMROSE

combination with our state flower, the bluebonnet. Make sure the location is a sunny one that drains well, in order for the duo to thrive together.

THE NATIVE ADVANTAGE

I write garden columns for several publications in the state and do live call-in radio shows as well. My readers and listeners often ask for my recommendations for fast-growing shade trees. I don't recommend these types of trees. Most, such as Arizona ash, *Fraxinus velutina*, tend to be loaded with problems. If you want to plant an ash, then look for our native Texas ash, *Fraxinus texensis*, a high-quality tree. For outstanding fall color, plant a sweetgum, *Liquidambar styraciflua*. If you're a fan of elm trees, try the cedar elm, *Ulmus crassifolia*. Most people become instant fans of this gorgeous native Texas elm in their landscape. (Read more about these in the "Trees" chapter.) All of these native trees normally have fewer problems than some imports.

And there are many, many other good choices. Properly selected, placed, and maintained, our native plants are a tough and relatively low-maintenance plant group.

FOR FURTHER INFORMATION

A great resource for Texas wildflower information is the Ladybird Johnson Wildflower Center outside Austin. You can call or write them for information on wildflowers, or you can go see this interesting place for yourself. Also note that our Department of Transportation (TXDOT) has information on some of the best locations for viewing wildflowers.

Remember that there are nurseries that specialize in native Texas plants. For more research on Texas native plants, contact the Native Plant Society of Texas (see page 258 for contact information). This organization is an excellent source for more recommendations. Find a chapter near you, and have fun with our native Texas plants!

CONEFLOWER

AGARITO
Berberis trifoliolata

Hardiness—Hardy throughout Texas

Color(s)—Yellow flowers; red berries in fall

Bloom Period—Spring

Mature Size (H x W)—3 to 6 ft. x 3 to 6 ft.

Water Needs—Water only as necessary to prevent complete soil dryness. Do not overwater.

Planting/Care—Plant in early fall or early spring in a well-drained location. Will grow in sand or clay. Plant no deeper than it was growing in its original container; planting too deep is sure death. Mulch. Fertilize once a year. Prune if desired, but it's much better to allow it to grow to its natural shape.

Pests/Diseases—None

Landscaping Tips & Ideas—Use this prickly native shrub wherever a minimum of water is available. Though the berries are a bit difficult to harvest, they are edible and make good jelly. The leaves may turn reddish or yellow from fall through winter.

AMERICAN BEAUTYBERRY
Callicarpa americana

Hardiness—Hardy throughout Texas

Color(s)—Greenish-white flowers; beautiful purplish berries in late summer to early fall

Bloom Period—Summer

Mature Size (H x W)—4 to 6 ft. x 5 to 8 ft.

Water Needs—Water as necessary to prevent soil dryness, especially during the blooming and fruiting stage.

Planting/Care—Plant in early spring or fall in a spot where it will have plenty of room to grow. Adapts to almost any soil. Fertilize in spring and again in fall. To keep it more compact, cut it back very severely just before spring growth.

Pests/Diseases—None

Landscaping Tips & Ideas—Use as a specimen plant or among perennials or other landscaping. Not good as a foundation plant because it is deciduous. However, its show of unusual color makes it worth planting in a secondary location. 'Lactea' has abundant creamy white berries.

AMSONIA
Amsonia tabernaemontana

Hardiness—Hardy throughout Texas

Color(s)—Blue

Bloom Period—Late spring

Mature Size (H x W)—2 ft. x 2 ft.

Water Needs—Water once or twice a week in hot summer weather.

Planting/Care—Plant in fall or early spring. Adapts to many soils; likes good drainage. A well-prepared planting area with added organic matter encourages vigorous growth. Fertilize established clumps each spring, but don't be too generous—overfertilizing causes floppy growth. Cut clumps back to the ground when they go dormant in the fall.

Pests/Diseases—No major problems

Landscaping Tips & Ideas—The light blue is easily overpowered by vibrant colors, so best with softer pastels. Works well with the yellows of late narcissus or pinks of azaleas. Excellent in mixed borders and perennial gardens. Sometimes the foliage turns an attractive yellow in the fall as the plant goes dormant.

AUTUMN SAGE
Salvia greggii

Hardiness—Hardy throughout Texas

Color(s)—White, pink, purple, and red

Bloom Period—Spring to fall

Mature Size (H x W)—1 to 3 ft. x 3 ft.

Water Needs—Water as necessary to prevent soil dryness. Do not overwater or keep wet.

Planting/Care—Plant in early spring or early fall. It prefers daylong sun, but if it must be in some shade, protect it from the hot west afternoon sun. Plant in well-drained ground. You may fertilize once a year. Prune rather severely in early spring to encourage new growth and maximum bloom. To encourage even more blooms, pinch, trim, or cut back periodically throughout the growing season.

Pests/Diseases—None (except for those that arise from poorly drained soil)

Landscaping Tips & Ideas—Spectacular in mass plantings of single colors. Outstanding color when placed along walkways going into your home. Try in large containers.

BLUEBONNET
Lupinus texensis

Hardiness—Hardy throughout Texas

Color(s)—Blue, pink, white, and maroon

Bloom Period—Spring

Mature Size (H x W)—15 to 24 in. x 10 to 12 in.

Water Needs—Water as necessary to prevent total soil dryness, especially at initial plant establishment.

Planting/Care—Plant treated (scarified) seed in the fall; plant transplants in early spring. Plant in grass-free areas that drain well and have full sun. For best results, lightly till the area and rake with a strong rake beforehand. No need to prune or fertilize.

Pests/Diseases—Uncommon. In areas where plant concentrations are heavy, there may be pillbugs, doodlebugs, or sow bugs. If this happens, seek pest-control options at local nurseries.

Landscaping Tips & Ideas—Allow the plants to die and go to seed for next year's crop—these areas will appear unkempt and untidy, so consider this when planning your garden design.

EVENING PRIMROSE
Oenothera spp.

Hardiness—Hardy throughout Texas

Color(s)—White, pale pink to rose, and yellow

Bloom Period—Summer

Mature Size (H x W)—6 to 24 in. x 3 ft.

Water Needs—Water as necessary to prevent soil dryness.

Planting/Care—Direct-seed in late summer to early fall in well-prepared beds; transplants can be planted in the fall or early spring. A sunny, well-drained location is ideal. Mulch. Fertilize each spring as new growth begins. Deadhead regularly.

Pests/Diseases—Few. If chewing insects become a problem, find control possibilities at your local garden center.

Landscaping Tips & Ideas—Plant along the curb, as border accents, or in meadows and rock gardens. There are various species and colors, some of which are short-lived perennials or biennials, plus a few annuals. Allow seedheads to mature to allow for future natural seeding in the garden.

INDIAN BLANKET
Gaillardia pulchella

Hardiness—Hardy throughout Texas

Color(s)—Yellow-and-red

Bloom Period—Late spring and summer

Mature Size (H x W)—1 to 2 ft. x 10 to 12 in.

Water Needs—Water as needed to prevent soil dryness; do not overwater.

Planting/Care—Direct-seed in late summer to early fall; set out transplants in early spring after the last frost. Full sun in a prepared bed with well-drained soil is best. Fertilizing is optional. Remove spent blooms to encourage a longer blooming season.

Pests/Diseases—None

Landscaping Tips & Ideas—Grow in any location in which you have perennial grasses (such as Bermuda) under control. It is attractive in rock gardens, or along natural gravel walks and trails. Use in native theme gardens or wherever a low-maintenance color plant is desirable.

INDIAN PAINTBRUSH
Castilleja indivisa

Hardiness—Hardy throughout Texas

Color(s)—White to slightly green; bracts, often mistaken for flowers, are intense shades of red to red-orange

Bloom Period—Spring to early summer

Mature Size (H x W)—6 to 16 in. x 4 in.

Water Needs—Water as necessary to prevent soil dryness.

Planting/Care—Direct-seed in late summer to early fall in a prepared seedbed. Plant in and among existing vegetation with special seed-planting drills; if sown on top of the ground, cut existing vegetation extremely short. Transplants may be set out in early spring. In either case, keep soil moist until plants become established. Will grow in clay, loam, or sandy soil if it is well-drained. No need to fertilize.

Pests/Diseases—None

Landscaping Tips & Ideas—May be used in clumps by themselves in land-scape beds. Wonderful mixed with bluebonnets. Try in large containers.

LANCELEAF COREOPSIS
Coreopsis lanceolata

Hardiness—Hardy throughout Texas

Color(s)—Yellow

Bloom Period—Summer

Mature Size (H x W)—18 to 36 in. x 12 to 18 in.

Water Needs—Water as necessary to prevent soil dryness.

Planting/Care—Sow seeds in early spring or early fall; set out transplants in early spring after frost. Needs six hours of sun a day. Space transplants about a foot apart in a checkerboard pattern if you want a solid bed. Divide overgrown plantings in fall or early spring. Fertilize each spring as new growth begins. Deadhead to encourage additional blooming.

Pests/Diseases—None

Landscaping Tips & Ideas—Useful in a dry landscape color garden or slope, and along sunny garden paths. Works well in stand-alone beds or in combination with other wildflowers, as well as with cultivated/hybrid plants. Attractive in clumps or drifts in a rock garden. Easy in containers.

MEALY BLUE SAGE
Salvia farinacea

Hardiness—Hardy throughout Texas

Color(s)—Purple and blue

Bloom Period—Late spring and summer

Mature Size (H x W)—2 to 3 ft. x 1 to 1½ ft.

Water Needs—Water as necessary to prevent soil dryness.

Planting/Care—Plant in spring in well-drained, well-prepared beds. Plant in a checkerboard style, a foot part, for mass effect. Mulch to conserve soil moisture and suppress weeds. Fertilize once a year in spring as new growth begins. No pruning is required, but some tip pinching will encourage more blooms.

Pests/Diseases—None serious

Landscaping Tips & Ideas—Try in planters in full-sun spots on your deck or patio. Other uses include borders, cut-flower gardens, color mixes, and meadows. For a striking combination, plant with gray dusty miller.

MEXICAN HAT
Ratibida columnifera

Hardiness—Hardy throughout Texas

Color(s)—Red-and-yellow

Bloom Period—Summer

Mature Size (H x W)—2 to 2½ ft. x 1 ft.

Water Needs—Maintain a moist (not wet) soil to encourage season-long blooming.

Planting/Care—Plant seed in late summer to early fall into a cleared, lightly tilled bed. Transplants can be set out in early spring. Choose a location that receives at least six hours of daily sun. If the soil drains well, no additional preparations are necessary. Mulch. Fertilize each year as new growth begins. Deadhead spent blooms.

Pests/Diseases—Uncommon

Landscaping Tips & Ideas—Great planted in drives, lanes, and slopes as well as cut-flower gardens. Plant as a stand-alone group planting or in combination with other native flowers such as Black-eyed Susan, gaillardia, coreopsis, verbena, and lantana. As a cut flower, it lasts a week or more.

PLAINS COREOPSIS
Coreopsis tinctoria

Hardiness—Hardy throughout Texas

Color(s)—Yellow with maroon

Bloom Period—Summer to fall

Mature Size (H x W)—up to 4 ft. x 1½ ft.

Water Needs—Water as needed to prevent soil dryness.

Planting/Care—You may direct-seed in late summer to early fall in a spot cleared of grasses, or set out transplants in spring. Mulch to conserve soil moisture. Usually requires no fertilizing or pruning. Deadhead spent blooms to tidy the plants and extend the bloom period, or allow it to go to seed—it is a prolific reseeder.

Pests/Diseases—None

Landscaping Tips & Ideas—Blooms all summer! Combine with smaller Texas flowers for stunning color combinations, such as with Indian blanket and Texas bluebells. 'Nana' is a stunning dwarf variety.

PRAIRIE VERBENA
Verbena bipinnatifida

Hardiness—Hardy throughout Texas

Color(s)—Blue, purple/lavender, and pink

Bloom Period—Early spring to fall

Mature Size (H x W)—6 to 16 in. x 18 in.

Water Needs—Water as necessary to prevent soil dryness.

Planting/Care—Sow seeds in late summer to early fall, or set out transplants in early spring. Will grow in clay, limestone, or sand as long as the soil is well-drained. Mulch after planting to conserve soil moisture. Fertilize in the spring as new growth begins. Remove spent blooms to encourage extra blooms, new growth, and new runners throughout the season.

Pests/Diseases—None

Landscaping Tips & Ideas—Offers striking color and will accent virtually any location. Plant a pure stand in a landscape bed, or plant with other wildflowers. May also be enjoyed in specialized locations, such as a rock garden or trailing over the edge of a flower bed.

TEXAS ASH
Fraxinus texensis

Hardiness—Hardy throughout Texas

Color(s)—Non-showy flowers; good fall foliage color

Bloom Period—Spring

Mature Size (H x W)—35 to 50 ft. x 25 to 35 ft.

Water Needs—Water regularly during establishment, and thereafter as needed to prevent soil dryness.

Planting/Care—Plant anytime, but fall is best. Make sure it has ample space and that the soil is deep, for best growth. It will grow in rather harsh conditions—such as restricted-root-zone areas and even compacted soil—but locations with better soil yield better results. Fertilize once in spring and once in fall, watering thoroughly after each application. Prune to remove dead or damaged limbs and correct growth habit.

Pests/Diseases—Aphids can visit; if they do, consult your local nursery for control advice.

Landscaping Tips & Ideas—A fast-growing, tough, durable, and drought-resistant landscape tree, it works well in smaller urban lots. Plant where its great fall colors can be viewed from the home, and where its dense shade will be a benefit in summer.

TEXAS BLUEBELLS
Eustoma grandiflorum

Hardiness—Hardy throughout Texas

Color(s)—Blue, purple, and white

Bloom Period—Summer

Mature Size (H x W)—24 to 30 in. x 8 to 10 in.

Water Needs—Maintain a moist soil, and mulch.

Planting/Care—Plant in a sunny, well-drained location in spring after the last frost. Although they can tolerate some shade from our hot western afternoon sun, they need a minimum of six hours of daily sun. Fertilize in spring as new growth begins, in mid-season, and once again in the fall; remember to water thoroughly after each application. Remove spent blooms to encourage more blooms throughout the season.

Pests/Diseases—None

Landscaping Tips & Ideas—Grow in large tubs, as border plantings, or in combination with other cut flowers. Its hard-to-find hue is a wonderful addition to your garden.

TEXAS LANTANA
Lantana horrida

Hardiness—Hardy throughout Texas

Color(s)—Yellow, orange, red, and combinations

Bloom Period—Spring, summer, and fall

Mature Size (H x W)—3 to 5 ft. x 4 to 8 ft.

Water Needs—Drought tolerant; water as necessary to prevent soil dryness.

Planting/Care—Sow seeds no later than the end of August. Or plant root tip cuttings. Or plant transplants in spring after the last frost. Because of the plant's wide spread, space at least four feet apart—you'll still have a mass planting. Prune back severely each spring to encourage new growth to begin at the base and to control size, then fertilize.

Pests/Diseases—If spider mites appear, consult with your local garden center about controls.

Landscaping Tips & Ideas—A colorful, care-free background or border plant for other summer annuals and perennials. Due to its size, allow adequate space or it may overpower its location.

TEXAS MOUNTAIN LAUREL
Sophora secundiflora

Hardiness—Hardy in warmer zones

Color(s)—Blue-grape

Bloom Period—Spring

Mature Size (H x W)—6 to 12 ft. x 2½ to 6 ft.

Water Needs—Do not keep the soil wet or damp, but provide extra irrigation as needed.

Planting/Care—Plant in fall or late winter/early spring, in well-drained soil. Disturb the root system as little as possible at planting time. It may take a year or more to become established. While considered a slow-growing native plant, it will respond to supplemental water and fertilizer (feed two or three times in spring and again in fall). Please note—and warn children—that, despite their appealing grape-soda fragrance, the beans are toxic.

Pests/Diseases—None

Landscaping Tips & Ideas—Works well with other natives, including Texas sage and agarito. They all are best used as focal points in beds away from the foundation of the house.

TEXAS WISTERIA
Wisteria macrostachya

Hardiness—Hardy throughout Texas

Color(s)—Lilac and purple

Bloom Period—Spring

Mature Size (H x W)—Vine to 20 ft. in all directions

Water Needs—Water as necessary to prevent complete soil dryness.

Planting/Care—Spring planting is ideal; fall planting is acceptable. Till or otherwise loosen the soil beforehand, and mulch after planting. Fertilization is not usually required. The bloom clusters appear after the foliage has developed. Prune and train as necessary to reach your desired goal.

Pests/Diseases—None

Landscaping Tips & Ideas—The combination of pretty, small blooms and nice, dark-green, glossy foliage makes this quite a showy plant. Grow it in any location where you wish to have a good-looking, easy-to-grow vine with fragrant blossoms. It works especially well on arbors, although pergolas, gazebos, and arches are all likely candidates for Texas wisteria.

TEXAS SAGE
Leucophyllum frutescens

Hardiness—USDA Zones 7b to 9

Color(s)—White, pink, and purple

Bloom Period—Summer

Mature Size (H x W)—4 to 8 ft. x 4 to 6 ft.

Water Needs—Water as necessary to avoid complete soil dryness.

Planting/Care—Plant in the spring or fall. It does extremely well in full sun, all day long (it can take only a little shade). It will grow in any well-drained soil. Mulch. Fertilizing is optional. Minimal or no pruning is recommended.

Pests/Diseases—None

Landscaping Tips & Ideas—This shrub is super in a dry garden. Try it as an accent planting in either the green or gray foliage. It bursts into outstanding bloom after a drenching rain—people stop to look and point at the beauty.

TURK'S CAP
Malvaviscus arboreus var. drummondii

Hardiness—Hardy throughout Texas

Color(s)—Red blooms and berries

Bloom Period—Spring through fall

Mature Size (H x W)—2 to 6 ft. x 3 to 5 ft.

Water Needs—Maintain a moist soil, and keep well-mulched.

Planting/Care—Easy to start from transplants, layering, or seed. Plant in early spring after the soil is warm. It will grow in most any soil if it is moist and well-drained. Improve the soil by adding organic matter for better growth. Once new growth begins in the spring, remove winter-killed growth—no other pruning is required. (It may die to, or nearly to, the ground each winter and regrow the following season.) To maximize blooms, fertilize two or three times through the growing season.

Pests/Diseases—None

Landscaping Tips & Ideas—This shrub works well planted in and among other landscape plants.

WAX MYRTLE
Myrica cerifera

Hardiness—Hardy throughout Texas

Color(s)—Not grown for flowers

Bloom Period—Not applicable

Mature Size (H x W)—12 to 20 ft. or more x 8 to 16 ft.

Water Needs—Maintain a moist soil, and mulch.

Planting/Care—May be planted year-round, but early fall is best and second best is early spring. Plant in any type of Texas soil, including sand, loam, or clay; it will even grow in relatively poorly drained areas. It will grow in sun and likes dappled, not heavy, shade. Fertilize once new growth begins in the spring, possibly once in mid-season, and once in the fall. Prune if you would like to maintain or create a desired shape.

Pests/Diseases—None serious

Landscaping Tips & Ideas—Good with groundcovers or other underplantings. It you want an extremely tall, dense, low-maintenance screening plant, it will also fit the bill. It may also be grown as a specimen plant.

WOOLLY BUTTERFLY BUSH
Buddleia marubifolia

Hardiness—Hardy throughout Texas

Color(s)—Orange

Bloom Period—Spring and summer

Mature Size (H x W)—2 to 4 ft. x 4 ft.

Water Needs—Maintain a moist, but not wet, soil.

Planting/Care—Plant in early spring or early fall. It will grow in sand or nice loam, as well as limestone soils, as long as the soil is well-drained. Fertilize two times during the growing season. For compactness, prune severely one time as spring begins. Otherwise, it is best to let it grow naturally.

Pests/Diseases—None serious

Landscaping Tips & Ideas—Works well when part of a design around courtyards, patios, or pools, and it grows especially well in large tubs or containers. Excellent for large border plantings. Can be combined with other Texas natives such as Texas mountain laurel, yaupon holly, and wax myrtle.

GO NATURAL—GROW A NATIVE OR MEADOW GARDEN

Perennials, grasses, and native plants offer more than just aesthetic appeal.

Whenever you opt for plants rather than pavement, the net effect is to cool your immediate area and provide a visual treat for you and your neighborhood as well.

Lawns are good. Trees are better. But I find something especially appealing about perennials, grasses, and native plants. They contribute shade, trap pollutants, and afford infiltration of rainwater like other plants. They are virtually care-free, providing a visual treat without being finicky, and their ease of culture may give the beginning gardener the confidence to try something different.

A perennial garden with native plants is a richly diverse habitat, perfect for butterflies, bees, and other beneficial wildlife to make use of. Better yet, once planted and established, it returns year after year.

I also love the look and feel of a prairie or meadow planting—a large, sunny spot filled with those native and other plants that practically take care of themselves—oxeye daisies, purple coneflowers, Black-eyed Susans, asters, native grasses, perennial sunflowers, beebalm, butterfly milkweed, or just about anything else that grows well (but not too well!) in your community.

Remember, some plants are considered invasive in some areas but not others. Plan to do a little research before committing to plants that may be considered overly enthusiastic in your area. Your County Extension Service is a good place to start your inquiries.

Native plants often require less of a space commitment, and you don't have to wait as long for them to reach maturity compared to trees. Another benefit is that they require less water, fertilizer, and care than lawns. For the time-challenged, most perennial, prairie, and meadow plantings need little more than an annual cutting back in late fall. Depending on where you garden, the plants may only need an occasional watering once established. Meadow and prairie plantings can often go without supplemental watering after the first year.

Native plantings perform well without repeated applications of fertilizers and chemicals to control disease and insect problems. Properly planted, natives are content with an annual topdressing of compost. The bonus is two-fold: Not only are you limiting the release of chemicals into the soil, but in the process of composting, you are contributing far less to landfill volume.

IN PRAISE OF DIVERSITY

Plant a bed or area of your landscape with diverse native plants and help make the world a better place!

- By growing a wide variety of plants in your garden, and avoiding monocultures whenever possible, you will enjoy a healthier garden with less need to use chemical controls. This in turn will promote insect and animal biodiversity.

- On a broader scale, when we avoid monocultures and encourage biodiversity, we promote the sustainability of fresh air, clean water, and healthy soil. We perpetuate plant life that is responsible for all of our food and much of our medicine. In turn, we foster a healthy economy and preserve our quality of life and the natural beauty of our planet.

JANUARY

- There are nurseries that specialize in native Texas plants. Find out if there is one or more near you, and visit.

- If there are certain native wildflowers you'd like to try, consider raising some from seed. Good, rooted, interesting plants may also be found at botanic garden plant sales, if you are near one. Call or check their website to see when their spring sale will be, and plan to attend.

- Although native plants are considered tough, many respond well to well-prepared soil. Incorporate 6 inches of organic matter in a landscape bed, blended with the top 8 inches of native soil.

- Prune to remove dead or damaged limbs on native trees and shrubs.

- Set aside space in your Texas gardening journal to document your foray into growing native plants. Make note of information you gather about ones that interest you.

FEBRUARY

- This is a fine month to start planting in many parts of Texas. Buy healthy plants and find appropriate locations in your landscape for them. If you are not sure of their soil or sun needs—many natives are widely adaptable, but have preferences—ask at the nursery where you bought the plants.

- When new growth starts to appear, you may fertilize your native shrubs and native trees. Follow label directions with care, and remember to water it in afterwards so the nutrients reach the root systems.

- Watch for signs of new growth in your native wildflowers, and be careful not to damage them when digging or hoeing.

- Newly planted natives, like any other new garden plant, need regular water to get growing. Water deeply and thoroughly if rainfall is sparse.

- Mulch your plants to a depth of 3 to 4 inches. This keeps weeds at bay, conserves soil moisture, and helps maintain an even soil temperature.

MARCH

- You may continue planting natives as the weather and soil start to warm up. Plan on where they will be planted based on the growing conditions and how they grow. Avoid ones that have little chance of thriving in the conditions you are able to provide.

- This is the month to fertilize shrubs and trees in your landscape. Granular fertilizers provide an easy and economical way to feed them.

- Although you can prune many native shrubs in the springtime, think twice. Part of the appeal of many of them, such as agarito and Texas mountain laurel, is their naturally casual look. It may be better to let them grow naturally, only trimming occasionally to shape a bit and encourage thicker growth.

- Established native perennials, like their cultivated counterparts, can be fertilized this month. Follow label directions, and water

the bed by hand to wash away any fertilizer granules off the foliage and down into the soil.

APRIL

- In April, the nurseries are full of plants. Choose larger plants in larger containers for planting this late.

- Pay careful attention to spacing perennial natives when planting. You may be tempted to plant them too closely, and many of them have wide-ranging growth habits that look best when allowed to grow as they would naturally. Allow elbow room, and mulch the open areas in between to suppress weeds.

- Although most natives are naturally healthy and resistant to common diseases and pests, keep an eye on them. If for some reason their growing conditions are stressful (crowding, for instance, or not enough water), they can fall prey just like any other garden plant.

- The weather is still relatively mild, but warm and sunny days and dry weather can mean that you need to water. Always water deeply and thoroughly. Sprinklers and soaker hoses can be very effective.

MAY

- For optimum growth, if rainfall falls short, provide extra irrigation.

- Cut bouquets! Mix native wildflowers with your other garden flowers for lively, intriguing flower arrangements.

- Pests are generally not a common problem for many of our native plants, but if any pest is brave enough to visit, have the invader identified at local nurseries and then take a recommended course of action.

- Happily growing native trees sometimes begin to hang too low over a patio, driveway, or public sidewalks or streets. Rather than wait for someone to break off obstructing limbs, prune these branches properly.

- If there is a nice, drenching rain, keep an eye on your Texas sage plants. These are amazingly responsive to a good soaking and burst into glorious bloom soon after.

- If you deadhead (remove spent blossoms) or pinch tips of some Texas wildflowers, it encourages them to make more flowers.

JUNE

- As blazing heat settles in, admire the natural toughness of the native plants in your landscape. They are well-adapted to the Texas climate and often amazingly drought tolerant. That said, it is still important not to neglect them. Wilting and tired plants require supplemental water, and you should give special attention to those you planted this season. They'll be tougher in years to come, but make sure they receive the water they need to survive and establish themselves.

- You may direct-seed warm-season native annuals even now. Just make sure they get the water and mulch they need to get growing well.

- Early one morning, or on a cooler day, stroll around your plantings with your Texas gardening journal and make notes on how your native plant selections have performed so far. Have they met your expectations? Are some doing very well? If yes, make a note to add more in the fall or next spring.

JULY

- Irrigate your native plants as necessary to prevent soil dryness. Many are drought tolerant, but not drought-proof!

- Deadhead the spent blooms on your native wildflowers to encourage extra blooms and a longer bloom season.

- If you are growing any natives in containers or tubs, especially out in direct sun, do not neglect watering. Plants in containers always dry out faster than those growing in the ground.

- Established shrubs that are otherwise healthy may show dead or wilted branches. Fungal infections have generally killed a portion of the root system that provided water to that section of the shrub. A shrub can wilt completely and die. You can pull back the mulch slightly to increase air spaces and allow the soil to dry out. To avoid the problem in the future, make sure beds drain well when they are being prepared. And don't overwater.

AUGUST

- Continue to provide supplemental water during these very hot weeks. Remember that deep, occasional watering is much better for your plants than light, regular watering.

- If you notice that the mulch you laid down months ago is getting rather thin and dispersed, replenish it. There's no need to scrape away the remains of the old mulch, just add more on top of it and spread it around. A depth of 2 to 4 inches is appreciated by most native flowers as well as the shrubs.

- Unlike many cultivated shrubs, native ones usually don't require that much fertilizing. You may be feeding the cultivated ones now or next month, but there's probably no need to fertilize the robust natives.

- Cut back old or spent flower stems on your native wildflowers such as Black-eyed Susan and Indian blanket, unless, of course, you want them to go to seed.

SEPTEMBER

- Plant bluebonnet seed in early fall. Choose a spot that is grass-free, sunny, and has well-drained soil. Don't just throw the seeds on the ground. Instead, lightly till the area and rake it. Sow approximately twelve seeds per square foot. "Treated seeds," also known as scarified seeds, germinate quickly and thrive with minimal irrigation. (Untreated seeds may take three years!)

- You can also direct-seed Indian paintbrush and others this time of year. Again, soil preparation and aftercare is needed.

- It's still a little too warm to plant native shrubs, even though you may see them offered at local retailers. If you must, just provide generous water and a mulch.

- Assess any young native trees you planted last spring. It is unlikely that pest control will be necessary this late in the year, but young trees need as much foliage for as long as possible to get established. So act quickly if you happen to spot problems.

OCTOBER

- Once the weather cools off, this is your final chance for the year to fertilize native shrubs and trees again if you think it's needed. Probably the newcomers will benefit, but established ones are unlikely to warrant it.

- Plant container-grown native plants if you find them for sale locally. The soil is still warm from summer but conditions are less stressful, and winter rains will soon be along to help them get established. In the meantime, water and mulch them. These plants will have a head start over their spring-planted counterparts and be even less work to care for next summer.

- An ideal time to plant Mexican hat from seed is late summer to early fall. Plant seeds in well-prepared seedbeds according to label directions. Choose a spot that is sunny and has well-drained soil and remove any existing, competing vegetation for easier germination.

- Migrating monarch butterflies may visit your butterfly weed.

NOVEMBER

- Visit your potted natives. If they filled their pots over the course of the spring and summer, and appear to be in good health, you could plant them out in your landscape now. As always, water and care for transplants as they settle in to their new homes.

- This is a fine time, in most parts of the state, to move plants around the landscape. If a native proved too tall or too robust for its spot, or seemed to need more or less sun, give it a new home.

- Do not fertilize any native plants this month. Also, there should be little or no need to water any of them.

- Continue to keep things neat. Taller native flowers that are still in bloom may need propping up or staking. Remember how windy some of those cold fronts can be. When they finish blooming, cut them back hard.

DECEMBER

- As the gardening year winds down, think about what you learned about the native plants you chose to grow. Were their colors and growth habits as billed? Do you wish you had massed some for greater impact? Did some look particularly well in the company of other plants, or did you spot combinations you would like to try? All these thoughts and ideas should go into your Texas gardening journal for later reference, and to help you plan to make better use of these plants in next year's garden.

- If you have questions about native plants, resolve to do some research this winter. Get some books, talk to more experienced gardeners and nursery staff, and seek out specialists for their catalogs or websites. Once you discover the joys of growing Texas natives, there's no turning back.

- Cool weather and regular rainfall now should make fussing over your garden, and especially your tough native plants, unnecessary.

EDIBLES: VEGETABLES, HERBS, BERRIES, &FRUITS
for Texas

There is something satisfying about putting fresh homegrown produce on the table—food you actually grew yourself. Some believe gardening was originally done in response to needs for food, seasonings, and medicine.

People decide to grow their own food for various reasons. For many, it is a way to have the freshest possible produce. Other gardeners crave types or varieties that are not available at the local supermarket. And, although economy is not always the main reason, the harvest from the home garden can save money.

Thanks to the relatively mild winters of our region, gardeners can harvest something from their vegetable, herb, and fruit gardens almost 365 days of the year. All that is needed is some planning, along with awareness of the many different types of edibles we can grow throughout the year. Naturally, gardeners in south Texas have more harvesting days than their counterparts in north Texas.

PLANNING THE VEGETABLE GARDEN

Choose a sunny, well-drained spot. Many vegetables, particularly those grown for their fruit or seeds (tomato, corn, cucumber, beans) need at least eight hours of direct sun for best production. Vegetables grown for their roots (carrot, turnip, radish) can do well with about six hours of direct sun. Most leafy crops (mustard, lettuce, chard, cabbage) can be productive with as little as four hours of direct sun.

Convenience in relation to the house is nice, but a nearby source of water is a more important consideration since irrigation will be necessary. Vegetable gardens can be beautiful at certain times, but the appearance is variable with the seasons and harvesting.

Think carefully about the size of the garden. If you are new to vegetable gardening, start off small and gradually enlarge the garden as you become more familiar with the amount of time and effort involved. Consider the size of your family and the space you have available, too. A 10-by-10-foot garden is a good starter size. If you can rely on help from other family members, a larger garden may be fine.

Whether to plant in traditional raised rows or raised beds is another decision to be made. Large gardens are usually laid out in rows because rows are easier to plant, cultivate, and harvest using mechanical equipment. Small gardens are much easier to handle when laid out in beds, which are suited to hand-tilling. Rows use space less efficiently than beds. Rows require one aisle per row, while beds require aisles only every 3½ to 4 feet. Rows necessitate spading the entire garden; only the beds are spaded, which saves work. You never walk on the soil in beds, and organic matter and soil amendments go only in the beds—there is no waste! With beds, more of the area is available for production than in rows, and the part that is not used for growing does not need fertilizing, weeding, or watering. In high-rainfall or relatively poorly drained areas, raised beds are advised.

If you decide to make raised beds, begin the first bed 18 inches from an edge of the garden. Set a pair of stakes to indicate two corners. Measure the width of the bed, 36 to 48 inches depending on the size of your garden and your reach, then set another pair of stakes at the other corners. These stakes mark out the first bed. Next, measure 18 inches to identify an aisle, measure the width of the next bed, and set another pair of stakes. Continue to delineate the rest of the beds. Rototill or spade the beds only, not the aisles. Work from the aisles, never walking on the beds. After you have worked up the soil, open furrows across the beds to plant. Placing boards or edging materials around each bed can be done, but is not necessary.

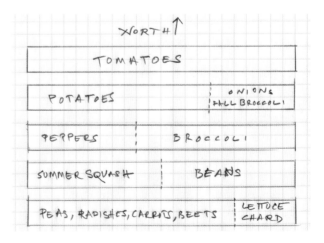

PEPPER

Next, decide on the vegetables you want to grow. Make a list of your favorites. The size of the garden is also a factor. Some large-growing vegetables such as pumpkins, brussels sprouts, corn, and okra occupy a lot of room and would not be as suitable for smaller gardens—unless you really want to grow them!

At this point, it helps to draw up a diagram of the garden you're planning—which vegetables will go where, and how many plants of each. Use graph paper and draw to scale if possible.

SELECTING VARIETIES

There are many varieties to choose from in every vegetable category. In the profiles ahead, a few are recommended, but don't feel bound by these suggestions. Ask around locally, at your favorite garden center as well as more experienced vegetable gardeners in your neighborhood. Your nearest Cooperative Extension Office can also recommend varieties that should do well for your particular area and microclimate.

New varieties are being developed each year, and catalogs are full of them. Many are worth trying, but before you devote your entire garden and a pile of money to try something new, try whatever piqued your curiosity on a smaller scale. Many home gardeners favor old standards, varieties that have been around a long time and have stood the test of time. Some of them have the same name but have been improved over the years. The 'Big Boy' tomatoes of the 1940s are not the same as those you are planting now. Improved disease resistance, plant habit, production, and weather resilience have been added.

Heirloom varieties, available from seed specialists, have become popular. These varieties have not been improved by plant breeders and many do not have the same disease resistance or the new varieties, but they retain the wonderful characteristics that made them popular in the past. These varieties may do very well in your garden if it is free of certain diseases.

All-America Selections (AAS) are awarded to varieties that have given outstanding performance in trial gardens throughout the country. These varieties are often worth trying in your garden.

Perhaps your best bet, space permitting, is to try a range of different types of vegetable varieties. Observe, taste, and enjoy them. Keep good notes, and make changes the following seasons as needed. Over time, you will develop favorites that do very well for you.

SOIL PREPARATION

Soil preparation is critical to successful vegetable gardening. Remove any existing unwanted vegetation. This includes weeds that have grown up between crops, or lawn grass in a new bed. Weed-control aids may be used prior to planting and are particularly useful in controlling perennial weeds such as Bermudagrass, Johnsongrass, nutgrass, and oxalis. Please note that these aids are not labeled for use in beds once the vegetables are growing there. Read and follow label directions carefully.

Use a shovel, garden fork, or tiller to turn the soil 8 to 10 inches deep. Rear-tined tillers work well for this, especially in heavy clay soils.

Spread a layer of organic matter such as compost, rotted leaves, manure, or Canadian

sphagnum peat moss 4 to 6 inches thick over the bed. If a soil test indicates the need for lime or sulfur, sprinkle the appropriate amount over the organic matter.

Thoroughly incorporate the amendments into the upper 8 to 10 inches of soil. Rake the bed smooth and you are ready to shape raised rows. About 3 feet across and 8 to 12 inches high works well for many crops.

PLANTING

Most vegetable gardeners purchase their transplants from local nurseries, but you can start your own. Transplants should be planted into the garden according to their recommended spacing.

Whether you raise them yourself or buy them, vegetable transplants should be compact, 4 to 6 inches tall, and have at least six fully developed leaves. They should have good green color and no pests on them. They should be well-rooted, which you can easily check by tapping them slightly out of their pot.

In direct-seeding vegetables, seeds are planted two to three times thicker than necessary for the number of plants needed. This ensures a good stand of seedlings. Once the seedlings are up and growing, the extras are pinched off with the thumb and forefinger, leaving behind seedlings at the proper spacing. This process is called thinning.

The timing of planting depends on the kinds of plants and the average date of the last frost (also called the frost-free date) in your part of the state. You can find out this date from your local garden center, on radio, television, or internet weather reports, or by asking at your nearest Cooperative Extension Office.

Some vegetables are completely hardy and can stand winter weather, or a freeze or two. Some can be planted as soon as the ground can be worked in spring. Seeds of some can be sown in the fall and will germinate in spring much earlier than the soil can be worked, giving them a nice head start. For some, you have to wait till there is no threat of frost. This basic information is provided in all the vegetable-plant profiles in the pages ahead, but should be reconfirmed locally if you are uncertain about when to plant.

WEEDS

The best defenses against weeds are to take care of any problems promptly, and to keep your beds mulched 3 to 4 inches deep.

Some effective mulches include bark, leaves, dry grass clippings, and pine straw. Commercial weed-blocking rolled aids/products and other materials are also useful in weed prevention.

Promptly pull or hoe any weeds that appear. Get them when they are small. Note: weeds pull best when the soil is moist.

PEST CONTROL

Pest control is necessary when it comes to vegetable gardening, especially during the late spring, summer, and fall growing seasons, in order to have successful crops. There are lots of bugs that would just love to eat your vegetables before you get a chance to harvest them. Major categories of insect pests include beetles, caterpillars, aphids, stinkbugs, and whiteflies. Although spider mites are not technically insects, they are generally grouped with them for pest-control purposes. Control is the same as for aphids, with the addition of mite-control aids.

Control nematodes by rotating crops, adding organic matter whenever beds are being prepared, and planting resistant cultivars. Snails and slugs chew holes in the leaves of many vegetables, especially leafy crops during the cool season. Baits, traps, and barriers are all worth trying.

The judicious use of pest-control aids, along with cultural techniques (such as planting early in the season and hand-picking) will generally prevent major outbreaks. Before using any pest-control aid, make sure you have properly identified the pest (insect, mite, fungus, bacteria). Help is also available from your local nursery and the Texas Cooperative Extension.

DISEASES

Fungi cause the majority of vegetable diseases, although viruses and bacteria can also be problems. Some tactics include crop rotation, spacing plants

ROSEMARY

properly for air circulation, and keeping beds mulched (which keeps soil-borne diseases from splashing up onto vegetables). Plant the best locally recommended, disease-resistant varieties. Fertilize and water as needed.

Controlling diseases is different from controlling insects. To be effective, disease-control aids must be used earlier, before much damage occurs, and then regularly after this first use. Always use aids (such as fungicides) according to label directions.

GROWING HERBS IN THE HOME GARDEN

Gardeners grow herbs for many uses, including cooking, creating fragrances, making medicines, and having attractive plants in the ornamental garden. The herbs profiled in the pages ahead are primarily culinary favorites that do well in our state.

Herbs add flavor and interest to our foods. Without them, foods would often be bland and not very interesting. Most cooks know how to use more common herbs, such as thyme, sage, and basil, which are readily available. Many other herbs which are used in other parts of the world have been introduced by people immigrating from those regions, and because of the recent interest in ethnic cooking, are becoming available here. Gourmet cooking shows on television have taught us about new herbs too. Most gourmet cooks never use dried herbs, but insist on freshly grown and harvested materials. Growing our own herbs enables those of us cooking at home to have the freshest ingredients for our dishes.

Fortunately, growing herbs is quite easy, often easier than growing many familiar vegetables. In fact, many thrive on minimal care and infertile soils. With too much tender, loving care, they become rank and less flavorful. For most gardeners, growing a few of each kind of herb is sufficient. Some herbs such as thyme and oregano are perennials, but most are generally grown as annuals (that is, you can plant them new each season). Some do well as potted plants (for example, chives and rosemary) and can be brought indoors for the winter in colder areas and used fresh throughout the cold part of the year.

PLANNING THE HERB GARDEN

Unlike vegetables, which require relatively large plantings in order to produce sufficient harvest, a single herb plant will often provide enough for a gardener's needs. Herbs may be grown in the vegetable garden, in their own area, or even among landscape plantings. Since few plants are needed, herbs are also excellent when grown in containers.

Most herbs require direct sun at least four to six hours a day (six to eight hours is best) and excellent drainage. Use raised beds or containers if drainage in your yard is questionable. Locate your herb-growing area as close to your kitchen as possible so the herbs are convenient to use while you are cooking.

PLANTING

Prepare the planting area as for vegetables. Containers are also excellent for growing herbs— use a lightweight potting mix that drains well. Because relatively few plants are needed, most gardeners buy herb transplants. You can, of course, plant seeds or raise your own transplants.

Cool-season annuals should be seeded or transplanted between September and February and include borage, celery, chervil, cilantro/coriander, dill, fennel, and parsley.

Warm-season annuals should be seeded or transplanted March through August, and include sweet basil, perilla, sesame, and summer savory. Actual planting dates will vary depending upon which zone you live in. Your local retailer can provide specific planting dates in your area.

Note that some common herbs, such as mint and oregano, are aggressive and will take over a garden if not restrained. Sometimes walling them off from the rest of the garden with timbers is a satisfactory solution. You could use 2-by-2-foot squares outlined by 2-by-4s on edge. Let your imagination go to work incorporating concrete blocks, bricks, clay tiles, or other masonry.

Planting seed is the way to start some herbs, but others are better obtained as started plants. Many garden centers carry herbs, but mail-order seed houses and specialty herb growers are excellent sources for the best varieties and selections of plants. You may also get herbs from fellow herb gardeners who are propagating their own plants. If you do, be sure to find out the correct name and properly label each plant, so you know how to grow it and use it.

HARVESTING HERBS

Harvest herbs frequently and regularly, being careful not to deplete all the plant's foliage. Cut off leaves or sprigs with a pair of scissors as needed. Generally, take no more than a third of the total foliage at any one time. Herbs are more attractive and compact in size when harvested regularly. Remember to rinse off the leaves before using.

As a rule of thumb, most herbs are ready to be harvested just as the flowers begin to open. The plants have the most flavor then. Early in the morning after the dew has dried is the best time to pick them, while they are still cool, fresh, and crisp. By later in the day, they may be warm and wilted.

DRYING HERBS

When the season begins to wind down, herbs can be harvested for drying. Note that dried herbs are usually three or four times as strong as fresh herbs. Leaves are best stored whole and crushed just before use. Seeds, too, should be stored whole and ground as needed. Cut annual herbs at the ground; cut perennial herbs about a third of the way down. To prepare the herbs for drying, rinse them in cold water and drain them on paper towels.

A favorite and effective way to dry herbs is to tie them loosely in bunches and hang them upside down in brown paper bags in a warm, dry place. In some homes, the attic may be a good place. This method works particularly well for seeds. After they dry, shake them in the bags until the seeds fall into the bags. Then store your harvest in airtight glass jars.

For other kinds of herbs, particularly fleshy-leaved ones such as sage, you can pick them, spread the herbs on a screen, and turn them every few days until they are dry. Then strip the leaves from the stems, and store the leaves in airtight glass jars. They do not require a dark place for storage, but should be placed out of direct sunlight.

You may prefer to dry herbs in the microwave, but you need to be aware of the downside of this method. Most shrink, and some—basil, chives, parsley, and French tarragon—lose up to 90 percent of their flavor. Others—rosemary, sage, and thyme—are unaffected by microwave drying. Prepare the herbs by rinsing, draining, and placing them between two layers of paper towel. Dry only four or five sprigs at a time. Turn on the microwave for about three minutes, then examine the herbs. If they are still too moist, turn them over and turn on the microwave for another two minutes or so. Repeat the process until the herbs are dry. There are charts for microwaving herbs, but they are only guides and provide a good starting place. After a few tries, you can determine the proper time for various herbs.

It is possible to freeze some herbs, such as dill, parsley, chives, and basil, for later use without blanching. Freeze the herbs quickly on a cookie sheet, and store them in airtight freezer bags. The herbs will be good six to eight months, or until the new crop comes in the next season.

PEST AND DISEASE CONTROL

Although they have a reputation for being resistant to attack from insects, herbs are occasionally damaged by various bugs. Diseases can be a problem during the hot summer months, especially during rainy periods when root and stem rots can occur.

Generally, though, pests do not bother most herbs. If you are growing only a few plants, bugs or diseases have a hard time finding them.

Usually, the best way to control pests is to pick off the infested sprig and discard it before the pests move on to the entire plant. Some, such as mites, aphids, or thrips can be controlled with insecticidal soap if they become troublesome. Always remember to carefully wash off insecticidal soap after you harvest the herbs.

Other than insecticidal soap, few pest-control aids have been labeled for use on herbs. Visit your local retailer for information and advice if warranted. And remember, herbs are generally chopped and added to dishes before cooking. So no one will know if there were a few holes in the leaves!

Prevent disease by planting your herbs in well-drained beds and spacing them properly for good air circulation. A mulch of light pebbles or marble chips seems to help herbs such as rosemary, thyme, sage, oregano, and catnip avoid stem and crown rots.

PLANNING THE FRUIT GARDEN

Growing small fruit, and especially tree fruit, adds another dimension to backyard gardening. Because all fruit plants are perennials and stay in the garden from a few years to a person's lifetime, planning a fruit garden is more important than planning a vegetable garden, which can be moved every year if necessary.

It is critical that you choose a variety that will prosper in your Texas zone and particular growing conditions—be sure to seek advice from a local nursery and/or your nearest Cooperative Extension Office when making these important choices.

After a fruit planting is started, it may take from one season to as many as several years to see results. Fruit gardeners must have patience to wait for a harvest, and while the plants are developing, they need a lot of care. Before starting, consider your time available to do all the pruning, fertilizing, watering, and controlling pests required to develop productive plants and to have clean, wholesome fruit.

Fruit plantings can fit into most backyard gardens, but each plant must have enough room to develop to its full size. (Strawberries are an exception—they are small enough to be easily squeezed into any available spot in the garden.) Air circulation is important for fruit crops, so the plants dry off quickly. This reduces disease problems and minimizes the chances of a late-season frost, which could kill blossoms.

Choose a location for the fruit garden in full sun and where it will not be disturbed by other activities in the yard. Also keep in mind that certain cultural necessities, such as spraying and pruning, may interfere with other things going on in the yard. For instance, fruit trees probably should not be planted where materials sprayed on them will cover other garden plants or drift into the house.

Cold air sinks into the lowest areas, so it will be colder in a low valley than on a hilltop or hillside. Planting in a valley is not recommended for this reason. Low winter temperatures are not as damaging as a freeze when the plants are in full bloom—you want to avoid that.

Planting

Spring planting is the preferred time for most fruit plants, just as the soil has dried enough to be worked. Fruit plants are usually sold bare root, and you'll have to protect the roots from drying out by keeping them moist, refrigerating them, or heeling them in. Soak mail-order plants in a bucket of water for several hours before planting to rehydrate them.

Since fruit plants will occupy the same spot for several years at least, take your time preparing the soil. If possible, start a year ahead of the planting date by killing off all vegetation. Regularly till the soil that year, adding organic matter such as compost, or seed and plow down a green-manure crop such as annual rye. Taking this extra time will significantly reduce a weed problem.

To plant, till the soil the same as you would for a vegetable garden (see previous instructions). Space plants according to their mature sizes, and apply remedial fertilizers as indicated by soil tests. Set the plants at the depth they grew in the nursery. Backfill with good topsoil, firming as you go. Soak thoroughly to settle the soil and force out any air pockets.

Pest and Disease Control

The days when wholesome fruit could be produced without insect-control measures have long passed away. Persistent treatment with the correct materials at the optimum times is essential.

New fruit cultivars are being developed to eliminate certain disease problems. When you select varieties for planting in your garden, choose those with enhanced disease resistance. Growing the plants in a well-drained soil and keeping foliage dry are most helpful. Fungicide applications are necessary to control some diseases.

Be sure to read and follow directions on aid labels. Keep all aids in their original containers with labels attached, and store them in a locked area out of reach of children.

Pruning

Pruning and renewal of fruit plantings are essential for maximum production. Annually prune fruit trees to develop fruitful wood. Prune brambles to remove old canes, and prune grapes to develop vigorous new growth each year. Shear back strawberries to remove old foliage and open up crowns to develop new foliage.

For specific pruning methods and requirements for your chosen fruits, consult the nursery where you purchased your plants and/or your local Cooperative Extension office.

APPLE
Malus cultivars

When to Plant—Plant in early spring as soon as the soil can be worked.

Where to Plant—A location in full sun with well-drained soil is ideal (cannot tolerate wet feet). Leave sufficient room to walk around the mature tree to spray it.

How to Plant—Buy as bare-root, two-year-old whips. Soak the roots to rehydrate them prior to planting in a large hole. Water well and provide stakes for support.

Water Needs—Water in dry weather, especially if it is growing in light soil that dries out quickly—apply an inch a week.

Care/Maintenance—Fertilize only if it does not seem to be growing vigorously. Get advice on proper pruning practices and their timing.

Pests/Diseases—Your local cooperative extension office can advise you on the products, amounts, and timing necessary for spraying so your apples remain healthy and bear tasty fruit.

Harvesting Tips—Taste, not color, is the only reliable test for ripeness.

Recommended Varieties—'Gala', 'Braeburn', 'Fuji'

BASIL
Ocimum basilicum

When to Plant—Plant seeds in spring after the last frost. Basil transplants should be planted into the garden no later than early September for a late crop.

Where to Plant—In full sun, in well-drained soil. If in a pot, use a light soil mix.

How to Plant—Plant 20 to 24 in. apart. Space rows 18 in. apart.

Water Needs—Water regularly; do not let soil dry out.

Care/Maintenance—Pinch out branch tips and regularly remove the flower spikes to encourage plants to continue producing leaves. Ultimately, the plants will begin to lose steam. If/when frosts occur, they will kill the plants.

Pests/Diseases—Aphids and mites can appear; pinch off affected shoots or treat with insecticidal soap.

Days to Maturity—60 to 70 or more, depending on the variety

Recommended Varieties—'Fino Verde', 'Sweet Genovese', 'Purple Leaf'

BEAN
Phaseolus vulgaris

When to Plant—Sow two weeks before last frost.

Where to Plant—Full sun is best (8 to 10 hours a day), in well-drained soil.

How to Plant—Sow bush beans 2 to 3 in. apart, pole beans 6 in. apart, then cover with an inch of soil. Add beneficial bacteria (legume inoculants), available from garden stores or catalogs, if needed.

Water Needs—Provide about an inch per week.

Care/Maintenance—Help pole beans get onto their supports (they twine counterclockwise). Weed and water regularly.

Pests/Diseases—Don't work in the beans when they are wet. Diseases include bean mosaic virus and bacterial blight. Leaf bean beetles may eat holes in the leaves.

Days to Maturity—50 to 70 days, depending on the type and variety

Recommended Varieties—Bush beans: 'Blue Lake', 'Bush Kentucky Wonder', 'Tendercrop'
Pole beans: 'Kentucky Blue', 'Kentucky Wonder', 'Romano'

BEETS
Beta vulgaris

When to Plant—Sow one month before the frost-free date.

Where to Plant—In well-prepared loamy, neutral-to-alkaline soil. Full sun and good drainage are key.

How to Plant—Fertilize the area, then work the soil into a fine seedbed. Sow seeds 1 in. apart and allow them 12 to 15 in. between rows. Cover with a half-inch of fine soil.

Water Needs—If no rain falls for 7 to 10 days, apply an inch of water.

Care/Maintenance—These plants require little care. Hoe or pull any weeds.

Pests/Diseases—Keep some out by covering the plants with netting or row covers. Leafminers, soil-borne maggots, and leaf-spot diseases are all potential problems that may be controlled with garden chemicals specifically labeled for this use.

Days to Maturity—48 to 60 days, depending on the variety

Recommended Varieties—'Big Red', 'Red Ace', 'Detroit Dark Red'

BLACKBERRY
Rubus cultivars

When to Plant—Plant in the spring as soon as the ground is dry enough to work.

Where to Plant—Provide full sun, well-drained soil, and ample space. Don't plant where solaneous crops (potatoes, tomatoes, etc.) grew in the last five years, due to soil-borne fungal disease.

How to Plant—Get one-year-old plants or tissue-cultured plugs. Plant in good soil in rows (2 ft. apart in rows 8 to 10 ft. apart) or in hills (4 to 5 ft. apart). They sucker extensively and will develop into a hedgerow on their own.

Water Needs—Water well at planting, and mulch to conserve soil moisture.

Care/Maintenance—Get training and pruning information from your local cooperative extension office; care varies with type.

Pests/Diseases—Buy only certified, disease-resistant varieties. Should any trouble occur, get advice from your local cooperative extension office.

Harvesting Tips—Color is the primary indicator: reds are red, blacks are black.

Recommended Varieties—'Chester Thornless', 'Darrow', 'Shawnee'

BLUEBERRY
Vaccinium corymbosum

When to Plant—Plant in spring as soon as the soil is workable.

Where to Plant—Blueberries will not prosper in alkaline (higher pH) soils. Plant in full sun in well-drained soil. For large plantings, a slope will improve air drainage.

How to Plant—Get vigorous two-year-old plants, and don't plant too deeply. The holes should be shallower than the depth of the roots and at least twice as wide. Water-in well, and mulch.

Water Needs—Water about once a week in dry weather.

Care/Maintenance—Be diligent with watering, mulching, and fertilizing throughout the growing season. Keep weeds away. For specifics on pruning, consult your local cooperative extension office.

Pests/Diseases—Blueberries are susceptible to a few diseases and some insects; consult your local cooperative extension office if you need advice. Protect ripening berries from hungry birds with netting.

Harvesting Tips—Pick when they are not only blue, but sweet to the taste.

Recommended Varieties—'Bluecrop', 'Bluetta', 'Patriot'

BROCCOLI
Brassica oleracea var. botrytis

When to Plant—Sow seed as early as the soil can be worked. Or sow seeds inside eight weeks of the last frost date.

Where to Plant—Full sun (8 to 10 hours per day) is best.

How to Plant—Plant in prepared, fertilized soil. Space transplants about 18 in. apart, with 36 in. between rows. In a bed, space plants 16 to 18 in. apart.

Water Needs—Water as necessary to keep the plants vigorous and growing—about an inch a week.

Care/Maintenance—When the plants are about half-grown, side-dress them with a complete fertilizer.

Pests/Diseases—Plant disease-resistant varieties, and practice crop rotation. Root maggots, cabbage worms, or sparrows can bother your crop—if they do, get advice and appropriate garden chemicals from your local garden center.

Days to Maturity—65 to 85 days, depending on the variety

Recommended Varieties—'Green Comet', 'Green Goliath', Purple Sprouting'

CABBAGE
Brassica oleracea var. capitata

When to Plant—Sow indoors eight weeks before last frost date, and set out about six weeks later.

Where to Plant—Full sun (a minimum of 8 hours per day) or partial shade (filtered sun all day or shade part of the day), in well-prepared soil with good drainage.

How to Plant—Space 12 to 18 in. apart, with 24 in. between rows.

Water Needs—They need about an inch of water a week; dry weather ruins them (causes cracking).

Care/Maintenance—Side-dress with a complete fertilizer when they are about half-grown.

Pests/Diseases—Cabbage are susceptible to various problems, which you can prevent or should treat quickly (get advice from your local garden center): root maggots, cabbage worms, and various leaf-spot diseases.

Days to Maturity—55 to 82 days, depending on the variety

Recommended Varieties—'Ruby Bull', 'Savoy Ace', 'Charmont'

CAULIFLOWER
Brassica oleracea var. botrytis

When to Plant—Grow as a spring or fall crop to avoid heat, cold, and dry weather. Start plants eight weeks before your last frost, and set out six weeks later.

Where to Plant—Deeply prepared, well-drained soil, in full sun.

How to Plant—Space transplants about 18 in. apart, 36 in. between rows. Water them in with a high-soluble phosphorus fertilizer.

Water Needs—Provide an inch per week as needed.

Care/Maintenance—When they are about half-grown, provide a dose of high-nitrogen fertilizer. Heads exposed to light will be off-color; blanch them by securing leaves around the heads when they are about 3 inches in diameter.

Pests/Diseases—Root maggots, cabbage worms, leaf-spot diseases, black rot and blackleg diseases, clubroot. Grow resistant varieties and/or take quick action (get control advice from a local garden center).

Days to Maturity—52 to 71 days, depending on the variety

Recommended Varieties—'Green Goddess Hybrid', 'Snowball Y Improved', 'Snow King'

CHIVES
Allium schoenoprasum

When to Plant—Sow seeds in early spring. Plant transplants when they become available in spring.

Where to Plant—For best growth, give them full sun (though they will tolerate some shade). Choose an undisturbed garden spot or grow in pots, so their spreading nature will not be a problem.

How to Plant—Sow seeds about 12 in. apart; cover lightly. Put started plants into well-prepared soil, about 12 in. apart.

Water Needs—Provide water if there is no rainfall.

Care/Maintenance—Little, if any, care is needed. Keep the plants clipped, both for harvesting and to prevent flowering, which affects the flavor and leads to often unwelcome self-sowing.

Pests/Diseases—Thrips and root maggots are possible. Seek local advice for combating, and remember to wash off insecticides after harvesting.

Days to Maturity—80 to 100 days

Recommended Varieties—The larger, related garlic chives, Allium tuberosum, yields a tasty harvest.

CILANTRO
Coriandrum sativum

When to Plant—Direct-sow in early spring; make successive sowings every three weeks till hot summer weather sets in.

Where to Plant—Plant seeds in a full-sun location that has well-drained, well-tilled soil.

How to Plant—Sow 1 in. apart in rows 2 ft. apart. In raised beds, sow the rows across the beds. Do not thin the seedlings.

Water Needs—Water weekly during dry weather to provide about 1 inch.

Care/Maintenance—Hoe or pull weeds that appear. The plants bolt very quickly in hot weather, so harvest early and often. To harvest the seeds, called coriander, allow seedheads to develop and turn tan (but gather before they begin to shatter).

Pests/Diseases—If mites become troublesome, spray them with insecticidal soap—and remember to wash it off after harvesting foliage.

Days to Maturity—45 to 60 days

Recommended Varieties—Slow-bolting varieties such as 'Santos' and 'Long-Standing'

CORN, SWEET
Zea mays var. rugosa

When to Plant—About the frost-free date in your area. Plant additional seedlings until early July if you wish a staggered harvest.

Where to Plant—Needs full sun (8 to 10 hours), good drainage, and lots of room.

How to Plant—Sow seeds in rich soil, 9 in. apart in rows, 24 to 36 in. between rows. Plant two or more rows of each variety side-by-side to assure pollination.

Water Needs—Water regularly, especially when the plants are tasseling, making silk, and during kernel development. Soaker hoses are a good idea.

Care/Maintenance—Control weeds. Side-dress with a complete fertilizer (such as 10-10-10) when they are about 1½ ft. tall.

Pests/Diseases—Plant disease-resistant varieties. Corn earworm, corn borers, and smut disease are potential problems; combat with advice from a local garden center.

Days to Maturity—64 to 92 days, depending on the variety

Recommended Varieties—'Butter and Sugar', 'Silver Queen', 'Earlivee'

COLLARDS
Brassica oleracea var. acephala

When to Plant—Early spring. Start seeds eight weeks before last frost, and set out about six weeks later. Or sow directly in the garden as soon as soil can be worked.

Where to Plant—Well-drained soil is a must, as is 8 to 10 hours of daily sun.

How to Plant—Plant in well-prepared soil. Space transplants 12 to 18 in. apart, with 30 in. between rows. Fertilize well.

Water Needs—Provide an inch a week if rainfall is lacking.

Care/Maintenance—When seedlings reach 12 inches high, thin to about 6 inches apart. If you prefer blanched leaves, tie up outer leaves.

Pests/Diseases—Possibly root maggots, cabbage worms, black rot and blackleg diseases, clubroot. Choose resistant varieties, and treat any problems quickly.

Days to Maturity—60 to 80 days, depending on the variety

Recommended Varieties—'Blue Max', 'HiCrop', 'Vates'

CUCUMBER
Cucumis sativus

When to Plant—Sow directly in the garden or set out transplants only after all danger of frost is past.

Where to Plant—Full sun and good drainage are key.

How to Plant—Bush types can go in the garden or in containers; train vining types on supports such as trellises. Plant in prepared soil, 36 in. apart, two or three per hill, and thin later.

Water Needs—Provide an inch of water a week.

Care/Maintenance—Protect plants from pests with row covers and/or insecticides. Keep area well-weeded.

Pests/Diseases—Cucumber beetles are a serious threat. A virus disease, cucumber mosaic, may cause misshapen, lumpy cucumbers. Grow resistant varieties.

Days to Maturity—48 to 63 days, depending on the variety

Recommended Varieties—'Salad Bush', 'Burpless', 'Marketmore 86'

DILL
Anethum graveolens

When to Plant—Sow seeds or set out started plants in early spring. Make successive sowings throughout the summer.

Where to Plant—Anywhere there is well-prepared, moist soil. Either full sun or partial shade is fine.

How to Plant—Sow seeds an inch apart in rows 1 ft. apart. Thin the seedlings when they are about 6 in. tall (and use the discarded seedlings in salad). Transplants may be set 1 ft. apart in beds or 2 ft. apart in rows.

Water Needs—Water when the weather is dry, providing an inch a week.

Care/Maintenance—Dill requires little care once it has started to grow.

Pests/Diseases—None serious. You may instead observe the larvae of the black swallowtail butterfly on your plants. These large black-and-yellow-striped caterpillars do not eat much and make spectacular butterflies.

Days to Maturity—50 to 70 days, depending on the variety

Recommended Varieties—'Fernleaf', 'Bouquet', 'Dukat'

EGGPLANT
Solanum melongena var. esculentum

When to Plant—Sow seeds indoors only two weeks before your last frost; set out in the garden six to eight weeks later, when soil and air have warmed up.

Where to Plant—Full sun (8 to 10 hours a day), in warm, well-drained, organically rich soil.

How to Plant—Sow seeds in hills 12 in. apart, with 24 to 30 in. between rows or even closer for small-fruited varieties; thin later to one per hill. Plant leggy transplants on their sides, and cover the long stems lightly with soil. The tips will turn upward and the buried stems will sprout new roots.

Water Needs—They need an inch of water a week.

Care/Maintenance—Side-dress them with high-nitrogen fertilizer at one foot tall. Mulch to conserve soil warmth.

Pests/Diseases—Plant resistant varieties. Typical problems are flea beetles and verticillium wilt.

Days to Maturity—52 to 80 days, depending on the variety

Recommended Varieties—'Black Beauty', 'Dusky', 'Ichiban'

FENNEL
Foeniculum vulgare

When to Plant—Start seed indoors six weeks before last frost or in late summer for a fall crop. Direct-sow after the last heavy freeze.

Where to Plant—Site in a sunny location with well-prepared soil. Since they get quite large and reseed vigorously, locate where they will have room and not shade out lower-growing plants.

How to Plant—Start in peat pots or direct-sow. When seedlings are about 4 in. tall, thin them to about 8 in. apart. Because they have taproots, they don't tolerate transplanting well.

Water Needs—Provide an inch of water a week during dry times.

Care/Maintenance—Cover the bulbs with soil to blanch them when they are 2 or 3 in. in diameter. Harvest before they bolt.

Pests/Diseases—Black-and-yellow striped caterpillars are not pests, but rather the larvae of the beautiful swallowtail butterfly. If they appear, they won't eat much anyway.

Days to Maturity—70 to 100 days

Recommended Varieties—*Foeniculum vulgare var. dulce*

HOT PEPPER
Capsicum spp.

When to Plant—Start seeds indoors two weeks before last frost, and plant in the garden after danger of frost is past.

Where to Plant—Full sun (8 to 10 hours per day) and prepared, well-drained soil is best.

How to Plant—In rows, space them 10 in. apart, 18 to 24 in. between rows. In beds, space plants 15 in. apart in all directions.

Water Needs—Provide an inch of water a week if rainfall is sparse.

Care/Maintenance—When the plants set fruit, side-dress with a complete fertilizer.

Pests/Diseases—Avoid common problems by planting disease-resistant varieties. If diseases or pests (such as aphids or caterpillars) appear, get advice locally on effective controls.

Days to Maturity—68 to 75 days or more, depending on the variety

Recommended Varieties—'Big Chili', 'Jalapeno', 'Habanero'

GRAPE
Vitis cultivars

When to Plant—Plant in spring as soon as soil is dry enough to work. The plants need time to become established before the stresses of summer afflict them.

Where to Plant—Well-drained but poor-quality soils tend to yield the best crops. Site where plants will warm up quickly, such as on the south side of a building.

How to Plant—Install supports beforehand; get advice from your local cooperative extension office. Set the plants at the same depth they were growing at the nursery (for grafted ones, make sure the graft is above ground).

Water Needs—Water if rainfall is sparse.

Care/Maintenance—Eradicate any weeds. No need to fertilize. For training and pruning advice, consult your local cooperative extension office.

Pests/Diseases—To maintain clean grapes, follow a regular spraying schedule—fungicides and insecticides, as needed.

Harvesting Tips—Pick when seeds and cluster stems turn brown and the berries attain maximum sweetness.

Recommended Varieties—'Red Flame Seedless', 'Thompson Seedless', 'Vanessa'

KALE
Brassica oleracea var. acephala

When to Plant—For a fall crop, sow in midsummer and set out six weeks later. For a spring crop, start seeds indoors eight weeks before the last frost, and set out six weeks later.

Where to Plant—Well-drained soil in full sun is best.

How to Plant—Space 12 in. apart, with 18 to 24 in. between rows. In a bed, space 12 in. apart. Fertilize.

Water Needs—Provide about an inch of water a week.

Care/Maintenance—Crop rotation and choosing disease-resistant varieties will make raising a good crop easier. Prevent cabbage worms with Bt. In the fall, wait till a frost before harvesting—the flavor is much better.

Pests/Diseases—Root maggots and cabbage worms are potential pests. Leaf-spot, yellows, black rot and blackleg diseases can occur. Take preventative steps or seek local advice about controls.

Days to Maturity—60 to 70 days, depending on variety

Recommended Varieties—'Dwarf Blue Curled Scotch', 'Dwarf Curled Vates', 'Winterbor'

LEEKS
Allium ampeloprasum

When to Plant—Start seeds in mid-February and transplant outdoors three weeks before last frost or as early as the soil is workable. Or direct-sow as early as the soil is workable.

Where to Plant—Plant in deeply prepared, well-drained soil. Full sun is preferred.

How to Plant—Prepare the bed deeply, adding organic matter and fertilizer. Space 4 in. apart, with 12 to 18 in. between rows. Set the plants somewhat deeper than they were growing.

Water Needs—Provide an inch of water a week.

Care/Maintenance—Leeks are heavy feeders, so side-dress them with nitrogen six weeks after transplanting. Blanch the lower parts of the stems by gradually hilling up soil around their bases.

Pests/Diseases—Use appropriate pest-control aids to combat onion maggots or thrips.

Days to Maturity—100 days or so

Recommended Varieties—'Alaska', 'Broad London', 'Titan' (for summer use)

LEMON
Citrus spp.

When to Plant—Plant in spring when soil and air are warm.

Where to Plant—Plant in your warmest spot, on the south or southeast side of your house, in full sun and well-drained soil. Allow the tree sufficient room, or grow a dwarf variety in a large container.

How to Plant—Rehydrate the roots prior to planting, then dig a hole twice as wide as the spread of the roots and the same depth that the tree grew at the nursery.

Water Needs—Provide an inch a week in dry weather, especially if grown in light soil.

Care/Maintenance—Weed the area. Get pruning and fertilizing advice from your local cooperative extension office. Rot occurs if you overwater your lemon tree or mulch its root zone too heavily. Protection from cold is critical—grow in the warmest parts of the state.

Pests/Diseases—Get pest-control advice from your local cooperative extension office.

Harvesting Tips—Pick when the fruit develops its full color; ripening time varies depending on the variety.

Recommended Varieties—'Eureka', 'Lisbon', 'Meyer'

LETTUCE
Latuca sativa

When to Plant—Plant early, in spring, before hot weather. Head lettuce should be started indoors earlier than leaf lettuce; consult seed packets for full information. Stagger plants to assure a continuous harvest.

Where to Plant—Excellent drainage is important. Site in full sun or part shade.

How to Plant—Space larger types (head lettuce) a foot apart, leaf types 4 to 6 in. apart.

Water Needs—Provide about an inch a week.

Care/Maintenance—Control weeds carefully with a hoe or hand-pulling, taking care not to uproot shallow-rooted plants. When plants are large enough, harvest every other one, leaving more room for the remaining ones.

Pests/Diseases—Earwigs and aphids are possible problems. Proper spacing and insecticidal soap can help.

Days to Maturity—50 to 90 days, depending on type and variety

Recommended Varieties—'Buttercrunch', 'Iceberg', 'Black-Seeded Simpson'

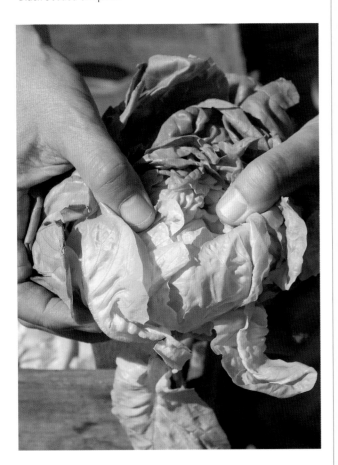

MINT
Mentha spp.

When to Plant—Set out started plants in spring.

Where to Plant—Most will thrive in full sun or partial shade. Plant where you can control them.

How to Plant—Plant in well-drained soil, separating various types by barriers. Contain plants with concrete blocks, timbers, and 12-inch clay drain tiles. Space plants 2 ft. apart in beds.

Water Needs—Keep the soil constantly moist, but not wet.

Care/Maintenance—Control weeds and watch that growth doesn't get out of hand. Mulch with straw in areas with cold winters and the plants will be protected; remove before they begin to grow the following spring.

Pests/Diseases—Verticillum wilt is the most damaging disease; do not plant mint where solanaceous crops (tomatoes, potatoes, etc.) have been grown because they all carry the disease and infect the soil.

Days to Maturity—Approximately 60 days

Recommended Varieties—Peppermint, Mentha x piperita; apple mint, Mentha saureolens; pineapple mint, *Mentha saureolens* var. *variegata*

MUSKMELON
Cucumis melo var. reticulatus

When to Plant—Sow seeds in peat pots a week before last frost. Direct-sow or set out transplants once the soil is warmed up and all danger of frost is past.

Where to Plant—Put in a full-sun location with well-drained soil and plenty of space.

How to Plant—Sow seeds an inch deep in hills 36 in. apart. In a bed, space them 36 in. apart down the middle.

Water Needs—They need at least an inch of water a week.

Care/Maintenance—Cover plants with row covers, for warmth as well as pest protection, until they begin to vine and to allow bees to pollinate the flowers. A trellis or fence must be strong enough; tie a little net or cloth parachute under each melon.

Pests/Diseases—Row covers and insecticides will fight off cucumber beetles.

Days to Maturity—75 to 96 days, depending on type and variety

Recommended Varieties—'Jenny Lind', 'Ambrosia', 'Saticoy'

MUSTARD
Brassica juncea

When to Plant—Direct-sow about 21 days before last frost.

Where to Plant—Site in well-drained soil, in full or part-day sun.

How to Plant—In rows, sow seed 15 to 20 in. apart. In beds, sow in rows 10 to 12 in. apart across the bed. Thin to 6 in. apart.

Water Needs—If rainfall is insufficient, provide an inch of water a week.

Care/Maintenance—Control weeds by carefully hoeing and pulling. Warm weather causes the plants to bolt; if this happens, pull them out, work the soil, and sow another crop in the fall.

Pests/Diseases—Cabbage worms can be prevented with Bt. Leaf-spot disease, black rot, and blackleg can be prevented by planting resistant varieties or treating with appropriate control aids.

Days to Maturity—35 to 50 days, depending on the variety

Recommended Varieties—'Green Wave', 'Savannah', 'Southern Giant Curled'

ONION
Allium cepa

When to Plant—Put them out as soon as the soil can be worked in the spring.

Where to Plant—Plant in full sun in well-prepared, well-drained soil.

How to Plant—In rows, space stick-outs 3 in. apart, with 12 to 15 in. between rows. Set transplants about an inch deeper than they were growing.

Water Needs—Apply an inch of water a week if the weather is dry.

Care/Maintenance—Control weeds carefully with hoeing or hand-pulling, to avoid disturbing the shallow roots. Try to get as much top growth as possible by the first day of summer; the size of the dry onions is determined by the tops. Side-dress when the plants reach 12 inches.

Pests/Diseases—Onion maggots and thrips may become troublesome; get control advice locally.

Days to Maturity—85 to 90 days, depending on the type and variety

Recommended Varieties—'Red Baron', 'Southport White Globe', 'Early Yellow Globe'

OREGANO
Origanum heracleoticum

When to Plant—Set out plants in early spring; they can stand a freeze. Divide them in the spring or fall.

Where to Plant—Locate in full sun in reasonably good garden soil—it should drain well and should not be puddled or compacted.

How to Plant—Put transplants in the garden 18 in. apart in 18-inch rows.

Water Needs—It needs little water—about an inch a week at most.

Care/Maintenance—True oregano is not invasive, though it is vigorous enough to squeeze out most weeds. Cut off flowers, as they appear to stimulate more production. Only the newer leaves are tender and flavorful. If the plant goes to seed, growth of new leaves stops. In cold-winter areas, it should survive the winter if you mulch it.

Pests/Diseases—None serious

Days to Maturity—60 to 90 days

Recommended Varieties—Pot marjoram (Origanum onites) is actually an oregano that has a bite to it.

PARSLEY
Petroselinum crispum

When to Plant—Sow seed indoors in midwinter, or direct-sow or plant seedlings when the soil outside can be worked.

Where to Plant—Site in deeply prepared soil, in full sun or partial shade. They only reach about a foot, so plant them wherever they fit.

How to Plant—Sow seeds an inch apart in rows a foot apart, and be patient, as germination sometimes takes four or more weeks. Then thin seedlings to a 5- or 6-inch spacing. Transplants can be spaced a foot apart in each direction in beds, or a foot apart in rows 2 ft. apart.

Water Needs—If rainfall is not sufficient, provide an inch a week.

Care/Maintenance—Parsley takes little care in the garden. Hoe or pull weeds as they appear.

Pests/Diseases—If mites occur, spray with insecticidal soap; rinse the treated leaves before use.

Days to Maturity—75 to 84 days, depending on the variety

Recommended Varieties—'Banquet', 'Giant Italian', 'Triple Curled'

PEA
Pisum sativum var. sativum

When to Plant—Only in cool weather! Sow as soon as the soil can be worked in spring. For a fall crop, use heat-tolerant varieties, and sow in midsummer so they mature in the cool weather.

Where to Plant—Plant in a part of the garden that drains well and dries out early in the spring. Partial shade shields the plants from intense heat and may prolong the season.

How to Plant—Sow seeds an inch apart and an inch deep into prepared, raked ground. Rows should be 12 to 18 in. apart. Thin seedlings to 8 to 10 in. apart.

Water Needs—Provide about an inch of water every 10 days if rainfall is sparse.

Care/Maintenance—Bush peas are self-supporting, but vining types need support such as short, slender branches ("pea sticks").

Pests/Diseases—Avert problems by choosing resistant varieties.

Days to Maturity—57 to 74 days, depending on type and variety

Recommended Varieties—'Alaska', 'Early Snap', 'Sugar Daddy'

PEACH
Persica vulgaris

When to Plant—Plant in spring, after all danger of frost is past—peach buds are vulnerable to cold.

Where to Plant—Choose a sheltered location in full sun with well-drained soil. Allow sufficient room, depending on whether you have a standard tree or one on dwarfing rootstock.

How to Plant—Rehydrate the roots prior to planting. Dig a hole twice as wide as the spread of the roots and of the same depth it was growing at the nursery. Water well.

Water Needs—Water well throughout the growing season if rainfall is sparse.

Care/Maintenance—Get advice from your local cooperative extension office on pruning techniques and timing. Apply fungicide in early spring.

Pests/Diseases—Peach leaf curl and borers are the most likely issues; get local advice on what to spray with and how often.

Harvesting Tips—Harvest when fruit is ripe or just a few days earlier. The taste test is the best means.

Recommended Varieties—'Loring', 'Dixiland', 'Texstar'

PEAR
Pyrus cultivars

When to Plant—Plant in the spring as soon as the soil is dry enough to work.

Where to Plant—Choose a site that receives full sun and has well-drained soil.

How to Plant—Buy as bare-root, two-year-old whips, rehydrate the roots, and plant in a hole twice as wide as the spread of the roots and the same depth that it was growing at the nursery.

Water Needs—Water regularly throughout the growing season if rainfall is sparse.

Care/Maintenance—A regular program of spraying and pruning is necessary for healthy trees and good crops, but not as intensive as for peach or apple trees. Consult your local cooperative extension office for the details. Fertilize if growth seems slow.

Pests/Diseases—Various insect pests may bother pears—see above.

Harvesting Tips—Ripe pears are soft and continue to ripen after picking. You may store them in the refrigerator.

Recommended Varieties—'Orient', 'Moonglow', 'Kieffer'

PEPPER, SWEET OR BELL
Capiscum annuum

When to Plant—Start seeds indoors about two weeks before last frost. Set transplants out after all danger of frost is past.

Where to Plant—Site in a well-drained part of the garden that receives full sun.

How to Plant—In rows, space plants 10 in. apart, with 18 to 24 in. between rows. In beds, space 15 in. apart in all directions. Plant leggy ones on their sides, cover the long stems lightly with soil; the tips will turn upward and the buried stems will sprout new roots.

Water Needs—Provide an inch of water a week if nature does not cooperate.

Care/Maintenance—Side-dress the plants with a complete fertilizer when they have set fruit.

Pests/Diseases—Aphids, mites, and whiteflies occur, and tobacco mosaic virus can be a problem. Insecticidal soaps and good garden hygiene can help.

Days to Maturity—65 to 90 days, depending on the variety

Recommended Varieties—'Bell Boy', 'Orobelle', 'Orange Sun'

PLUM
Prunus cultivars

When to Plant—Plant in spring as soon as soils are dry enough to work.

Where to Plant—Site in well-drained soil in full sun. Allow space—don't let them grow into each other or into nearby structures.

How to Plant—Choose one on dwarfing rootstock, available as bare-root, two-year-old whips. Rehydrate the roots, then plant in a hole twice as wide as the spread of the roots and the same depth as it was growing at the nursery. Soak well.

Water Needs—Water regularly throughout the growing season.

Care/Maintenance—Different types are trained and pruned differently; get specific advice from the nursery or your local cooperative extension office.

Pests/Diseases—Black knot fungus causes large black galls on the stems. Rot and borers can also be problems. Get advice on proper spraying chemicals and timing.

Harvesting Tips—The fruit continues to ripen after full color appears, so rely on the taste test.

Recommended Varieties—'Morris', 'Ozark Premier', 'Methly'

POTATO
Solanum tuberosum

When to Plant—Plant about three weeks before last frost.

Where to Plant—Well-drained, well-tilled soil in full sun is ideal.

How to Plant—Potatoes are started from seed pieces, not from actual seeds. Use certified seed potatoes from a reliable outlet. Space 12 to 15 in. apart, with 24 in. between rows. Plant 2 to 3 in. deep with the eyes up.

Water Needs—Even, consistent moisture is key—provide an inch of water a week.

Care/Maintenance—When sprouts are 6 in. high, begin (carefully) hilling soil around them. The hills eventually should be about 6 in. high and a foot wide.

Pests/Diseases—Floating row covers can protect your crop from various pests, including leaf hoppers, potato beetles, and flea beetles. Scab disease affects potatoes grown in alkaline soil; buy resistant varieties.

Days to Maturity—100 to 130 days, depending on the variety

Recommended Varieties—'Norland', 'Kennebec', 'Yukon Gold'

PUMPKIN
Cucurbita pepo

When to Plant—Sow seeds indoors one month before last frost, in peat pots. Set plants in the garden after danger of frost is past.

Where to Plant—A sunny spot with well-drained soil is best (light shade may be tolerated). Room to spread out is important!

How to Plant—Start out by sowing six seeds or two or three seedlings in hills about 5 ft. apart, with rows 10 ft. apart. The tiny roots are easily damaged, so work with care. Thin to two or three seedlings per hill when they are big enough to handle.

Water Needs—Provide an inch of water per week.

Care/Maintenance—After they set fruit, pumpkins need lots of water and fertilizer.

Pests/Diseases—The worst pest is squash-vine borers. Cucumber beetles and squash bugs can also occur. Control with appropriate insecticides.

Days to Maturity—100 to 120 days, depending on the variety

Recommended Varieties—'Connecticut Field', 'Baby Bear', 'Jack Be Little'

RADISH
Raphanus sativus

When to Plant—In spring, sow seeds as soon as the soil is dry enough to work. For a fall or winter crop, sow in late summer or fall.

Where to Plant—Choose a well-drained site in full sun or partial shade.

How to Plant—Work the soil into a fine seedbed. Sow about three per inch in rows 8 to 10 in. apart, and cover with ¼ in. of fine soil. Thin spring radishes to 1 inch; thin winter radishes to 3 or 4 inches. In beds, broadcast, then thin to 2 or 3 inches.

Water Needs—Apply an inch of water a week when rainfall is sparse.

Care/Maintenance—Hoe or pull weeds so they don't compete.

Pests/Diseases—Soil-borne maggots may damage the roots; treat with an insecticide.

Days to Maturity—22 to 28 days for spring; 55 to 70 days for winter

Recommended Varieties—Spring: 'Easter Egg', 'Champion', 'French Breakfast'; Winter: 'Black Spanish', 'Chinese White', 'Tama'

RASPBERRY
Rubus cultivars

When to Plant—Plant in spring as soon as the ground can be worked.

Where to Plant—Site in full sun in well-drained, prepared, weed-free soil, with room around the beds to mow the suckers. Don't plant where solanaeous (potatoes, tomatoes, etc.) crops grew in the last five years.

How to Plant—Rehydrate the roots before planting. Space 2 ft. apart in rows that are 8 to 10 ft. apart, or space in hills 4 or 5 ft. apart. Dig holes at least the diameter of the root spread. Install supports or trellises.

Water Needs—Water regularly if rainfall is sparse.

Care/Maintenance—Get training and pruning advice for your specific cultivar from your local cooperative extension office.

Pests/Diseases—Various problems are possible: virus, mites, scale insects, anthracnose, and spur blight. Get advice on cultural practices and pest-control regimens from your local cooperative extension office.

Harvesting Tips—Ripe berries will achieve full color.

Recommended Varieties—'Heritage', 'Autumn Britten', 'Caroline'

ROSEMARY
Rosmarinus officinalis

When to Plant—Set starts in the garden after danger of frost is past.

Where to Plant—Grow in pots on a patio, or set plants directly in the garden. The soil must be well-drained, though it need not be fertile, and full sun is best.

How to Plant—Start from seed indoors in midwinter. Set plants in the garden 18 in. apart. If growing in a pot, one plant per 12-inch container is about right.

Water Needs—Make sure they never dry out completely.

Care/Maintenance—Rosemary requires very little attention in the garden and withstands all but the most severe drought. You may fertilize once in the spring and once in the summer. Dig up if freezing weather is expected.

Pests/Diseases—Soggy soil may cause root and stem rots; correcting drainage solves the problem.

Days to Maturity—75 to 85 days

Recommended Varieties—'Arp', 'Hill's Hardy', 'Prostrata'

SAGE
Salvia officinalis

When to Plant—Start seed indoors in peat pots in late winter. Seedlings may go in the ground as soon as the soil can be worked in spring; they can withstand a frost.

Where to Plant—Well-drained soil and full sun is important. Also, because the plants will eventually become quite big, place them where they will not shade or interfere with other plants or foot traffic.

How to Plant—Prepare the soil deeply and well. Set out the started plants 15 to 18 in. apart so they have room to develop.

Water Needs—If there is no rain for one or two weeks, apply an inch of water.

Care/Maintenance—Sage is low-maintenance, requiring only a bit of weeding and pruning. Keep weeds under control.

Pests/Diseases—Use insecticides to control pesky mites. Wet weather and damp soil can lead to rot.

Days to Maturity—80 to 90 days

Recommended Varieties—Pineapple sage, Salvia elegans

SQUASH
Cucurbita spp.

When to Plant—Start seeds in peat pots a week before last frost. Set out transplants or direct-sow after danger of frost has passed.

Where to Plant—Site in full sun in well-drained soil. Grow bush types in beds or containers.

How to Plant—Sow six seeds or set two or three transplants in hills about 5 ft. apart, with rows 10 ft. apart. Thin to two or three per hill.

Water Needs—Apply an inch of water a week.

Care/Maintenance—Squash require lots of water and fertilizer after they set fruit. Side-dress with nitrogen.

Pests/Diseases—If squash-vine borers appear, slit invaded stems lengthwise, then bury so new roots can form. Insecticides may be needed for these and for cucumber beetles and squash bugs.

Days to Maturity—Summer: 50 to 65 days; Winter: 111 to 120 days

Recommended Varieties—Summer: 'Black Zucchini', 'Scallopini', 'Early Yellow Summer Crookneck'; Winter: 'Table King Acorn', 'Buttercup', 'Baby Hubbard'

STRAWBERRY
Fragraria cultivars

When to Plant—Plant in early spring as soon as the soil dries enough to be workable.

Where to Plant—Well-drained soil and full sun are essential, as is good air circulation. Don't plant where solanaceous crops (potatoes, tomatoes, etc.) grew in the last five years.

How to Plant—Prepare the soil as you would for a vegetable garden. June-bearing strawberries are usually planted in matted rows: set plants 18 in. apart in rows at least 3 ft. apart. Everbearing and day-neutral ones are best planted in hills, 12 in. apart.

Water Needs—Water regularly and thoroughly.

Care/Maintenance—Mulch with straw to keep weeds at bay and conserve soil moisture. Fertilize, but avoid getting any on the foliage.

Pests/Diseases—Most insect problems are solved with a timely application of insecticides.

Harvesting Tips—They're ready about 30 days after the first bloom, when fully red.

Recommended Varieties—'Chandler', 'Sequoia', 'Douglas'

SWISS CHARD
Beta vulgaris var. cicla

When to Plant—Start seeds indoors about six weeks before last frost, or sow directly into the garden or set out transplants after the frost-free date.

Where to Plant—Good drainage and well-drained soil are important. A location with 8 to 10 hours of sun is best.

How to Plant—Seeds are actually dried-up fruits containing two or more seeds, so don't plant too close together, and thin to 4 to 6 in. apart. Final spacing should be 8 to 10 in. apart, allowing 18 in. between rows.

Water Needs—Provide an inch of water a week.

Care/Maintenance—Cover plantings with cheesecloth or commercial row covers. Try to keep the foliage dry when watering.

Pests/Diseases—Very susceptible to leafminer damage, as well as beet leaf spot. Cover the plants as suggested above and/or get control advice locally.

Days to Maturity—About 40 days, depending on the variety

Recommended Varieties—'Bright Lights', 'Ruby', 'Winter King'

THYME
Thymus vulgaris

When to Plant—Spring. Use plants that have been grown in containers, or divide existing plants.

Where to Plant—Grow in well-drained but not overly fertile soil. Full sun is best, partial sun is tolerated. Thyme also grows well in containers and makes an attractive porch, patio, or windowbox plant.

How to Plant—Set plants on 12-in. centers in rows or beds. Erect barriers if you want to distinguish between varieties or control rampant growth.

Water Needs—Excess moisture easily damages thyme, so water only if rain has not fallen for several weeks.

Care/Maintenance—Trim thyme to keep it in bounds. When plants become overgrown and woody, take cuttings.

Pests/Diseases—Mites can occur on indoor plants, and are best treated with insecticidal soap (wash them thoroughly before use).

Days to Maturity—70 to 90, depending on the variety

Recommended Varieties—English thyme, French thyme, Lemon thyme

TOMATO
Lycopersicon lycopersicum

When to Plant—Sow or set out transplants at the frost-free date.

Where to Plant—Well-prepared, well-drained soil, in full sun, is ideal.

How to Plant—Sow seeds of smaller ones in hills 2 ft. apart; for larger staked and caged ones, sow 36 to 42 in. apart (put support in place at planting time). Thin to one plant per hill.

Water Needs—Supply an inch of water a week.

Care/Maintenance—Row covers will protect from cold weather and some pests. Maintain even soil moisture and mulch. Feed when fruit is the size of golf balls, and repeat every three or four weeks.

Pests/Diseases—Foliar diseases may be prevented by good garden hygiene and watering on the ground; if they occur, combat with recommended controls. Aphids and mites can be combated with insecticidal soap.

Days to Maturity—58 to 81 days, depending on the variety

Recommended Varieties—'Better Boy', 'Celebrity', 'Beefmaster'

WATERMELON
Citrullus linatus

When to Plant—Sow seeds indoors in peat pots a month before last frost. Direct-sow or set out transplants after danger of frost is past.

Where to Plant—Site in full sun, in well-drained soil, with ample room to spread.

How to Plant—Set two or three plants to a hill, 26 in. apart. Bush types may be grown in large containers. Black plastic mulch is a good idea since it traps soil warmth.

Water Needs—Supply an inch of water a week.

Care/Maintenance—Use floating row covers to warm the plants and keep out pests. Remove when flowers appear so bees can pollinate. Support rampant vines.

Pests/Diseases—The main enemy is cucumber beetles—fight them with covers and/or insecticides.

Days to Maturity—80 to 90 days, depending on the variety

Recommended Varieties—'Bush Sugar Baby', 'Jack of Hearts', 'Charleston Grey'

ANNUAL HERBS

Common Name Scientific Name	Spacing Height	Row	Plants	Cultural Hints	Uses
Anise *Pimpinella anisum*	24 in.	18 in.	10 in.	Grow from seed. Plant after frost. Sun.	Leaves for seasoning, garnish; use dried seed as spice.
Basil, Sweet *Ocimum basilicum*	20–24 in.	18 in.	12 in.	Grow from seed. Plant after frost. Sun.	Season soups, stews, salad, omelets.
Borage *Borago officinalis*	24 in.	18 in.	12 in.	Grow from seed, self-sowing. Best in dry, sunny areas.	Young leaves in salads and cool drinks.
Caraway *Carum carvi*	12–24 in.	18 in.	10 in.	Grow from seed. Biennial seed-bearer. Sun.	Flavoring, especially bakery items.
Chervil *Anthriscus cerefolium*	10 in.	15 in.	3–6 in.	Sow in early spring. Partial shade.	Aromatic leaves used in soups and salads.
Coriander *Coriandrum sativum*	24 in.	24 in.	18 in.	Grow from seed. Sow in spring, in sun or partial shade.	Seed used in confections. Leaves in salad.
Dill *Anethum graveolens*	24–36 in.	24 in.	12 in.	Grow from seed sown in early spring. Sun or partial shade.	Leaves and seeds used for flavoring and pickling.
Fennel (Florence Fennel) *Foeniculum vulgare*	60 in.	18 in.	18 in.	Grow from seed sown in early spring. Sun, partial shade.	Has anise-like flavor for salad. Stalk eaten raw or braised.
Parsley *Petroselinum crispum*	5 in.	18 in.	6 in.	Grow from seed started in early spring. Slow to germinate. Sun. Biennial.	Brings out flavor of other herbs. Fine base and seasoning.
Summer Savory *Satureja hortensis*	18 in.	18 in.	18 in.	Grow in well-worked loam. Sow seed in spring. Sun.	Use leaves fresh or dry for salads, dressings, stews.

PERENNIAL HERBS

Common Name Scientific Name	Spacing Height	Row	Plants	Cultural Hints/Uses
Catnip *Nepeta cataria*	3–4 in.	24 in.	18 in.	Hardy. Sun or shade. Grow from seed or by division. Leaves for tea or seasoning.
Chives *Allium shoenosprusum*	12 in.	12 in.	12 in.	Little care. Divide when overcrowded. Grow from seed or by division. Favorite of chefs. Snip tops finely. Good indoor pot plant.
Horehound *Marrobium vulgare*	24 in.	18 in.	15 in.	Grow in light soil, full sun, intense heat. Protect in cold climates in winter. Grow from seed, cuttings, or division. Leaves used in candy or seasoning.
Hyssop *Hyssopus officinalis*	24 in.	18 in.	15 in.	Grow in poor soil, from seed. Hardy. Sun. A mint with highly aromatic, pungent leaves.
Lavender *Lavandula* spp.	24 in.	18 in.	18 in.	Grows in dry, rocky, sunny locations with plenty of lime in soil. Fresh in salads, or flowers dried for sachets, potpourri.
Lovage *Levisticum officinale*	3–4 ft.	30 in.	30 in.	Rich, moist soil. From seed planted in late summer. Sun or partial shade. Of the carrot family; cultivated in European gardens as a domestic remedy.
Oregano *Origanum vulgare*	24 in.	18 in.	9 in.	Grows in poor soil from seed or division. Sun. Flavoring for tomato dishes, pasta.
Peppermint *Mentha piperita*	36 in.	24 in.	18 in.	Can start from seed, but cuttings recommended. Sun or shade. Cut before it goes to seed. Sun. Aromatic; used as flavoring oil used in products such as chewing gum, liqueurs, toilet water, soap, candy.
Rosemary *Rosmarinus officinalis*	3–6 ft.	18 in.	12 in.	Grows in well-drained non-acid soil. From cuttings or seed. Sun. Leaves flavor sauces, meats, and soups.
Sage *Salvia officinalis*	18 in.	24 in.	12 in.	From seed or cuttings. Full sun. Grows slow from seed. Renew bed every 3–4 years. Seasoning for meats, herb teas; used either fresh or dried.
Spearmint *Mentha spicata*	18 in.	24 in.	18 in.	Grows in moist soils. Hardy. From cuttings, divsion. Sun. Aromatic, for flavoring, condiments, teas.
Sweet Marjoram *Marjorana hortensis*	12 in.	18 ft.	12 in.	From seed or cuttings, as annual, or overwinter as pot plant. Sun. Seasoning, fresh or dried.
Sweet Woodruff *Asperula odorata*	8 in.	18 in.	12 in.	Keep indoors or in cold frame over winer. Semi-shade. Flavoring in drinks.
Tarragon *Artemisia dracunculus*	24 in.	24 in.	24 in.	Does best in semi-shade. By division or root cuttings. Protect during cold winters. European herb of aster family; aromatic seasoning.
Thyme *Thymus vulgaris*	8–12 in.	18 in.	12 in.	Grows in light, well-drained soil. Renew plants every few years. By cuttings, seed, division. Sun. Aromatic foliage for seasoning meats, soups, and dressings.
Winter Savory *Satureja montana*	24 in.	15 in.	18 in.	Grows in light, sandy soil. Trim out dead wood. From cuttings or seed. Sun. Seasoning for stuffing, eggs, sausage; accents strong flavors.

SUGGESTED CONTROLS OF COMMON VEGETABLE PESTS

INSECT	CONTROLS
Aphids, mites, thrips—tiny, slow-moving insects that affect shoot tips or foliage of most garden crops.	Apply insecticidal soap. Pick off infested shoots.
Bean leaf beetles—affect beans.	Apply Sevin when damage (small holes eaten in leaves) is noticed.
Beetles, cutworms, grasshoppers, leafhoppers—affect most crops.	Apply Sevin, rotenone, or permethrin when insects are observed on the plants.
Cabbage worms—green worms that affect all cole crops and related herbs eat holes in leaves.	Apply *Bacillus thuringiensis kurstaki* when white butterflies are seen in the garden.
Colorado potato beetles—affect potatoes, tomatoes, eggplant.	Apply *Bacillus thuringiensis* 'San Diego'. Handpick from plants.
Corn borers—affect sweet corn, tomatoes, peppers.	Apply Sevin insecticide when damage (holes eaten in stems or in fruit) is noticed.
Corn earworms—affect sweet corn.	Apply Sevin insecticide when damage is noticed on tips of the ears.
Cucumber beetles—affect vine crops.	Cover plants with floating row covers until bloom begins. Apply Sevin insecticide.
Earwigs—nocturnal insects with pincers on posterior end eat holes in leaves.	Apply Sevin, rotenone, or permethrin when insects are observed on the plants or damage is noticed.
Potato leafhoppers—affect potatoes, beans.	Apply Sevin when damage (brown spots in leaves or brown dry leaf margins) is noticed or when leafhoppers are seen.
Slugs—slimy, snail-like creatures eat holes in leaves or fruit of all crops.	Remove mulches and debris. Pick slugs when seen. If damage is severe, apply metaldehyde bait.
Soil insects, maggots—affect all crops by fly larvae damaging stems or roots.	Apply Diazinon in irrigation water. Cover rows with screen after sowing seed and until seedlings are sizable.
Squash bugs—affect squash, pumpkins.	Trap them under boards. Apply sabidilla.
Squash vine borers—affect squash by shredding stems at soil line.	Cover plants with floating row covers until bloom begins. Apply Sevin insecticide.
Whiteflies—affect tomatoes, squash.	Apply insecticidal soap when adults are seen in garden (clouds of tiny white insects scatter when the plants are disturbed).

Insecticides are safe to use on food crops if you follow the directions on the label. Be sure to wear the proper protection when mixing the materials, and keep the containers securely locked where children cannot get to them. Sevin® is a wettable powder that is not absorbed by plants, and Diazinon is not absorbed by plants. These chemicals, applied at the recommended rates, break down in the time between application and harvest.

SUGGESTED CONTROLS OF MAJOR FRUIT PESTS

INSECTS	CONTROLS
Aphids, mites, thrips—tiny, slow-moving insects that affect shoot tips or foliage of nearly all fruit plants.	Apply insecticidal soap or multipurpose spray when noticed.
Apple maggots, fruit worms, coddling moths, plum circulio—larvae mine their way through the fruit, destroying its value.	Apply multipurpose spray following regular 10- to 14-day schedule beginning at petal fall.
Crown borers—white grubs infest crowns of strawberry plants, which die at soil line.	Apply multipurpose spray at 7- to 10-day intervals until 3 days before harvest begins.
San Jose Scale insects—small, immobile insects cause leaf drop and dead branches, and damage surface of tree fruits.	Apply dormant oil before leaves emerge in spring, and apply multipurpose spray every 10 to 14 days after petal fall

DISEASES	CONTROLS
Mildew—white powder-like fungus covers surfaces of apple leaves.	Apply sulfur when mildew appears.
Rust—fungus causes orange spots on leaves, damages fruit.	Apply multipurpose spray beginning as leaves emerge in spring and every 7 to 10 days until 2 weeks before harvest.
Scab—fungus disease causes spots on fruit tree leaves and fruit, and severe leaf drop.	Apply multipurpose spray beginning as leaves emerge in spring and every 7 to 10 days until 2 weeks before harvest.
Verticillium wilt—causes branches or whole plants to wilt and die.	Buy certified, disease-free stock. Plant in soil that has not grown solanaceous vegetables. Destroy infected plants.
Virus diseases—cause undersized leaves and small, distorted fruit.	Buy certified, disease-free plants. Destroy infected plants

JANUARY

- Review records in your Texas gardening journal of last year's garden, choose the vegetables and herbs you want to grow this year, and secure your seeds—either by ordering from catalogs or from local shops.

- Dreaming about juicy vine-ripened tomatoes? Transplants will not become available in local nurseries until March. But if you want to grow your own transplants, plan on getting seeds planted this month.

- Place a sheet or tarp over young and newly germinated vegetable seedlings if temperatures lower than the upper 20s are predicted.

- Many of the cool-season crops such as broccoli, cabbage, cauliflower, collards, and other greens are heavy feeders and need a constant supply of nutrients to do their best, so sidedress them now.

- A home fruit garden needs to be large enough to produce the kinds of fruit you want, but not so large that it becomes a burden. Plan realistically and with care.

FEBRUARY

- February can be intensely cold or remarkably mild. This month separates the gamblers from the more conservative gardeners. In south Texas, a few brave souls will set out early tomato transplants in late February, preparing to protect them should a frost threaten.

- Early plantings have fewer insect and disease problems. Corn planted in late February, for instance, will have very few earworms.

- Tender, succulent foliage is what we want from greens such as mustard, Chinese cabbage, kale, collards, turnips, and spinach. Applications of fertilizers containing nitrogen will encourage lush, tender growth that is best for eating.

- Holes in leaves may mean caterpillar or snail and slug activity. Identify the culprit, and put out traps or handpick.

- The best time to plant fruit trees is in early spring as soon as the soil can be worked, which might be sometime this month.

MARCH

- Harvest root crops before the roots become too large and tough.

- Harvest leafy vegetables regularly. Harvest the lower leaves first.

- Vegetables to plant now in Zones 8 and 9 include: collards, kohlrabi, lima beans, mustard, radish, snap beans, and Swiss chard. Wait till late March or early April to plant cantaloupe, corn, cucumbers, eggplant, peppers, Southern peas, pumpkin, summer squash, tomatoes, watermelon, and winter squash.

- Blend fertilizer into garden beds, along with organic matter, when preparing them for planting. Water-in transplants with a fertilizer solution mixed at half strength with water or a root stimulator according to label directions.

- If you order bare-root berry bushes or young fruit trees and aren't ready to plant them immediately, you can refrigerate them, or heel them into a temporary spot.

APRIL

- All of the warm-season vegetables can continue to be planted this month. Cool-season vegetables still growing in the garden should be finished in April, or at least May in Zone 6. Make plans now on which warm-season vegetables you will plant in those areas.

- Herbs to plant now include basil, perilla, sesame, lemon balm, mints, and rosemary—as day and nighttime temperatures reach into the 70s or more.

- Stake or cage young tomato plants now. Train the plants to one or two main shoots by pinching off side shoots or "suckers."

- If you grow vegetable and herb plants in containers, pay careful attention to proper watering. Containers dry out faster than you may realize, and the results of even one severe wilting can be disastrous.

- Blackberries sucker profusely. Each spring, you should rototill the perimeter of the planting to eliminate those that have grown outside the row.

MAY

- Dry, hot weather is not unusual in May. Drought-stressed vegetables may drop flowers and young fruit and are more susceptible to pest damage. Vegetable gardens need 1 to 2 inches of water per week, and when rain is insufficient, you must make up the difference.

- If you used standard types of granular fertilizer, it is time to sidedress vegetables planted in March if you haven't already done so.

- You may begin harvesting various vegetables this month: bell peppers, tomatoes, snap beans, squash, cucumbers, and sweet corn. Some are so prolific they need to be harvested every day.

- Fruit trees and bushes, especially newly planted ones, must have regular, deep watering in order to survive and thrive. Mulch at their bases to conserve soil moisture and help keep weeds down.

JUNE

- Vegetables to plant this month include: cantaloupe, collards, eggplant, luffa, okra, peanuts, peppers, pumpkin, Southern peas, sweet potato (slips), Swiss chard, and watermelons. Even though cucumbers and squash can be planted in June and July, production is difficult in midsummer due to pest problems.

- Continue to keep records on the performance of your edible crops in your Texas gardening journal. These notes will be invaluable.

- Transplants of eggplants, peppers, and tomatoes may be planted this month.

- Mulches are especially important in midsummer. They shade the soil and keep it cooler, in addition to controlling weeds and conserving moisture. A cooler soil is healthier for vegetable roots.

- Water as needed, in the early morning. Do not be fooled by quick light showers that do little to thoroughly water the garden.

- Different fruits are susceptible to different pests and diseases. Get specific information and advice on whatever you are growing from your local Cooperative Extension office.

JULY

- Though it is blazing hot outside, it is not too soon to be looking ahead to your fall kitchen garden. Seeds for cole crops such as cabbage, broccoli, and cauliflower can be planted this month to produce transplants.

- This is the last month to plant such heat-loving vegetables as okra, peanuts, luffa, and, in south Texas, sweet potato. They should all be planted within the first week of the month.

- The squash vine borer can be very destructive to pumpkins and squash planted at this time of year. If you have had major problems with them in the past, treat plants regularly with appropriate insect-control aids.

- Provide at least an inch of water per week if rainfall is scarce.

- Keep up with the weeds. Maintain mulch 3 to 4 inches deep as a deterrent.

- Pick fresh strawberries as they ripen; if you have too many, make jam!

AUGUST

- Vegetables to plant in August include: broccoli, brussels sprouts, bunching onions, cabbage, cauliflower, Swiss chard, Chinese cabbage, collards, cucumbers, lima beans, Southern peas, peppers, Irish potatoes, rutabagas, shallots, squashes, tomatoes, and turnips.

- When a crop is finished, pull it up promptly and throw it in your compost pile. (Note: if your tomatoes have southern blight, do not compost the dead plants.)

- If your plants need water, don't wait for possible rain. Continue to water regularly, especially newly planted seeds and transplants.

- You may incorporate fertilizer when preparing beds for new plantings.

- If birds are after your ripening fruit, there are numerous tactics to try: scare objects like balloons, noisemakers, and motion-sensitive water sprayers. But netting is ultimately the most effective way to keep the harvest for yourself.

SEPTEMBER

- Cooler weather may begin, bringing welcome relief. You may go ahead now and plant: beets, broccoli, cabbage, carrots, cauliflower, Chinese cabbage, collards, English and snow peas, potatoes, kale, leek, lettuce, mustard, onion, radish, rutabagas, shallots, snap beans, and Swiss chard.

- Regularly remove the flower spikes from basil to encourage the plants to continue producing leaves.

- If herbs such as sage, lavender, thyme, and catnip managed to make it through the summer, they should begin to revive as the weather gets cooler. Remove any dead parts, and fertilize lightly to encourage new growth.

- Pay careful attention to the water needs of your edible plants, especially newly planted things. Water deeply and less frequently to encourage a deep root system.

- Grapes are now maturing. Full color is not the only indicator that they are ready to eat. Watch carefully for the time when the seeds and cluster stems turn brown—that's when they have maximum sweetness.

OCTOBER

- Fall is an excellent time to plant many hardy perennial herbs in the garden. Plan the location and think how many you would like to plant. A few herb palnts provide a lot of harvest, so don't plant more than you can use.

- Many shade trees drop their leaves. Save these for use in the vegetable garden, either for compost or as a mulch material.

- Beds you do not intend to replant now may be planted with a cool-season "green manure" crop. These are seeded into the beds, allowed to grow for a few months, and then turned under to provide organic matter to the soil.

- October is typically relatively dry. Water established vegetables and herbs deeply and thoroughly as needed. Newly planted ones will usually need more frequent irrigation.

- Harvest from your fruit trees promptly and often. Ripe fruit on the ground isn't just a shame, it can attract bees and yellow-jackets.

NOVEMBER

- Some additional plantings of cool-season vegetables can continue into late winter and early spring. If you live in Zone 9, try: beet, cabbage, carrot, collard, garlic, kale, kohlrabi, leek, lettuce, mustard, onion, radish, rutabaga, spinach, Swiss chard, shallot, and turnip.

- Direct-seed root crops such as beets, carrots, radishes, and turnips.

- When planted early so they will have time to establish and grow, lettuces are very productive in the cool-season garden.

- Don't overlook the ornamental qualities of many cool-season vegetables and herbs. Curly parsley makes a great edging for flower beds. Curly leaf mustard and red leaf mustard are outstanding when mixed with cool-season bedding plants.

- If you aren't growing fruit trees or bushes now, but would like to in the future, pave the way ahead of time. Get a soil test and indicate what you are thinking of growing—the results will include recommendations on amendments. Add lots of organic matter and/or plant a green manure crop.

DECEMBER

- Take time to make plans in your Texas gardening journal this month for the new year.

- December is a good month to have the soil in your vegetable garden tested.

- The following crops are very hardy and will survive temperatures in the low 20s and teens: beets, Brussels sprouts, carrots, celery, collards, garlic, kale, onions, leeks, and shallots.

- Long stretches of cold weather will slow the growth of vegetables and reduce the need for additional fertilizer. On the other hand, an unusually mild winter may encourage vigorous growth, requiring additional fertilizer. Watch the weather and use your best judgment.

- Dreaming of growing your own berries or fresh fruit? Now is a good time to do some research on what is involved, and which kinds (and specific cultivars) do best in your area. Books and catalogs are fine resources, but your nearest Cooperative Extension Office can really fill you in on what's best and what's involved.

ROSES
for Texas

eople have been cultivating roses for several thousand years. It's even possible that very early humans appreciated the edible and medicinal qualities of the hips and delighted in the color and fragrance of the flowers. This long history (as well as the flower's extraordinary beauty) has created a special relationship between gardeners and roses. Indeed, it would be difficult to find a flower as universally loved. The rose is now our nation's floral emblem.

PLANNING

First decide how you want to use roses in the landscape and why you intend to grow them. The trend these days is to incorporate roses into landscape plantings just like any other shrub. This works particularly well with the old garden, shrub, floribundas, climbers, miniatures, and some species.

If you want to grow roses with perfect flowers on long stems for cutting, you will probably choose the hybrid teas and grandifloras. These rosebushes often have rather unusual shapes that do not combine easily with other plants. That, along with their cultural requirements, is why they are often grown in separate beds.

If you want to train roses on a trellis, arbor, or fence, you'll want to grow rose cultivars from the climbers, ramblers, and old garden roses that produce long, vigorous canes.

Hybrid teas, grandifloras, and floribundas, the most popular and widely available groups of roses, can be relatively high-maintenance plants. Keep this in mind when planning how many roses you want to include in your landscape and where you want to plant them.

PLANTING

Roses must have at least six to eight hours of sun daily to perform up to your expectations. Any shade they receive should ideally come in the afternoon. Morning sun helps dry the foliage early, reducing disease problems. Roses need excellent drainage; avoid low areas that stay wet.

Bed preparation is important:

1. Remove unwanted vegetation from the area. If this is a new bed, remove the sod or eliminate it with a weed-control aid. In an existing bed, remove weeds.

2. Turn the soil at least 8 to 10 inches deep.

3. Spread amendments over the turned soil. Add at least 4 inches of organic matter such as compost, sphagnum peat moss, rotted manure, or finely ground pine bark. If the soil is heavy clay, a 2- to 3-inch layer of sand should be spread next. Add sulfur or lime if a soil test indicates they are needed.

4. Thoroughly blend the amendments into the existing soil and rake smooth.

To plant roses:

1. Dig a hole in a well-prepared bed as deep and wide as the roots or rootball. In a clay soil, use a mixture of 25 percent soil and 75 percent organic matter to fill the hole. In a sand soil, a 50-50 mixture of soil and organic matter works well. These are also ideal mixed to use when you are constructing a complete rose bed.

2. For bare root roses, place a cone of soil in the hole, remove the roots from the wrapper, position the plant over the cone, and spread the roots out over it. Hold the plant in place so the graft union (large knob on the lower part of the plant) is about 2 inches higher than the soil of the bed. Use your other hand to push and firm soil into the hole to cover the roots.

3. For container roses, slide the plant out of the container. Put the rootball in the hole. Its top should be level with the soil of the bed. Make sure the graft is 2 inches above soil level. Fill in around the rootball and firm with your hand.

4. Water plants in thoroughly to finish settling the soil.

5. A root stimulator may be applied using label directions.

6. Mulch the plants 3 to 4 inches deep, filling in all space between them with your favorite bark mulch. Maintain this mulch year-round.

WATERING

Irrigation will be necessary when rain does not occur regularly, especially in the warm to hot months of April through November. An occasional thorough soaking is preferred to light, frequent irrigation. If done properly, irrigation should not be necessary more than once or twice a week during dry periods. Use soaker hoses if practical. They apply water without wetting the foliage, which helps reduce disease problems.

A 3- to 4-inch layer of mulch (like cypress mulch or pine bark) or 4 to 6 inches of pine needles, clean hay, or dry leaves will help retain soil moisture and reduce the need for irrigation by preventing surface evaporation.

During our long growing seasons, roses usually need 1 to 1½ inches of water per week. If this isn't supplied by rain, it's up to the gardener to irrigate as needed.

FERTILIZATION

Roses require an adequate supply of available nutrients to produce vigorous bushes and high-quality flowers. Begin to fertilize in mid- to late February or early March in Zones 8b and 9. In Zones 8a, 7b, 7a, and 6, start fertilizing in late March/early April or as new growth begins and all dangers of frost have passed. In areas where the phosphorus levels in the soil are high, choose a premium-quality, slow-release granular fertilizer with about a 3:1:2 ratio, such as 15-5-10. Where phosphorus levels are low, use a premium-quality, granular rose fertilizer according to label directions. If needed, apply granular fertilizers every six to eight weeks throughout the growing season until late August or early September.

If you wish to fine-tune your fertilization program, follow the recommendations from a soil test.

PEST CONTROL

If you want to minimize the use of pest-control aids in your landscape, roses may not be your best choice. Texas's hot, humid to dry climate creates perfect conditions for a variety of insects and diseases that attack roses. That said, you can enjoy success if you do your homework and pick roses that have a proven track record of being tougher than most and resistant to common problems. Ask at your local nursery, ask rose-gardening neighbors, or contact a regional rose or garden club for advice.

For roses in general, hybrid teas, grandifloras, and floribundas, in particular, controlling the fungal disease blackspot may require weekly spraying from late March to November. Other fungal diseases you may see are powdery mildew and stem canker, while downy mildew and rust are less common. To control these diseases by preventing them, it is advised that a spray program be started early and continued on a regular basis.

Insects are not generally as destructive as fungus, and control can be provided on an as-needed basis. Thrips damage flowers in April through October. Aphids attack new growth and flower buds in early spring, early summer, and any other time tender new growth and flower buds arise. Leaf-cutter bees cut neat, round holes from the edges of rose leaves to line their nests. Beetles and caterpillars are occasional problems. Spider mites attack rose foliage and are generally worst during hot, dry weather.

As with diseases, wide selections of aids to control insect pests are available at local retailers, including nurseries and garden centers. After making your decisions on which aids to purchase, be sure to follow label directions.

PRUNING

In Texas, roses may be pruned twice a year—in early to mid-February, rather severely, and again, lightly, in mid-August to early September. The classic pruning technique for hybrid teas and grandifloras is designed to encourage the production of high-quality flowers with long stems for cutting. This involves rather hard pruning, back to 18 to 24 inches or as much as half the plant's height in late winter, and 30 to 36 inches or less in the late summer. Floribundas, shrub roses, miniatures, old garden roses, and others require only moderate pruning to shape them.

Cut the bush back to the desired height. Remove all the dead wood, diseased canes, and twiggy growth. Cut each remaining cane back to just above a bud (preferably one facing away from the middle of the bush).

Some rose cultivars (ramblers, some climbers, and old garden roses) bloom prolifically in the spring and early summer, then stop. These roses bloom on growth they made the summer before and generally are not as popular as repeat-blooming roses that bloom all summer. They should be pruned as needed in early to midsummer soon after they finish their bloom season.

TREE ROSE

ABRAHAM DARBY
Rosa cultivar

Type—English/Austin

Color/Bloom Size—Pink, 4½ to 5 in.

Fragrance—Rich and romantic

Bloom Period—Midseason, repeats

Mature Height—5 to 6 ft.

Water Needs—Water regularly throughout the growing season.

Planting/Care—Plant in spring in deeply prepared soil, in full sun. Mulch well and fertilize to boost health and performance.

Disease Resistance—Resistant to mildew, but may require treatment for blackspot.

Landscaping Tips & Ideas—This is a tough, durable plant and grows rather tall—in fact, its long, arching stems are easy to train on a small trellis or along and over a fence. Just watch out for the thorns, which are up to an inch long.

ALTISSIMO
Rosa cultivar

Type—Climber/Rambler

Color/Bloom Size—Crimson, 4 to 5 in.

Fragrance—Mild, sweet

Bloom Period—All season

Mature Height—8 to 12 ft.

Water Needs—Water regularly throughout the growing season.

Planting/Care—Plant in spring in deeply prepared soil, in full sun. Mulch well and fertilize to boost health and performance.

Disease Resistance—Moderate

Landscaping Tips & Ideas—The canes need to be trained where you want them to go, and on this rose they are nice and pliable. Show off this lavish bloomer on a pillar, clambering up a porch support, or trained against a wall trellis.

175

ANGEL FACE
Rosa cultivar

Type—Floribunda

Color/Bloom Size—Lavender-purple, 3 ½ to 4 in.

Fragrance—Intense, citrusy

Bloom Period—Midseason, repeats

Mature Height—2½ to 3 ft.

Water Needs—Water regularly throughout the growing season.

Planting/Care—Plant in spring in deeply prepared soil, in full sun. Mulch well and fertilize to boost health and performance.

Disease Resistance—Good

Landscaping Tips & Ideas—Low-growing, it is ideal for mixed borders, where it settles in, spreads out a bit, and dependably produces those enchanting flowers all summer long. The coppery, dark-green foliage is also attractive in such a setting.

BELINDA'S DREAM
Rosa cultivar

Type—Shrub

Color/Bloom Size—Pink, 3 to 4 in.

Fragrance—Rich and heady

Bloom Period—All season

Mature Height—4 to 6 ft.

Water Needs—Water regularly throughout the growing season.

Planting/Care—Plant in spring in deeply prepared soil, in full sun. Mulch well and fertilize to boost health and performance.

Disease Resistance—Excellent

Landscaping Tips & Ideas—A gorgeous fragrant bloomer for Texas; an outstanding performer even in highly alkaline clay soils. A big shrub, it makes a colorful contribution to mixed flower beds, or can be used as a hedge rose (it is thorny).

BLAZE
Rosa cultivar

Type—Climber/Rambler

Color/Bloom Size—Cherry red, 2 to 3 in.

Fragrance—Mild, fruity

Bloom Period—All season

Mature Height—10 to 15 ft.

Water Needs—Water regularly throughout the growing season.

Planting/Care—Plant in spring in deeply prepared soil, in full sun. Mulch well and fertilize to boost health and performance.

Disease Resistance—Good

Landscaping Tips & Ideas—A shorter climber with heavy-blooming ability. The stems are easy to manipulate; well-suited to adorning wooden fences or draping over stone walls. It is also a fine choice for backing a mixed flower garden with season-long color.

BONICA
Rosa cultivar

Type—Shrub

Color/Bloom Size—Pink, 1 to 2½ in.

Fragrance—None

Bloom Period—All season

Mature Height—2 to 4 ft.

Water Needs—Water regularly throughout the growing season.

Planting/Care—Plant in spring in deeply prepared soil, in full sun. Mulch well and fertilize to boost health and performance.

Disease Resistance—Generally trouble-free

Landscaping Tips & Ideas—These tough plants tolerate cold winters and blazing summers. Well-suited to screen, hedge, and foundation plantings. Individual plants are a lovely, no-nonsense addition to a flower border.

CALDWELL PINK
Rosa cultivar

Type—Polyantha Shrub

Color/Bloom Size—Lilac-pink, 2 in.

Fragrance—Slight

Bloom Period—All season

Mature Height—4 to 7 ft.

Water Needs—Water regularly throughout the growing season.

Planting/Care—Plant in spring in deeply prepared soil, in full sun. Mulch well and fertilize to boost health and performance.

Disease Resistance—Good

Landscaping Tips & Ideas—This exuberant bloomer is covered with clusters of small flowers for most of the growing season, making it popular where dependable color is desired. Adding to its popularity is the fact that it tolerates our oppressive summer heat so well—it's a real trooper. Big enough to be used in a shrub border, or spilling over a fence or wall, but manageable enough to be a good citizen in a mixed flower bed. Its romantic color gives a nice cottage-garden feel.

CAREFREE BEAUTY
Rosa cultivar

Type—Shrub

Color/Bloom Size—Rosy-pink/4 to 4 ½ in.

Fragrance—Moderate, sweet perfume

Bloom Period—Midseason, repeats well

Mature Height—5 to 6 ft.

Water Needs—Water regularly throughout the growing season.

Planting/Care—Plant in spring in deeply prepared soil, in full sun. Mulch well and fertilize to boost health and performance.

Disease Resistance—Good to excellent

Landscaping Tips & Ideas—A tough rose with a splashy personality, making it welcome wherever a durable pink rose is required. It becomes a full, substantial bush, so be sure to give it ample room. A row makes an excellent, very tough hedge planting.

CHRYSLER IMPERIAL
Rosa cultivar

Type—Hybrid Tea

Color/Bloom Size—Deep red, 4½ to 5 in.

Fragrance—Spicy, rose-clove scent

Bloom Period—Midseason, repeats well

Mature Height—4 to 5 ft.

Water Needs—Water regularly throughout the growing season.

Planting/Care—Plant in spring in deeply prepared soil, in full sun. Mulch well and fertilize to boost health and performance.

Disease Resistance—DISEASE RESISTANT in most of Texas (mildew can occur in cool, wet weather)

Landscaping Tips & Ideas—This is a classic old rose that has been used in breeding newer and arguably better ones, but it remains beloved for its intense fragrance and great beauty. The long, strong stems, with one glorious bloom each, make it perfect for a cutting garden. It's also a natural for any formal rose garden or flower bed.

DOUBLE DELIGHT
Rosa cultivar

Type—Hybrid Tea

Color/Bloom Size—Pink-yellow-cream, 5½ in.

Fragrance—Strong and spicy

Bloom Period—All season

Mature Height—3½ to 4 ft.

Water Needs—Water regularly throughout the growing season.

Planting/Care—Plant in spring in deeply prepared soil, in full sun. Mulch well and fertilize to boost health and performance.

Disease Resistance—Susceptible to mildew in cool, wet climates, otherwise resistant and healthy

Landscaping Tips & Ideas—In the garden, it forms a medium-size, irregularly bushy plant and wafts intense fragrance for many feet in all directions. So place where it can be appreciated—in a frontyard flower bed, as the star of a mixed display, next to a patio, deck, or terrace, or even in a large container in any sunny spot.

DREAMGLO

Rosa cultivar

Type—Miniature

Color/Bloom Size—Dark pink, 1 in.

Fragrance—Slight, sweet

Bloom Period—Midseason, with good repeat

Mature Height—18 to 24 in.

Water Needs—Water regularly throughout the growing season.

Planting/Care—Plant in spring in deeply prepared soil, in full sun. Mulch well and fertilize to boost health and performance.

Disease Resistance—Good

Landscaping Tips & Ideas—A very handsome and healthy plant for gardens that lack space for larger rose bushes. Excellent in containers, too. Provides reliable, glorious color for months.

FIRST PRIZE
Rosa cultivar

Type—Hybrid Tea

Color/Bloom Size—Pink, 5 to 5½ in.

Fragrance—Moderate, old-rose perfume

Bloom Period—All season

Mature Height—3 to 5 ft.

Water Needs—Water regularly throughout the growing season.

Planting/Care—Plant in spring in deeply prepared soil, in full sun. Mulch well and fertilize to boost health and performance.

Disease Resistance—Spray to prevent mildew and blackspot.

Landscaping Tips & Ideas—A spectacular and especially long-lasting bloom, in the garden or in a vase. The shimmering, pretty color is at home in any romantic garden scheme. Don't crowd the plant, though, as good air circulation helps to keep it healthy.

FRAGRANT CLOUD
Rosa cultivar

Type—Hybrid Tea

Color/Bloom Size—Coral-red, 5 in.

Fragrance—Powerful tea rose

Bloom Period—All season

Mature Height—4 to 5 ft.

Water Needs—Water regularly throughout the growing season.

Planting/Care—Plant in spring in deeply prepared soil, in full sun. Mulch well and fertilize to boost health and performance.

Disease Resistance—Good

Landscaping Tips & Ideas—A big, gorgeous bloomer, with a bold, dramatic color to match. Not always easy to place in a garden, as a result—your best bet is to include it in a bed with other hot-colored flowers.

GOLD MEDAL
Rosa cultivar

Type—Grandiflora

Color/Bloom Size—Golden yellow with red, 3½ to 4½ in.

Fragrance—Moderate, fruit-and-spice

Bloom Period—All season

Mature Height—4 ft.

Water Needs—Water regularly throughout the growing season.

Planting/Care—Plant in spring in deeply prepared soil, in full sun. Mulch well and fertilize to boost health and performance.

Disease Resistance—Vulnerable to blackspot, otherwise good

Landscaping Tips & Ideas—Abundant blossoms cloak a tough, handsome bush in clusters and singles, making for an impressive show. Thorns are sparse on the long stems, which makes them easy for cutting bouquets. Feature in a prominent spot where you can enjoy the cheerful color.

JEAN KENNEALLY
Rosa cultivar

Type—Miniature

Color/Bloom Size—Pink-apricot, 1 ½ in.

Fragrance—Soft, mild

Bloom Period—Midseason, repeats well

Mature Height—1 ½ to 2 ft.

Water Needs—Water regularly throughout the growing season.

Planting/Care—Plant in spring in deeply prepared soil, in full sun. Mulch well and fertilize to boost health and performance.

Disease Resistance—Good

Landscaping Tips & Ideas—A perky, pastel beauty of a miniature, lovely in a big container on a patio or deck. Or tuck one into a pastel-themed flower border, where it will be a source of constant and lovely color.

KNOCK OUT
Rosa cultivar

Type—Shrub

Color/Bloom Size—Ruby-red, 3 to 3 ½ in.

Fragrance—Light, sweet

Bloom Period—All season

Mature Height—3 ft.

Water Needs—Water regularly throughout the growing season.

Planting/Care—Plant in spring in deeply prepared soil, in full sun. Mulch well and fertilize to boost health and performance.

Disease Resistance—Exceptional DISEASE RESISTANCE (it appears to be impervious to blackspot)

Landscaping Tips & Ideas—A super-tough, super-prolific shrub rose developed a few years ago (it now has some equally laudable siblings, including a very full-petaled double red, a pink, and even a yellow). Ideal for use where roses have done poorly in the past, and a wonderful source of summerlong color. Excellent in a perennial garden, or any cottage-garden planting scheme.

LADY BANKS' ROSE
Rosa banksiae 'Lutea'

Type—Old Garden/Species

Color/Bloom Size—Yellow, 1 to 1 ½ in.

Fragrance—Mild, sweet

Bloom Period—Several weeks in early summer

Mature Height—to 20 or 30 ft. or more

Water Needs—Water regularly throughout the growing season.

Planting/Care—Plant in spring in deeply prepared soil, in full sun. Mulch well and fertilize to boost health and performance.

Disease Resistance—Disease-free!

Landscaping Tips & Ideas—Not a rose for the faint-hearted, but easy and wonderful in the right spot. To enjoy this glorious, carefree, nearly thornless rose, give it room to roam. Let it cover an old dead tree or give it a sturdy garden shed to scramble up and over.

MUTABILIS
Rosa chinensis var. mutabilis

Type—Old Garden/Species/China

Color/Bloom Size—Changeable, 4 in.

Fragrance—Slight, sweet

Bloom Period—All season

Mature Height—6 to 10 ft.

Water Needs—Water regularly throughout the growing season.

Planting/Care—Plant in spring in deeply prepared soil, in full sun. Mulch well and fertilize to boost health and performance.

Disease Resistance—Maybe a little blackspot in late summer

Landscaping Tips & Ideas—Nicknamed the "butterfly rose" because its bright, single blossoms change color as they age and a bush in bloom displays all stages of this feature—thus making it look like it is covered in multicolored, fluttering butterfly wings. The petals begin yellow, darken to orange, then turn deep pink and finish crimson. Use as a backdrop for a multicolored flower border, or feature as an informal but delightful specimen plant where it can be the center of attention.

NEW DAWN
Rosa cultivar

Type—Climber/Rambler

Color/Bloom Size—Pink, 3 to 3½ in.

Fragrance—Moderate, fruity

Bloom Period—All season

Mature Height—12 to 20 ft.

Water Needs—Water regularly throughout the growing season.

Planting/Care—Plant in spring in deeply prepared soil, in full sun. Mulch well and fertilize to boost health and performance.

Disease Resistance—Good

Landscaping Tips & Ideas—Seeking a very pretty and dependable climber? 'New Dawn' is justly popular, thanks to its long, pliable canes (though it is thorny). Train it onto an arch, let it cascade over a fence, or drape it over a front-porch railing. Just be sure to put it where its beauty and wonderful fragrance—reminiscent of ripe peaches—can be enjoyed.

QUEEN ELIZABETH
Rosa cultivar

Type—Grandiflora

Color/Bloom Size—Pink, 3½ to 4 in.

Fragrance—Mild, tea scent

Bloom Period—Midseason, repeats

Mature Height—5 to 8 ft.

Water Needs—Water regularly throughout the growing season.

Planting/Care—Plant in spring in deeply prepared soil, in full sun. Mulch well and fertilize to boost health and performance.

Disease Resistance—Good

Landscaping Tips & Ideas—A tall and robust plant, she looks regal flanking a doorway or garden entrance, or grown against the side of a house or other building in need of spectacular, reliable color. Would also make a good background for a big, sunny, pastel-themed flower bed.

SEA FOAM

Rosa cultivar

Type—Shrub

Color/Bloom Size—Pale pink to white, 2 to 3 in.

Fragrance—Slight

Bloom Period—Midseason, repeats

Mature Height—8 to 12 ft.

Water Needs—Water regularly throughout the growing season.

Planting/Care—Plant in spring in deeply prepared soil, in full sun. Mulch well and fertilize to boost health and performance.

Disease Resistance—Good

Landscaping Tips & Ideas—A rugged plant of great beauty. Often used as an informal but pretty climber. But due to its sprawling growth habit, this is a rose you can use as a groundcover, trailing over a rock wall or covering a hillside or bank.

SIMPLICITY
Rosa cultivar

Type—Shrub

Color/Bloom Size—Pink, red, white, yellow, or lavender, 3 in.

Fragrance—Light, sweet

Bloom Period—All season

Mature Height—4 to 5 ft.

Water Needs—Water regularly throughout the growing season.

Planting/Care—Plant in spring in deeply prepared soil, in full sun. Mulch well and fertilize to boost health and performance.

Disease Resistance—Vulnerable to blackspot; spray to prevent

Landscaping Tips & Ideas—This is the classic informal hedge rose, dependably full of flowers all summer and very resilient. Plant in a long row below a porch, to outline a garden room or establish a border backdrop, or along a property line.

SOMBREUIL
Rosa cultivar

Type—Climber/Rambler

Color/Bloom Size—Creamy white, 3½ to 4 in.

Fragrance—Rich, honeysuckle-like perfume

Bloom Period—Early to midseason, repeats

Mature Height—12 to 15 ft.

Water Needs—Water regularly throughout the growing season.

Planting/Care—Plant in spring in deeply prepared soil, in full sun. Mulch well and fertilize to boost health and performance.

Disease Resistance—Good

Landscaping Tips & Ideas—This gorgeous, old-fashioned climber is an inspired choice for a pillar or porch railing. It prospers in mild climates (is not very cold-hardy).

SUNSPRITE
Rosa cultivar

Type—Floribunda

Color/Bloom Size—Yellow, 3 in.

Fragrance—Strong, sweet licorice

Bloom Period—Midseason, repeats

Mature Height—2½ to 3 ft.

Water Needs—Water regularly throughout the growing season.

Planting/Care—Plant in spring in deeply prepared soil, in full sun. Mulch well and fertilize to boost health and performance.

Disease Resistance—Good

Landscaping Tips & Ideas—Because it has such excellent, bright, dependable color, it is often used as a hedge plant. But single plants make a cheerful addition to a mixed flower bed.

TROPICANA
Rosa cultivar

Type—Hybrid Tea

Color/Bloom Size—Orange, 5 in.

Fragrance—Heady, richly fruity

Bloom Period—All season

Mature Height—4 to 5 ft.

Water Needs—Water regularly throughout the growing season.

Planting/Care—Plant in spring in deeply prepared soil, in full sun. Mulch well and fertilize to boost health and performance.

Disease Resistance—Good

Landscaping Tips & Ideas—A classic beauty for a formal rose garden, cutting garden (nice long cutting stems, ideal for big bouquets!), or mixed flower bed with pretty perennials. Its unique and striking orange color looks great with purple- or white-flowered companions.

WINSOME
Rosa cultivar

Type—Miniature

Color/Bloom Size—Pink, 2 in.

Fragrance—None

Bloom Period—Midseason, repeats

Mature Height—16 to 22 in.

Water Needs—Water regularly throughout the growing season.

Planting/Care—Plant in spring in deeply prepared soil, in full sun. Mulch well and fertilize to boost health and performance.

Disease Resistance—Excellent

Landscaping Tips & Ideas—The plant is quite bushy and grows vigorously, so it's a good mini for growing in the ground rather than a container. Its good health and sweetheart blooms would be a welcome addition to a mixed flower border or cutting garden.

COMMON ROSE PESTS

Symptom: Young leaves are curled up or distorted; sooty mold on leaves.

Possible diagnosis: Aphids—tiny, pear-shaped, sucking insects.

Remarks: These insects love new growth! They excrete honeydew, a sticky, sweet substance that can turn black as sooty mold grows on it. Ants may dine on the honeydew but not otherwise harm the plant.

Recommended less-toxic treatments: Knock the aphids off with a blast from the hose. Treat with neem or pyrethrin. Spray with insecticidal soap.

Recommended chemical controls: Spray with malathion.

Symptom: Nibbled leaves and flowers.

Possible diagnosis: Japanese beetles—half-inch long, metallic copper-and-green bugs.

Remarks: They travel in groups—if you see one, there are more.

Recommended less-toxic treatments: Pick off and kill individual beetles—evening is best, and you can drop them in a bucket of soapy water (don't squash them since that releases pheromones that attract other Japanese beetles). Go after their larvae by treating your lawn (where they live before they grow up and attack your roses with milky spore or parasitic nematodes). Use rotenone. Use pyrethrum.

Recommended chemical controls: Use carbaryl (Sevin).

Symptom: Wilting, dying canes.

Possible diagnosis: Borers—tiny, worm-like larvae.

Remarks: Entry holes are usually visible, often lower down on the canes. These insects like young canes or recently cut ones.

Recommended less-toxic treatments: Immediately cut out and destroy affected canes.

Recommended chemical controls: None.

Symptom: Stunted growth.

Possible diagnosis: Nematodes in the soil—microscopic worms.

Remarks: Check the roots for telltale galls.

Recommended less-toxic treatments: Pull out and destroy infected plants and do not replant in that area for a few seasons. Apply chitin or a chitin-containing product to the soil.

Recommended chemical controls: None.

Symptom: Tiny, shell-like bumps "glued" to the stems.

Possible diagnosis: Scale insects—tiny bugs that create a protective scaly or crusty shell over themselves.

Remarks: These insects suck plant juices from the stems, sometimes also the leaves.

Recommended less-toxic treatments: Spray with horticultural oil when the pest is in its crawling stage. Try releasing parasitic wasps in the rose garden.

Recommended chemical controls: Spray with malathion or carbaryl (Sevin).

Symptom: Leaves are mottled yellow, especially during hot, dry spells; over time, you can see a silver stippling or sheen.

Possible diagnosis: Spider mites—tiny spider relatives, specks the size of pepper grains, in green, red, or yellow.

Remarks: The pests themselves are almost too tiny to see, but you can observe their webs on an infected plant, particularly on the undersides of the leaves. They thrive during hot, dry summers on dusty plants.

Recommended less-toxic treatments: Hit the bush with blasts of hose water, aiming especially for leaf undersides. Spray with insecticidal soap, sulfur, or horticultural oil. Try releasing predatory mites in the rose garden.

Recommended chemical controls: Spray with a miticide such as Avid or Ortho Isotox Formula IV.

Symptom: Misshapen leaves, deformed buds, flowers discolored and with brown spots.

Possible diagnosis: Thrips—tiny yellow or brown insects.

Remarks: Most common in early summer. Most common on light-colored roses.

Recommended less-toxic treatments: Spray with insecticidal soap. Spray with neem, rotenone, or pyrethrum.

Recommended chemical controls: None.

Symptom: No flowers. Buds shrivel and turn black.

Possible diagnosis: Rose midges—tiny insects.

Remarks: These insects are barely visible.

Recommended less-toxic treatments: Spray with insecticidal soap.

Recommended chemical controls: Combat the soil-borne larvae with an organophosphate insecticide.

COMMON ROSE DISEASES

Symptom: Small black spots on the leaves, with fringed edges.

Possible diagnosis: Blackspot.

Remarks: Common in hot, humid weather.

Recommended less-toxic treatments: Promptly remove and destroy affected leaves. Prune the bush to improve air circulation. Deliver water to the soil; do not let it splash on the leaves. Water in the morning so the plant can dry out over the course of the day. Spray with summer oil. Spray with a dormant spray that includes lime sulfur. Spray with neem.

Recommended chemical controls: Spray with chlorothanonil (Daconil).

Symptom: White powdery residue on the leaves, sometimes also on flower petals; leaves and flowers become crinkled and distorted.

Possible diagnosis: Powdery mildew—a fungus.

Remarks: Thrives in dry conditions.

Recommended less-toxic treatments: Spray with summer oil. Spray the foliage with an antidessicant (antitranspirant) product, which makes a thin, waxy layer over the leaves that shields them from this disease.

Recommended chemical controls: Spray with a fungicide. Sulfur-based ones are the most effective.

Symptom: Yellow-edged purple blotches on leaf surfaces; grayish fuzz on the undersides.

Possible diagnosis: Downy mildew—a fungus.

Remarks: Often seen in cool, damp weather.

Recommended less-toxic treatments: Prune the bush to improve air circulation. Deliver water to the soil; do not let it splash on the leaves. Water in the morning. Spray with a dormant oil.
Recommended chemical controls: Spray with a sulfur- or copper-based fungicide.

Symptom: Undersides of leaves develop rusty spots; yellow spots appear on the tops.
Possible diagnosis: Rust—a fungus.
Remarks: Often seen in dry areas. Thrives when there are warm days coupled with cool nights.
Recommended less-toxic treatments: Remove and destroy affected leaves. Deliver water to the soil; do not let it splash on the leaves. Spray with a dormant oil.
Recommended chemical controls: Spray with a lime-sulfur fungicide.

Symptom: Deformed new growth, yellow mottling on leaves.
Possible diagnosis: Rose mosaic virus.
Remarks: Can't spread from plant to plant contact (but will pass on via pruners used on diseased roses).
Recommended less-toxic treatments: Remove and destroy affected leaves. Severely affected plants should be destroyed and you should contact the nursery where you got the rose and get a replacement.
Recommended chemical controls: None.

JANUARY

- Make decisions on how many roses and which types and cultivars you want to add to your landscape, as well as where you want to add them. Early planting, this month or next month, is especially important for bare-root roses.

- Late December through early February is the best time to transplant roses. To move a bush to a new location, prune it back appropriately, dig it with as much of the roots as possible, and plant immediately.

- Blackspot may be active if the weather is mild and the roses have not gone dormant. Most gardeners take a break from spraying this time of year. Defoliation is not as debilitating as it would be during the summer.

- Mulch 3 to 4 inches deep to suppress winter cool-season weeds. If any pop up, handpull while small.

- No fertilizer should be applied to roses this month.

FEBRUARY

- When planning the location of roses in your landscape, keep in mind the extraordinary fragrance of many cultivars. Plantings of fragrant roses are especially nice around porches, patios, and entrances.

- This is a good month for both planting and transplanting roses. Finish transplanting in the early part of the month, especially in the southern part of the state. Plant rosebushes in well-prepared beds with good drainage and plenty of sun.

- Roses generally do better with good air circulation. When they are used in mixed plantings, nearby shrubs, vines, and even large perennials should not be allowed to crowd them. When pruning your rosebushes, trim or snip back shoots or branches from nearby plants that are growing into the roses' space.

- Newly planted roses should be watered in thoroughly. Maintain a moist soil.

- Finish pruning during the early to middle part of this month.

MARCH

- If you plan to regularly spray your roses, check out your supply of pest-control aids this month. Spraying should begin soon, and you will need materials on hand when the time comes.

- Continue to plant roses purchased in containers. If you are expecting a mail-order shipment of bare-root roses, hope they arrive soon; plant them immediately.

- Evaluate your roses carefully. They will begin active growth this month. Any bushes that are dead, sprouting poorly, or have only a few weak living canes may need to be replaced.

- Roses throughout the state should be fertilized this month when new growth begins. Use a premium-quality rose fertilizer and follow label directions.

- Prune immediately if you have not already done so. Pruning this late will not hurt your bushes, but your roses will bloom later.

APRIL

- Make some notes in your Texas gardening journal about when various roses started blooming. Note how many weeks had passed since you pruned. You can manipulate, to some degree, when your roses bloom by pruning earlier or later within the recommended period.

- Blooming roses are available in containers at nurseries. You can pick out the color, shape, fragrance, and size of flowers that you want. There is a price, however. Planting roses now means they have to establish themselves while blooming.

- Supplemental water is usually needed this month. Water until the soil is moistened at least 5 to 6 inches down. Use sprinklers or soaker hoses.

- Blackspot, powdery mildew, aphids, and others can start up now. Begin spraying as soon as possible and spray every seven to ten days through November. Many rose gardeners use products that combine two or three aids for effective control of diseases and insects. These are usually great.

MAY

- Stop and smell the roses. Forgive the cliché, but this is one of our best blooming months. Record comments on each in your Texas gardening journal; these will help tremendously when, at the end of the growing season, you are deciding which roses to keep.

- Ramblers and climbers should be in full bloom. Pay attention to training and tying these to the arbor, fence, trellis, or other structure they are to grow on.

- More heat means that the need for water is more likely. From now on, a week or ten days without a good rain means turning on the irrigation.

- You can fertilize again this month (six to eight weeks after your spring application).

- Are you spraying regularly? If not, expect to see blackspot on virtually every type of rose.

- Other than deadheading and pruning off suckers below the graft union, no pruning is required this month.

JUNE

- Regularly collect and dispose of diseased leaves that yellow and drop from your rosebushes. This may help reduce blackspot problems. And it helps to make the entire planting area look better.

- The intense heat this time of year can dry out beds surprisingly fast. Roses planted this year need a deep watering whenever we go five to seven days without a good rain. Older,

more established plants should be watered seven to ten days after the last good rain. Bottom line: maintain a moist soil.

- If you did not fertilize last month, you may this month.

- Hot, dry weather may encourage spider mites to attack. If you use a combination pest-control aid, make sure it will control mites as well as the other pests.

- Keep weeds under control by regular handpulling and mulching 3 to 4 inches deep.

- If your rose is not a repeat-blooming type, go ahead and prune now.

JULY

- Plan on gardening during the cooler early-morning and late-afternoon hours. Heat is brutal this time of year for gardens and gardeners alike.

- This month's heat may lower the vigor of many roses. Despite your best efforts at proper care, you will notice the flowers are now often smaller with less-vivid colors.

- Blooms seem to fade as soon as they open. Hang in there and don't give up! Continue regular care, especially watering.

- Mulching 3 to 4 inches deep with your favorite bark mulch and maintaining it through the summer reduces the required frequency of irrigating, conserves soil moisture, and moderates soil temperatures.

- Do not fertilize this month.

- Blackspot, spider mites, leaf-cutter bees, caterpillars, beetles, and weeds are the most common problems this time of year—keep after them all.

- Other than deadheading and pruning out diseased or dead growth, no pruning is required this month.

AUGUST

- Plan on fertilizing late this month. Extra nutrients now will encourage vigorous growth and flowering over the next three months.

- This is also a good time to evaluate how your roses did over the summer. By now, they will show how well they endured the heat, drought, rain, and humidity of a Texas summer. Any rose that has performed poorly for two seasons should probably be replaced.

- Prune roses to get them in shape for the fall blooming season. After a long summer of growth, most are rather overgrown. Top the bushes back to the desired height. Remove all dead wood, diseased canes, and twiggy growth. Cut back each remaining cane to just above a bud (preferably facing away from the center of the bush).

- Blackspot continues to be the number one problem. Continue a regular spray program to control it, and keep yellow, fallen leaves raked or picked up from rose beds.

SEPTEMBER

- Rose hips may appear on some of your bushes this month. They make great wildlife food and various types are used to make jelly. Rose petals are also edible. Use petals or hips only from flowers that have not been sprayed with pest-control aids.

- During this growing period before their fall bloom, pay careful attention to rainfall amounts and water if 1 to 1½ inches of rain has not fallen for about a week.

- If fertilizing this month, use the same types/ratios/analysis as used earlier this season. This is the last fertilization required for this season.

- Roses that were not cut back in late August should be cut back in early September. Pruning roses later generally means they will come into bloom a little later.

OCTOBER

- Plan on enjoying all the beautiful roses blooming this month. Pleasant weather makes it delightful to be outside.

- Fall planting is certainly possible in Texas. Roses are hardy and will not mind winter's cold. Container-grown ones can go into the ground from late October through winter.

- Now that flower production has resumed, it's time to start deadheading again.

- Although the weather is mild to cool, October can be one of our driest months. Water roses deeply as needed, based on rainfall. Avoid wetting the foliage, as this encourages blackspot. Maintain a moist soil condition.

- No fertilizer is needed for the rest of the growing season.

- Cooler, drier weather will reduce blackspot. If the weather cooperates, reduce spray frequency to once every ten days or more. If the weather is warm and wet, spray weekly.

- Prevent cool-season weeds with a pre-emergent weed-prevention aid. Use on the rose bed prior to mulching.

NOVEMBER

- Little has to be done to prepare roses for the coming winter. Mild winters in south Texas often prevent roses from going dormant at all. Full dormancy is most likely in north Texas.

- Planting roses in fall is a good idea for most of Texas because it allows a plant to grow roots and become established during the cool season. Fall-planted roses are more likely to be stronger and more vigorous during their first summer. The container roses available at local nurseries may be left over from last spring.

- Rose flowers provide a great deal of pleasure when cut and brought indoors. Cut just as the buds start to open, with stems long enough for arranging.

- Other than deadheading, no pruning is needed now.

DECEMBER

- Need more roses? Check out the new catalogs to see what new ones are being offered. If you mail-order your roses, specify that you need to receive them for planting in January (south Texas) or February (north Texas).

- Early to mid-December after a killing freeze or frost is a good time to transplant roses to a new location. Dig it with as much of the root system as possible and plant immediately.

- Slower growth, cool to cold temperatures, and abundant rainfall generally make watering unnecessary this month. Newly planted or transplanted roses, however, should be watered as needed if sufficient rain does not occur.

- Update your Texas gardening journal. List all the pests you encountered an which cultivars seemed to have the worst problems. How effective were pest-control efforts, and how might they have been improved?

- Make sure all your rosebushes have labels with their proper names stuck in the ground at their bases.

SHRUBS
for Texas

Shrubs are woody perennial plants that produce multiples stems from the soil or multiple branching close to the ground and grow smaller than trees, generally no taller than about twelve feet. They may be evergreen or deciduous. In Texas, relatively mild winters allow us to grow a wide variety of evergreen shrubs and a few deciduous shrubs, which are really popular. Shrubs are generally grown for their colorful flowers or attractive foliage, but they may also provide fragrance and ornamental or edible fruit.

PLANNING

Shrubs are a fundamental and essential part of most landscape designs. They are the primary plant material used to shape spaces, create structure in the landscape, enhance the home and other buildings, provide privacy, screen views, and guide traffic patterns.

Planting the right shrubs in the right location is critical to the plant's health and your happiness with the planting. Every gardener has favorite shrubs he or she wants to plant in the landscape. By all means, choose shrubs you like, but it is also important that you consider the growing conditions of the area, size limitations, the purpose of the planting, and the characteristics you want the shrubs to have.

First evaluate the site. Is it shady or sunny? Well-drained or damp? Is the soil acid or alkaline? You must choose shrubs that will thrive in the growing conditions in which they will be planted.

Next consider the purpose of the planting. Is it to beautify the house, screen a view, provide colorful flowers, create privacy, or another one of the many reasons why shrubs are planted?

List the characteristics the shrubs must have to satisfy your taste and the purpose they will serve. Decide on the mature size needed, between evergreen and deciduous, whether or not you will want flowers (and if so, what color and when), and any other features you feel are important.

Finally, choose the shrubs that will most closely fit the growing conditions, purpose, and desired characteristics. Choose your favorite shrub if it's the

AZALEA

best choice, but if not, plant another shrub. Planting a shrub that will grow too large for its location is the most common mistake gardeners make. Always ask about or find out the mature size of the plants you intend to plant. If someone says, "You can always keep it pruned to whatever size you want," walk away and choose a smaller-growing shrub.

PLANTING SHRUBS

The ideal planting season for shrubs in Texas is October through March. Fall planting in October through early December is especially good. Roots grow readily at that time of year. Shrubs then have until May to make root growth and get established before hot weather. Shrubs are almost always sold as container-grown plants. On occasion, larger specimens are available balled-and-burlapped. Shrubs are generally planted into well-prepared beds.

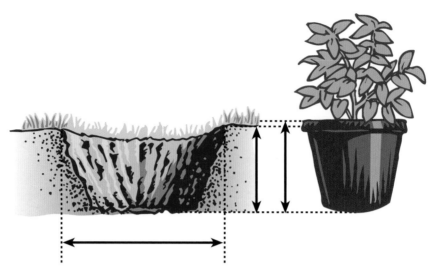

BED PREPARATION

1.   Remove unwanted vegetation from the bed area. Weeds or turfgrass may be removed physically or eliminated with a weed-control aid (follow label directions carefully) and turned under.

2.   Turn the soil to a depth of at least eight to ten inches with a shovel, spade, or garden fork.

3.   Spread desired amendments over the turned soil. Have your soil tested through your local extension service office to find out what it needs. You should always add four to six inches of organic matter, such as compost, sphagnum peat moss, rotted manure, or finely ground pine bark. Depending on your soil and the type of shrubs that will be planted, additional materials might include sand, lime, or sulfur.

4.   Thoroughly blend the amendments into the soil, rake the bed smooth, and shape the edges. The level of the soil in the bed will be higher than it was before. This is good, as it will improve drainage.

PLANTING

1.   Place shrubs in their containers atop the soil where they will be planted. Make sure the spacing and arrangement are proper before going to the next step.

2.   Push down slightly on a pot to make a shallow depression, and set the shrub—in its container—aside.

3.   Dig a hole into the depression deep enough to accommodate the rootball and a little wider.

4.   Remove the shrubs from the container. If the roots are tightly packed in a solid mass, cut or pull apart the root system slightly. This will encourage the roots to grow into the surrounding soil.

5.   Place the rootball into the hole. It is crucial for the top of the rootball to be level with or slightly above the soil surface.

6.   Use your hands to push and firm soil into the space between the rootball and the sides of the hole.

7.   After planting all the shrubs in the bed, water them thoroughly by hand to finish settling the soil.

8.   Apply a root stimulator using label directions now (this is optional, but helpful).

9.   Finally, mulch the bed 3 to 4 inches deep.

WATERING

Newly planted shrubs will need careful attention to watering the first year after planting. Water as needed during hot summer weather if adequate rain does not occur. Established shrubs will need supplemental irrigation only during the hottest, driest weather. It is important to water thoroughly enough to moisten the soil 4 to 6 inches down. This is best accomplished with sprinklers or soaker hoses.

FERTILIZING

Shrubs are best fertilized in early spring and, where rapid growth is desired, again in midsummer. Standard granular fertilizers will feed for about six to eight weeks. Applied in early spring, they supply nutrients to shrubs during their primary growth period from spring to early summer. This is adequate in most circumstances. Young shrubs that are being encouraged to grow rapidly, or shrubs in low vigor, may be fertilized again in midsummer or early fall.

A premium-quality, long-lasting, slow-release granular fertilizer is fine for most situations. Fertilizers with a 3:1:2 ration such as 15-5-10, 18-6-12, or 21-7-14 work well. Always read and follow label directions when applying fertilizers.

Acid-loving shrubs, such as azaleas, camellias, and gardenias, will occasionally have problems with iron deficiencies when grown in too-alkaline soils, and may require fertilizers rich in available or chelated iron.

PEST CONTROL

Insects are an occasional problem on some shrubs. A few popular shrubs have fairly common pest problems, lacebugs on azaleas and whiteflies on gardenias, for instance, but most of the time we simply monitor shrubs and deal with pest problems as they occur. Common insect pests on shrubs are lacebugs, scale, whiteflies, caterpillars, and aphids. Insect-control aids commonly used to control these pests are widely available at local retailers.

Spider mites are an occasional problem during hot, dry weather.

Diseases can be very destructive, particularly root rots. The best defense against root rot is choosing well-adapted plants and providing good drainage. Leaf spots are not uncommon, but generally are not severe enough for you to worry about spraying if shrubs are vigorous and otherwise healthy. Powdery mildew creates a thin, white, powdery film on the foliage of certain shrubs. It can be fairly easily controlled with fungus disease-control aids or by planting in locations where the air movement is good.

PRUNING

Pruning is a regular part of shrub care. Done primarily to keep shrubs attractively shaped, make them bushier and fuller, rejuvenate old, overgrown specimens, or control size, pruning can be minimized with careful plant selection.

Specially shaped shrubs, such as topiary and clipped hedges, require the most pruning. Shrubs that grow too large for their location may require almost constant pruning to keep the right size. Do not plant shrubs that will grow significantly larger than needed for a location.

Hedges, topiaries, and shrubs not grown for flowers can be pruned anytime between mid-March and September. Prune hedges so that the base is slightly wider than the top. This will keep the hedges full at the bottom.

Shrubs that bloom from January through April should be pruned after they finish flowering, but before late June. Shrubs that bloom from May through September should be pruned January through March (except hydrangeas and gardenias, which are pruned right after they finish flowering in June or July). Prune flowering shrubs at the wrong time and you may prevent them from flowering during the ensuing growing season.

ABELIA
Abelia x grandiflora

Hardiness—Hardy throughout Texas

Color(s)—White, pink; bronze fall foliage

Bloom Period—Summer to fall

Mature Size (H x W)—3 to 8 ft. x 3 to 8 ft.

Water Needs—Deep, infrequent irrigation is best; drip irrigation works very well.

Planting/Care—Will grow in light, sandy soil or heavy clay, so long as it gets full sun. Plant in early spring or early fall. Fertilize as needed.

Pests/Diseases—No pests; disease is not a problem in full-sun locations that have good air movement.

Landscaping Tips & Ideas—A tall, wide blooming shrub, not suitable in front of porches, low windows, narrow beds, or in limited spaces. Annuals may be planted outside its spread if desired. White-flowered 'Prostrata' remains a mere three feet tall. 'Sunrise' has cream and pink variegated foliage. And there are good new cultivars with variegated or chartreuse foliage, on dwarf plants, that may capture your fancy.

ALTHEA
Hibiscus syriacus

Hardiness—Hardy throughout Texas

Color(s)—White, pink, red, purple, and blends

Bloom Period—Summer

Mature Size (H x W)—8 to 12 ft. x 3 to 6 ft. or more

Water Needs—Water well at planting time and to aid establishment. Mulch to conserve soil moisture.

Planting/Care—In the Panhandle, plant in very early spring. In the rest of Texas, plant at any time (fall is best). Grows in all types of soils that drain well; full sun is best. Use slow-release fertilizer.

Pests/Diseases—Aphids occasionally visit tender new growth. In July and August, when humidity is very low, spider mites may appear. Consult your local retailer for controls.

Landscaping Tips & Ideas—Use as a summer-blooming screen planting. Or grow in a container, trained into a tree form. Groundcovers, perennials, and annuals may all be planted in a bed of althea.

ARALIA
Fatsia japonica

Hardiness—Hardy only in Zones 8a to 9b

Color(s)—Not grown for flowers; grown for evergreen foliage

Bloom Period—Not applicable

Mature Size (H x W)—5 to 7 ft. x 4 to 5 ft.

Water Needs—Keep moist but not wet.

Planting/Care—In Zone 8a, plant in early spring through early fall; in warmer zones, plant anytime. An eastern exposure with sun until 10 a.m. (or daylong dappled sun) is best. Will tolerate a poorly drained clay or sandy soil. Responds well to fertilizing. Keep mulched.

Pests/Diseases—None serious

Landscaping Tips & Ideas—Use as a mass background planting in shady bed locations with ferns to create a pleasing effect under trees. Works well with ferns and aucuba to create interesting tropical effects. Use as a stand-alone or in mass plantings in large containers. Also works well as a corner foundation planting.

AUCUBA
Aucuba japonica

Hardiness—Hardy in USDA Zone 7b, borderline hardy in Zone 7a

Color(s)—Green foliage flecked or splashed with gold

Bloom Period—Not grown for flowers

Mature Size (H x W)—4 to 8 ft. x 4 to 6 ft.

Water Needs—Maintain a moist but not wet soil throughout the growing season.

Planting/Care—Plant anytime, though fall is best. Shade is the key! Will grow in heavy clay or sandy soils, but must have good drainage. Responds well to regular, light applications of fertilizer. Prune selectively because pruning scars remain visible longer than on most other landscape plants.

Pests/Diseases—None

Landscaping Tips & Ideas—Makes a wonderful foundation planting; just remember that it gets tall. Try planting it on the inside of a protected courtyard, atrium, or solarium. It also does well in beds of shade-loving ferns, and may be grown in a container.

AZALEA
Rhododendron spp. and cultivars

Hardiness—Hardy in all zones except USDA Zone 6a

Color(s)—Red, coral, salmon, pink, white, and lavender

Bloom Period—Spring

Mature Size (H x W)—3 to 10 ft. x 3 to 8 ft.

Water Needs—Keep soil moist but not wet.

Planting/Care—Best planted in early spring in prepared, acidic ground. Fertilize after bloom, mid-season, and early fall. Prune to maintain desired shape after blooms drop.

Pests/Diseases—Mites, lace bugs, and scale are potential pests. Leaf gall, leaf spots, and flower or petal blight are potential diseases. Chlorosis is also possible. Keeping plants healthy will prevent most, but if a problem arises, consult your local garden center for control recommendations.

Landscaping Tips & Ideas—Utilize in mass effect with outstanding results. Camellias and gardenias make good companions. Plant lower-growing types under low windows.

BARBERRY
Berberis thunbergii

Hardiness—Hardy throughout Texas

Color(s)—Vibrant red fall foliage

Bloom Period—Not grown for flowers/ not applicable

Mature Size (H x W)—I to 6 ft. x 2 to 7 ft.

Water Needs—Maintain a moist, but not wet, soil; drip irrigation is ideal.

Planting/Care—Plant at any time, in full sun in good, organic soil. Make beds a minimum of 5 feet wide, larger if possible. Apply 3 to 4 inches of mulch. During the growing season, fertilize and prune as needed.

Pests/Diseases—Aphids may visit new growth, but usually aren't much of a problem. Get advice from your local garden center.

Landscaping Tips & Ideas—Use as a special planting in color beds, or use as foundation plants. For best effect, mass planting is recommended. Its colors are often enhanced in landscape plantings by white periwinkle or other white blooms.

BOXWOOD
Buxus microphylla

Hardiness—Most varieties are hardy throughout Texas.

Color(s)—Evergreen foliage; not grown for flowers

Bloom Period—Not applicable

Mature Size (H x W)—I to 20 ft. x I to 6 ft.

Water Needs—Keep soil moist but not wet.

Planting/Care—Fall is the best time to plant. Site in shade; well-drained soil is a must or root rot will occur. Provide 3 to 4 inches of bark mulch. Fertilize as needed.

Pests/Diseases—Do not plant if your soil has root-knot nematodes (have your soil tested for these pests). Leafminers and spider mites may visit but usually aren't a problem for healthy plants. Control products are available at your local garden centers.

Landscaping Tips & Ideas—Use as foundation plantings, screens, or specimens. For year-round green beauty, 'Winter Gem' is hard to beat in Texas.

BURNING BUSH
Euonymus alata

Hardiness—Hardy throughout Texas (may struggle in coastal areas)

Color(s)—Red foliage; red-orange fall fruit

Bloom Period—Not grown for flowers

Mature Size (H x W)—4 to 10 ft. x 8 to 12 ft.

Water Needs—Water as needed to prevent dry soil.

Planting/Care—Plant anytime (fall is best) in moist, well-drained, fertile soil in full sun. For best fall color, it needs at least six hours of full sun a day. Provide 3 or 4 inches of bark mulch. Fertilize as needed. Prune as desired, although spring is best for radical pruning.

Pests/Diseases—None serious

Landscaping Tips & Ideas—Popular as a screening hedge. For a super look, plant in front of dark green, broadleaf evergreen shrubs such as tall-growing hollies. Works well in large tubs or containers. May be trained into a multiple-stemmed small tree suitable for sunny patios and other limited-space applications.

BUTTERFLY BUSH
Buddleia davidii

Hardiness—Hardy throughout Texas

Color(s)—White, pink, yellow, and purple

Bloom Period—Summer

Mature Size (H x W)—3 to 8 ft. x 4 to 6 ft.

Water Needs—Water to keep the soil from drying out. More frequent watering is needed during the first year, less in the following years.

Planting/Care—Plant anytime, though early spring is best. Select a full-sun, well-drained, and fertile location. Provide a 3- to 4-inch mulch layer. Fertilize as needed. Prune to shape. May be radically pruned just before new spring growth, if desired.

Pests/Diseases—None serious; rot occurs in poorly drained sites

Landscaping Tips & Ideas—Not good for a foundation planting. Instead, use in mass bed plantings and in combination with perennials or relatively large blooming specimens. Plant where your family can enjoy its fragrance, color, long bloom period, and its ability to attract butterflies.

CAMELLIA
Camellia japonica

Hardiness—Hardy in USDA Zones 7a to 9b, depending on the variety

Color(s)—Red, pink, white, rose, and blends

Bloom Period—Fall through spring

Mature Size (H x W)—6 to 8 ft. x 6 to 8 ft. or more

Water Needs—Maintain a moist, but not wet, soil.

Planting/Care—Plant in spring or fall, in well-drained, fertile, acidic soil. Dappled sun throughout the day is ideal. Provide 4 inches of pine bark mulch. Fertilize with granular azalea/camellia fertilizer as needed.

Pests/Diseases—Tea scale is usually the only problem, and a once-a-year application of dormant oil will take care of it. Leaf spot may appear. Camellias in good health rarely have problems.

Landscaping Tips & Ideas—Spectacular in beds underneath the canopies of large shade trees. Great in large containers or trained into patio trees, screens, hedges, or color beds.

CHERRY LAUREL
Prunus caroliniana

Hardiness—Hardy in USDA Zones 7b to 9b

Color(s)—White

Bloom Period—Spring and summer

Mature Size (H x W)—18 in. to 25 ft. x 3 to 16 ft.

Water Needs—Water as needed to prevent dry soil.

Planting/Care—Plant in spring/fall. Prefers well-drained locations in moist, fertile soils, with sun and good air movement. Maintain 3 to 4 inches of bark mulch. Fertilize as needed.

Pests/Diseases—Grasshoppers may visit during the summer, and leaf spots occur if air movement is poor and humidity is high. Controls are available at your local garden centers.

Landscaping Tips & Ideas—Use as individual specimens, as screen plantings, or trained into patio trees. Don't use as foundation plantings or site near walkways or driveways or in front of entrances or windows, as they will quickly outgrow these areas.

CLEYERA
Ternstroemia gymnanthera

Hardiness—Hardy in USDA Zones 7a to 9b

Color(s)—Yellow blooms, red to purple fruits, bronze winter foliage

Bloom Period—Summer

Mature Size (H x W)—6 to 8 ft. x 4 to 8 ft. or more

Water Needs—Maintain a moist soil during the growing season.

Planting/Care—Fall planting is best, spring planting is fine. Best in areas that do not receive the hot direct western sun. Prefers dappled shade, well-drained soil, and ample space. Maintain a 3- to 4-inch bark mulch layer. Fertilize as needed. Pruning is rarely needed, but if you must, spring and early summer are the best times.

Pests/Diseases—None serious

Landscaping Tips & Ideas—A slow-grower, great planted in groups, corners, or alcoves. Not as good for a hedge or screen. Make interesting plantings in beds under tall trees. A good companion for dwarf hollies.

COTONEASTER
Cotoneaster spp. and cultivars

Hardiness—Hardy throughout Texas

Color(s)—White, pink flowers; red fruit

Bloom Period—Spring

Mature Size (H x W)—1 to 8 ft. x 3 to 10 ft.

Water Needs—Water to prevent dry soil.

Planting/Care—Plant at any time, but fall is best. Install in partially shady locations with good air movement and moist, fertile soil. Do not plant next to a solid fence or in an area where there is reflected heat. Make beds a minimum of 5 feet wide. Mulch. Fertilize as needed.

Pests/Diseases—Susceptible to fire blight; your local garden centers will have control products if you need them.

Landscaping Tips & Ideas—The lower-growing ones are suitable for rock gardens and as groundcovers. The larger-growing varieties may be trained into interesting tree forms. Cotoneaster is compatible with holly, nandina, Indian hawthorn, and others.

CRAPEMYRTLE
Lagerstroemia indica, and hybrids of L. indica x L. fauriei

Hardiness—Hardy in USDA Zones 7 to 9

Color(s)—White, pink, red, lavender, purple, and magenta; colorful fall foliage

Bloom Period—Summer

Mature Size (H x W)—18 in. to 25 ft. x 3 to 25 ft.

Water Needs—Water as needed to maintain moist soil. Will tolerate dry conditions, but doesn't like them.

Planting/Care—Plant anytime, though fall is best. Do not plant in shady areas! Plant in full sun in a well-drained spot, where they can be easily watered. Mulch. Fertilize as needed. Prune to shape in late winter.

Pests/Diseases—Powdery mildew may visit during very humid conditions with poor air movement. Aphids may visit as well. Your local retailer can offer you several controls.

Landscaping Tips & Ideas—Works well as a specimen, in mass plantings, in large containers, in extended foundation beds, and in stand-alone beds developed in sunny locations.

ELEAGNUS
Elaeagnus pungens

Hardiness—Hardy in USDA Zones 7a to 9b

Color(s)—Evergreen foliage, non-showy flowers, red fruit

Bloom Period—Summer

Mature Size (H x W)—8 to 12 ft. x 8 to 10 ft.

Water Needs—Water as needed to keep soil from drying out.

Planting/Care—Plant anytime, though fall planting is best. It prefers a moist, loamy, fertile soil. Mulch. Fertilize as needed. Pruning can be a chore if you maintain the plant short and narrow; better to allow to grow to its natural shape/size, and little additional pruning will be needed.

Pests/Diseases—Spider mites may visit; your local retailer will have control solutions.

Landscaping Tips & Ideas—An excellent plant for large screening or as a large specimen. Because of its large size, it is not recommended for a foundation. Various annuals may be planted at the outside edges if desired.

EUONYMUS
Euonymus japonica

Hardiness—Hardy throughout Texas

Color(s)—Colorful evergreen foliage

Bloom Period—Not applicable

Mature Size (H x W)—1 to 10 ft. x 1 to 6 ft.

Water Needs—Water as needed to prevent the soil from drying.

Planting/Care—Plant anytime, though fall is best. Though it is adaptable, six to eight hours of daily sun, along with shade from the hot western afternoon sun, is most desirable. Prefers moist, fertile soils. Mulch. Fertilize as needed. Lends itself well to shearing and training into various shapes.

Pests/Diseases—An application of dormant oil once a year in late winter will usually control scale. Powdery mildew can occur; seek controls at local nurseries.

Landscaping Tips & Ideas—Because of its leaf colors and ability to re-grow, it is a good candidate for screens, hedges, foundation plantings, and specimens. Use in large containers.

FLOWERING QUINCE
Chaenomeles japonica

Hardiness—Hardy throughout Texas

Color(s)—White, red, pink, and coral

Bloom Period—Early spring

Mature Size (H x W)—3 to 4 ft. x 5 ft.

Water Needs—Water as needed to prevent soil dryness.

Planting/Care—Plant anytime, but fall is ideal. Plant in full sun where there is adequate moisture and fertile soil. Mulch. Fertilize as needed. Prune as desired; do severe pruning in the spring just after blooming.

Pests/Diseases—Aphids may visit new top growth, but they usually aren't a long-term problem; see your local retailer for control options.

Landscaping Tips & Ideas—In sunny areas where azaleas are difficult to grow, try flowering quince. It may be clipped to form an interesting hedge. It also works well in color beds, and its blooms are a standout in wide beds in front of tall-growing broadleaf evergreens like holly.

GARDENIA
Gardenia jasminoides

Hardiness—Hardy in USDA Zones 8b to 9b

Color(s)—White, creamy white

Bloom Period—Summer

Mature Size (H x W)—6 in. to 6 ft. x 3 to 6 ft.

Water Needs—Maintain a moist soil—not wet or dry. Drip irrigation is good.

Planting/Care—Plant in very early spring or early fall, in moist, sandy, acidic soil. A spot with morning sun and shade from the direct hot afternoon sun is ideal. Mulch. Fertilize as needed.

Pests/Diseases—Aphids, whiteflies, nematodes, mites, scale, sooty mold, and leaf spot can all hit gardenias. Get control advice from your local retailer.

Landscaping Tips & Ideas—For small spaces, try one of the smaller varieties as an indoor/outdoor container planting. The taller-growing varieties make interesting foundation plantings. Good as mass plantings, specimens, hedges, groundcovers, and container plants. They also work well in beds of azaleas and camellias.

FORSYTHIA
Forsythia x intermedia

Hardiness—Hardy throughout Texas

Color(s)—Gold, yellow

Bloom Period—Early spring

Mature Size (H x W)—6 to 8 ft. x 6 to 10 ft.

Water Needs—Soil moisture is important, even during our winters.

Planting/Care—Fall is best for planting. Sun is essential (after six hours of full sun, it may be shaded for the rest of the day). A heavy mulch is beneficial. Fertilize up to three times during the growing season. Prune to shape in the spring after blooming is complete. Though it is winter-hardy, it isn't fond of dry conditions at any time.

Pests/Diseases—None serious

Landscaping Tips & Ideas—Makes a wonderful show of color in large beds with early-spring blooming bulbs planted outside the drip line. Because of their size, the plants may be trained into specimens or hedges.

HOLLY
Ilex spp. and cultivars

Hardiness—Hardy throughout Texas

Color(s)—Evergreen foliage, fall to winter red berries

Bloom Period—Spring

Mature Size (H x W)—3 to 50 ft. x 3 to 20 ft.

Water Needs—Water as needed to prevent dry soil.

Planting/Care—Plant any time, though fall is best. Some varieties prefer full sun, others do better in more shade. All will grow in acidic soils, some grow well in alkaline ones. Hollies like a moist, well-drained spot. They respond well to regular fertilizing. For severe pruning, early spring is best.

Pests/Diseases—Scale and grasshoppers are potential problems; a local nursery can recommend remedies.

Landscaping Tips & Ideas—Dwarf varieties work well in front of low windows and porches and along walkways. Hollies may be utilized with any other landscape shrub, and can have annuals and perennials planted in front of them.

HYDRANGEA
Hydrangea macrophylla

Hardiness—Hardy throughout Texas

Color(s)—White, red, pink, and blue; some varieties have multicolored foliage

Bloom Period—Spring, summer, and fall

Mature Size (H x W)—5 to 7 ft. x 6 to 8 ft.

Water Needs—Maintain a moist soil, especially during bud-forming and blooming periods.

Planting/Care—Plant in very early spring or fall, in fertile, deep, moist soil that drains well. Eastern or northern exposures are preferred. For pink blooms, grow in alkaline soil and use granular rose fertilizer. For blue, grow in acidic soil and feed with azalea fertilizer. Prune if needed to shape after peak bloom.

Pests/Diseases—None serious

Landscaping Tips & Ideas—Grow beneath tall shade trees, or display in containers on shady decks or patios. A stand-out with holly growing behind it. Shade-tolerant annuals such as wax begonias, coleus, and hardy perennial ferns work well around hydrangeas.

INDIAN HAWTHORNE
Raphiolepsis indica

Hardiness—Hardy in USDA Zones 7b to 9b

Color(s)—White, pink, and rose-red

Bloom Period—Spring

Mature Size (H x W)—3 to 8 ft. x 3 to 6 ft.

Water Needs—Water when establishing; drought tolerant thereafter.

Planting/Care—Plant in fall or very early spring. A minimum of six to eight hours of full sun without reflected heat is ideal. Best in deep, fertile, well-drained soil. Mulch, and feed as needed. Perform any severe pruning in spring after bloom is finished, and selective pruning as needed.

Pests/Diseases—Leaf spot may appear. Choose disease-resistant cultivars.

Landscaping Tips & Ideas—Some of the taller varieties make top-notch foundation plantings against relatively tall walls. Use other varieties in mass plantings or under low windows or other structures. Good companions include salvia and lantana.

JAPANESE YEW
Podocarpus macrophyllus

Hardiness—Hardy in Zones 7a to 9b

Color(s)—Evergreen foliage

Bloom Period—

Mature Size (H x W)—8 to 12 ft. x 3 to 10 ft.

Water Needs—Irrigate as needed to maintain a moist soil.

Planting/Care—Fall planting is best, early spring is good. Does best in deep, loose, moist soils with at least six to eight hours of full sun. It tolerates considerable shade but loses foliage density in heavy shade. Mulch well. Fertilize as needed. Japanese yew lends itself to shearing almost anytime. Severe pruning, if needed, should be done in early spring.

Pests/Diseases—No serious pests; root rot can occur in poorly drained locations.

Landscaping Tips & Ideas—Plant any place tall, dense, upright shrubs are desired. When planted relatively close together, these shrubs will make very tall screens and/or hedges.

JUNIPER
Juniperus chinensis

Hardiness—Hardy throughout Texas

Color(s)—Foliage in various shades of green, also golden-yellow, frosty blue and silvery blue

Bloom Period—Spring

Mature Size (H x W)—1 to 20 ft. x 3 to 15 ft.

Water Needs—Irrigate to prevent dry soil; deep irrigation is great for growing junipers.

Planting/Care—Plant early fall or very early spring, in well-drained soils and full sun. Mulch. Fertilize as needed. Prune lightly to shape as new growth appears; do not perform radical pruning on older stems without foliage, or they may not regrow.

Pests/Diseases—Spider mites could be a problem in hot, dry locations. See a local retailer for control options.

Landscaping Tips & Ideas—Use as hedges, corner plantings, foundation plantings, or screens. Work well in manipulated forms such as bonsai, twists, spirals, and pom-poms. Can grow in large containers. Companions include lantana and Mexican bush sage.

LOROPETALUM
Loropetalum chinense

Hardiness—Hardy throughout Texas

Color(s)—Pink, red-violet, and white flowers; foliage features scattered reddish-purplish leaves

Bloom Period—Mainly spring and summer

Mature Size (H x W)—10 ft. x 6 ft.

Water Needs—Water as needed to maintain a moist soil. Not drought tolerant.

Planting/Care—Plant late fall or early spring. The ideal site offers moisture-retentive, sandy loam soil where surface water disappears quickly after a rain. Likes acidic soil. Mulch after planting. Fertilize in spring and replenish the mulch then as well. Prune as needed in late winter to maintain good form and to control size.

Pests/Diseases—Uncommon

Landscaping Tips & Ideas—Use large hollies, Japanese yew, or waxleaf ligustrum as a backdrop for a grouping of these. Plant groundcover junipers or bedding annuals in front of them. 'Burgundy' is an excellent cultivar. In smaller spaces, keep pruned low or they will outgrow their bounds.

MAHONIA
Mahonia bealei

Hardiness—Hardy throughout Texas

Color(s)—Yellow

Bloom Period—Winter

Mature Size (H x W)—4 to 6 ft. x 3 to 5 ft.

Water Needs—Maintain a moist soil.

Planting/Care—Fall and spring planting are best. Will grow in light to heavy Texas soils as long as they aren't wet or poorly drained. Does best in moist, fertile, improved locations. Apply a layer of bark mulch. Fertilize as needed.

Pests/Diseases—None serious

Landscaping Tips & Ideas—For a great look, prune back one or more stems of each plant at different levels in very early spring. Use as foundation plantings in two or more rows, in masses under trees, or in containers. When used as multiple-row foundation plantings, alternate in a checkerboard pattern for a very interesting look. It does well in shaded areas with companions such as aucuba, aralia, English ivy, and ferns.

NANDINA
Nandina domestica

Hardiness—Hardy throughout Texas

Color(s)—White flowers, red berries, colorful fall foliage

Bloom Period—Summer

Mature Size (H x W)—5 to 7 ft. x 3 to 6 ft.

Water Needs—Water to prevent soil dryness.

Planting/Care—Plant in early spring or early fall, in sunny locations without reflected heat and shade from the afternoon sun. It responds with vigor to deep, fertile, moist soils. Mulch. Fertilize as needed. Prune each spring. (If plant is leggy, cut back half of the stems to the points where new branching is desired. After the stems have produced new foliage, cut back the remaining ones to the desired height.)

Pests/Diseases—None

Landscaping Tips & Ideas—Use in masses as foundation plantings, stand-alone yard beds, backgrounds, and confined areas such as planters. This tough plant can be used in beds around trees with annuals, bulbs, and perennials.

OLEANDER
Nerium oleander

Hardiness—Hardy in USDA Zones 8a to 9b, some in Zone 7

Color(s)—White, pink, red, coral, and yellow

Bloom Period—Spring to fall

Mature Size (H x W)—4 to 15 ft. x 5 to 12 ft.

Water Needs—Water to prevent excessive soil dryness. Very drought tolerant.

Planting/Care—Plant in early spring or any time when there is no danger of frost. It will tolerate almost any Texas soil, but prefers deep, moist, fertile, loose soil. The plant needs a well-prepared soil. After planting, mulch. Fertilize as needed during the growing season. Remove dead stems every spring.

Pests/Diseases—Caterpillars may visit but are easily controlled; consult a local retailer for possibilities.

Landscaping Tips & Ideas—Always more attractive when allowed to grow into their natural shape and size. Make a great natural-looking screen or hedge. Display dwarf types in containers on patios, poolsides, or decks.

PHOTINIA
Photinia x fraseri

Hardiness—Hardy throughout Texas, except USDA Zone 6

Color(s)—White flowers; new leaf growth is red

Bloom Period—Spring

Mature Size (H x W)—10 to 15 ft. x 8 to 10 ft.

Water Needs—Water as needed to prevent soil dryness, at the soil line.

Planting/Care—Plant in early fall or early spring, in full sun, in well-drained soil, with ample room and good air movement. Mulch. Fertilize as needed. Minimal pruning is needed when growing into a natural form; pruning at least every week is needed when growing clipped hedges.

Pests/Diseases—Prone to leaf spot problems in some areas; may be controlled with sprays.

Landscaping Tips & Ideas—Can be grown as tall screens, hedges, or specimens. May be trained into a tree form and grown in a container. Because it grows quickly, do not plant in front of standard windows, porches, walks, or as foundation plants.

PYRACANTHA
Pyracantha coccinea

Hardiness—Hardiness varies with species and cultivars.

Color(s)—White flowers, red-orange berries in fall/winter

Bloom Period—Spring

Mature Size (H x W)—2 to 10 ft. x 2 to 10 ft.

Water Needs—Maintain a moist, but not wet, soil during the growing season.

Planting/Care—Early fall and very early spring are both good planting times. Prefers fertile, moist, well-drained locations. Mulch, and fertilize as needed. Requires minimal pruning (espaliers may require several prunings during the growing season to train and maintain their form).

Pests/Diseases—Lace bugs and spider mites may visit; your local retailer will have several controls.

Landscaping Tips & Ideas—Low-growing varieties work as groundcovers. Others work as screens, accents, bank plantings, specimens, and espaliers (on walls, fences, and landscape structures in formal patterns). Various low-growing annuals look good in front of pyracantha plantings.

SPIREA
Spirea japonica

Hardiness—Hardy throughout Texas

Color(s)—Pink, rose-pink, purplish-pink, white, and red

Bloom Period—Spring through midsummer

Mature Size (H x W)—1 to 6 ft. x 3 to 5 ft.

Water Needs—Maintain a moist soil during growth and bloom periods. Prevent dryness during the rest of the year.

Planting/Care—Plant in fall or very early spring, in full sun and moist, well-drained, fertile soil. This plant will tolerate some shade and almost any Texas soil. Mulch. Fertilize as needed. After blooming, minimal pruning may be necessary to aid in natural shaping.

Pests/Diseases—None serious

Landscaping Tips & Ideas—The lower-growing varieties will add color and interest to extra-wide foundation plantings. The blooms stand out when planted in front of taller-growing broadleaf evergreens such as holly. Use taller varieties as informal hedges or screens. Spirea specimens are often standouts in the landscape.

VIBURNUM
Viburnum spp. and cultivars

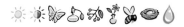

Hardiness—Hardy in USDA Zones 7 to 9, depending on variety

Color(s)—White, cream, pink, pinkish-white, and rose-tinted white

Bloom Period—Spring

Mature Size (H x W)—3 to 18 ft. x 3 to 16 ft.

Water Needs—Soil moisture is needed, but don't overwater.

Planting/Care—Best planted in fall or very early spring. Site in sun, with some afternoon shade. All viburnums prefer deep, fertile, moist, well-drained soil. Mulch well. Fertilize as needed. Prune as needed to shape; do major pruning after the main bloom flush.

Pests/Diseases—None serious

Landscaping Tips & Ideas—Medium-size ones, like V. davidii, make good low, wide foundation plantings or hedges. Taller ones, such as V. japonicum, make outstanding specimens or very tall, wide screens. Add annual or perennial color in front of the evergreen types if the beds are wide enough.

WAX-LEAF LIGUSTRUM
Ligustrum japonicum

Hardiness—Hardy in USDA Zones 7b to 9b

Color(s)—White

Bloom Period—Spring and summer

Mature Size (H x W)—10 to 14 ft. x 8 to 12 ft.

Water Needs—Water as needed to prevent soil dryness.

Planting/Care—Early fall or early spring is best. This is a tough, rapid-growing shrub that will grow in almost any soil type. Mulch. Fertilize as needed. When training as a hedge, prune weekly during the growing season (don't prune in late fall or winter).

Pests/Diseases—None serious

Landscaping Tips & Ideas—Lends itself well to horticultural training in forms such as patio trees, pyramids, and pompoms. It may be used as an accent, specimen, or large container plant. It is easily trained into various hedge shapes, including square, round, and oval.

WINTER JASMINE
Jasminum nudiflorum

Hardiness—Hardiness varies by variety

Color(s)—Yellow

Bloom Period—Winter and early spring

Mature Size (H x W)—3 to 4 ft. x 4 to 6 ft.

Water Needs—Maintain a moist soil throughout the growing season.

Planting/Care—Fall and winter plantings are best. Never plant in heavily shaded spots; it prefers daylong full sun. Make planting beds at least 5 feet wide. Mulch. Fertilize as needed. Shear to shape in spring, after bloom is complete.

Pests/Diseases—None serious

Landscaping Tips & Ideas—Plant on hillsides, in large wide beds with other colorful shrubs, or grouped together in masses. It is great for a low shrub planting. It also works well cascading over walls or on banks, or in spots where erosion may cause problems. The color really stands out if planted in front of dark-green, broadleaf evergreen companions.

SHRUBS

Name	Size (H × W) and Type	Light	Flowers and Comments
American Beautyberry *Callicarpa americana*	6 by 4 feet; deciduous.	Full to part sun.	Native shrub suitable for relaxed landscape styles; purple berries in clusters along stems in late summer.
Aucuba *Aucuba japonica* 'Variegata'	5 by 3 feet; evergreen.	Shade.	Dark green and yellow variegation, coarse texture. Looks tropical but is quite hardy.
Azaleas *Rhododendron* spp. and cultivars	2 by 2 to 10 by 10 feet, depending on cultivar; mostly evergreen.	Part shade to sun, depending on cultivar.	Many different cultivars of this very popular spring-flowering shrub exist. Indica types are largest and easy to grow. Azalea cultivars that bloom at times other than spring are becoming more popular.
Banana Shrub *Michelia figo*	15 by 6 feet; evergreen.	Full sun to part shade.	Very fragrant, banana scented, creamy yellow flowers in April.
Barberry *Berberis thunbergii*	1½ by 2 to 6 by 7 feet; mostly deciduous, depending on variety.	Full to part sun.	Colorful leaves during the growing season and in the fall.
Boxwood *Buxus microphylla*	1 by 1½ to 20 by 6 feet; evergreen.	Part sun to shade.	Bright-green to dark-green leaves depending on variety. Great as formal hedges.
Butterfly Bush *Buddleia alternifolia* *B. davidii*	6 by 6 feet to 10 feet by 10 feet; deciduous.	Full to part sun.	Long summer blooming season; spikes of fragrant purple, pink, or white flowers are attractive to butterflies; tends to be short-lived. Native and non native varieties.
Camellia *Camellia japonica*	12 by 8 feet; evergreen.	Part sun to part shade.	Large flowers of striking beauty in shades of red, pink, or white December to March. Acid-loving, depending on variety.
Cherry Laurel *Prunus laurocerasus*	1½ by 3 to 25 by 16 feet; evergreen	Full to part sun.	Dark, glossy green leaves and fragrant white blooms; good screening plant.
Chinese Holly *Ilex cornuta* and many cultivars	3 by 3 to 12 by 10 feet, depending on cultivar; evergreen.	Full sun to part shade.	Most cultivars produce bright red berries fall to spring. Leaves are prickly. Watch for white scale inssects, especially on the back sides of leaves.
Chinese Mahonia *Mahonia fortunei*	3 by 3 feet; evergreen.	Part morning shade to shade.	Excellent small shrub for shady areas; flowers are not significant.
Cleyera *Ternstroemia gymnanthera*	8 by 5 feet; evergreen.	Morning sun to part shade.	Slow growth; good for a hedge in part shade; new growth is burgundy; flowers not significant; best in acidic soils.

SHRUBS

Name	Size (H × W) and Type	Light	Flowers and Comments
Crapemyrtle *Lageratroemia indica*	1½ by 3 to 25 by 25 feet; deciduous.	Full sun.	Medium-green leaves, many bloom colors. Great as accents, speciments, and hedges.
Dwarf Yaupon *Ilex vomitoria* 'Nana'	3 by 3 feet; evergreen.	Sun to part shade.	Tough, widely planted shrub with small leaves and a neat growth habit; no berries are generally produced.
Fatsia *Fatsia japonica*	5 by 4 feet; evergreen.	Part shade to shade.	Large tropical leaves on a plant hardy to the mid- to low teens; striking large clusters of small white coral, flowers in early December.
Flowering Quince *Chaenomeles speciosa*	8 by 6 feet; deciduous.	Full to part sun.	Showy flowers in shades of red, pink, or white produced in late winter/early spring before the foliage; often called "Japonicas."
Gardenia *Gardenia jasminoides*	6 by 5 feet; evergreen.	Morning full to part sun.	Very fragrant, white flowers in May; some flowers in fall; acid-loving; watch for whiteflies.
Glossy Abelia *Abelia × grandiflora*	3 by 3 to 10 by 10 feet, depending on cultivar; semi-evergreen.	Full to part sun.	Long summer blooming season, small white flowers in clusters; pest-free; evergreen in all but the coldest winters.
Hydrangea *Hydrangea macrophylla*	4 by 4 feet; deciduous.	Part shade to shade; no afternoon sun.	Large, showy flower clusters in shades of blue, lavender, or pink in May; prune before the end of July; blue in acidic soils, pink in alkaline soils.
Indian Hawthorne *Raphiolepsis indica*	2 by 2 to 5 by 4 feet, depending on cultivar; evergreen.	Part sun to full sun.	Clusters of pink or white flowers in April. White cultivars generally more more resistant to fireblight; watch for scale.
Japanese Viburnum *Viburnum japonicum*	12 by 6 feet; evergreen.	Full sun to part shade.	Excellent hedge plant; watch for thrips during summer; flowers not significant.
Japanese Yew *Podocarpus macrophyllus*	15 by 6 feet; evergreen.	Full sun to part shade.	Useful as a hedge or screen; grows well in part shade; flowers not significant.
Junipers *Juniperus* spp. and cultivars	1 by 3 to 10 by 10 feet, depending on type; evergreen.	Full sun.	Large group of plants of various sizes and growth habits; full sun and good drainage are important; spider mites are common.
Mock Orange *Philadelphus coronarius*	10 by 6 feet; deciduous.	Full sun to part shade.	Large, arching branches produce showy fragrant, white flowers in late spring.

SHRUBS

Name	Size (H × W) and Type	Light	Flowers and Comments
Sweet Olive *Osmanthus fragrans*	15 by 10 feet; evergreen.	Full sun to part shade.	A "must have" for gardeners looking for fragrance; will slowly grow into a small tree; tiny, creamy white flowers are produced from fall to spring. Grow in zones 8b and 9.
Spirea, Bridal Wreath *Spirea × vanhoutei*	6 by 5 feet; deciduous.	Full to part sun.	Often planted where a smaller shrub would be a better choice; beautiful fountain of white flowers in April.
Virginia Willow *Itea virginica*	5 by 4 feet; deciduous.	Full sun to part shade.	Spikes of small white flowers in late spring and outstanding burgundy red fall foliage make this native shrub worth planting.
Wax-leaf Ligustrum *Ligustrum japonicum*	15 by 10 feet; evergreen.	Full sun to part shade.	Fast-growing shrub popular for hedges and screens; clusters of fragrant white flowers in summer. Grow in zones 8b and 9.

JANUARY

- This is a good month for planting and transplanting shrubs. They are as dormant as they will get this month and the weather is cool to cold and moist.

- If temperatures reach the low teens, some shrubs (such as certain varieties of azalea and pittosporum) may experience bark-splitting. Check your shrubs a week or two after a severe freeze.

- Should the weather be dry and mild, water newly planted shrubs as needed to maintain a moist soil. If a hard freeze is expected and the soil is dry, water thoroughly before the freeze arrives.

- Winter is an excellent time to apply horticultural oil sprays to shrubs that are prone to scale. These include camellias, hollies, magnolias, euonymus, privets, and cleyera.

- Some of the earliest-flowering shrubs, such as flowering quince, may bloom in January in south Texas. Cut a few branches and place in them in a vase.

FEBRUARY

- You might want to pay visits to nurseries or public gardens where you can see shrubs you are considering planting "in person." Once you see them, you might like them even better, or you may decide not to plant them.

- It would be great to finish up planting shrubs this month, giving them even more time to get established before hot weather arrives. They should be planted in well-prepared beds.

- February can have spells of bitter cold. Make sure shrubs are well-watered prior to a freeze if the ground is dry. Cover tender shrubs such as hibiscus or Mexican heather.

- It is still a little early for fertilizing most shrubs. Although some, like camellias, star magnolia, and flowering quince may be blooming, encouraging new growth with fertilizer may cause plants to be damaged by a late freeze.

MARCH

- Plan on getting your shrub planting finished up this month in south Texas. Don't panic. Shrubs may be planted from containers throughout the year, but they like it so much better when they have a chance to make some root growth before hot weather arrives.

- Check the mulch situation in your shrub beds. If it has broken down and gotten thin over time, now is a good time to replenish it. There is no need to remove the old mulch; just add new mulch on top of it—a 4-inch layer is recommended.

- This is the month to fertilize shrubs. Most respond well to 3:1:2 or 4:1:2 ratio fertilizers. Use slow-release granular fertilizer for good results.

- Apply aluminum sulfate around the roots of hydrangeas now if they are pink and you want them to be blue.

- Finish up pruning summer-flowering shrubs such as althea, oleander, vitex, and crapemyrtle by the end of this month.

APRIL

- Newly planted shrub beds may need to be watered once or twice a week if five to seven days pass without a good rain. These plants do not yet have well-established root systems and are very susceptible to drought stress.

- When you water shrubs, make sure the soil is moistened 4 to 6 inches down. If you use a soaker hose, make sure it passes within several inches of the base of each shrub in the bed.

- Fertilize now if you did not last month. Your shrubs can use the extra nutrients during the next six to eight weeks when they do much of their growing for the year.

- Insects become much more common as warmer weather settles in. Treat promptly before any damage becomes too severe. Spray, especially under the leaves, with appropriately labeled insect-control aids. Make applications every ten days until June. Follow label directions.

- Prune spring-flowering shrubs after they finish flowering.

MAY

- Although planting shrubs from containers may continue, increasingly stressful weather conditions mean that extra care will be needed. If you do plant now, do not disturb the root system, even if it is rootbound. Shrubs will not tolerate damage to their root systems when it is hot.

- Overcrowded shrub plantings can create stress through competition, and increased insect and disease problems may occur. In extreme cases, you may have to take out some to make room for the rest. Sometimes regular pruning can keep things from getting out of hand.

- As temperatures rise, shrubs absorb water faster from the soil. Those planted within the last six months need water once or twice a week in dry weather.

- This is a major month to prune spring-flowering shrubs that need it. About the only shrubs you wouldn't prune now are those that bloom in summer. Prune with a definite vision of what you are trying to accomplish.

JUNE

- Keep records about your shrubs in your Texas gardening journal: pest problems, treatments that were effective or ineffective, blooming times, when shrubs were planted, and where they were purchased are all valuable bits of information.

- Keep your summer-flowering shrubs tidy. Pull or trim off faded flowers as they occur. In the case of dwarf crape myrtles, oleanders, and others, trimming off the faded flowers will encourage more blooms to form.

- A shrub can pull all the water out of its rootball and get desperately thirsty even when the soil of the bed feels moist, so check the rootball rather than the soil to determine if it is dry.

- Control powdery mildew on your shrubs with fungus-control aids.

- Control whiteflies on gardenias, citrus trees, and any other shrubs with aids specifically labeled to control them. Follow label directions. Make three applications ten days apart, and spray during the cooler early-morning hours.

JULY

- Shrubs that always seem to have something wrong or need constant work to be kept attractive may not have been good choices. Decide if there is a problem that can be corrected, or plan to replace with lower-maintenance types this fall.

- Even well-established shrubs need to be watered if there is little rain. Because they are shallow-rooted, azaleas are one of the most drought-vulnerable shrubs we grow.

- You may fertilize established shrubs that were last fed in the spring. This is recommended for shrubs you want to grow as much and as fast as possible. This is not recommended for those that have already outgrown their space and need to be cut back frequently.

- Finish pruning spring-flowering shrubs this month. Do not prune camellias; their flowerbuds for fall and winter bloom are already set.

- Prune hedges as needed to keep them neat and thick.

AUGUST

- Late-summer stress can occasionally cause shrubs to drop some of their older leaves. This is generally not a major problem and no cause for alarm.

- Keep beds mulched to a depth of 3 to 4 inches. Not only does this help control weeds and conserve soil moisture, but it also helps prevent the soil from building up so much heat.

- August can be very hot and dry. Provide deep, thorough irrigation with sprinklers or soaker hoses. Water as needed if rain has not occurred in the last five to seven days for new plantings, in the last ten days for established plantings.

- Spider mites can be a problem on shrubs such as azaleas and junipers during hot, dry weather. The foliage will become faded and tan as they feed. Combat them with pest-control aids from your local retailers.

- Finish shearing hedges or pruning shrubs not grown for flowers.

SEPTEMBER

- Planning on planting some shrubs this fall? If we do get some beautiful cool weather and you feel like digging in the garden, go ahead and start preparing beds now for planting shrubs next month. Dig in generous amounts of organic matter.

- Now that the hottest weather is probably coming to an end, take time to evaluate the shrubs growing in your landscape. What would you do differently regarding pest control? Sometimes we decide to let a problem go untreated, then regret the decision when a lot of damage occurs. Make notes in your Texas gardening journal.

- Although temperatures may become milder, September weather can still be sweltering and dry. Apply water as needed to your shrub plantings to maintain a moist soil.

- This is usually the last month to fertilize shrubs in most of Texas. If you live in the Rio Grande Valley, fertilization may take place even later. Always apply fertilizers using label directions.

OCTOBER

- Shrub planting can begin this month, but there is no hurry. Take time to consider your needs and develop a plan for a landscape that will be attractive, functional, and successful.

- It's still too early to transplant, but you can begin to plant container-grown shrubs. Remember proper bed preparation.

- Although cooler, October can be one of our driest months. Established shrubs may not need much attention, but continue to water shrubs planted in the past year as needed if expected rainfall does not occur.

- Apply fertilizer during plant installation, but usually no fertilizer is applied to existing shrub plantings this month.

- Azalea lacebugs will be active through November. They feed from the underside of leaves, causing small white dots on the upper sides and dark brown spots on the back. Do not let a lot of damage occur before you treat.

NOVEMBER

- Planting shrubs in November or early December is particularly recommended. The weather is generally mild and pleasant,

and rainfall typical of our winters allows the new plantings to settle in and adjust with little stress (and less work for you).

- Plant shrubs in well-prepared beds. Avoid preparing beds and planting if the soil is wet. Wait a couple of days after a heavy rain before digging in the soil.

- If you notice scale on camellias, hollies, euonymus, or other plants, the cool season is an ideal time to treat with oil sprays. During cooler temperatures, heavier oils are safe to use.

- Be very cautious about what you prune and how. November can be relatively mild, and shrubs often do not get a strong signal to go dormant. Shearing or heading back shrubs might still stimulate growth, which is not a good idea just before winter.

DECEMBER

- If planted now, shrubs will have about five months to get established before dealing with high temperatures next summer. This makes them better prepared to survive their first Texas summer in the ground.

- Transplanting or moving shrubs in your landscape to a new location can also begin now. If you plan on moving a deciduous shrub, wait until it has dropped its leaves.

- In south Texas along the coast, gardeners often plant various tropical shrubs. The chance of severe injury or loss during cold winters makes it generally unwise to include too many tropicals in landscape plantings in most of the state.

- Water newly planted shrubs and those that have been transplanted if the weather turns dry and mild. Keep the soil moist.

- By mid-December, shrubs are pretty much dormant, and pruning them now will not stimulate new growth. Feel free to trim hedges and other shrubs, unless they bloom in the spring.

VINES
for Texas

No other plants can do what vines can do in the landscape. They are indispensable for growing up a pillar, covering an unattractive fence, softening architectural features, or creating screens. A vine-covered arbor provides a shady retreat.

Vines are a remarkably diverse group of plants. They include annuals and perennials and can be woody or herbaceous, evergreen or deciduous. Perennial vines are the most important group, as they become a permanent part of the landscape. Before you use them (and you really should), there are a couple of things you should understand about vines.

HOW THEY CLIMB

First, they're lazy. Rather than putting the considerable effort it takes into growing a strong stem, they use another plant or structure to provide support. Where does all that unused energy go? Into the fastest-growing plants in your landscape! You must be prepared for the extraordinary rate of growth of which vines are capable, and be willing to control them when necessary.

Second, vines climb in two distinct ways: by twining and by clinging. It is very important to know how a vine you want to use climbs.

Twining vines climb by wrapping their stems, leaves, or tendrils around a support. They must have string, wire, latticework, trellises, piles, or other support structures they can twist around.

Clinging vines can grow on flat surfaces by using roots along their stems, or "holdfasts." They are useful for covering the sides of buildings or walls without having to build a support.

CHOOSING A VINE

Vines are grown for their attractive foliage and colorful flowers. Some provide ornamental or edible fruit, and several produce fragrant flowers. When you determine a vine is needed in your landscape, the selection process is the same as for any plant. Decide on the characteristics you would like the vine to have, determine the growing conditions in the area where it will be planted, and choose the vine that most closely fits.

Finally, bear in mind that caring for vines involves controlling and training them more than anything else, as well as—on occasion—watering, fertilizing, and pest control.

CONSIDER THE NATIVES

If vines are your passion, a native vine with an exotic-looking blossom is the maypop or passionvine, *Passiflora incarnata*. At garden shows these actually stop traffic, as visitors inquire about them with a mixture of excitement and wonder.

For you hummingbird lovers, a platting of coral honeysuckle, *Lonicera sempervirens*, is highly recommended. They love this baby!

If you like wisteria, but are concerned about it taking over your landscape, try Texas wisteria, *Wisteria macrostachya*. It has wonderful flowers and is much easier to manage than the imported wisterias. This beauty works well on garden structures in the landscape including, but not limited to, arbors, pergolas, and arches.

SUPPORTS FOR VINES

Vines are versatile in our Texas landscapes, but can always be relied upon to contribute vertical interest for much of the year, depending on your selection.

Here are some ideas of ways to use vines:

On a fence: Whether it's to disguise an ugly fence or view, or just for decoration, many vines do very well on fences. Plant at the base and a little away, and train the vine up onto the fence.

On a house, shed, or other building: Be careful! A bad match may mean the vine straggles or damages a building, while a good match makes an enchanting sight. Choose the vine for this job with care and with an eye to how willing you are to intervene as needed to train or prune the growth.

On a tree: This is best done on a dead tree that you'd rather not remove, but still appears stable. Live trees can get choked by vigorous vines, or the vine may struggle to get the sunlight and air it

PASSION FLOWER

needs to thrive. In general, lighter-weight vines are best for this job.

On a trellis or lattice: Whether homemade or store-bought, a flat support can make a beautiful support for the right vine. Make sure the two are a good match, that the vine is not too vigorous or heavy for the support. Also be sure to anchor or secure the support very well—the earlier the better.

On an arch, arbor, or pergola: Flowering and fragrant vines are especially wonderful on these sorts of stylish supports. Again, make sure the vine is not too heavy for the support, and make sure the support is strong enough for the job. Access is also an issue—at times, you may have to climb a ladder to prune or to harvest flowers or fruit.

On the ground: Some vines with no handy support can make a decent groundcover. English ivy is often in this role, but Virginia creeper and wintercreeper can also do. This could be a good solution for a steep bank/embankment.

In a pot: Smaller and lighter vines can be very pretty in a large pot, provided they are in an appropriate location and support is close by or even inserted into the pot itself. Remember that potted plants dry out quickly; be diligent about watering a potted vine or it can wilt dramatically.

PLANTING

The best time to plant most vines is springtime. Prepare the spots by removing any unwanted plants (weeds or turf-grass), and turn over the soil. Add about 4 to 6 inches of organic matter, and thoroughly dig it in.

When you plant the vine, make sure the top of the rootball is even with the soil level, firm the soil around it, and water it in.

Apply a premium-quality, long-lasting, slow-release granular fertilizer. Mulch 3 to 4 inches deep around the plant to control weeds and conserve moisture.

Name	Size/Type	Light	Flowers and Comments
Carolina Yellow Jessamine *Gelsemium sempervirens*	to 20 feet; Evergreen, twining	Full sun to part shade	Yellow, fragrant flowers in late winter to early spring; one of the best vines; vigorous; prune regularly to control; native; hardy in all Texas zones except zone 6.
Chinese Wisteria *Wisteria sinensis*	to 50 feet; Deciduous, twining	Full to part sun	Dangling clusters of fragrant lilac-purple flowers in March–April; vigorous, rampant vine that must be carefully controlled; keep away from trees and houses.
Confederate Jasmine *Trachelospermum jasminoides*	to 20 to 60 feet; Evergreen, twining	Full sun to part shade	Very fragrant clusters of white flowers in early summer; may be severely damaged or killed by temperatures in the mid- to low teens; usually hardy in zones 8b and 9.
Coral Honeysuckle *Lonicera sempervirens*	15 to 20 feet; Evergreen, twining	Full to part sun	Clusters of tubular coral red flowers in spring to early summer and scattered through the year; attractive blue-green foliage; easy to control; native.
Crossvine *Bignonia capreolata*	to 50 feet; Semi-evergreen, twining	Part sun to part shade	Showy clusters of large tubular yellow and red flowers; large vine not suitable for a small trellis; native.
English Ivy *Hedera helix*	to 60 feet; Evergreen, clinging	Part sun to shade	Excellent clinging vine; flowers insignificant; many cultivars with different leaf shapes, sizes, and variegations. Root rot can be a problem in poorly drained locations.
Passion Vine *Passiflora incarnata*	to 20 feet; Deciduous, twining	Full morning to part sun	Dark-green 3- to 5-point leaves; exotic look; intricate blooms, pale to pinkish lavender with 3-inch-diameter fruits; native.
Texas Wisteria *Wisteria macrostachya*	to 20 feet; Deciduous, vigorous, robust	Full sun to shade	Sweet fragrance from grapelike clusters of lilac to bluish purple blooms; hardy statewide; native.
Virginia Creeper *Parthenocissus quinquefolia*	40 to 50 feet; Deciduous, climber	Full sun to shade	Large 5-part dark-green leaves changing to brilliant red in early fall; hardy statewide; native.

AKEBIA
Akebia quinata

Hardiness/Type—Hardy throughout Texas; evergreen

Color(s)—Purple, white

Bloom Period—Spring

Mature Height—Up to 25 ft.; twining

Water Needs—Once established, supplemental watering is rarely necessary.

Planting/Care—Plant in fall in mild zones so it can get established in the cool, moist winter weather. Start containerized ones in the summer. In a pot or in the ground, site in full to part sun; vines in too much shade do not bloom. Fertilization is not recommended—this plant can become invasive. Prune as needed during the summer to control growth and to train. Since it blooms on new growth, you can prune in late winter or early spring.

Pests/Diseases—None

Landscaping Tips & Ideas—Flower clusters hang downward, so the vine is particularly effective when used to cover an arbor over a sitting area. The edible fruit is seldom produced in cultivation.

BOSTON IVY
Parthenocissus tricuspidata

Hardiness/Type—Hardy throughout Texas (may struggle in coastal areas); deciduous

Color(s)—Fall foliage in orange and red

Bloom Period—Not applicable

Mature Height—Up to 40 ft.; clinging

Water Needs—Water as necessary to prevent soil dryness.

Planting/Care—Best planted in early spring or early fall. Performs best with morning sun and some shade from the hot, western afternoon sun. Mulch. You may feed once in early spring, but most vines are fast-growing, so do not overfertilize. Prune as necessary to shape and train. On walls, prune yearly to prevent it from growing into the wooden parts of your home.

Pests/Diseases—In late summer, spider mites may visit in hot, full-sun locations; consult your local garden center for controls.

Landscaping Tips & Ideas—Needs ample space. May be used as a groundcover, is excellent on trellises, and may also be grown directly on brick walls.

CAROLINA JESSAMINE
Gelsemium sempervirens

Hardiness/Type—Hardy in USDA Zones 7 to 9; evergreen

Color(s)—Yellow

Bloom Period—Late winter to early spring

Mature Height—Up to 20 ft.; twining

Water Needs—Water sufficiently to prevent soil dryness, especially in late summer.

Planting/Care—Plant in spring or fall, in full sun or shade (blooming is reduced in shady areas). Will grow in sandy, loamy, and clay soils, will tolerate damp conditions, and has moderate drought resistance. Mulch the root zone year-round. Fertilize regularly. Prune and train as necessary; growth is especially rapid in spring, so pay close attention to directing and training then.

Pests/Diseases—None serious

Landscaping Tips & Ideas—Grow on trellises or other large structures, tying to the support with elastic stretch ties. Does well in large tubs or planters on decks and balconies. May also be used to cover the ground and spill over slopes.

CLEMATIS

Clematis spp. and cultivars

Hardiness/Type—Hardy throughout Texas; deciduous

Color(s)—Purple, red, white, pink, blue, and bicolors

Bloom Period—Varies with species and variety

Mature Height—Up to 20 ft.; twining

Water Needs—Keep soil moist with regular watering.

Planting/Care—Plant in late winter or early spring when weather stress is reduced. Plants should receive full morning sun, but must escape the afternoon's cruel heat. An eastern exposure is preferred. Best in fertile, well-drained, alkaline soil. Mulch to keep roots cool and moist. Fertilize regularly. Pruning times vary with species/type; check with your nursery. Handle these fragile vines carefully when pruning. Tie to their support in the early stages of development.

Pests/Diseases—Consult your local garden centers for advice, should problems appear.

Landscaping Tips & Ideas—A wide range of colors and flower forms makes clematis a perfect accent for numerous annuals and perennials that favor morning sun.

CONFEDERATE STAR JASMINE

Trachelospermum jasminoides

Hardiness/Type—Hardy in USDA Zones 7b to 9; evergreen

Color(s)—White

Bloom Period—Spring

Mature Height—60 to 80 ft.; twining

Water Needs—Water as necessary to prevent soil dryness; drip irrigation is beneficial.

Planting/Care—Plant in early spring in a location that has moist, well-drained beds enriched with organic matter. Do not plant in full shade or in a spot that is difficult to water. Fertilize when new growth begins in spring. Prune and train as required to obtain desired effect.

Pests/Diseases—None

Landscaping Tips & Ideas—Outstanding fragrance, handsome dark-green foliage, fast-growing. Nice as a backdrop on growing structures or with lantana and ruellia planted below it. It's a good accent in a large container with a frame on decks, poolside, and on patios. It's a good choice for framing and accenting gates and entrances.

CORAL HONEYSUCKLE

Lonicera sempervirens

Hardiness/Type—Hardy throughout Texas; evergreen

Color(s)—Coral flowers; blue-gray-green foliage

Bloom Period—Spring and summer

Mature Height—Up to 20 ft.; twining

Water Needs—Water to prevent soil dryness, especially in late summer.

Planting/Care—Plant in early spring so it will have the entire growing season to establish itself. A preferred location would be an eastern exposure with shade from the hot afternoon sun. Mulch. If planted in deep, rich soil, fertilization is seldom necessary. Prune and train as necessary to reach desired goals; use elastic stretch ties to tie to a structure.

Pests/Diseases—None serious

Landscaping Tips & Ideas—If you like to have blooming plants that require minimal care but do not have a lot of square footage, try this plant on wires or upright structures. It also does well when allowed to weep over rock walls.

CORAL VINE
Antigonon leptopus

Hardiness/Type—Hardy in USDA Zones 8 and 9; deciduous

Color(s)—Pink, white

Bloom Period—Summer to fall

Mature Height—10 to 15 ft.; twining

Water Needs—While it is quite drought tolerant, it will appreciate an occasional long, deep drink of water.

Planting/Care—Plant in early spring after all danger of frost has passed, in improved, well-drained soil. (When planting seeds, make sure the soil temperature is above 70 degrees F.) Mulch. Fertilize regularly. Prune if necessary to train and direct its growth. It may freeze to ground level in the winter, to return in the spring. So it may be necessary to prune away winter kill.

Pests/Diseases—None

Landscaping Tips & Ideas—This beauty usually is not overpowering and can be utilized anywhere a tough blooming vine is desired. May be grown in a large container. Looks great as a backdrop for flower beds.

ENGLISH IVY
Hedera helix

Hardiness/Type—Hardy throughout Texas; evergreen

Color(s)—Evergreen foliage

Bloom Period—Not applicable

Mature Height—Up to 60 ft.; clinging

Water Needs—Water as necessary to maintain moist growing conditions.

Planting/Care—Plant in early spring or early fall. For best results, plant in well-prepared beds where it will receive morning sun and afternoon shade or dappled sun throughout the day. Mulch. Fertilize regularly. Prune as necessary to maintain and train.

Pests/Diseases—In high humidity or where air circulation is poor, bacterial leaf spot may visit. In hot, dry locations, spider mites may visit. Visit your local garden center for control possibilities.

Landscaping Tips & Ideas—May be grown as an espalier—trained by routine pruning in desired patterns and designs against a flat, vertical surface. Makes pleasing evergreen forms on many different types of structures, including trellises, arbors, fences, and archways. It is welcomed in cottage-type gardens.

FIG IVY
Ficus pumila

Hardiness/Type—Hardy in USDA Zones 8a to 9b; evergreen

Color(s)—Evergreen foliage

Bloom Period—Not applicable

Mature Height—Up to 40 ft.; clinging

Water Needs—Water as necessary to maintain a moist soil. Do not let it get totally dry, but do not keep it wet.

Planting/Care—Does best planted in early spring, especially in locations where its hardiness is marginal. Do not plant in total shade. For best results, start in well-prepared beds. Fertilize each spring when new growth begins. Prune to improve appearance, to encourage new growth, and to maintain desired direction of growth.

Pests/Diseases—None serious

Landscaping Tips & Ideas—Quite attractive as it clings neatly to its support, offering a green, vertical mat of fine-textured foliage. Outstanding on native stone walls, forming a wall covering. A good companion would be lantana.

HYACINTH BEAN
Lablab purpureus

Hardiness/Type—Tropical vine, grown as an annual

Color(s)—Lilac-purple flowers; purple seedpods

Bloom Period—Summer

Mature Height—6 to 10 ft.; twining

Water Needs—Maintain a moist soil throughout the growing season.

Planting/Care—Plant seeds directly into well-drained soil after danger of frost is past (planting indoors is not better than direct-seeding). Mulch. Supplemental feedings are seldom needed unless planted in poor soils (do not go overboard with fertilizing, however, or the plants will be all vine and no flowers or pods). Pinch or cut the plant to keep it within bounds.

Pests/Diseases—None serious

Landscaping Tips & Ideas—Make a good, tall garden backdrop. Also work well on fences to hide eyesores. Will grow up most anything by weaving their vines around and through the support system, similar to pole beans. The flower and pod clusters are great in flower arrangements.

JAPANESE HONEYSUCKLE
Lonicera japonica

Hardiness/Type—Hardy throughout Texas; evergreen

Color(s)—White, yellow, or purple

Bloom Period—Spring to fall

Mature Height—Up to 20 ft.; twining

Water Needs—Maintain a moist growing condition.

Planting/Care—Plant anytime, though early spring is best. Though adaptable, it does best in prepared beds. Mulch. Due to its fast rate of growth, it may not require fertilizer. Prune and train as necessary to achieve the form you desire.

Pests/Diseases—None

Landscaping Tips & Ideas—Because this plant is aggressive and can be invasive, plant it where it will have room to grow, be easy to maintain, yet not overgrow its location. It is outstanding in open, full-sun locations, planted by itself or on large structures. It thrives on large arbors, providing wonderful shade, fragrance, and blooms. It makes an excellent evergreen vertical screen. Do not plant on your home or trees.

MALABAR SPINACH
Basella rubra

Hardiness/Type—Grown as an annual

Color(s)—Red stems, dark green leaves

Bloom Period—Summer (very inconspicuous)

Mature Height—Up to 10 ft.; twining

Water Needs—Provide supplemental water during dry spells; the plants are not very drought-tolerant.

Planting/Care—Sow the seeds in spring after danger of frost is past (or start them indoors three or four weeks earlier). It takes about 60 days from sowing until you have some substantial, harvestable growth. Mulch, but avoid the stems. Fertilize regularly, but don't overdo. Trim to keep the plant growing to your desired shape and space.

Pests/Diseases—Rare, but watch for spider mites; local nurseries can advise you on controls.

Landscaping Tips & Ideas—This heat-loving annual vine hides unsightly areas or provides an upright backdrop. It grows easily on fences and provides ornamental qualities in the vegetable garden. (Only the young leaves are eaten.)

MAYPOP
Passiflora incarnata

Hardiness/Type—Hardy in USDA Zones 7 to 9; deciduous

Color(s)—Lavender-purple

Bloom Period—Summer

Mature Height—Up to 20 ft.; twining

Water Needs—Maintain a moist soil; prevent soil dryness.

Planting/Care—Plant in spring after all danger of frost is past, in well-drained soil. Mulch. Fertilize yearly, in spring, as new growth begins. Prune only as needed to achieve your training goal.

Pests/Diseases—Rare; if you happen to have problems, seek advice at local garden centers.

Landscaping Tips & Ideas—May be used with other vining plants, or at the back of screening-type shrubs that will allow the vine to grow up and above them. It will also grow on any structure, including fences, pergolas, gazebos, and lattice.

MORNING GLORY
Ipomoea purpurea

Hardiness/Type—Annual

Color(s)—White, purple, pink, red, blue, scarlet, and crimson

Bloom Period—Spring, summer, and fall to frost

Mature Size (H x W)—8 to 30 in. x to 12 ft. or more; twining

Water Needs—Water as necessary to prevent wilting.

Planting/Care—A well-drained location and sandy soils are preferred, with six hours of sun a day. Train a plant by tying the vine to a structure with a plastic stretch tie or nylon stocking. One application of rose fertilizer early in the spring is beneficial.

Pests/Diseases—Virtually pest- and disease-free. If grasshoppers or other pests visit your plants, take a trip to your local retailer for appropriate controls.

Landscaping Tips & Ideas—These plants are extremely useful for summertime flowering screens. They may be used on any type of structure such as trellises, mailboxes, gazebos, or fences, and are often used for quick shade on porches, or to shade hot, western exposures.

PORCELAIN VINE
Ampelopsis brevipedunculata

Hardiness/Type—Hardy in USDA Zones 6 and 7; deciduous

Color(s)—White flowers, followed by green to purple berries

Bloom Period—Spring to early summer

Mature Height—10 to 20 ft.; twining

Water Needs—Provide supplemental irrigation during severe droughts.

Planting/Care—Plant as a dormant plant in early spring, or as a containerized plant in late spring or early summer. Some afternoon shade is welcome. It adapts to poor soils, which are sometimes better for keeping the plant under control. Feed only sparingly. Prune in summer to keep the vine within the confines of its support system. Dormant pruning should not include too much one-year-old wood or stems.

Pests/Diseases—In heavy shade, look for the occasional aphid and mildew.

Landscaping Tips & Ideas—Use it for arbors, fences, pergolas, and trellises. Grow on a fence in the garden to attract birds and pollinators.

TRUMPET VINE
Campsis radicans

Hardiness/Type—Hardy throughout Texas; deciduous

Color(s)—Orange-scarlet

Bloom Period—Summer into fall

Mature Height—Up to 30 ft.; twining

Water Needs—Keep the soil moist during establishment, but afterwards, natural rain should suffice.

Planting/Care—Plant in early winter to early spring. It tolerates just about any soil type, and prefers full sun. Fertilize early in the growing season. You may prune it occasionally to confine it to desired spaces. Do any required pruning in late winter. Roots invading shrub areas and flower beds must be dug up and removed; cutting deep roots is only a temporary measure, as suckers will form. The vine is self-clinging.

Pests/Diseases—Seldom enough to warrant control

Landscaping Tips & Ideas—If there's a bare fence around that could use a touch of color, consider this location for trumpet vine. Because it is so aggressive, beware of planting it too near other trees, shrubs, or flowers. In rural areas, it enhances the appearance of barns, sheds, and other such structures.

VIRGINIA CREEPER
Parthenocissus quinquefolia

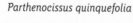

Hardiness/Type—Hardy throughout Texas; deciduous

Color(s)—Red fall foliage; blue berries

Bloom Period—Summer (inconspicuous)

Mature Height—Up to 50 ft.; clinging

Water Needs—Water during establishment; after that, water occasionally to prevent soil dryness.

Planting/Care—Plant in spring or early fall. It will grow in virtually any type of Texas soil, including clay and sand, as long as the soil is well-drained. Fertilization is usually not required. Prune to maintain desired shape and size.

Pests/Diseases—None

Landscaping Tips & Ideas—When used as a vine covering a large garden structure or cottage, it will provide shade in the summer and gorgeous color in the fall, and it will allow sunlight in during the winter. Can also be used in expansive areas, under trees, as a thick groundcover, and allowed to weep over stone walls.

WISTERIA
Wisteria sinensis

Hardiness/Type—Hardy throughout Texas; deciduous

Color(s)—Blue, purple, white, and rose

Bloom Period—Spring

Mature Height—Up to 35 ft.; twining

Water Needs—Water as needed to prevent soil dryness.

Planting/Care—The best time to plant is early fall. It grows well in full sun or dappled sun/shade, in most soils. Best results are achieved in well-prepared beds on strong structures. No fertilization is usually required. Prune to keep it from taking over other plants in confined locations. In alkaline soils, yellow (chlorotic) leaves may occur; apply iron and sulphur as needed to correct this situation.

Pests/Diseases—None serious

Landscaping Tips & Ideas—Because wisteria has been known to literally take over other plantings, plant it on strong structures that are separate in the landscape, such as a freestanding arbor. It is elegant in a large planter, too. 'Purpurea' is great for fragrance and color.

WISTERIA

JANUARY

- Virtually all the hardy perennial vines can be planted or transplanted this month.

- Do not prune spring-blooming vines now, or you will reduce or eliminate their flowers.

FEBRUARY

- Water newly planted, transplanted, or divided vines thoroughly when they go in the ground.

- Thoroughly irrigate existing plantings throughout the month as needed.

- Keep an eye out for scale insects on various vines. Spray with a dormant or lightweight horticultural oil or other scale-control aid.

MARCH

- There are wonderful vines available at local nurseries. Here, we can look at each plant "in person" before purchasing and choosing individual plants if desired.

- Plant vines this month. Prepare the spots by removing any unwanted plants (weeds or turfgrass) and turn over the soil. Add about 4 to 6 inches of organic matter and thoroughly dig it in.

- When you plant a vine, make sure the top of the rootball is even with the soil level, firm the soil around it, and water it in.

- After planting a new vine, apply a slow-release granular fertilizer, then mulch 3 to 4 inches deep around the plant to control weeds and conserve soil moisture.

- Water new plantings as needed to maintain a moist soil, especially those in full sun.

- Fertilize vines moderately and only if you need to stimulate new growth.

- Carolina jessamine should be finished blooming by now. Trim it back if necessary.

APRIL

- Give vines a try this season as container plantings. Look around your landscape for places where a container would make a nice addition, such as patios, porches, or decks. Vines will need some sort of support.

- If you use a vine to cover a fence or trellis and want it to be full at the bottom, this can be a problem. When you plant, weave the long stems horizontally along the lower portion of the fence or trellis. As the vine grows upwards, continue to weave it back and forth through the support.

- When it reaches the top of its support, don't just cut it off. Take the ends of the vine and weave them back downward.

- Fertilizing vines is optional and not recommended if they have a history of vigorous growth.

- Prune spring-flowering vines such as Carolina jessamine and wisteria after they finish flowering.

MAY

- Walk through your landscape as often as you can. Using snips or handpruners, stop and lightly prune vines.

- Established vines are often included in beds with other plant materials. If you water them enough to keep the other plants happy, the vines should be happy, too.

- Vines don't usually need much fertilizer, but if you are trying to stimulate growth, they can be fertilized.

- Watch for disease and insect problems. Aphids may show up on the new growth of many kinds of vines. If present, caterpillars are only a minor problem. Control aids are available at local retailers.

- Vines that we use as groundcovers (such as Asian jasmine and English ivy) don't have the good sense to stop at the edge of their beds and will grow out onto sidewalks or other areas they are not wanted. Prune back the edges of those plantings occasionally.

JUNE

- Evaluate how well vines are growing on the support provided for them. Whether the vine is trained on an arch, fence, pole, trellis, or latticework—is it turning out as you intended? If there are problems, decide on a solution.

- Replace a weak or inadequate support, if practical, with one that is stronger or larger.

- Prune a vine regularly to keep it the size and shape desired.

- Some vines will be under tremendous stress as the weather grows hotter. They may need to be watered every day. Check them often and water as needed.

- Hot, muggy weather and lots of rain make diseases worse this time of year. Leaf spot diseases caused by various fungal organisms can attack. Trim off any badly damaged foliage and spray with your selected pest-control aid according to label directions.

- Wisteria is a very heavy vine; make sure you have adequate support for it.

JULY

- Record information on the performance of your vine plants in your Texas gardening journal. It is the best way to avoid repeating past mistakes and helps you do a better job of caring for your plants.

- Water is especially critical this time of year. Most established plantings can get by with an occasional deep watering when the weather is dry. Recent plantings should be watered thoroughly whenever a week passes without rain.

- Some vines, such as coral honeysuckle, bloom sporadically during the summer. The more you snip these, the fewer flowers you will have. Rather than trimming off shoots, try weaving them back into the main part of the vine or the support.

AUGUST

- Vines planted this season may grow slowly, then speed up as they become better established.

- If you watch the trellis disappear under a mound of green foliage, and tendrils are reaching for you as you walk by, it's time to do some serious pruning.

- Proper watering is critical during this time of year. Morning is the best time, so that plants will be well-supplied going into the hottest time of the day.

- Vines that bloom in the spring, such as wisteria and Carolina jessamine, need time to grow and set flowerbuds before winter. Avoid much pruning after this.

SEPTEMBER

- September can be hot and dry, so continue to water when necessary. When watering, do a thorough job. Water deeply and occasionally rather than lightly every day.

- Pests have had all summer to build up population levels. Inspect your vines frequently, and spray only infested plants.

- Minimize pruning now to avoid flushes of new growth. Remove excessively long shoots from vines but do not shear back the whole plant.

OCTOBER

- October begins the fall-planting season, especially for hardy perennial vines. Prepare the area well beforehand, including digging in plentiful organic matter.

- The weather may be dry and mild to hot some years, so watch the weather and water if needed.

- Keep pruning to a minimum. Any pruning done now to spring-flowering vines will reduce the number of flowers next spring.

NOVEMBER

- Deciduous vines like wisteria will begin to look tired, and the foliage will begin to die before it drops.

- Continue to plant hardy perennial vines. They will not grow over the winter, but they will send out new roots and get existing roots established. As a result, they will outgrow plants that are planted next spring and have to be tended so much next summer.

- If you planted one of the more tender tropical vines such as mandevilla, allamanda, or bougainvillea, you now have three choices. The first is to let winter do what it will. Plant new ones next spring if they don't make it through the winter. The second choice is to mulch them thickly over their roots and lower stem. The third is to dig them up, pot them, and try overwintering them indoors.

- Check vines for the presence of scale insects, and control if needed.

DECEMBER

- You can plant hardy perennial vines throughout the winter, but early December is an especially good time. The weather is still generally mild, and the soil is warm from summer. If planted now, plants will make strong root growth and be ready to grow vigorously next spring and summer. The weather conditions over the next several months mean you can just about water them in and walk away.

- Cut back the dead growth of vines after freezes kill them back. Put some mulch over the roots to protect them from the cold.

- Water in newly planted or transplanted vines; then water as needed to maintain a moist soil.

- No fertilizing is required until next spring.

TREES
for Texas

Trees are a vital part of most landscapes. They provide shade, privacy, windbreaks, fruit or nuts, and flowers, and can increase real-estate value as well. Select them carefully. They will be around for a long time. Proper placement is very important, as mistakes are not easily corrected later on when trees are large.

PLANNING

There is no one perfect tree for all of Texas. Trees have advantages and disadvantages, depending on their planting locations and desired characteristics. Here are some points you need to consider:

1. Select a tree that will mature at a size right for its site. This cannot be stressed enough. Planting trees that will grow too large for their locations is one of the most common mistakes people make (along with planting too many trees). Generally, small trees are those that grow from 15 to 25 feet tall, medium-size trees grow from 30 to 55 feet tall, and large trees are those that grow 60 feet or taller.

2. Think about the purpose of the tree and why you feel it is needed. This will help you determine what characteristics the tree should have, such as its shape, size, and rate of growth. Ornamental features such as flowers, attractive berries, brightly colored fall foliage, or unusual bark should also be considered.

3. Decide if you want a tree that retains its foliage year-round (evergreen) or loses its leaves in the winter (deciduous). Deciduous trees are particularly useful where you want shade in the summer and sun in the winter.

4. Choose trees that are well-adapted to our growing conditions. They must be able to tolerate long, hot summers and mild/cold winters. A number of northern species of beech, maple, conifers, and others you might see in catalogs are often unsuitable for our state. Trees that are not completely hardy are not good choices either.

5. Check the location of overhead power lines, and if you must plant under them, use small, low-growing trees. Consider underground water lines and septic tanks as well as walks, drives, and paved surfaces that may be damaged by the roots of large trees. Locate large trees at least 15 to 25 feet away from your house.

PLANTING AND TRANSPLANTING

Planting trees properly can make the difference between success and failure. Whether the tree is balled-and-burlapped or container-grown, dig the hole at least twice the diameter of the rootball, and no deeper than the height of the rootball.

Remove the tree from the container and place it gently in the hole. A rootball tightly packed with thick, encircling roots indicates a rootbound condition. Try to unwrap or open up or even cut some of the roots to encourage them to spread into the surrounding soil. Once the tree is in the hole, remove any nylon twine or wire supports that may have been used, and fold down the burlap from the top of the rootball. The top of the rootball should be level with or slightly above the surrounding soil. It is critical that you do not plant the tree too deep.

Thoroughly pulverize the soil dug out from the hole and use this soil, without any additions, to backfill around the tree. Add soil around the tree until the hole is half-full, then firm the soil to eliminate air pockets—but do not pack it tight.

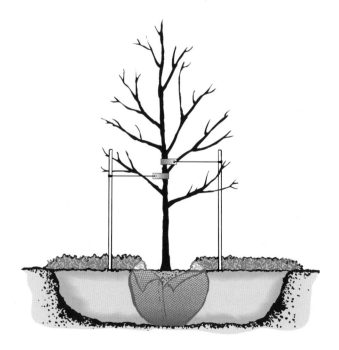

Finish filling the hole, firm again, and then water the tree thoroughly to settle it in. Generally, we do not add fertilizer to the planting hole. The use of a root-stimulating solution is optional.

If the tree is tall enough to be unstable, it should be staked—otherwise, it's not necessary. Do not drive the stake into place directly against the trunk and then tie the tree to it. Two or three stakes should be firmly driven into the ground just beyond the rootball. Tie cloth strips, old nylon stockings, or wire (covered with a piece of garden hose where it touches the trunk) to the stakes and then to the trunk of the tree. Leave the support in place no more than nine to twelve months.

CARING FOR YOUR TREES

Keep the area one or two feet out from the trunk of a newly planted tree mulched and free from weeds and grass. This will encourage the tree to establish faster by eliminating competition from grass roots. It also prevents lawn mowers and string trimmers from damaging the bark at the

JAPANESE MAPLE

base of the tree, which can cause stunting or death. The mulch should be about four inches deep.

People tend to think of established trees as almost indestructible. Trees do not need a great deal of care compared to other plants in the landscape, but they do occasionally need water, fertilizer, and pest control.

Perhaps the greatest threat to trees is people. A common conception is that tree roots are located deep in the soil and so are well-protected from damage. Actually, tree roots are remarkably shallow. The majority of the root system responsible for absorbing water and minerals is located in the upper eighteen inches of soil, and it spreads out at least twice as far as the branches. As a result, many people damage or kill their trees in a variety of ways. Tree roots are vulnerable to damage from soil compaction caused by excessive foot traffic or vehicular traffic. Whether building a new home on a lot with existing trees, an addition to an existing home, or a new patio, construction work kills lots of trees. Even repairing driveways, sidewalks, and streets may cause extensive damage to tree roots. If filling is needed, no more than two inches of fill per year should be spread over a tree's root system.

WATERING

Water a newly planted or transplanted tree whenever the soil is dry. This is the single most important thing you can do to ensure its survival, especially during the first summer after planting. To properly water a tree in its first year, turn a hose on trickle and lay the end on top of the ground within six inches of the trunk. Let the water trickle for about 30 to 45 minutes. This should be done as needed during hot, dry weather.

Older, established trees rarely have to be watered, but exceptionally dry weather during the months of July, August, and September may place enough stress on trees to make watering necessary. Lawn sprinklers are good devices for watering the expansive root systems of established trees. Set the sprinkler to apply about an inch of water, and water about once a week until sufficient rain occurs.

FERTILIZING

In the first five to ten years after planting, young trees can be encouraged to grow significantly faster if fertilized annually. Older trees can be fertilized less often. In fact, for older trees with good vigor, color, and rate of growth, fertilization is optional.

Trees are generally fertilized in late February in south Texas in anticipation of growth beginning in February or March. In north Texas, fertilize two to four weeks later.

PEST CONTROL

Although they require less pest control than other plants in the landscape, trees do occasionally have pest problems that need to be controlled. The best trees are relatively free from pest problems or will not be badly damaged or killed by pests that do attack them. This is fortunate, as the average gardener does not have the proper equipment to spray a large tree.

When selecting a tree for your landscape and before purchasing, be sure you are familiar with its potential pest problems: how serious they tend to be and how often they are likely to occur.

REDBUD

PRUNING

For a variety of reasons, virtually all trees are pruned at some time. Lower branches are gradually removed from a young, growing tree to lift its canopy to an appropriate height. Dead or diseased branches should occasionally be removed. Fruit trees are pruned in a variety of specialized forms. Problems with poorly placed branches or an unattractive shape may need to be fixed.

Pruning needs to be done correctly. Except for certain types of fruit trees, pruning is generally kept to a minimum, but should certainly not be avoided when necessary.

PRUNING EXAMPLES

Open center for peaches

Central leader for apples

227

ARBORVITAE
Thuja occidentalis

Hardiness—Hardy throughout Texas

Color(s)—Evergreen foliage

Bloom Period—Not applicable

Mature Size (H x W)—3 to 40 ft. x 3 to 15 ft.

Water Needs—Water as needed to maintain sufficient moisture for growth (a drip irrigation system is ideal).

Planting/Care—Plant any time of the year. It grows in all Texas soils, including loose blow sand and compact clay. A full-sun location is best. Mulch. Fertilize regularly. May be sheared into all sorts of shapes.

Pests/Diseases—Juniper blight, spider mites, and bagworms are more of a problem on Oriental than on Eastern varieties. The gardening aid industry has products to help control these.

Landscaping Tips & Ideas—Use as tall screening, windbreak, or specimen plantings. Not for use as foundation plantings, and they don't work well with companion plants.

BALD CYPRESS
Taxodium distichum

Hardiness—Hardy throughout Texas

Color(s)—Fall foliage is copper to bronze

Bloom Period—Spring, nonshowy

Mature Size (H x W)—50 to 100 ft. x 20 to 50 ft.

Water Needs—Maintain a moist-to-damp soil.

Planting/Care—Fall is the best planting time; early spring is second best. Prefers moist, full-sun areas, but will grow in any standard lawn area. Don't plant in areas that are dry, difficult to water, or shady. Mulch. Temporary staking may be required. Responds with vigor to regular fertilizing. No pruning required.

Pests/Diseases—None serious

Landscaping Tips & Ideas—If you want a tree in an area that is both sunny and a bit damp, this is a great choice. Needs room to grow—spacing of 25 to 50 feet may be necessary to obtain an attractive result. Will adapt to street plantings and confined urban areas.

CEDAR
Juniperus virginiana

Hardiness—Hardy throughout Texas

Color(s)—Evergreen foliage

Bloom Period—Summer (nonshowy blooms)

Mature Size (H x W)—20 to 40 ft. x 20 to 30 ft.

Water Needs—Requires minimal water (even when the tree is establishing itself).

Planting/Care—Plant in fall or early spring. Will grow in all types of Texas soil, as long as it is well-drained. Mulch. Responds well to regular fertilizing. Prune in spring; don't severely prune branches that have no foliage or they will fail to produce new foliage.

Pests/Diseases—Spider mites, bagworms, juniper scale or blight, and cedar apple rust are potential problems. Consult your local garden centers for help.

Landscaping Tips & Ideas—Good for windbreaks, privacy screens, and as a specimen. Groundcovers may be used in their shadow. Cedars are good transitional plants to unify natural plantings and more formal groupings.

CEDAR ELM
Ulmus crassifolia

Hardiness—Hardy throughout Texas

Color(s)—Yellow fall leaves

Bloom Period—Spring (nonshowy)

Mature Size (H x W)—60 to 80 ft. x 40 to 50 ft.

Water Needs—Water to prevent soil dryness—especially during the two-year establishment period.

Planting/Care—Plant in fall or very early spring. If you buy a tree larger than 20 gallons (or in a very large ball), have a landscape contractor plant it for you. Add no soil amendments. Construct a berm to hold water. Stake temporarily to prevent top movement. Mulch. Begin regular fertilizing after the first year. Prune to shape in very early spring.

Pests/Diseases—Elm leaf beetles may visit but are not a big problem.

Landscaping Tips & Ideas—A prime location is on the west side of your home, where it will provide shade in summer but allow warming sun in the winter months.

CHINESE PISTACHIO
Pistacia chinensis

Hardiness—Hardy throughout Texas

Color(s)—Vivid fall foliage

Bloom Period—Spring (nonshowy)

Mature Size (H x W)—20 to 40 ft. x 20 to 30 ft.

Water Needs—Water as needed, and especially in July and August.

Planting/Care—Plant container-grown plants in fall or early spring, in any sunny location. Mulch. Fertilize regularly. Pruning may be desired when the tree is young in order to train its growth, but is usually unnecessary after this early stage.

Pests/Diseases—None

Landscaping Tips & Ideas—Will grow in confined or hot areas. Due to its size and deep roots, you may plant it close to your home, but allow enough room for it to reach its normal form. It offers light shade that will allow you to grow other plants—like St. Augustine grass—beneath it. Use as a single accent or in a line planting or informal natural grouping.

DOGWOOD
Cornus florida

Hardiness—Hardy throughout Texas

Color(s)—White, red, and pink flowers; red/orange fall foliage

Bloom Period—Spring

Mature Size (H x W)—20 to 30 ft. x 25 ft.

Water Needs—Water to prevent soil dryness. Because of their shallow root systems, dogwoods cannot tolerate dry soil for prolonged periods.

Planting/Care—Plant in early fall or early spring from containers, in well-drained soil. Mulch. Fertilize once in spring when new growth begins and once in fall. Prune to shape in early spring after blooming.

Pests/Diseases—Should leaf spot, borers, or other insects or diseases become a problem, visit your local garden center for controls.

Landscaping Tips & Ideas—Group several dogwoods together in a multiple planting, perhaps beneath some taller-growing oak trees or elms. Or plant in a patio area near your home, near garden structures, or on your landscape's border.

FLOWERING PEAR
Pyrus calleryana

Hardiness—Hardy throughout Texas

Color(s)—White flowers; glorious fall foliage

Bloom Period—Spring

Mature Size (H x W)—30 to 50 ft. x 20 to 40 ft.

Water Needs—Water to establish, and provide extra water in July and August.

Planting/Care—Plant in fall or early spring, in sunny locations with fertile, well-drained, moist soil. Mulch. Fertilize at least in early spring and in fall, and more often if your tree is growing in challenging conditions or poor soil. Prune to ensure strong branch/limb structure (failure to do so can lead to splitting in an ice storm).

Pests/Diseases—None serious

Landscaping Tips & Ideas—Line a property entrance, driveway, or use as a street tree (acceptable in urban lots). Utilize as a single specimen, as accent plants, in formal line plantings or groupings, and in Japanese gardens.

FLOWERING CRABAPPLE
Malus spp.

Hardiness—Hardy throughout Texas

Color(s)—White, pink, red, and blends; small fruits are red to red-orange

Bloom Period—Spring

Mature Size (H x W)—10 to 25 ft. x 15 to 30 ft.

Water Needs—Provide supplemental water during July and August.

Planting/Care—Plant in fall or early spring. They grow best in deep, fertile, moist soils. Mulch, and provide temporary staking if needed. Fertilize three times a year. Prune to shape in spring after blooms drop.

Pests/Diseases—Maintaining a healthy tree is the best way to prevent fire blight, powdery mildew, and apple scab; if these problems occur, consult local retailers.

Landscaping Tips & Ideas—Plant in rows along drives or walkways in groups of three or more. In a triangular pattern, they are great for sunny corners. Great near decks and gazebos with plantings of annuals or perennials.

GINKGO
Ginkgo biloba

Hardiness—Hardy throughout Texas

Color(s)—Lemon/golden yellow fall foliage

Bloom Period—Spring (nonshowy)

Mature Size (H x W)—50 to 70 ft. x 20 to 50 ft.

Water Needs—Water during establishment. Provide long, slow, deep drinks during July and August.

Planting/Care—Plant in fall or spring, ideally in deep, fertile, moist soil in full sun. It will tolerate (though grow slowly) in a wide range of urban conditions. Mulch. Fertilize regularly starting in its second year. Pruning is rarely needed.

Pests/Diseases—None

Landscaping Tips & Ideas—An outstanding lawn tree and a knockout in the fall once maturity is reached. Best as a stand-alone specimen; make sure there is ample room. Plant one near the street so everyone passing by may enjoy it. Ginkgos may be used in large planters and in Japanese gardens.

GOLDEN RAIN TREE
Koelreuteria paniculata

Hardiness—Hardy throughout Texas

Color(s)—Yellow blooms; pink to mauve seedpods; golden fall foliage

Bloom Period—Spring

Mature Size (H x W)—20 to 40 ft. x 20 to 35 ft.

Water Needs—Water to prevent dry soil, especially in July and August.

Planting/Care—Plant in fall or spring. They will grow in a wide range of Texas soils, but prefer loose, moist, fertile soils. Don't plant in poorly drained areas or in spots that are difficult to water. Mulch, and provide temporary staking if necessary. Fertilize regularly. Prune when young to ensure strong branching.

Pests/Diseases—Box elder bugs may appear in the fall; local retailers offer control possibilities.

Landscaping Tips & Ideas—Wonderful in areas where space is limited. Works well along the sides of walkways and driveways of single-story homes or small urban lots.

GREEN ASH
Fraxinus pennsylvanica

Hardiness—Hardy throughout Texas

Color(s)—Golden yellow fall foliage

Bloom Period—Spring (nonshowy)

Mature Size (H x W)—40 to 70 ft. x 30 to 50 ft.

Water Needs—Water as needed to prevent soil dryness, especially in July and August.

Planting/Care—Plant in fall or spring in deep, moist, non-heavy clay, in a soil pH of 6.5 to 7.5. Mulch and stake. Apply root stimulator during the first year. Begin regular fertilizing in the second season. In very late winter, remove dead growth.

Pests/Diseases—Borers may visit unhealthy trees.

Landscaping Tips & Ideas—Give it room to spread. If you have a septic system, plant 20 feet or more from your field lines to prevent the roots from plugging them. For maximum cooling effects, site on your home's west side. Best utilized as a stand-alone specimen.

JAPANESE MAPLE
Acer palmatum

Hardiness—Hardy throughout Texas

Color(s)—Red or red-orange fall foliage

Bloom Period—Spring (nonshowy)

Mature Size (H x W)—2 to 20 ft. x 3 to 20 ft.

Water Needs—Keep the soil moist during the growing season.

Planting/Care—Plant in early fall or very early spring, in acidic soil. Maintain a year-round mulch. Fertilize regularly. Prune only to remove dead or damaged branches.

Pests/Diseases—Aphids may visit new growth. Tip growth may suffer freeze damage if exposed to severe cold.

Landscaping Tips & Ideas—In most Texas locations where there are spring azalea and/or spring flower trails, this tree adds extra excitement. It's a real knockout interplanted with pink dogwood. Plant in groups under the canopies of tall shade trees. Make outstanding accent plants. May be grown in containers, as bonsai, and in Japanese gardens. Spectacular with beds around them.

LACEBARK ELM
Ulmus parvifolia

Hardiness—Hardy throughout Texas

Color(s)—Pale yellow fall foliage

Bloom Period—Early spring (nonshowy)

MATURE SIZE (H x W)

40 to 60 ft. x 30 to 50 ft.

Water Needs—Water if needed to maintain vigor; young trees may need supplemental water in July and August.

Planting/Care—Plant in fall, winter, or early spring. Tolerates poor soils, including deep sand or heavy clay. Does best in deep, moist soil. Site away from landscape beds (at least 30 feet), due to the invasive, shallow, fibrous roots. Mulch. Fertilize annually. Prune to remove dead twigs at any time.

Pests/Diseases—Aphids may visit new growth.

Landscaping Tips & Ideas—A fast-growing shade tree in Texas. It will grow almost anywhere, including parking areas, street plantings, and confined locations. Makes a dense canopy of wonderful summertime shade.

LEYLAND CYPRESS
x Cupressocyparis leylandii

Hardiness—Hardy throughout Texas

Color(s)—Evergreen foliage

Bloom Period—Not applicable

Mature Size (H x W)—20 to 40 ft. x 15 to 20 ft.

Water Needs—Drought tolerant once established. Give a deep, slow drink in July and August.

Planting/Care—Plant in fall, winter, or spring. Prefers well-drained, relatively loose, fertile, moist soils. Mulch. Fertilize regularly. Prune in spring to maintain desired shape.

Pests/Diseases—Bagworms may visit; they may be handpicked off and disposed of; visit your local retailers for additional options.

Landscaping Tips & Ideas—Don't attempt to use as foundation plants, but do use as specimens or accents. Excellent as a wind, privacy, or noise screen. Because of its soft foliage, may be used near pedestrian traffic. In very wide beds, use groundcovers if shade is too heavy to grow grass under the tree's foliage.

MIMOSA
Albizia julibrissin

Hardiness—Hardy throughout Texas

Color(s)—Pink, rose-red

Bloom Period—Summer

Mature Size (H x W)—230 to 40 ft. x 30 to 40 ft.

Water Needs—Provide supplemental water during establishment.

Planting/Care—Plant in early fall or early spring, in well-drained, fertile, moist soil. Mulch and, if necessary, stake. Fertilize regularly. Prune young trees to encourage strong branching. Don't perform radical pruning of limbs on a yearly basis—this is harmful to the tree's long-term health and life span.

Pests/Diseases—Aphids and their secretions can be a problem. Mimosa webworms may visit. There are several controls available at your local retailer.

Landscaping Tips & Ideas—Don't plant near landscape beds because of large crops of mimosa seedlings. Provide space between a pool, deck, or gazebo and a mimosa to avoid fallen blooms. Use to line both sides of driveways and around yard structures.

OAK
Quercus spp.

Hardiness—Hardy throughout Texas

Color(s)—Fall foliage can be colorful.

Bloom Period—Spring (nonshowy)

Mature Size (H x W)—20 to 100 or more ft. x 15 to 80 ft.

Water Needs—Provide supplemental water during establishment, and give a long, slow drink in July or August.

Planting/Care—Plant anytime in deep, fertile, well-drained soil. Trees in containers larger than 20 gallons should be planted by a contractor. Mulch, and stake if necessary. Oaks respond with vigor to regular fertilizing, especially in their early years. Prune to train, thin, or correct, and remove dead limbs as needed.

Pests/Diseases—May have leaf galls or aphids. Some variet-ies such as pin or water oak are vulnerable to mistletoe.

Landscaping Tips & Ideas—Oaks are great as specimens, yard trees, or shade trees. Allow sufficient space from structures, driveways, and walkways based on their normal spread.

PALM, CALIFORNIA FAN
Washingtonia filifera

Hardiness—Hardy in USDA Zones 8 and 9

Color(s)—Grayish-green evergreen foliage

Bloom Period—Not applicable

Mature Size (H x W)—30 to 45 ft. x 5 to 15 ft.

Water Needs—Water to prevent soil dryness during establishment; drought tolerant when established.

Planting/Care—Plant in early spring after any possible frost date, or in early summer. Well-drained soil is required. Have large plants put in by a contractor. Mulch, and stake temporarily if needed. Fertilize twice a year. Remove dead leaves/fronds.

Pests/Diseases—No serious pests. To prevent root rot and suffocation, make sure your selected planting location drains well.

Landscaping Tips & Ideas—Because they are dominant landscape plants, place carefully or they may overpower your garden. Use for lining driveways, framing structures, as specimens, or in groups. Do well in containers or planters. Good as accents in swimming pool areas or entry courts.

PECAN
Carya illinoiensis

Hardiness—Hardy throughout Texas

Color(s)—Yellow fall foliage

Bloom Period—Spring (nonshowy)

Mature Size (H x W)—60 to 125 ft. x 100 ft.

Water Needs—Prevent soil dryness; drip irrigation works well.

Planting/Care—Plant in the fall or early spring, in deep, well-drained soil. Don't plant in shallow or rocky soil. Mulch, and stake temporarily if necessary. Fertilize annually. Prune to maintain strong branching. Remove deadwood.

Pests/Diseases—Potential problems include pecan scab, aphids, webworms, and casebarer. Ask your local cooperative extension office for a recommended spray schedule for pecans.

Landscaping Tips & Ideas—Plant where they will have sufficient room to grow. Space away from driveways, pools, your home, and other structures. Discuss which variety you should choose with your local nursery.

PINE
Pinus spp.

Hardiness—Hardy throughout Texas

Color(s)—Evergreen foliage

Bloom Period—Spring (nonshowy)

Mature Size (H x W)—20 to 125 ft. x 15 to 70 ft.

Water Needs—Water as necessary, especially during establishment.

Planting/Care—Plant in early fall, or early spring. Depending on the variety, pine trees will grow in light and sandy soils to heavy clay soils—make a match with your yard's conditions. Mulch, and stake temporarily if necessary. Fertilize regularly. Prune to remove deadwood and maintain desired shape.

Pests/Diseases—If pine bark beetles or pine tip moths appear, ask your local garden center for controls.

Landscaping Tips & Ideas—Placement, including proximity to your home, depends on the ultimate height and width of the tree you choose. Some tall-growing pines can create a windbreak, or you may wish to use a small one for a patio tree.

PURPLE LEAF PLUM
Prunus cerasifera

Hardiness—Hardy throughout Texas

Color(s)—White and purple blooms; purple foliage

Bloom Period—Spring

Mature Size (H x W)—15 to 25 ft. x 10 to 20 ft.

Water Needs—Water to prevent soil dryness.

Planting/Care—The best planting times are fall, winter, and early spring. It prefers moist, fertile, well-drained soil. Mulch, and provide temporary staking if needed. Fertilize regularly throughout the growing season. Prune to remove dead branches and twigs, or shape in very early spring.

Pests/Diseases—Fireblight may occur. Peach tree borers can visit unhealthy trees. Consult your local nursery for control advice.

Landscaping Tips & Ideas—A colorful addition for patios, decks, and gazebos. Can be grown in large containers or planters. Due to their relatively small size, may be located rather close to structures, walks, and drives—just not too close, or growth will be deformed.

REDBUD
Cercis canadensis

Hardiness—Hardy throughout Texas

Color(s)—Pink blooms; yellow fall foliage

Bloom Period—Spring

Mature Size (H x W)—15 to 30 ft. x 15 to 25 ft.

Water Needs—After establishment, water only during dry periods to help maintain healthy trees.

Planting/Care—Plant in fall, winter, or early spring, in moist, fertile, well-drained soil. Mulch. Fertilize regularly. Prune when young to prevent narrow, weak-angled branches; very little pruning is needed afterwards. The fast-growing redbud is relatively short-lived (20 to 25 years).

Pests/Diseases—Aphids may occur on spring foliage; visit area retailers for controls.

Landscaping Tips & Ideas—Use as lawn trees, specimens, or courtyard or patio plantings. They also work well near yard swings, decks, gazebos, and other garden structures. In group plantings, they provide a great spring show. Can be used to line driveways and walks without damage.

SWEET BAY MAGNOLIA
Magnolia virginiana

Hardiness—Hardy throughout Texas

Color(s)—Creamy white flowers; cherry red seeds in fall

Bloom Period—Spring to summer

Mature Size (H x W)—20 to 40 ft. x 15 to 25 ft.

Water Needs—Maintain a moist soil—do not let the soil become dry.

Planting/Care—Early fall or spring are great planting times. Plant in moist-to-damp, but not wet, areas. They tend to do better when protected from our hot afternoon sun and southwesterly summer winds. Mulch, and stake if necessary. Fertilize three times a year. Prune only to shape or remove dead or damaged branches.

Pests/Diseases—None

Landscaping Tips & Ideas—This is definitely not an ornamental tree for hot, dry locations. It works well in large beds of groundcovers or low-growing shrubs. Cultural requirements are similar to azaleas, and sweet bay will do well planted among them.

SWEETGUM
Liquidambar styraciflua

Hardiness—Hardy throughout Texas

Color(s)—Vivid fall foliage

Bloom Period—Spring (nonshowy)

Mature Size (H x W)—45 to 50 ft. or more x 60 ft.

Water Needs—Water to prevent soil dryness.

Planting/Care—Best planted in fall so you can determine leaf color. Will grow in loam or clay, as long as the soil is deep and moist. Mulch, and stake temporarily if necessary. Fertilize regularly. Prune to remove dead branches; no other pruning is usually needed.

Pests/Diseases—Tent caterpillars and aphids may visit. In hot, dry seasons, spider mites may appear. Your local nursery can advise you.

Landscaping Tips & Ideas—Because of the falling debris and the tree's size potential, don't plant it next to structures, walkways, or patios. Use it as a specimen tree in west locations in the landscape or as part of a large landscape bed.

WEEPING WILLOW
Salix babylonica

Hardiness—Hardy throughout Texas

Color(s)—Yellow fall foliage

Bloom Period—Spring (nonshowy)

Mature Size (H x W)—40 to 60 ft. x 30 to 40 ft.

Water Needs—Keep moist at all times during the growing season.

Planting/Care—Plant in fall or early spring. Select a site in full sun with moist to damp soil (even in our hot months). Mulch well to retain soil moisture. Fertilize regularly. Prune during establishment and in the early years to produce a straight trunk; little pruning is needed thereafter. Remove deadwood as it presents itself.

Pests/Diseases—Aphids and thrips may visit, but they usually aren't a concern. Borers may hit unhealthy trees.

Landscaping Tips & Ideas—This striking tree is best used as an accent. Pick planting spots carefully and don't locate near known sewage lines, homes, walks, or drives. Willows have invasive fibrous roots.

PALMS FOR TEXAS

After visiting the Gulf Coast or the Rio Grande Valley, you may be one of the visitors wishing for palm trees in your own backyard. While this is not possible in all areas of Texas, it is possible in approximately 40 percent of the state. This is especially true if you take the time to select winter-hardy palms for your particular area. By making this extra effort, you, too, may enjoy a backyard tropical (or at least semi-tropical) planting of palms.

The following is a list of palms, including common and scientific names, suggested USDA plant hardiness zones, and suggested cold tolerances. Know this about palms—cold hardiness is often a combination of lowest temperatures and how long sustained. If temperatures drop low and rise quickly, little damage may occur, but if the lower temperatures remain for several hours, or on into days, freeze damage is more likely.

For the most part, growing palms in Texas landscapes is part of what I call "gardening on the edge!" Should you decide to go for it, be aware of my cautions listed above.

Palm Name	Botanical Name	Hardiness Zones	Suggested Cold Tolerances
Spiny Fiber Palm	Trithrinax acanthocoma	8-9	10 deg. F.
South American Needle Palm	Trithrinax campestris	8-9	20 deg. F.
Takil Palm	Trachycarpus takil	8-9	10 deg. F.
Dwarf Windmill Palm	Trachycarpus nanus	8-9	10 deg. F.
Sikkim or Windamere Palm	Trachycarpus latisectus	8-9	10 deg. F.
Windmill or Chusan Palm	Trachycarpus fortunei	8-9	10 deg. F.
Mexican Blue Palm	Brahea armata	8-9	15 deg. F.
Guadalupe Palm	Brahea edulis	8-9	15 deg. F.
Chilean Wine Palm	Jubaea chilensis	8-9	15 deg. F.
Mazari Palm	Nannorrhops ritchieana	7b-9	20 deg. F.
Needle Palm	Rapidophyllyum hystrix	7b-9	10 deg. F.
Bermuda Palmetto	Sabal bermudana	8-9	15 deg. F.
Florida Scrub Palmetto	Sabal etonia	8-9	15 deg. F.
Mayan Palm	Sabal guatemalensis	8-9	15 deg. F.
Texas or Mexican Palmetto	Sabal mexicana	8-9	15 deg. F.
Dwarf Palmetto	Sabal minor	7b-9	15 deg. F.
Cabbage or Florida Sabal Palm	Sabal palmetto	8-9	15 deg. F.
Sonoran Blue Palmetto	Sabal uresana	8-9	15 deg. F.
Brazoria Palm	Sabal x texensis	8-9	15 deg. F.
Yatay Palm	Butia yatay	8-9	15 deg. F.
Wooly Butina Palm	Butia eriospatha	8-9	15 deg. F.
Pindo or Jelly Palm	Butia capita	8-9	15 deg. F.
Canary Island Date Palm	Phoenix carariensis	8b-9	25 deg. F.

Remember, the low temperatures listed here are for short durations only, and there is no guarantee damage won't occur.

TREES

Name	Type	Height × Width	Comments
American Holly *Ilex opaca*	Evergreen	40 to 50 by 15 to 30 feet	Excellent medium-sized tree; red berries on females in winter are eaten by birds; native; 'Savannah' is a popular smaller-growing hybrid cultivar. Great in eastern one-third of Texas.
Bald Cypress *Taxodium distichum*	Deciduous	50 to 100 by 20 to 50 feet	Narrow cone shape when young; knees rarely produced in cultivation, remove if desired; an unuaual conifer that drops its needles in winter; native.
Cabbage Palm *Sabal palmetto*	Evergreen	25 by 6 feet	Hardy in zones 8b and 9; may be damaged or killed by temperatures below 15 degrees; slow rate of growth. A palm for the coast and Rio Grande Valley.
Cedar *Juniperus virginiana*	Evergreen	20 to 40 by 20 by 30 feet	Attractive fine-textured conifer; trunk with peeling bark has great character; good source of wildlife food; spider mites and bag worms may occur; native.
Cedar Elm *Ulmus crassifolia*	Deciduous	60 to 80 by 40 to 50 feet	Dark-green 1- to 2-inch-long, almost shiny leaves with some light yellow fall color. Hardy in all zones; native.
Chinese Parasol Tree *Firmiana simplex*	Deciduous	35 by 15 feet	Large leaves and a smooth, green trunk make this tree distinctive; appropriate for use fairly close to buildings and patios; unusual seedpods; prone to white scale. Tropical looking tree.
Chinese Pistachio *Pistacia chinensis*	Deciduous	25 to 40 by 20 by 35 feet	Brilliant orange-red to gold fall color; excellent shade tree; leafs out relatively late—early to mid-April; a different species from the one that produces edible nuts. Great tree for Texas landscapes.
Deodar Cedar *Cedrus deodara*	Evergreen	40 to 60 by 20 to 30 feet	Looks like it belongs up North but does very well in in zones 8 and 9; silvery-green needles; branches form graceful tiers; pyramidal shape more irregular with age.
Flowering Crab Apple *Malus* spp.	Deciduous	10 to 25 by 15 to 30 feet	Bright to dark-green or red to red-purple leaves during growing season. Showy white, pink, red, or blends of these colors; blooms in early spring. Fruits are deep red or red-orange. Hardy in all Texas zones.
Flowering Dogwood *Cornus florida*	Deciduous	20 to 30 by 25 feet	Beautiful spring flowers before the foliage in shades of white, pink, or rose; prefers some shade; best used where there is excellent drainage and acid soils; prone to several pests; native.
Flowering Pear *Pyrus calleryana*	Deciduous	30 to 50 by 20 to 40 feet	Narrow upright growth when young becomes broader as trees age; white flowers in spring and brilliant fall foliage not as prominent in warmer portions of the state; older trees prone to branch splitting; 'Aristocrat', 'Bradford', 'Capital', and other cultivars are available.

TREES

Name	Type	Height × Width	Comments
Fringe Tree *Chionanthus virginicus*	Deciduous	20 to 25 by 15 to 20 feet	Also called grancy graybeard; greenish-white fringe-like flowers in spring as foliage emerges; excellent small ornamental tree; native. The Chinese fringe tree (*C. retusa*) is also recommended; the white flowers are more showy. Use in eastern third of Texas.
Ginkgo *Ginkgo biloba*	Deciduous	50 to 70 by 20 to 50 feet	Attractive fan-shaped foliage reliably turns a beautiful yellow in fall; plant grafted males to avoid undesirable fruit; slow rate of growth; tough tree with no problems.
Golden Rain Tree *Koelreuteria paniculata*	Deciduous	20 to 40 by 20 to 35 feet	Medium-green to blue-green foliage during the growing season with yellow fall colors. Also has golden-yellow blooms during the growing season. Hardy in all zones.
Green Ash *Fraxinus pennsylvanica*	Deciduous	40 to 70 by 30 to 50 feet	Excellent fast-growing shade tree; yellow fall color in north Texas. A much better tree than Arizona ash.
Japanese Maple *Acer palmatum*	Deciduous	2 to 20 by 3 to 20 feet	Graceful, tiered growth habit; many, many cultivars with various leaf shapes and colors (yellow-green, green, bronze, burgundy); excellent specimen tree; small and relatively slow growing; prefers some afternoon shade. Needs deep moist soils. Not drought tolerant. Hardy in all Texas zones.
Lacebark Elm *Ulmus parvifolia*	Deciduous to semi-evergreen	40 to 60 by 30 to 50 feet	Very fast-growing shade tree; vase to umbrella shaped; attractive trunk with peeling bark; reliable and relatively pest-free; leafless for a short time in late winter. 'Drake' is a super variety.
Leyland Cypress x *Cupressocyparis leylandii*	Evergreen	20 to 40 by 15 to 30 feet	Pyramidal or conical with dark-green foliage. Hardy in all Texas zones.
Live Oak *Quercus virginiana*	Evergreen	40 to 80 by 60 to 100 feet	An outstandingly beautiful but very large tree; popular, but often planted where a smaller species would be more appropriate; destructive roots; best adapted to south Texas; salt tolerant; native.
Mimosa *Albizia julibrissin*	Deciduous	30 to 40 by 30 to 40 feet	Light-green, feathery compound leaves during the growing season; non-showy fall color. Old favorite with pink to rose-pink blooms. Hardy in all zones.
Parsley Hawthorn *Crataegus marshallii*	Deciduous	15 to 30 by 15 to 20 feet	Clusters of white-pink spring flowers and red fruit in the fall are outstanding features of this small flowering tree; thorny when young; birds eat the fruit; plant in small areas; native. Cedar apple rust could be a problem in poor-air-movement locations.

TREES

Name	Type	Height × Width	Comments
Pecan *Carya illinoiensis*	Deciduous	60 to 125 by 40 to 100 feet	Edible nuts; 'Choctaw', 'Desirable', 'Cheyenne', and 'Caddo' are good varieties; large trees need a lot of room; brittle wood very prone to breakage; prone to webworms; native.
Pines *Pinus* spp.	Evergreen	20 to 125 by 15 to 70 feet	Various species including short leaf pine, loblolly pine, slash pine; tall trees that are best planted in areas with sandy, acid soils; Southern pine borer and pine bark beetles can be problems; native and non native.
Purple Leaf Plum *Prunus cerasifera*	Deciduous	15 to 25 by 10 to 20 feet	Soft red-purple to purple leaves during the growing season; non-showy fall color. Small ornamental red-purple to purple fruits follow a show of white early-spring flowers. Very hardy in all Texas zones.
Redbud *Cercis canadensis*	Deciduous	15 to 30 by 15 to 25 feet	Small pinkish-purple flowers in great profusion in spring before the foliage emerges; attractive heart-shaped leaves turn yellow before dropping; needs excellent drainage; native. The 'Oklahoma' variety is super.
Saucer Magnolia *Magnolia* x *soulangiana*	Deciduous	20 to 25 by 20 to 30 feet	Large, fragrant pinkish-purple to white flowers in late winter to very early spring before the foliage; often grown multitrunked; numerous cultivars available; scale an occasional problem. In zone, 7 late freezes may occasionally damage.
Shumard Oak *Quercus shumardii*	Deciduous	80 to 100 by 50 to 60 feet	Relatively fast growth, especially if fertilized when young; shiny, dark-green foliage turns red in fall; excellent large shade tree; strong wood resists wind damage; native.
Silver Bell *Halesia diptera*	Deciduous	25 by 20 feet	Bell-shaped, white flowers in spring just as the foliage emerges; adaptable and easy; often used as a substitute where dogwoods do not thrive; good for small areas in east Texas. Is not drought resistant.
Southern Magnolia *Magnolia grandiflora*	Evergreen	50 to 100 by 30 to 50 feet	Beautiful tree with dark-green shiny foliage; fragrant, white flowers in May and June; considered messy because of leaf drop; numerous pests; scale is possible; difficult to grow plants underneath due to heavy shade; destructive roots; native.
Swamp Red Maple *Acer rubrum* 'Drummondii'	Deciduous	50 to 80 by 40 to 60 feet	Excellent fast-growing shade tree; tolerant of poor drainage; females produce attractive burgundy flowers and fruit in February; better adapted to Texas than northern red maples; native. Plant in moist areas. Best used in far east Texas.

TREES

Name	Type	Height × Width	Comments
Sweet Bay Magnolia *Magnolia virginiana*	Semi-evergreen	20 to 40 by 15 to 25 feet	Generally does not lose all leaves in winter; striking silvery backed foliage; fragrant flowers resemble Southern magnolia but smaller; upright form; tolerates poor drainage; native.
Sweet Gum *Liquidambar styraciflua*	Deciduous	45 to 50 by 40 to 60 feet	Upright pyramidal shape when young, broader with age; star-shaped leaves very reliably turn purple, orange, burgundy, or yellow in fall; prickly fruit can be a nuisance; native. Some may reach 100 feet tall in Texas. Plant in deep soils only.
Texas Ash *Fraxinus texensis*	Deciduous	35 to 50 by 25 to 35 feet	Long dark-green leaves changing to yellow, copper, rose, tangerine, and lime in the fall; hardy in all Texas zones. Native; best ash tree for Texas.
Vitex, Chaste Tree *Vitex agnus-castus*	Deciduous	9 to 15 by 10 to 15 feet	Spikes of lavender-purple, white, or pink in early summer, reblooming in late summer; attractive star-shaped foliage drops early; excellent fast-growing, small ornamental tree. Tough and hardy statewide. Good drought tolerance; native.
Weeping Willow *Salix babylonica*	Deciduous	40 to 60 by 30 to 40 feet	Narrow medium-green leaves turning yellow in early fall. Very hardy in all Texas zones. Many varieties available. Relatively short-lived accent trees.
Willow Oak *Quercus phellos*	Deciduous	80 to 100 by 40 to 60 feet	Excellent, fast-growing upright oak with narrow leaves; deserves more use; good for urban sites; leafless for brief period in late winter. Grow in acidic soils only; native.
Windmill Palm *Trachycarpus fortunei*	Evergreen	20 by 6 feet	Beautiful palm with a hairy trunk; good in small areas; reliably hardy in south Texas in zones 8b and 9. A palm for the Texas coast and Rio Grande Valley.

JANUARY

- January is an excellent month to plant trees. Deciduous trees are leafless this time of year, so when you go to the nursery to make your selection, expect to see bare branches. Don't be afraid to purchase and plant these trees, especially balled-and-burlapped specimens.

- Ice storms in north Texas sometimes create heavy ice buildup on branches, causing them to break. Either prune off the ragged stubs yourself or have a professional tree surgeon do it.

- Water newly planted trees thoroughly. Normally they do not need to be fertilized.

- Established trees in their first five to ten years after planting can be encouraged to grow faster with annual moderate fertilization. A granular fertilizer with a 3:1:2 ratio such as 15-5-10 works well; follow directions on the label about amount.

- January is an appropriate time to prune most fruit trees; pruning is rather specific and you can get detailed information from your local cooperative extension service.

FEBRUARY

- Although considered evergreen, live oaks drop some, most, or all of their leaves in late February or early March. Rake them up and use as mulch, put them in your compost pile, or store them in plastic bags for later use.

- If your patio is too hot and sunny to use during the summer, consider planting a small- to medium-size tree to the south or southwest of the patio.

- Stake newly planted trees if they seem unstable once planted.

- Finish fertilizing most trees in late February in Zones 8 and 9. It is important for the nutrients to be available to a tree as it begins spring growth.

- If your oaks have had heavy infestations of oak leaf blister in the past, spray them with a disease-control aid (or have a tree-care company do it if the tree is large) just as the dormant buds swell and begin to grow.

MARCH

- This is the last month of the ideal planting season when balled-and-burlapped trees are purchased and planted.

- Keep the area one to two feet out from the trunk of a newly planted tree mulched and free of weeds and grass. People are often tempted to plant a small flower bed around the base—but just leave the area mulched. The young tree will not appreciate your digging around it every few months to replant bedding plants.

- There is no need to water established trees. If the weather is mild and dry, water newly planted trees thoroughly as needed.

- Fertilize trees as soon as possible if you didn't last month in south Texas. Now is a good time to fertilize in north Texas.

- Continue to spray trees such as magnolias, Chinese parasol tree, and hollies if infested with scale. Use a lightweight horticultural oil, making two or three applications per label instructions.

APRIL

- Keeping simple records about your trees can be very helpful. Record such information as when trees are planted, their names, where they were purchased, what kind of pest problems occur (including when they occur and what treatments are used), and other information you think will be helpful.

- Sunny, warm days and dry weather can mean you need to water. Run a hose on low trickle for 30 to 45 minutes, a few inches from the trunk. Do this for each newly planted tree about once a week if needed.

- Iron deficiencies can show up in several types of oaks and pines growing in alkaline soils. Symptoms include yellowing of the foliage, especially the newer leaves. Treat the tree with chelated or other forms of iron now. Apply sulfur or copperas (iron sulfate) to the area where the roots are located to help acidify the soil.

- Prune spring-flowering trees this month and next month if needed.

MAY

- You may plant container-grown trees this month, but they are at a great disadvantage to trees planted earlier. Do not disturb the roots of container-grown trees planted this late, even if they are rootbound. Pay careful attention to watering late-planted trees.

- Promptly remove any branches that begin to hang too low over public sidewalks or streets.

- Magnolias are one of the most drought-susceptible trees we commonly grow. As they come into bloom in May, they may appear wilted if the weather is dry. They may drop their old leaves now. Put out the sprinkler and water the tree thoroughly if the soil is dry.

- Fertilizers will still be beneficial if applied this month.

- If you find cut-off small branches with green leaves under your shade tree, don't be alarmed. It's squirrels building their nests, and the damage they cause is usually minor.

JUNE

- June marks the beginning of hurricane season. Now is the time to hire professional arborists to remove heavy limbs and prune to balance out the weight distribution of the canopy. Consider also removing those that hang over the house near the roof.

- Because of their tropical nature, palms are best planted in summer, between May and August.

- Bald cypress is a popular yard tree. It rarely produces knees in home landscapes, but if it does and they are a problem, use a saw to remove them just below the soil surface. This will not injure the tree.

- Use lawn sprinklers to apply one inch of water to your established trees. It's most important to apply water at the dripline at the edge of the canopy.

- Recently planted trees should be thoroughly watered anytime rain does not occur for five to seven days—continue this practice for the rest of the summer.

JULY

- This is a great month to walk around your landscape and see where additional shade is needed. Enter your observations, thoughts, and decisions in your Texas gardening journal.

- Do not dig up and transplant trees now. The chances of their surviving are poor.

- If it has not rained for several weeks, apply one inch of water to the roots of mature trees every two weeks until it rains.

- Young trees, trees in stress, or trees in low vigor may benefit from a second fertilizer application this month. Use half the rate that was applied in January or February.

- Webworms attack a wide variety of trees but seem especially fond of pecans. Although it looks terrible, the damage is generally not significant. There may be multiple generations through the summer, so it would require repeated spraying from midsummer to fall to control these pests. If a nest is low enough, just prune it off.

AUGUST

- Finish planting palms this month. They will need the remaining warm weather to become established before winter. If a palm tree is tall, it will generally need to be staked with strong supports.

- Even with good care and regular watering, recently planted trees may look stressed at this time of year. This is not unusual, and you should not be overly alarmed. Keep up good care. Until these trees establish a good root system, they may continue to show late-summer stress for the next several years.

- Water newly planted trees once or twice a week until it rains. Older, established trees rarely need to be watered.

- Fertilizer containing quick-release nitrogen should not be applied to trees for the rest of the year. It may stimulate late growth, which could reduce the hardiness of a tree and promote winter injury.

- Trim faded flower heads off vitex to stimulate another flush of flowers.

SEPTEMBER

- Summer thunderstorms can damage trees with high, gusty winds and lightning. Storm-damaged trees often need pruning. This should include sawing off damaged limbs immediately after damage occurs.

- Lightning strikes are not unusual. As soon as they occur, take pictures and contact your homeowner's insurance company. Trees damaged by acts of nature are usually covered.

- Although temperatures may become milder, September weather can also be sweltering and dry. Keep up the watering, especially on newly planted trees. The most important maintenance item for newly planted trees this month is maintaining a moist soil at the root zone area.

- This is the last month to fertilize in north Texas for the year. South Texas gardeners may fertilize through October. Apply according to label directions.

- If grass is not prospering under your trees, you can selectively prune lower branches and some of the inner branches to allow more light to reach the lawn below.

OCTOBER

- The fall planting season gets started this month. Take your time and select just the right tree for each situation. If you are planning on purchasing a large tree, check with your local nurseries on delivery and installation prices since it may be too big for you to handle. Shop around.

- If you have identified a tree you want to move, root pruning it now is a good idea. By cutting some of the long roots this month, new fibrous ones are formed closer to the trunk with the area of the soil to be moved with the plant. Use a sharp-bladed shovel for this work.

- Trees that suffer root damage due to soil compaction show low vigor, dieback, and an unusual number of dead branches in the tree. Talk to a professional arborist about injecting water under high pressure into the soil of the root zone to loosen it and improve air content.

NOVEMBER

- When deciding on which trees to plant in your landscape, try to find mature specimens to observe—in local public gardens or arboretums as well as other people's yards.

- November and early December are perhaps the best times to plant trees in Texas. The soil is still warm from summer, which encourages vigorous growth. At the same time, the weather is cool, and the trees are going dormant, which reduces stress. Generous rainfall during the winter makes constant attention to watering unnecessary.

- Water in newly planted trees thoroughly.

- No fertilizer needs to be applied to trees this month.

- Deciduous trees drop their leaves this month and into December. Check them and evergreens such as holly for signs of scale. Spray with lightweight horticultural oil or other pest-control aids if needed.

- Identify pruning needs and take care of the pruning.

DECEMBER

- Spend some time catching up on your Texas gardening journal entries. Record unusual weather, new tree plantings, and anything else you think might be useful later on.

- Any recently planted tree whose stakes have been in place for nine to twelve months should have the support removed now. If you have newly planted trees that will remain staked, check where the ties come into contact with the trunk and make sure they are not causing damage.

- Water in trees when planted, and if the weather is mild and dry, water as needed. Established trees will not need to be watered this time of year.

- Winter is an ideal time to prune trees. Deciduous trees are leafless; this allows you to more clearly see the structure of your trees, and you don't have the weight of the foliage to deal with. Evergreen trees may be pruned this time of year as well.

APPENDIX

SUMMARY OF PEST-CONTROL OPTIONS

According to the dictionary, a pest is defined as "a person or thing that causes trouble, annoyance, discomfort, etc.; nuisance; specifically, any destructive or troublesome insect, small animal, weed, etc." Additionally, the suffix cide is defined as "killer, killing." Put the two together, and we have pesticide, or any aid used to kill, eliminate, control, or prevent pests. Pest encounters by Texas gardeners include insects, mites, diseases, weeds, plus, at times, small animals such as gophers and moles. For some, our hot, dry summers are a pest.

While we can't control the weather, we can help ourselves and our gardening goals by planting the best locally-adapted plants and their varieties, plus provide proper care for them as suggested in this book. Remember, healthy well-adapted plants have fewer problems with any pest.

The aids/controls/products listed in this section are some that are available to the gardener in today's marketplace. These products can be found at local nurseries, garden centers, farm stores, hardware stores, and mass merchandizers. The market is constantly changing, and because of this, some products, brand names, active ingredients, and uses also change. Utilize local retailers, as they can be an invaluable information source when deciding which aids, if any, will be used. Not all products, active ingredients, packaging, and forms are available at every retailer.

Review the following information on Insect Pests, Disease Pests, and Weed Pests, and use it as a guide when visiting local retailers.

INSECT PESTS AND SOME CONTROLS

Aids/controls/products are listed alphabetically and not in order of preference or recommendation by the authors. The following list is compiled from available information and is believed to be accurate and correct. But it is not an absolute list. Common and/or trade names of aids/controls/products are capitalized, and active ingredients are in lower-case letters. Insect-control aids/products are constantly changing. Texas gardeners may utilize any of the various aids/controls/products listed if available at local or area retailers.

Remember, not all insects are pests. Only use insect aids/controls/products when and if needed to help you achieve your personal gardening goals. Always read and follow label directions/instructions when utilizing any of these. Insecticides derived from naturally occurring components and compound ingredients are also pesticides.

DISEASE PESTS AND SOME CONTROLS

Aids/controls/products are listed alphabetically not in order of preference or recommendation by the authors. This list is compiled from available information and believed to be accurate and correct, but it is not an absolute list. Common and/or trade names of aids/controls/products listed are capitalized, and active ingredients are lowercased. Disease-control aids/products are constantly changing. All aids/controls/products listed may or may not be available at your local or area retailers.

To prevent plant diseases, plant disease-resistant varieties when possible. Maintaining the health of plants also helps prevent plant diseases. Remember, it is better to prevent plant diseases than to cure them. Always read and follow label directions when applying any disease-control aid.

Before treating for plant diseases, it is wise to identify the specific pests. If you are unable to identify the problem(s), take samples to local retailers. They can correctly identify the problem(s) and recommend specific treatments to control the disease pest(s) if controls are needed.

Should you wish to confirm a retailer's identification or simply wish to handle the problem without consulting local retailers, there is a third method to identify plant diseases. Contact your County Extension Agent's office and ask for a Texas Plant Disease Diagnostic Laboratory form number D-1178.

Complete the form as accurately as possible. Follow all the instructions for collecting plant specimens as well as packaging and mailing. When you receive the diagnosis, it is your decision to

Continued Page 249

INSECT PESTS

Name	Controls	Plants Affected	When Pest Active
Ants and fire ants	**See below for control details	Few if any plants are affected; nuisance to people	Year-round, especially in warm seasons

**Baits—Hydramethylnon (amidinohydrazone) and sulfluramid (n-ethyl perfluorooctanesulfonamide); Avermectins (abamectin); Spinosyns (spinosad); Insect Growth Regulators (fenoxycarb, methoprene, pyriproxyfen).

**Contact Insecticides—Botanicals (d-limonene—a citrus oil extract, pyrethrum, pyrethrin, rotenone, pine oil, turpentine); Derivatives of Pyrethrin (allethrin, resmethrin, sumithrin, tetramethrin); Carbamates (bendiocarb, carbaryl); Organophosphates (acephate, dichlorvos, fenthion, isofenphos, malathion, propetamphos, propoxur, trichlorfon); Inorganic Compounds—Boric acid, Diatomaceous earth products (D.E., silicone dioxide).

Name	Controls	Plants Affected	When Pest Active
Aphids	acephate, azadirachtin (neem), bifenthrin, cyfluthrin, deltamethrin, esfenvalerate, fluvalinate light horticultural oils, imidacloprid, insecticidal soap, permethrin, pyrethrin, pyrethrum	Any plant with tender new growth	Year-round when plants are actively growing
Armyworms	acephate, bifenthrin, *Bacillus thuringiensis* (Bt), carbaryl, cyfluthrin, esfenvalerate,permethrin, pyrethrin, pyrethrum, spinosad	Texas lawn grasses	Usually summer; may occur spring and fall
Bagworms	Same as armyworms	Cedar, juniper, and arborvitae	Usually in active growing season; remain year-round if not physically removed
Beetles	acephate, azadirachtin (neem), bifenthrin, cyfluthrin, deltamethrin, esfenvalerate, fluvalinate, light horticultural oils, imidacloprid, permethrin, pyrethrin, pyrethrum	Vegetables, some trees, and flowers	Usually in warm seasons
Billbugs	acephate, bifenthrin, cyfluthrin, fluvalinate	Plants with tender shallow root systems, usually annuals	Year-round; most active in warm, moist times
Borers, **Woody Plants**	bifenthrin, imidacloprid, thiodan	Trees and old large shrubs	Most active in spring and summer
Caterpillars	Same as armyworms	Many plants with tender growth, vegetables, and annuals	Most active in spring; also active through fall
Chiggers	fluvalinate, malathion	None; nuisance to people	Warm seasons
Chinch bugs	acephate, bifenthrin, carbaryl, cyfluthrin, fluvalinate, isofenphos	Texas lawn grasses	Hot, dry summers

INSECT PESTS

Name	Controls	Plants Affected	When Pest Active
Crickets (common and mole)	carbaryl, isofenphos, pyrethrin, resmethrin	Mole: any plants they cut the roots of; Common: nuisance to people	Warm and especially moist seasons
Cutworms	acephate, bifenthrin, carbaryl, cyfluthrin, esfenvalerate, pymethrin pyrethrin, pyrethrum, spinosad	Vegetable transplants most affected	Most active in spring
Earwigs	propoxur, malathion, metaldehyde baits, resmethrin, pyrethrin	Plants not normally affected; nuisance to people	Year-round; most active in warm seasons
Fleas	bifenthrin, carbaryl, pyrethrin, propoxur	None; nuisance to people and pets	Year-round; most active in warm seasons
Fungus gnats	Bt/H-14, malathion pyrethrum, pyrethrin	Usually not harmful to plants; most often found in houseplants; may be a nuisance to people	Year-round; most active in growing season
Grasshoppers	acephate, bifenthrin, carbaryl, pyrethrin	Almost any plant	Summer, especially when hot and dry
Grubs	isofenphos, imidacloprid, ethoprop	Texas lawn grasses	May be active year-round; most damage in cool seasons
Lacebugs	acephate, fluvalinate, light horticultural oil, imidacloprid, malathion	Ornamental shrubs, such as azaleas and pyracanthas	Summer
Leaf cutter bees	carbaryl, malathion, propoxur, pyrethrum, resmethrin	Any plant in the landscape with relatively tender leaves	Warm seasons
Leaf hoppers	acephate, bifenthrin, carbaryl	Vegetables and ornamentals, including roses	Warm active growing season
Leaf miners	acephate, malathion, spinosad	Trees to vegetables	Active growing season
Leaf rollers	Same as armyworms	Various plants in the garden, including cannas	Active growing season
Mealybugs	acephate, light horticultural oils, malathion, pyrethrum, pyrethrin	Any tender plant; houseplants	Year-round indoors; active growing season outdoors
Millipedes and centipedes	carbaryl, bifenthrin, pyrethrin, resmethrin	None; nuisance to people	Year-round; most active in warm, moist seasons
Pecan nut casebarer	*Bacillus thuringiensis* (Bt), carbaryl, malathion	Pecans and hickory	Active growing season
Pecan phylloxera	dormant oils, malathion	Pecans and fruits	Active growing season

INSECT PESTS

Name	Controls	Plants Affected	When Pest Active
Plant bugs	acephate, azadirachtin (neem), bifenthrin, carbaryl, cyfluthrin, permethrin, pyrethrin	Vegetables	Active growing season
Scales	acephate, bifenthrin, dormant horticultural oil, light horticultural oil, imidacloprid	From trees to houseplants	Year-round; most active in growing season
Scorpions	propoxur, malathion, pyrethrin	None; nuisance to people	Warm, moist seasons
Slugs and **snails**	Various traps (beer), copper metal strips, iron phosphate baits (Sluggo), metaldehyde baits.	Young tender shallow-rooted foliage plants, including hosta	Warm growing season
Sod webworms	Same as armyworms	Texas lawn grasses	Summer heat
Sowbugs/pillbugs	bifenthrin, carbaryl, fluvalinate	Annuals and vegetables	Warm, moist seasons
Spider mites	bifenthrin, imidacloprid, kelthane, light horticultural oil, malathion, pyrethrin	From trees to houseplants	Year-round indoors; hot, dry times outdoors
Spiders	No control is normally needed; bifenthrin, pyrethrin, resmethrin	None; nuisance to people	Year-round indoors; most active in growing season
Squash bug	pyrethrum, pyrethrin, carbaryl, rotenone	All types of squash	Warm growing season
Squash vine borer	*Bacillus thuringiensis* (Bt), carbaryl, spinosad	All types of squash	Warm growing season
Stinkbugs	rotenone/pyrethrum combination, malathion, carbaryl	Primarily vegetables, including squash	Warm growing season
Thrips	acephate, azadirachtin (neem), bifenthrin, carbaryl, cyfluthrin, permethrin, pyrethrin	Roses are main plants affected	Active growing season
Ticks	bifenthrin, carbaryl, pyrethrin, propoxur	None; nuisance to people and pets	Year-round; primarily in warm seasons
Wasps, **hornets**, and **yellow jackets**	permethrin, pyrethrin, resmethrin, carbaryl	None; nuisance to people	Warm seasons
Webworms, **fall** and **tent caterpillars**	acephate, bifenthrin, *Bacillus thuringiensis* (Bt), carbaryl, cyfluthrin, esfenvalerate, permethrin, pyrethrum, spinosad	Trees and shrubs sometimes; Texas lawn grasses	Warm seasons

INSECT PESTS

Name	Controls	Plants Affected	When Pest Active
Whiteflies	acephate, bifenthrin, light horticultural oil, malathion, pyrethrin	Primarily ornamentals, including gardenia and lantana	Warm growing season
Woolly oak galls	No control is necessary	Oak trees	Year-round

INSECT PEST BIO-CONTROL OPTIONS

Bacillus thuringiensis (BT): A specific control for several larvae/caterpillars/worms.

Green lacewings: Their larvae feed on numerous insect pests.

Ladybugs/beetles: they prefer certain sucking insect pests, including aphids, mealybugs, and spider mites.

Natural insecticides: Diatomaceous earth (DE), neem, nicotine, pyrethrum, rotone, and sabadilla are used to control insect pests.

Nosema Locustae: A protozoan spore specifically utilized for grasshopper control.

Praying mantis: Prefers grasshopers, crickets, bees, wasps, and flies as their food sources.

Trichogramma wasp: A miniature wasp that attacks the eggs of 200+ insect pests.

follow their suggestion/recommendations or decline. This has proven to be a very accurate method of identifying plant disease pests in Texas.

WEED PESTS AND SOME CONTROLS

Aids/products are listed alphabetically and not in order of preference or recommendation by the authors. This list is compiled from available information and is believed to be accurate and correct. But it is not an absolute list. Common and/or brand names are capitalized, and active ingredients are in lowercase letters. Texas gardeners may utilize any of the various names listed if available at local or area retailers. Always read labels before purchasing, and follow application instructions when using any weed-control aid.

Generally, there are far more varieties or types of broadleaf weed pests than grassy ones in Texas landscapes and/or gardens. To be effective, a pre-emergent should be applied before weed seeds emerge or germinate. A post-emergent is utilized after weed pests have emerged and are actively growing.

DEER-RESISTANT LANDSCAPES AND GARDENS

Deer will eat almost anything if they are hungry enough—it is important for gardeners to remember this. Wouldn't you? Most of the deer are whitetail that are doing the damage in Texas. The key words here, folks, are "deer-resistant." Not "deer-proof."

If you want to help keep them out of your areas of concern, do not feed them. This actually increases the damage to landscapes and gardens. Feeding them increases their numbers in your area, and the deer will prune your plants in addition to taking the food offered. Bottom line, don't feed the deer in your neighborhood because it also affects your neighbor's property.

Various types of fences may be used to prevent deer from visiting your gardens and landscape. Specific plans for them are available from local sources including the Extension Service, the Texas Parks and Wildlife Department, and retailers specializing in "game-proof" fences. Certainly, it's up to you to fence or not. Done correctly, fences nearly always provide the desired results.

DISEASES

Name	Controls	Plants Affected	When Pest Active
Algae	Bordeaux Mixture, Daconil, Dithane, dry conditions, Fore, Mancozeb DG, Minicure 6 F, and Thalonil 4 L	Almost any plant in warm, moist, high humidity locations	Warm, moist seasons/ conditions
Anthracnose	Bordeaux Mixture, Daconil, and Manab	Trees, vegetables, lawn grasses, and berries	Spring
Bacteria	Agrimycin, Bordeaux Mixture, and Kocide 101	Pears, pyracanthas, and apples	Spring and summer
Blackspot	Bayleton, Daconil, Fung Away, Funginex, and Daconil	Roses	Active growing season
Brown patch	Bayleton, Defend, Fung Away, Manab, Penstar, Rubigan, and Terraclor	Texas lawn grasses	Usually spring and/or fall
Cotton root rot	No controls available; plant resistant varieties	Trees, especially dogwood; shrubs, especially wax ligustrum	Year-round; most active in warm seasons
Crown rot	Daconil, good soil drainage, and Terraclor	Any plant especially those rosette form, especially African violets	Year-round; most likely in warm, moist seasons
Downy mildew	Bordeaux Mixture, captan Folpet, Manab, Manzate, sulfur, and Zineb	Vegetables	Active growing season
Fruit rot	benomyl, Bordeaux Mixture, captan, Daconil, Funginex, Maneb, and sulphur	Stone fruits	Throughout fruiting seasons
Gray mold (Botrytis)	Banner Maxx, Daconil 2787, Thiram, and Zineb	Annuals and perennials, especially amaryllis, carnations and geraniums	Active growing season
Gray leafspot	Bayleton, and Fung Away	Texas lawn grasses	Warm, moist seasons
Leaf spots	Bordeaux Mixture, Daconil 2787, Funginex, Heritage, Terraclor, and Thalonil	Flowers, especially roses; shrubs, especially red tips; trees, especially redbud	Warm growing season
Oak leaf blister	Copper Sulfate	Oak trees	Active growing season
Phytophora	No controls; practice good cultural technique techniques; rotate crops	Annual vinca, petunias, and other annuals	Warm growing season

DISEASES

Name	Controls	Plants Affected	When Pest Active
Powdery mildew	Banner Maxx, Bayleton, Daconil 2787, Funginex, Rubigan A. S., and sulfur	Roses, crape myrtles, and vegetables	Warm growing season, especially with humid conditions
Pythium blight	Alliette, Banol, Heritage, Mancozeb, Koban, Prodigy, and Subdue	Texas lawn grasses	Warm growing season
Root rot	Daconil 2787, Terraclor, and well-drained growing conditions	Any plant	Year-round; most likely in cool/coldseasons
Rusts	Hlorothalonil, Maneb, Myclobutanil, Terraclor, Zineb	Vegetables, roses, and Texas lawn grasses	Warm growing season
Rhizoctonia	Bayleton, Daconil 2787, Defend, Fore, Penstar, and Terraclor	Vegetables	Active growing season
Scab	Benlate, Benomyl, captan, Daconil, sulfur, and Topsin M	Pecans and hickory apples	Spring, summer, and fall
Soil-borne diseases (living in the soil)	Daconil and Terraclor	See rhizoctonia and phytophora	See rhizoctonia and phytophora (both are soil-borne diseases)
Stem canker	No controls available; remove infected small plants and dead parts of large plants	Roses and trees	Year-round
Stem rot	Good cultural practices; Terraclor, and Zineb	Plants with herbaceous stems	Warm growing season
Take-all patch	Banner Maxx, Heritage, Patchwork, Rubigan, and Rubigan A. S.	Texas lawn grasses	Fall and winter
Viruses	No controls available; plant resistant varieties	All plant groups	Year-round; most active in warm growing season

WEEDS

Broadleaf Weed Pests	Pre-Emergent Controls	Post-Emergent Controls
Bur clover, chickweed, dandelion, dock, field bindweed (wild morning glory), henbit, wood sorrel, plantain, purslane, and wild onion	Betasan, Dacthal, and Gallery	Banvel 4S, Confront 3L, and 2, 4-D, glyphosate, Prompt 5L, Sencor, and Trimec

Grassy Weed Pests	Pre-Emergent Controls	Post-Emergent Controls
Bahiagrass, crabgrass, dallisgrass, goosegrass, Johnsongrass, nutgrass (nutsedge), poa annua (annual bluegrass), quackgrass, and sandbur or grassbur	Balan, Barricade, Betasan, Dacthal, Dimension, Surflan 4AS, and Team	Acclaim Extra, betazon, DSMA, Fusilade II, glyphosate, illoxan, Image, and MSMA

Another possible deterrent is a dog. If your dog is outside a great deal, especially in the evening or early-morning hours when hungry deer may be on the prowl, a protective dog may keep them away just by his or her active presence or barking.

SOME EXTRA HELP

In addition to plants, fences, and trained dogs, there are commercial aids available also. Check with your local nursery or home and garden center. Should you decide to try one, always read and follow label directions.

When using repellent products, it is best to utilize them before feeding habits are established. It is also wise to change products from time to time, to keep deer guessing.

The following is a list of deer "resistant" and not deer "proof" plants for Texas landscapes and gardens. Some are more resistant than others. Deer can't read nor do they respect your landscape and gardening efforts. It is up to you to fence and plant less-desirable plants to prevent the damage. This list should be an aid.

ANNUALS AND PERENNIALS

Ageratum *Ageratum* spp.
Angel Trumpet *Datura* spp.
Annual Sunflower *Helianthus* annuus
Artemisia *A. ludoviciana*
Autum Sage *Salvia greggii*
Beargrass *Nolina* spp.
Begonia *Begonia* spp.
Black-eyed Susan *Rudbeckia hirta*
Blackfoot Daisy *Melampodium leucanthum*
Bluebonnet *Lupinus texensis*
Candytuft *Iberis sempervirens*
Cardinal Flower *Lobelia cardinalis*
Cedar Sage *Salvia roemeriana*
Chrysanthemum *Dendranthema* spp.
Columbine *Aquilegia* spp.
Copper Canyon Daisy *Tagetes lemonii*
Coreopsis *Coreopsis* spp.
Drummond's Skullcap *Scutellaria drummondii*
Cosmos *Cosmos bipinnatus*

Dusty Miller *Centaurea cineraria*
Flame Acanthus *Anisacanthus wrightii*
Four-o'Clock *Mirabilis* spp.
Foxglove *Digitalis* spp.
Gayfeather *Liatris* spp.
Hardy or Mallow Hibiscus *Hibiscus moscheutos*
Hummingbird Bush *Anisacanthus wrightii*
Indian Blanket *Gaillardia pulchella*
Indigo Spires *Salvia* spp.
Iris *Iris* spp.
Jerusalem sage *Phlomis fruticosa*
Lantana *Lantana horrida*
Larkspurs *Delphinium carolinianum*
Marigolds *Tagetes* spp.
Maximilian Sunflower *Helianthus maximiliani*
Mealy Blue Sage *Salvia farinacea*
Mexican Bush Sage *Salvia leucanthia*
Mexican Hat *Ratibida columnaris*
Mexican Mint Marigold *Tagetes*
Mountain Pink *Centaurium beyrichii*
Milkweeds *Asclepias* spp.
Nightshades *Solanum* spp.
Oxeye Daisy *Luecanthemum*
Penstemons *Penstemon* spp.
Periwinkle *Vinca rosea*
Pink Wood Sorrel *Oxalis drummondii*
Plumbago *Plumbago auriculata*
Prickly Pear Cactus *Opuntia lindheimeri*
Purple Coneflower *Echinacea angustifolia*
Red Salvia *Salvia vanhouttei*
Rock Rose *Pavonia lasiopetala*
Rosemary *Rosemarinus officinalis*
Savory *Satureia* spp.
Snow-on-the-Mountain *Euphorbia marginata*
Snow-on-the-Prairie *Euphorbia bicolor*
Sedum *Sedum acre*
Texas Sage *Salvia texana*
Texas Betony *Stachys coccinea*
Wedelia *Wedelia triobata*
Verbena *Verbena* spp.
Yarrow *Achillea filipendulina*
Yellow Wood Sorrel *Oxalis dillenii*
Zexmenia *Wedelia hispida*
Zexmenia *Zexmenia hispida*
Zinnia *Zinnia* spp.

BULBS
Hardy Red Amaryllis *Hippeastrum × Johnsonii*
Lily of the Nile *Agapanthus* spp.

GRASSES
Gulf Muhley *Muhlenbergia capillaris*
Inland Sea Oats *Chasmanthium latifolium*
Lindhreimer's Muhley *Muhlenbergia lindheimeri*
Maidengrass *Miscanthus sinensis*
Pampas Grass *Cortaderia selloana*
Purple Fountain Grass *Pennisetum setaceum*

GROUNDCOVERS, HERBS, AND FERNS
Aaron's Beard *Hypericum calycinum*
Asian Jasmine *Trachelospermum asiaticum*
Carpet Bugle *Ajuga reptans*
Germander *Teucrium chamaedrys*
Gray Santolina *Santolina chamaecyparissus*
Green Santolina *S. virens*
Holly Fern *Cyrtomium falicatum*
Lemon Mint *Monarda citriodora*
Lavender *Lavandula* spp.
Maidenhair Fern *Adinatum capillus-verneris*
Mexican Oregano *Poliomintha longifolia*
Mondo Grass *Ophiopogon japonica*
Sword Fern *Nephrolepis* spp.
Spearmint *Menta spicata*
Thyme *Thymus* spp.
Vinca *Vinca major*
Wood's Fern *Dryopteris* spp.

SHRUBS
Abelia *Abelia* spp.
Acuba *Acuba japonica*
Autumn Sage *Salvia greggii*
Barberry *Berberis thunbergii*
Boxleaf Euonymus *Euonymus japonica* 'Microphylla'
Boxwood *Buxus microphylla*
Ceniza/Texas Sage *Leucopyllum* spp.
Cherry Laurel *Prunus caroliniana*
Cotoneaster *Cotoneaster* spp.
Damianita *Chrysactinia* mexicana
Deciduous or Possomhaw Holly *Ilex decidua*
Dwarf Chinese Holly *Ilex cornuta*
Eleagnus *Eleagnus* spp.
Evergreen Sumac *Rhus virens*

Fragrant Mimosa *Mimosa borealis*
Germander *Teucrium* spp.
Goldcup *Hypericum* spp.
Japanese Aralia *Arelia sieboldii*
Japanese Boxwood *Buxus microphylla*
Japanese Yew *Podocarpus macrophyllus*
Jerusalem Cherry *Solanum pseudocapsicum*
Juniper *Juniperus* spp.
Lavender *Lavandula* spp.
Mexican Buckeye *Ungnadia speciosa*
Mexican Silktassle *Garrya lindheimeri*
Nandina *Nandina* spp.
Oleander *Nerium oleander*
Pineapple Guava *Fijoa sellowiana*
Pomegranate *Punica granatum*

TREES
Note: None are truly resistant when the unwanted visitors decide to rub on them for whatever purposes, including shaping up their antlers. It is usually best to construct individual protective barriers around any desired tree not protected inside your yard. These structures may include steel posts on three or four corners with panels or wire installed on them to prevent deer from reaching the protected tree(s). This is especially important for newly planted and young trees.

VINES
Carolina Jessamine *Gelsemium sempervirens*
Clematis *Clematis* spp.
Crossvine *Bignonia capreolata*
Confederate Star Jasmine *Trachelospermum jasminoides*

GRASSHOPPER-RESISTANT PLANTS
People ask for assistance in controlling grasshoppers in their lawns, gardens, and landscapes. Yes, there are plenty of products to "kill" these plant-eating pests, but total control may be elusive. True, there are wizards who claim to have . . . the answer.

There are many varieties of grasshoppers and they don't all have the same eating habits, rates of growing, or reproducing. One size does not fit all in controlling grasshoppers. For example, some bait products are attached to bran, and not all grasshoppers eat bran. Because of this, products attached to bran are not effective on these specific grasshoppers.

With the assistance of horticulturists and Master Gardeners, here is a list of plants that have been proven (by experience) to be grasshopper-resistant.

Keep in mind that this list of grasshopper-resistant plants is based on subjective observations, and not scientific studies. Depending on grasshopper populations and available "food" for the pests, plants that normally have light damage may be consumed more heavily.

NORMALLY NOT PREFERRED

American Beautyberry
Artemisia
Bouncing Bet
Bridal Wreath Spirea
Bur Oak
Camellia
Carolina Jessamine
Catalpa
Chinese Pistachio
Confederate Star Jasmine
Coralberry
Crossvine
Crapemyrtle
Dwarf Burning Bush
Euonymus (evergreen varieties)
Evergreen Sumac
Fig Ivy
Flame Acanthus
Elderica or Afghan Pine
Fall Aster
Forsythia
Gaura
Goldenrod
Gregg Dahlia
Indian Hawthorne
Juniper
Lacebark Elm
Lantana
Lemon Mint
Leyland Cypress
'Lady in Red' Salvia

Live Oak
Loblolly Pine
Maximilian Sunflower
Mealy Blue Sage
Mexican Mint Marigold
Mexican Oregano
Obedient Plant
Oleander
Passion Vine
Pavonia (Rock Rose)
Perennial Verbena
Portulaca
Privet
Purslane
Pygmy Barberry
Rosemary
Rue
Sage (Autumn)
Scott's Pine
Shumard Red Oak
St. John's Wort
Texas Bluebells
Texas Red Oak
Turk's Cap
Vitex
Wax Myrtle
Weigela
'Winter Gem' Boxwood
Wisteria
Yaupon Holly (standard and dwarf)

CONSUMED

Althea (Rose-of-Sharon)
Amaryllis
Bachelor Buttons
Bush Honeysuckle
Butterfly Bush
Canna
Carissa Holly
Cherry Laurel
Daylily
Dianthus
Dwarf Burford Holly
Eleagnus
Flowering Quince
Hardy Hibiscus

Iris
Liriope
Mondo Grass
Moss Rose
Mums
Needlepoint Holly
Nellie R. Stevens Holly
Passion Vine
Peach
Privet
Purslane
Roses
Russian Sage
Tradescantia
Weigela
Wisteria

WATERWISE PRINCIPLES AND PLANT LIST

As sure as the sun rises and sets, we Texans know that July and August will be hot and dry. It's not only hot and dry during these months, but the hot weather begins in June and may continue through September.

By employing a method of landscaping known as "xeriscape," or "waterwise gardening," Texans may enjoy interesting landscapes and reduce water usage. It involves low water usage once plants are established—but it does not mean using only cactus, agave, or all native plants.

THE BASICS

- Have a plan before shopping. This plan or design should include selecting plants that, after initial establishment, are well-adapted for local use with relatively low water usage. These plants should also be known to have minimal, if any, pest and disease problems. If you are not aware of this detailed information, be sure to ask your local nursery before choosing the plants in your design.
- Perform thorough soil preparation prior to planting. If you cannot provide what a plant needs in the way of soil preparation—don't plant it!
- Install your plants properly and at the recommended time for relatively quick establishment. Fall is the best time for initial planting of all winter-hardy woody landscape plants in Texas. The statement "fall is for planting" is very true.
- Mulch, mulch, and mulch! Mulch after initial planting and continue doing it on a year-round basis. Most of the soil around my plants is covered with a 3- to 4-inch layer of bark mulch. Mulch is a layer or a blanket of material on top of the ground. No mulch is good if you are not using it. Good organic mulches may be preferable to materials such as pea gravel, lava rock, or other crushed-stone products.
- Properly maintain your plants. This includes fertilizing, pruning, controlling pests (including weeds, insects, and diseases), maintaining your selected mulch layer, and watering wisely. Drip irrigation systems are more efficient than standard systems for landscape plantings. However, standard sprinkler irrigation systems may also be used, especially in lawn areas. Water only when plants need irrigating, then do so thoroughly. Don't water on a preset schedule, but do water when plants need a drink.

It's always important to remember two words: "once established." When you read or hear about plants that are drought tolerant or will fit into a xeriscape plan, remember that most plants need, require, and benefit from a little help during initial establishment.

Just because a plant is drought tolerant doesn't automatically mean it is winter-hardy in your zone or would do well in your type of native soil. It's always wise to ask your local nursery if a plant is winter-hardy and does well in our native soils before purchasing and planting.

The following is a list of plants recommended for Texas water-wise or xeriscape landscapes and gardens. Remember, Texas is diverse, so check with your local nursery if you have a question about a specific plant.

ANNUALS
Black-eyed Susan
Bluebonnet
Coneflower (clasping-leaf)
Copper Plant
Coreopsis (Plains)
Gomphrena
Indian Blanket
Phlox drummondii
Texas Bluebells

BULBS
Canna
Crinum
Daylily
Iris (bearded)

GRASSES
Bermuda (Common, Tex turf
10™ and Coastal)
Buffalo
Fountain Grass
Maidengrass
Pampas Grass

GROUNDCOVERS
Artemisia
Jasmine (Asian and Confederate
Star)
Liriope
Ophiopogon
Prostrate Rosemary
Santolina
Sedum
Wintercreeper
Vinca major

PERENNIALS
Artemisia
Bouncing Bet
Butterfly Weed
Coneflower (Purple)
Coreopsis (Lanceleaf and Sunray)
Evening Primrose
Four-o'Clock
Gaillardia
Gayfeather

Lantana
Mexican Firebush
Mexican Hat
Phlox pilosa
Plumbago (white and blue)
Prairie Verbena
Ruellia
Salvia/Sage (Scarlet coccinea,
    Mealy Blue farinacea,
    Mexican bush leucantha,
    Autumn greggii)
Skullcap

ROSES
Most rose species

SHRUBS
Abelia
Agarito
Althea (Rose-of-Sharon)
American Beautyberry
Arborvitae
Barberry
Boxwood (Winter Gem
    and Japanese)
Butterfly Bush
Cacti
Cenzino (Texas Sage)
Cherry Laurel
Crapemyrtle
Eleaganus
Evergreen Sumac
Flowering Quince
Forsythia
Gray Cotoneaster
Holly (Burford, Dwarf Burford,
    Chinese Horned, Dwarf
    Chinese Horned, Willowleaf,
    Nellie R. Stevens, Carissa,
    Yaupon, Dwarf Yaupon,
    Possomhaw, and American)
Indian Hawthorn
Nandina (*domestica, compacta,*
    Harbor Dwarf, Gulf Stream,
    and Firepower)
Oleander
Palmetto

Pittosporum
Rosemary
Spirea
Texas Mountain Laurel
Vitex
Wax Myrtle
Woolly Butterfly Bush
Yucca

TREES
Ash (Texas and Green)
Bald Cypress
Bois 'd Arc/Osage Orange
Deodar Cedar
Desert Willow
Elm (Cedar and Lacebark)
Flowering Pear
Ginkgo
Golden Rain Tree
Juniper (Alligator, Ashe, Eastern
    Red, and Weeping)
Mesquite
Mexican Buckeye
Oak (Blackjack, Bur,
    Chinquapin, Chisos Red,
    Escarpment Live, Lacey,
    Live, Texas Red, and Vasey)
Parkinsonia/Paloverde
Pecan
Persimmon
Pine (Aleppo, Eldarica, Loblolly,
    Mexican, Pinyon, Slash)
Pistachio (Chinese and Texas)
Poinciana
Redbud (Texas and Oklahoma)

VINES
Boston Ivy
Carolina Jessamine
Honeysuckle (Coral, Flame,
    Hall's, and Purpurea)
English Ivy
Fig Ivy/Creeping Fig
Silverlace Vine
Trumpet Vine
Virginia Creeper
Wisteria (Chinese and Texas)

WATERWISE PRODUCT RECOMMENDATIONS

Here are some products that can make watering your garden and landscape cheaper, more efficient, and more effective. Shop for them at local retailers or from mail-order or Internet garden suppliers.

RAIN BARRELS

Rain barrels are an easy way to harvest rainwater from your roof. They provide a convenient (and free) supply of water whenever you need it or when water restrictions make your normal sources unavailable. In fact, you might be surprised to know just how much water can be harvested from the roof of even a modest-size home.

Ready-made rain barrels are available from a wide range of sources, including gardening catalogs, Internet sources, and some garden centers and home improvement stores. Barrels can also be recycled and easily adapted for rainwater harvesting as a do-it-yourself project. However, if you take this route, you should consider the barrel's original use before deciding to use it to harvest and store water that will eventually go into your garden and landscape.

Whether you are making your own, or purchasing a ready-made one, be sure that the outlet is placed at the very bottom of the barrel. Otherwise too much water can accumulate below the outlet and become stagnant and putrid.

When installing rain barrels, there are a few things you should know to get the most benefit from them. First, don't have all gutters leading to just one or two downspouts. Rain barrels under these will fill rapidly, often resulting in overflow. Instead, have multiple downspouts inserted where you want them. Having rain barrels under multiple downspouts will increase the opportunity for collecting the maximum amount of water possible.

Downspouts that lead directly into a rain barrel can contain a lot of debris. What doesn't get filtered out ultimately affects what comes out of the spigot, and can limit flow. Direct connections also allow an entry for mosquitoes. A good solution to both problems is to install an inlet drain to stop large debris and a mosquito screen as a barrier.

Even with covers and screens, water collected in a rain barrel will have debris from pollen, dust, etc. This is harmless to your plants but can eventually affect and clog watering emitters. Check and clean it periodically to provide the best flow rate over time.

SOAKER HOSES

Watering directly at the soil level is the most efficient way to irrigate, for two reasons. First, it cuts down on wasted water tremendously. Water is delivered directly to the soil. Because water is not shot in the air before falling back to earth, all water is utilized right where the plant needs it most—at the roots. With this method, there's no drift or evaporation. Furthermore, the water isn't deflected away or suspended on the foliage where it is exposed to wind and sun, the two biggest culprits of evaporation.

Second, by watering at the soil level, the foliage stays dry. Keeping foliage dry is an important step in minimizing plant diseases. That's an important point when it comes to water conservation because a healthy plant requires fewer resources to keep growing strong. That includes water!

Soaker hoses are widely available. They are made of porous plastic and "sweat" the water slowly out onto the soil when water is running through them.

Like any other hose, soaker hoses need to be kept free of dirt and clogs inside, and replaced when they break down over time—which they will, because they are exposed to weather and sunlight.

Snake soaker hoses carefully through garden beds and around the bases of tree or shrub plantings. It is best to do this early in the season, both so you can begin to use it as needed, and also so you don't trample on growing plants. At first, the hose may be exposed (even if it's black or you try to disguise it with mulch), but as plants grow, you won't see it as much. You can move it at any time to adjust where the water goes.

DRIP-IRRIGATION SYSTEMS

For the most precise and efficient watering of individual plants (such as trees, shrubs, groundcovers, perennials, vegetables, and containers), drip irrigation is the ideal way to go. In fact, it's so efficient that many water municipalities exempt landscape watered with drip irrigation from restrictions during drought. The concept has been used since ancient times when buried clay pots were filled with water and the water gradually seeped into the soil.

Although modern technology has provided improvements to the original design, the concept is still the same. A plastic supply line is connected to the water supply. Along the line, microtubes (¼-inch, flexible, spaghetti-like tubing) are inserted into the supply line and emitter tips are attached to the ends of the microtubes. The emitters allow the water to drip from the end. Based on the emitter tip selected, the rate of flow can vary from a few ounces to several gallons per hour while using much less water than conventional impact sprinklers.

Drip irrigation parts and accessories are readily available at garden centers and home improvement stores, as well as online and in catalogs. They can be purchased piecemeal or in kits. In permanent systems, a backflow prevention device is installed at the beginning of the line to prevent contaminated water from being sucked back into the water source should a reverse-flow situation occur. In any event, if you don't have the time or confidence to install a system yourself, hire a reputable local contractor to do it for you.

RAIN SENSOR
This is one of the easiest ways to conserve a precious natural resource.

We've all seen it. It's pouring rain as we drive by a house where the irrigation system is dutifully doing its job. Thank the timer for that. Unfortunately, a brain is not part of the standard equipment on an irrigation system.

Fortunately, this scenario doesn't have to be the rule. For a small extra cost, rain sensors can be included in or added to many in-ground irrigation systems. These sensors are typically mounted on or near the gutters and are designed to detect rainfall. The sensors are designed to override the cycle of an automatic irrigation system when adequate rainfall has been received. If the system happens to be operating at the same time as the rain falls, the sensor shuts the irrigation system off.

Many sensors must accumulate a certain amount of water before overriding the system to shut off. That can waste ¼ to ½ inch of water. However, current technology is available that overrides an operating irrigation system at the first indication of rain. It's well worth having this water-saving option.

COOPERATIVE EXTENSION
The Cooperative Extension Service in this state is now called the Texas AgriLife Extension Service of the Texas A&M University. At http://texasextension.tamu, you will find a comprehensive list of local offices as well as tour of the many services, publications, and workshops offered.

MASTER GARDENERS
If you would like to find a Master Gardener in your area, or are interested in becoming one, refer to http://mastergardener.tamu.edu, or contact Jayla Fry, Master Gardener Program Coordinator, or Dr. Douglas Welsh, Associate Head for Extension Programs, 225 Horticulture/Forest Science Building, College Station, TX 77843. (979) 845-5341.

WATER DISTRICTS
If you would like to find/get in touch with your Texas water district, please search for it at http://www10.tceq.state.tx.us/iwud/dist/index.cfm.

NURSERY & LANDSCAPE ASSOCIATION
This is a good place to start if you are seeking professional advice or help with a garden or landscaping project: http://www.tnlaonline.org.

GARDEN CENTERS
Texas abounds in good garden centers and nurseries, which you can find in your regional yellow pages or online. A good site to explore is: http://www.tnlaonline.org.

NATIVE PLANTS

Learn about our state's bounty of native plants, and good ones for your garden and how to find, grow, propagate, and otherwise enjoy them. You can start here, at the Native Plant Society of Texas's main website: http://npsot.org/.

GARDEN TOURS

Many Texas public gardens have docents (trained volunteers) and/or knowledgeable staff to show you around and answer your questions, or you may be able to manage or enhance your visit with provided maps, brochures, and plant lists. See the list on the following pages. If you are interested in seeing private gardens, check with local garden clubs and watch for event listings in your local media.

FLOWER AND GARDEN SHOWS

A directory of these justly popular events is available online at http://www.lasr.net/events.php?State=Texas&State_ID=TX&Keyword=Flower%20Shows, and http://flowers.boomja.com/Flower-Shows-Texas-24565.html. If you go to one, remember to bring a camera and notebook to capture good ideas, plant names, and so forth.

FLOWER FESTIVALS

We love to celebrate our bluebonnets and our roses, but there are others. Find listings online at http://gotexas.about.com/od/flowerfestivals/Flower_Festivals.htm, or watch for listings in your local media.

TEXAS PUBLIC GARDENS TO VISIT

We also highly recommend the book *Texas Public Gardens* by Elvin McDonald (Pelican Publishing Co., 2009; hardcover). It features detailed, personal observations and descriptions of all these gardens and more, by one of the country's most respected horticulturists, accompanied by glorious photography.

Amarillo Botanical Gardens
www.amarillobotanicalgardens.org
1400 Streit Dr.
Amarillo, TX 79106-1731
(806) 352-6513

Antique Rose Emporium
www.antiqueroseemporium.com
9300 Lueckemeyer Rd.
Brenham, TX 77833
(There are additional locations/retail nurseries in Independence and San Antonio.)
(800) 441-0002

Bayou Bend Collection at the Museum of Fine Arts, Houston
www.mfah.org
1 Westcott St.
River Oaks/Houston, TX 77007-7009
(713) 639-7750

Beaumont Botanical Gardens
www.beaumontbotanical-gardens.com
6088 Babe Zaharias Drive
Beaumont, TX 77705
(409) 842-3135

Bell Park Cacti Garden, Hale Ave K (at FM 1424 and FM 1914)
Hale Center, TX 79041

Brackenridge Park
(adjacent to San Antonio Zoo)
3910 N. Saint Mary's Street
San Antonio, TX 78212-3172
(210) 736-9534

Cullen Sculpture Garden
5100 Montrose (Montrose Boulevard at Bissonnet Street)
Houston, Texas 77006
(713) 845-1000

Dallas Arboretum & Botanical Garden
www.dallasarboretum.org
8525 Garland Road
Dallas, TX 75218
(214) 515-6500

El Paso Desert Botanical Garden, Keystone Heritage Park
www.elpasobotanicalgardens.org
4200 Doniphan Dr.
El Paso, TX 79912
(915) 584-0563

Forbidden Gardens
www.forbidden-gardens.com
3500 Franz Rd.
Katy, TX 77493
(281) 347-8000

Ft. Worth Botanical Garden
www.fwbg.org
3220 Botanic Garden Blvd
Fort Worth, TX 76107
(817) 871-7686

Hermann Park
www.hermannpark.org
6201 A Golf Course Dr.
Houston, TX 77030
(713) 524-5876

Lady Bird Johnson Wildflower Center

http://www.wildflower.org
4801 La Crosse Ave.
Austin, TX 78739
(512) 232-0100

Mast Arboretum
http://arboretum.sfasu.edu
Stephen F. Austin State University
Nacogdoches, TX 75962
(936) 468-4343

Mercer Arborteum
www.hcp4.net
22306 Aldine Westfield Rd.
Humble, TX 77338
(281) 443-8731

Moody Gardens
www.moodygardens.com
One Hope Boulevard
Galveston, TX 77554
(800) 582-4673

Texas Discovery Gardens
www.texasdiscoverygardens.org
3601 Dr. Martin Luther King
Dallas, TX 75210
(214) 428-7476

Tyler Municipal Rose Garden
www.texasrosefestival.com
420 Rose Park Dr.
(Highway 31 West
at Rose Park Drive)
Tyler, TX 75702
(903) 597-3130

Zilker Botanical Garden
www.zilkergarden.org
2220 Barton Springs Rd.
Austin, TX 78746
(512) 477-8672

TEXAS GARDEN OR PLANT-RELATED CLUBS AND ORGANIZATIONS

These groups are always worth seeking out and joining! You will find valuable information, fun and educational activities, new plant sources, and like-minded new friends.

Supplement this list by searching on the internet, in regional gardening publications, and in your local telephone book; also check bulletin boards at markets, garden centers, and plant shows.

A&M Garden Club
College Station, TX

African Violet Society
of America, Inc.
Box 3609
Beaumont, TX 77704-3609

Alamo Bromeliad Society
110 Palo Duro Dr.
San Antonio, TX 78232-3027

American Begonia Society,
Astro Branch
4513 Randwick
Houston, TX 77092

American Begonia Society,
Houston Satellite Branch
1423 Lasky
Houston, TX 77034

American Begonia Society,
San Jacinto Branch
2314 Straight Creek Dr.
Houston, TX 77017

American Hibiscus Society
Lone Star Chapter
9715 Oasis Dr.
Houston, TX 77096

American Hibiscus Society,
Space City Chapter
Pasadena, TX

Arlington Men's Garden Club
128 Peyton Place
Arlington, TX 76010

Arlington Organic Garden Club
Box 173954
Arlington, TX 76003-3954

Athens Master Gardener
Texas A&M University
Athens, TX

Austin Bonsai Society
2220 Barton Springs Rd.
Austin, TX 78746

Austin Butterfly Forum
Austin, TX

Austin Cactus & Succulent
Society
Austin, TX

Austin Fern & Cycad Society
Austin, TX

Austin Hemerocallis Society
1213 Southwood Rd.
Austin, TX 78704

Austin Herb Society
Austin, TX

Austin Pond Society
Austin, TX

Austin Rose Society
Austin, TX
Big Country Bonsai Club
300 N. Westwood
Abilene, TX 79603-6807

Big Tree Registry
Texas A&M University
College Station, TX

Bloomin' Buds Club
San Antonio, TX

Bonsai Society of Dallas
Richardson Family YMCA
Dallas, TX

Botanical Research Institute
of Texas
509 Pecan St.
Fort Worth, TX 76102-4060

Brazosport Daylily Society
Box 167
Waller, TX 77484

Bromeliad Society of Austin
Austin, TX

Cactus & Succulent Society
of Kerr County

Carnivorous Plants of Texas
Dallas, TX

Central East Texas
Orchid Society
Tyler, TX

Central Texas Herb Society
307 West Ave. East
Lampasas, TX 76550-1821

Collin County Rose Society
1409 Hillside Drive
Plano, TX 75074

Corpus Christi Bonsai Club
3206 Sonoma Dr.
Corpus Christi, TX 78414-3914

Corpus Christi
Bromeliad Society
125 Lake Shore Dr.
Corpus Christi, TX 78413

Corpus Christi
Daylily Society
4814 Lansdown Dr.
Corpus Christi, TX 78411-2718

Corpus Christi Rose Society
Corpus Christi, TX

Cryptanthus Society
2355 Rusk
Beaumont, TX 77702

Cypress Creek Daylily Club
8914 Pine Ln.
Magnolia, TX 77355-2111

Dallas Area Historical Rose
Society
Richardson, TX

Dallas Historic Tree Coalition
Dallas, TX

Dallas Koi Kichi Group
Dallas, TX

Dallas Rose Society
Dallas, TX

Daylily Growers of Dallas
302 Meadowcreek Dr.
Mesquite, TX 75150-8006

East Texas Arboretum
1600 Patterson Rd.
Athens, TX 75751

East Texas Daylily Society
11294 FM Rd 3226
Arp, TX 75750-9535

El Paso Native Plant Society
7760 Maya Ave.
El Paso, TX 79912

El Paso Rose Society
El Paso, TX

First Men's Garden Club of Dallas
1711 Rainbow Dr.
Richardson, TX 75081-4612

Floriculture Horticulture Society
Texas A&M University
College Station, TX 77843-2133

Fort Worth Bonsai Society
3130 Woodland Heights
Colleyville, TX 76034

Fort Worth Orchid Society
Fort Worth, TX

Fort Worth Rose Society
Fort Worth, TX

Fredericksburg Garden Club
161 Schattenbaum
Fredericksburg, TX 78624

Galveston Orchid Society
Galveston, TX

Garden Club of Austin
1615 CR 107
Hutto, TX 78634

Garden Clubs of Lubbock
Lubbock, TX

Garden Gate Club
Burleson, TX

Gardeners of Amarillo
32 Tascocita Rd.
Amarillo, TX 79124

Golden Spread Daylily Society
107 Sunset
Amarillo, TX 79106

Golden Triangle Bromeliad
Society
Box 100
Mauriceville, TX 77626

Golden Triangle Rose Society
Beaumont, TX

Grapevine Garden Club
Grapevine, TX

Greater Dallas/Ft. Worth
Bromeliad Society
508 Aspen Incline
Hewitt, TX 76643

Greater Fort Worth Herb Society
Fort Worth, TX

Greater North Texas Orchid Society
Dallas, TX

Gulf Coast Daylily Society
5390 Fairview
Beaumont, TX 77705-6016

Gulf Coast Fruit Study Group
2 Abercrombie Dr.
Houston, TX 77084

Gulf Coast Horticulture Society
4267 S. Judson
Houston, TX 77005

Heart O'Texas Orchid Society
Austin, TX

Herb Association of Texas
Hallettsville, TX

Herb Society of America
Pioneer Unit
P. O. Box 23
Round Top, TX 78954

Herb Society of America
South Texas Unit
Box 6515
Houston, TX 77265

Heritage Rose Foundation
Richardson, TX

Houston Amaryllis Society
15319 Vandalia Way
Houston, TX 77053

Houston Bonsai Society, Inc.
Houston Garden Center
Houston, TX

Houston Cactus &
Succulent Society
3214 N. Peach Hollow Circle
Pearland, TX 77584

Houston Camellia Society
7815 Burgoyne
Houston, TX 77063

Houston Hemerocallis Society
1002 Village Brook
Livingston, TX 77351-2866

Houston Orchid Society
Houston, TX

Houston Rose Society
Houston, TX

Huntsville Muddy Boots Daylily
Society
1327 15th St.
Huntsville, TX 77340

Ikebana International,
Dallas and Fort Worth Chapters
Dallas, TX
International Bulb Society
550–10 South, Suite 201
Beaumont, TX 77707

International Oleander Society
Box 3431
Galveston, TX 77552

Johnson County Iris &
Daylily Society
Rte. 1, Box 348
Hico, TX 76457-9633

Koi & Water Garden Club
of North Texas
Carrollton, TX

Lone Star African Violet Council
5235 Kingston Dr.
Wichita Falls, TX 76310-3029

Lone Star Chapter of the
American Hibiscus Society
Houston, TX

Lone Star Daylily Society
Pearland, TX 77581-4808

Lone Star ZNA Koi Club
Houston, TX

Lufkin Hemerocallis Society
1302 Tom Temple Dr., #302
Lufkin, TX 75904-5552

Magnolia Garden Club
Beaumont, TX

Men's Garden Club
of Houston
9502 Meadowvale Dr.
Houston, TX 77063-5204

Men's Garden Club of Plano
824 Weeping Willow Ct.
Allen, TX 75001

Moto Kara Koi Kai
1840 Portsmouth
Houston, TX 77098

Nacogdoches Daylily Society
Box 22
Douglas, TX 75943-0022

NASA Area African Violet
Society
4334 Plover Dr.
Seabrook, TX 77586

Native Plant Society of Texas
Austin Chapter
Austin, TX

Native Plant Society of Texas
Collin County Chapter
812 Fairlawn St.
Allen, TX 75002

Native Plant Society of Texas,
Georgetown Chapter
Georgetown, TX

Native Plant Society of Texas
Houston Chapter
Box 131254
Houston, TX 77219-1254

Native Plant Society of Texas
Post Oak Chapter
Post Oak, TX

Native Plant Society of Texas
Red River Chapter
Wichita Falls, TX

Native Prairies Association
of Texas

North Texas Daylily Society
Fort Worth
991 Quail Run
Azle, TX 76020-6421

Organic Garden Club
of Fort Worth
Fort Worth, TX

Palm Society of South Texas

Pioneer Plant Society
Navasota, TX

Plumeria Society of America

Rio Grande Valley Bonsai Society
2415 East Hwy. 83
Weslaco, TX 78596

River Oaks Garden Club
Houston, TX

Rockport Herb & Rose
Study Group
Rockport, TX

Rockwall-Rowlett
Garden Club
502 Shoretrail Dr.
Rockwall, TX 75087

San Antonio Bonasi Society, Inc.
Ruble Center
San Antonio, TX

San Antonio Botanical Society
San Antonio, TX

San Antonio Daylily Society
6122 John Chapman
San Antonio, TX 78240-5311

San Antonio Herb Society
San Antonio, TX

South Texas Golf Course
Superintendents Association
Southeast Texas Bonsai Club
Box 7975
Beaumont, TX 77726-7975
Southside Preservation
Association
Fort Worth, TX

Southwest Koi & Pond Society
El Paso, TX

Space City Chapter of the
American Hibiscus Society
Pasadena, TX

Spring Branch
African Violet Club
2015 Bauer
Houston, TX 77080

Star Flowers Garden Club
2311 Perkins Rd.
Arlington, TX 76016

Texas Association of
Landscape Contractors

Texas Bamboo Society
Austin, TX

Texas Botanical Garden Society
Austin, TX

Texas Gulf Coast Fern Society

Texas Horticulture Society
College Station, TX

Texas Koi &
Fancy Goldfish Society
Marion, TX

Texas Native Plant Project
Box 2742
San Juan, TX 78589

Texas Nursery &
Landscape Association
7730 S IH-35
Austin, TX 78745-6621

Texas Organic Growers
Association
Box 2637
Wimberley, TX 78676

Texas Pecan Growers Association
Drawer CC
College Station, TX 77841

Texas Rose Rustlers
9730 Harrowgate
Houston, TX 77031

Texas Turfgrass Association

Texoma Herb &
Old Rose Society
Denison, TX

Tree Folks
Austin, TX

Turfgrass Producers of Texas

Tyler Men's Garden Club
17424 CR 46
Tyler, TX 75704

Violet Crown Garden Club
2220 Barton Springs Rd.
Austin, TX 78746

Waco Pond Society
Waco, TX

Water Garden Club
of South Texas
San Antonio, TX

INDEX OF COMMON NAMES

summer savory, 164
sunflower, 37
swamp red maple, 240
sweet bay magnolia, 236, 241
sweetgum, 236, 241
sweet marjoram, 165
sweet olive, 207
sweet pepper, 158
sweet woodruff, 165
Swiss chard, 162
switch grass, 116

T
Takil palm, 237
tall fescue, 93
tarragon, 165
Texas ash, 131, 241
Texas bluebells, 132
Texas lantana, 132
Texas mountain laurel, 132
Texas palmetto, 237
Texas sage, 133
Texas wisteria, 133, 213
thyme, 162, 165
tickseed, 49, 60
tiger flower, 79
tiger lily, 79
tigridia, 79
tomato, 163
torenia, 37
trumpet vine, 220
tuberose, 79
tulbaghia, 79
tulip, 77, 78
Turk's cap, 133

V
variegated Japanese silver grass,
    115, 119
verbena, 37
veronica, 59, 62
viburnum, 203
Virginia creeper, 213, 220
Virginia willow, 207
vitex, 241

W
watermelon, 163
wax begonia, 38
wax-leaf ligustrum, 204, 207
wax myrtle, 134
weeping willow, 236, 241
wild ageratum, 61

wild ginger, 60
wild oats, 116
willow oak, 241
windamere palm, 237
windmill palm, 237, 241
wintercreeper, 117
winter jasmine, 204
winter savory, 165
wisteria, 220
woolly butterfly bush, 134
wooly Butina palm, 237

y
yarrow, 59–60
Yatay palm, 237

Z
zebra grass, 117, 119
zephyranthes, 79
zingiber, 79
zinnia, 38
zoysia, 87, 93

BOTANICAL INDEX

Dan Gill earned B.S. and M.S. degrees in horticulture from Louisiana State University in Baton Rouge, and is an Associate Professor in Consumer Horticulture with the LSU AgCenter. He is the spokesperson for the LSU AgCenter's Get It Growing project, a statewide educational effort in home horticulture utilizing radio, Internet, TV and newsprint. Gardeners throughout Louisiana read his columns in local newspapers, watch his gardening segments on local TV stations, and listen to him on local radio. In the New Orleans area, Dan appears weekly on the Channel 4 *Morning News,* writes a weekly gardening column for *The Times-Picayune,* and hosts the Saturday morning "Garden Show" on WWL 870-AM, a live call-in radio program. In addition to *Month-By-Month Gardening in Texas,* Dan is also co-author of the *Louisiana Gardener's Guide* and author of *Month-By-Month™ Gardening in Louisiana.* His "South Louisiana Region Report" and "Only in Louisiana" columns appear monthly in the *Louisiana Gardener Magazine.*

A horticulturist and native Texan, **Dale Groom** is nationally known as an accomplished author, radio and television host, speaker, consultant, and columnist whose column, "Ask the Plant Groom™" is syndicated. Dale also produces and hosts *The Plant Groom™* television series which airs nationwide, and he hosts "The Plant Groom™," a live call-in radio program. The author is an Extension Horticulturist, a certified professional nurseryman, and a plant and flower show judge. Dale received his Bachelor of Science degree in agriculture from Stephen F. Austin State University and a Master of Science degree in horticulture from East Texas State University. He also established the Ornamental Horticultural program at Tyler Junior College.

Horticulturist **Steve Dobbs** joined the University of Arkansas at Fort Smith as Director of Grounds and Landscape in April 2002. In 2005, Steve was appointed Plant Operations Director where he coordinates the maintenance efforts related to some 44 buildings and 168 acres of grounds. Under Steve's direction, UA Fort Smith has been recognized numerous times for their landscape and beautification efforts. Steve is the author of *The Southern Lawn Series* and the *Oklahoma Gardeners Guide.* From 1990–1995 Steve was host and producer of the popular television show "Oklahoma Gardening," which was selected as the Best TV Gardening Program in the Nation in 1992 by the Garden Writers Association of America.

James Fizzell has more than fifty years of hands-on horticultural experience, making him the source other experts turn to with their toughest turf, vegetable, landscape, and plant problems. Fizzell is well known to Midwest gardeners through numerous appearances on radio and TV and from articles for neighborhood weekly newspapers. He has been the popular host of his own radio and TV gardening programs. Mr. Fizzell has been featured often in leading trade journals, and as a celebrated speaker at industry seminars and horticultural associations throughout the Midwest. Jim has written twelve books for Midwest gardeners for Cool Springs Press. Jim and his wife, Jane, currently reside and garden on Garden Street in Northern Illinois.

Joe Lamp'l, (aka joe gardener®) is the host of two National television shows: GardenSMART on PBS and DIY Network's Fresh from the Garden. His latest project includes producing and hosting a brand new series on PBS, Growing a Greener World. He's also a syndicated columnist and author, including his latest book: The Green Gardener's Guide: Simple Significant Actions to Protect & Preserve Our Planet. Joe's passion and work related to gardening, sustainable living, and environmental stewardship through multiple media platforms has positioned him as one of the most recognized personalities in the "green" sector today. Find out more information about Joe and his work online at www.joegardener.com.

An experienced horticulture expert, **Dr. Joe White** has been both a student and a teacher of Louisiana plant life for more than thirty years. Whether serving as the LSU-area horticulture agent, or writing his popular weekly columns for the *Shreveport Times* (until retirement), White has worked to enrich the public knowledge and understanding of horticulture. Dr. White has been honored by many organizations including the LCES Program of Excellence and the Professional Achievement Award from the Louisiana Nursery and Landscape Association.